School & College
CURRICULUM
DESIGN

Book Two:
IMPLEMENTATION

Matt Bromley

Spark
BOOKS

ISBN: 9798645689537

DEDICATION

I am lucky: my job affords me the opportunity to visit countless schools and colleges in the UK and overseas. Ostensibly, I do so to share my expertise and experience which, let me tell you, gives me a sense of imposter syndrome. I'm particularly surprised when a school or college invites me back because they wish to hear more! But in so doing, I get to talk to and learn from so many wonderful colleagues – teachers, leaders, support staff all – who are dedicated to the education profession and determined to make a difference for the pupils and students in their charge.

It is fair to say my thoughts and ideas are continually reshaped and refined as a consequence of these inspiring interactions. Sometimes, my opinions are solidified because I see and hear hard evidence of their truth. At other times, my opinions are challenged and changed as they meet with the resistance of reality.

I therefore dedicate this book to the thousands of hard-working people who work in education every day and who have helped shape the ideas I share within these pages. They can take the credit; I will accept the blame for any errors or omissions.

This is Book Two in a three-volume series and I have been overwhelmed by the positive response I've received to the first book on 'intent'. As a consequence of that book, I've been invited into so many schools and colleges and to speak at countless conferences. And with each engagement, I have learned more.

Lots of schools and colleges have used my book as the blueprint for their curriculum developments and it is beyond humbling to see my advice enacted in practice and already making a positive difference to pupils' lives. I'd therefore like to add my thanks here to those colleagues who've bought the first book – or even bought a set for their staff - and have contacted me to tell me how it's helped them. And I'd also like to thank those colleagues who've approached me at conferences and asked me to sign a copy, thus fulfilling one of my lifelong dreams!

CONTENTS

PART ONE:

FRONT MATTER

Matt Bromley

CHAPTER ONE:
A NOTE ON THE TEXT

This is Book Two in a three-part series. It tackles 'curriculum implementation'. Book One explored 'curriculum intent' whilst Book Three will examine 'curriculum impact'.

The series title is 'School *and College* Curriculum Design' because it is aimed at leaders and teachers in primary, secondary and further education settings.

At times, as in Book One, I will refer to 'pupils and students' to make clear my advice applies equally to young children *and* older learners. I will also make reference to both the schools inspection handbook and the further education and skills inspection handbook, articulating the differences between the two.

However, for the sake of brevity, I will often default to the terms 'pupils' and 'schools'.

I wish to make clear, therefore, that all of the advice contained within this book – and indeed in the series as a whole – relates to schools *and* FE colleges, even if the language does not always feel inclusive.

Of course, at times I will talk about strategies specific to schools such as the Pupil Premium Grant but all the advice – if not the illustrated examples – is, I think, relevant to all readers.

I have worked extensively – as a teacher, leader and advisor – in all three phases (primary, secondary and FE) and have enacted the advice I share in this series of books in all three phases and so I know it can work in all.

Yes, there are clear differences; but all three phases have more in common than that which divides them.

Two further notes about the text you're about to read before you do so...

Firstly, although I think it likely that many readers of this book will have already enjoyed (or perhaps endured?) Book One in the series, I don't wish to presume this is the case for all. As such, there will be some repetition from the previous volume whenever I think it important to call-back some core ideas before expanding upon them in this volume. Where there is a significant overlap between the two books, I will explicitly note it and advise returning readers where they can to skip to. Although I am wary of needless repetition and wish to provide good value for money (which, at c145,000 words, I hope you feel this book delivers), I have decided that, when all's said and done, there is no harm in revisiting some of the key ideas I expounded in the first book in the series.

Secondly, the middle sections of this book that detail the three steps of teaching for long-term learning are updated, adapted and abridged versions of a text that was – as indicated on the cover of this book - first published as How to Learn (2018). Readers who have purchased and read that book may still find these sections useful as part of the overall narrative about curriculum implementation and, if nothing else, it will provide a useful retrieval practice activity. But I will understand if those readers choose to skip these chapters or indeed – if reading this as a sample – decline the purchase of this book altogether.

CHAPTER TWO:
THE STORY SO FAR...

This is the second of three guides to the school and college curriculum design process.

Taken together, this series seeks to navigate the reader through the process of redesigning their school or college curriculum, in order to ensure that it is broad and balanced, ambitious for all, and prepares pupils and students for the next stages of their education, employment and lives.

The journey began in Book One with **curriculum intent** – the *'Why?'* and the *'What?'* of education.

This book, meanwhile, tackles **curriculum implementation** – the *'How?'* of education.

Book Three will conclude with **curriculum impact** – the *'How successfully?'*.

The story so far...

Book One was about 'intent' – all the planning that happens before teaching happens.

In *Part One* of Book One, we defined that slippery term 'curriculum' and argued that a curriculum is not a single entity; rather, it is a composite of at least four different elements: the national, the basic, the local, and the hidden curriculums.

We also defined the words 'broad' and 'balanced' and explored what a broad and balanced curriculum looked like in practice.

We examined the primacy of the curriculum over teaching, learning and assessment, and defended curriculum's role as the master, as opposed to the servant, of education.

We considered the true purpose of an education and, by so doing, articulated the intended outcomes of an effective school and college curriculum.

We explored the vital role that senior leaders can play in the curriculum design process whilst also defending the rights of middle leaders and teachers – those with subject specialist knowledge – to create their own disciplinary curriculums with a degree of freedom and autonomy.

We analysed the importance of creating a culture of high aspirations where each pupil is challenged to produce excellence.

We considered the centrality of social justice to effective curriculum design, too; and concluded that a curriculum is a means of closing the gap between disadvantaged pupils and their more privileged peers.

In *Part Two* of Book One, we examined *why* designing a knowledge-rich curriculum was important because, contrary to popular opinion, pupils can't 'just Google it'. We discussed *what* knowledge mattered most to our pupils' future successes and how to identify the 'clear end-points' or 'body of knowledge' of a whole-school or college - and indeed subject-specific - curriculum.

Also in *Part Two*, we discussed ways of ensuring our curriculum is ambitious for all, including by adopting (and possibly adapting) a mastery approach whereby we set the same destination for all pupils and students, irrespective of their starting points and backgrounds, rather than reducing the curriculum offer or 'dumbing down' for some. We talked, too, of modelling the same high expectations of all, albeit accepting that some pupils will need additional and different support to reach that destination.

In *Part Three* of Book One, we discussed how to assess the starting points of our curriculum, both in terms of what has already been *taught* (the previous curriculum) and what has actually been *learnt* (our pupils' starting points – their prior knowledge, and their knowledge gaps and misconceptions).

We explored the importance of curriculum continuity, too, and considered the features of an effective transition process. And we looked at ways of instilling a consistent language *of* and *for* learning.

In *Part Four* of Book One, having identified both our destination and our starting points, we plotted a course between the two, identifying useful waypoints or check-points at which to stop along the way – which might take the form of 'threshold concepts' – through which pupils must travel because their acquisition of these concepts (be they knowledge or skills) is contingent on them being able to access and succeed at the next stage.

We explored the importance of having a planned and sequenced curriculum, ensuring we revisit key concepts several times as pupils travel through the education system but, each time, doing so with increasing complexity, like carving a delicate statue from an alabaster block, each application of hammer and chisel revealing finer detail and, in the case of curriculum sequencing, more - and *more complex* - connections to prior learning (or schema) that, in turn, help pupils to learn more and cheat the limitations of their working memories in order to move from novice and towards expert. This is something we will return to in more detail in this book.

We explored how these 'waypoints' or threshold concepts might be used as a means of assessment so that curriculum knowledge – rather than something arbitrary such as scaled scores, national curriculum levels, GCSE or A Level grades, or passes/merits/distinctions on vocational qualifications – is what we assess, by means of a progression model. We will return to this in Book Three.

In *Parts Five* and *Six* of Book One on curriculum intent, we turned to the subject of differentiation – arguing again that all pupils deserve access to the same ambitious curriculum, no matter their starting points and backgrounds, and no matter the opportunities and challenges they face in life.

We accepted that, of course, some pupils need more support and more time in order to reach the designated end-points of our curriculum, or to master the 'body of knowledge' we assign them, and not all will do so, but we argued that we should not 'dumb down' or reduce our curriculum offer for disadvantaged or vulnerable pupils, pupils with SEND, or learners with High Needs, because by so doing we only perpetuate the achievement gap and double their disadvantage. Rather, we should ensure that every pupil is plotted a course for the same destination, albeit accepting that the means of transport and journey time may differ.

Accordingly, in *Part Five* we defined excellence and explored the importance of 'teaching to the top'. We looked at how to model high expectations of all pupils. And we looked at ways of 'pitching' learning in pupils' 'struggle zones' (delicately balanced between their comfort zones and their panic zones where work is hard but achievable with time, effort and support).

Then, in *Part Six*, we looked at ways of diminishing disadvantage - accepting that if we want to offer all pupils the same ambitious curriculum, we must also identify any gaps in their prior knowledge and skills, and support those pupils with learning difficulties or disabilities to access our curriculum and have a fair – if not equal – chance of academic success.

We looked at the role of cultural capital in closing the gap, arguing that vocabulary instruction (particularly of Tier 2 words) is a useful means of helping disadvantaged pupils to access our curriculum, but that this, in and of itself, is not enough. Rather, we asserted that cultural capital took myriad forms and had different definitions, and, as such, we should also plan to explicitly teach pupils how to speak, read and write in each subject discipline, and fill gaps in their world knowledge. We will return to this subject later in this book.

We also looked at how to make a success of in-class differentiation and additional interventions and support. And we looked at how to develop pupils' literacy and numeracy skills in order to help disadvantaged learners to access our curriculum. Finally, we examined ways of developing pupils' metacognition and self-regulation skills to help them become increasingly independent, resilient learners. We will also return to these ideas within these pages.

In short, Book One in this three-volume series followed a six-step process of curriculum design which went as follows:

1. Agree a vision
2. Set the destination
3. Assess the starting points
4. Identify the waypoints
5. Define excellence
6. Diminish disadvantage

Book One – as I said earlier – was about all the planning that happens before teaching happens.

This book, meanwhile, is about the teaching that happens next. In other words, it deals with curriculum **implementation**, the way in which teachers translate curriculum plans in practice with pupils and students in classrooms. In the next chapter we will define 'implementation' in more detail...

CHAPTER THREE:
WHAT IS CURRICULUM IMPLEMENTATION?

At the time of writing, curriculum design is a hot topic in England's schools and colleges, thanks at least in part to Her Majesty's Inspectorate. In 2019, Ofsted – the Office for Standards in Education which inspects state-run schools and colleges in England - published a new Education Inspection Framework (EIF).

Although teachers and education leaders in England cannot ignore Ofsted (to do so would, in my view, be foolish rather than brave because inspection outcomes matter in all sorts of ways), we should never forget that Ofsted are not why we do what we do. As teachers and leaders, we do what we do for our pupils and students and if we do what is right for them, acting with integrity at all times, we should have nothing to fear from Ofsted.

Nor are Ofsted the reason for this series of books – indeed, the manuscript for Book One began life long before Ofsted consulted upon and published its EIF – although, perhaps shamefully, in the final draft of that book I 'borrowed' (at my publisher's shrewd request) Ofsted's 3I's of intent, implementation and impact as a means of articulating the curriculum design process.

Having said this, the new inspection framework does, I think, provide a logical way of thinking about curriculum design and its focus on 'the real substance of education' is to be commended.

We will examine what the EIF means for curriculum design in more detail in Chapter Four but for the purposes of this chapter, let's focus on how Ofsted defines 'implementation'...

In the schools' inspection handbook, Ofsted defines implementation as the way in which "the curriculum is taught at subject and classroom level".

Accordingly, during an inspection, Ofsted will want to see how teachers enable pupils to understand key concepts, presenting information clearly and promoting appropriate discussion, how teachers check pupils' understanding effectively, identifying and correcting misunderstandings, and how teachers ensure that **pupils embed key concepts in their long-term memory** and apply them fluently.

Further, Ofsted will want to see if the subject curriculum that classes follow is designed and delivered in a way that allows pupils to transfer key knowledge to long-term memory and if it is sequenced so that **new knowledge and skills build on what has been taught before** and towards defined end points.

We will unpack those two paragraphs in a moment.

In the further education and skills inspection handbook, Ofsted argues that teachers need sufficient subject knowledge, pedagogical knowledge and pedagogical content knowledge to be able teach learners effectively.

Effective teaching and training should, Ofsted argues, ensure that learners in further education and skills settings **know more and remember what they have learned** within the context of the approach that teachers have selected to serve the aims of their curriculum. Consequently, learners will be able to apply vocational and technical skills fluently and independently.

In both schools and FE settings, Ofsted says that inspectors will want to see evidence that teachers use assessment to check pupils' understanding, and they will evaluate how assessment is used in a school or college to support the teaching of the curriculum, but – crucially – not in a way that substantially increases teachers' workloads. By including reference to the report of the Teacher Workload Advisory Group, 'Making data work', which recommends that school leaders should not have more than two or three data collection points a year, Ofsted implies – I think – that it will expect schools to follow this advice or have a solid rationale for not doing so.

In short, Ofsted's definition of effective curriculum implementation is high quality teaching which leads to long-term learning.

So, let's unpack those ingredients...

How the curriculum is taught at subject level

Here, we might consider how curriculum plans are written to ensure the subject is taught in a planned and sequenced manner, and in a way that ensures all teachers within a department are consistent in the content they deliver, as well as in the broad pedagogical approaches they apply to teach their subject.

It might help to consider the following questions:

What makes our subject different to other subjects on the timetable? For example, how do scientists think, as distinct from mathematicians? How do scientists speak, read and write? How is this explicitly taught to pupils?

What shape does the subject curriculum take? Is it linear or spiral? What does progress look like in this subject? Can it be extrapolated by assessing pupils' knowledge and skills at two points in time? Or is it more complex than this? Can some skills be observed? What about knowledge, how do you know when pupils have acquired it securely and can apply it in a meaningful way? Indeed, can you know this?

What form do the key concepts (end points or body of knowledge) take in this subject? For example, are they worded as big questions, ideas, concepts, values, behaviours, facts, or skills? Or a combination of all these and more?

How do these key concepts develop other time? Do they get reinforced each term and year? Do they get built upon and added to as pupils progress through the curriculum and as subject content is returned to with increasingly complexity? How are explicit links made between what pupils already know and can do, and what they need to learn next?

Is the subject content the same regardless of which teacher a pupil has? What value judgments are made about what knowledge and skills are most important and which aspects of the subject can be dropped? Are such decisions made as a department or by individual teachers? Is subject content taught in the same or broadly similar ways by all teachers in the department? For example, where appropriate, do all teachers use the same presentation slides, textbooks and worksheets? Do they all use the same schemata or aides memoire?

What cross-curricular links are made? Do subject teachers work with other departments to identify commonalities and themes where relevant? Do subjects liaise on their sequencing to maximise the potential to support each other's delivery? When maths is needed in science, do science teachers use the same mathematical methods as maths teachers? Do all teachers ensure they teach tier 2 vocabulary in ways that do not contradict other subjects but that make explicit the differences that exist in the meanings of, say, command words such as 'analyse' between subject disciplines?

How the curriculum is taught at classroom level

Here, we might consider the way curriculum plans are translated into practice by individual teachers. In so doing, the following questions may prove useful:

What does our subject-specific learning environment, including classrooms and corridors, look and sound like? What makes the teaching of this subject different to the teaching of other subjects? How is the learning environment organised? What do all classrooms contain? How are the walls used? What layout is optimal? How is the space utilised including the use of displays to aid learning? What of the social environment? What do interactions look like and why? Does the way the classroom is run mirror expectations in the subject field? Are explicit links to the subject discipline made?

What rules and routines are particular to this subject? How are they articulated, reinforced, enforced? In subjects with a practical element, such as design and technology, engineering, and construction, how are health and safety taught and high standards upheld?

What does the teacher do in this subject? What is the balance between teacher-led and pupil-led activities? What do teacher explanations look like in practice? How does the teacher make use of modelling and thinking aloud? How do they make their subject expertise explicit to pupils so what is invisible to the novice learner becomes visible?

Is pair and group work used in this subject? How and why? What guidelines are established? How and how often? Are they routinely upheld? Does self- and peer-assessment and feedback feature in this subject? How is this managed?

What does assessment look like in our subject? What is assessed, by whom, when and how? How is feedback given? What is done with it?

How teachers enable pupils to understand key concepts

Here, we might consider the ways in which teachers articulate the end points or body of knowledge to be learned in their subject discipline. In so doing, we might pose the following questions:

What are the key concepts? Who decides? When are they taught? How and how often are they returned to and expanded upon? Do key concepts feature in learning objectives or intended outcomes? Do key concepts feature in knowledge organisers or unit summaries? Are they used in low-stakes quizzes, hinge questions, exit tickets, homework tasks and so on in order to ensure they form part of retrieval practice activities?

How do teachers in our subject discipline routinely – and unobtrusively – assess pupils to ensure they have understood the key concepts they've taught? Do they return to this to ensure that what pupils know today, they still know tomorrow?

How teachers present information clearly

Here, we might consider what effective teacher instruction looks like in each subject discipline. In some subjects, teacher explanations might be the most effective and efficient means of imparting information, whereas in other subjects a more hands-on approach for pupils (such as pair or group work, or problem-based learning etc.) might be preferable. In many subjects, of course, a combination of the two approaches probably works best because it provides a varied diet for learning activities for pupils and moves them towards independence.

The following questions may be helpful here:

Where teacher explanations are used, do teachers present information with clarity? Do they explicitly teach the vocabulary that pupils need to know, and do they 'front load' their explanations with the key facts or ideas pupils need?

Do teachers made good use of modelling, constructing and deconstructing examples of excellence for pupils rather than showing 'one I made earlier'? Do they accompany these models with 'thinking aloud' to ensure pupils are exposed to an expert's decision-making processes and to ensure they can see that producing work of high quality is rarely easy and without error, rather it is an iterative process that involves learning from mistakes, taking two steps forward and one step back?

Do teachers check their pupils' understanding of these key concepts routinely and regularly and use the information this gleans to adapt their teaching pace and style?

How teachers promote appropriate discussion

Here, we might consider how class discussion and debate are managed. As such, the following questions may be of use:

When are classroom discussions used? Does the teacher use whole-class, group or pair discussion, or a combination? When group work is used, is this is the best means of promoting discussion and are guidelines established to ensure all pupils are engaged and that no one gets a 'free ride'? Are roles assigned to ensure each pupil has a responsibility and is accountable to the group for its success?

Does the teacher explicitly teach effective debating skills and is this within a subject-specific context? Are the rules and routines for effective debate and discussion regularly and consistently reinforced? Are these rules the same in each classroom and with each teacher in a department? What about across the whole school or college curriculum? Do these rules help pupils to comment on others' contributions without it becoming a personal attack? Are active listening skills taught?

Do pupils know there is no hiding place in the classroom and that they will be expected to contribute? But is the classroom a safe place for pupils to take risks and make mistakes, and are reluctant speakers helped to develop confidence and resilience over time? Is there a safety net to catch pupils when they fall? Do discussions help pupils to make progress? Are discussions and question-and-answer sessions inclusive of all pupils?

How teachers check pupils' understanding effectively, identifying and correcting misunderstandings

In addition to what I say above about enabling pupils to understand key concepts including through assessment and by routinely returning to concepts to ensure that what pupils know today, they still know tomorrow, it's important that teachers also discover and unpack any misunderstandings and misconceptions that pupils develop. Assessment therefore needs to identify when pupils get it wrong or when gaps remain, and the results of these assessments need to be used to inform the teacher's planning and teaching.

Accordingly, I would add the following questions:

Do teachers ensure that any misconceptions and gaps are addressed? Do they ensure that pupils have acquired the requisite key concepts to enable them to move on to the next part of the curriculum? Do they use this information to inform their planning and teaching?

How teachers ensure that pupils embed key concepts in their long-term memory

Information has only been learned if it has been encoded in long-term memory. Indeed, the educational psychologist Paul Kirschner defines learning simply as a change in long-term memory. Information is encoded in long-term memory (in other words, it is transferred from the short-term or working memory into the long-term memory from where it can be accessed and used later) when pupils have actively attended to the information.

Pupils are more likely to attend to information if it is stimulating and if it requires them to think – in other words, the work must be challenging. However, as working memory is very small, it is also important that pupils are helped to make good use of that limited space and avoid overloading it with too much information at once.

As such, here we might consider the following questions:

How do teachers in each subject discipline 'hook' pupils and gain the active attention of their working memories? How do teachers ensure pupils focus on the curriculum content they need to encode and avoid unhelpful distractions?

How do teachers pitch learning so that it falls within pupils' struggle zones, meaning it is hard and requires thinking, but is also within their capability and does not overload their working memories?

How teachers ensure that pupils can apply key concepts fluently

Once information has been encoded in long-term memory, it has been learned. However, this is not enough if we are to achieve long-term learning. If information is left dormant, it will become increasingly hard to recall later. In other words, pupils may learn something today but be unable to recall it and apply it tomorrow.

Here, therefore, we might consider the following questions:

How and how often do teachers return to prior learning to keep it active and accessible? What do teachers do with that prior learning when they do return to it? As long-term memory is practically limitless, it is helpful for pupils to do something different with their prior learning each time they return to it, thereby encoding new information in long-term memory.

How are pupils helped to apply prior learning in different ways and in different contexts so that learning becomes transferable? How do teachers help pupils to see connections within and across the curriculum so that they can apply what they learn in one topic to another related topic, or what they learn in one subject to another related subject, and so on?

Above all else, it is important that pupils are afforded the opportunity to apply their newfound knowledge and skills – to do something with it beyond sitting exams. As such, we should ask:

How are knowledge and skills placed within a wider context so pupils can see why that knowledge and those skills are useful and usable both now and in the future? Do teachers articulate the purpose of learning in each subject and each topic, because with purpose comes motivation?

How the subject curriculum is designed and delivered in a way that allows pupils to transfer key knowledge to long-term memory

In addition to what I say above about encoding information in long-term memory, it is important that – at a subject level and in long- and medium-term teaching plans – opportunities for pupils to engage in retrieval practice activities are baked into the curriculum and not left to chance or to individual teachers' discretion.

One way to do this well is to adopt a progression model such as the one I outlined in Book One in this series which makes use of threshold concepts. A progression model is not only a useful means of assessing pupils' progress, it is also a way to ensure that concepts are returned to often and are built upon with increasingly complexity.

How the subject curriculum is sequenced so that new knowledge and skills build on what has been taught before

Another advantage of the progression model is that it helps to ensure the curriculum is planned and sequenced. Sequencing is a means of ensuring that curriculum content is taught in a logical order and that concepts are returned to and developed over time.

Here, therefore, we might consider the following:

In what order is subject content taught and how is the subject curriculum taught over time?

Is there curriculum continuity, including between the different phases and key stages of education?

Do teachers in each year group and key stage know what went before and what follows?

In this sense, we might regard the subject curriculum as a novel and each teacher as being responsible for writing one or two chapters. Each teacher must know the plot arc of the whole book and must understand how their chapters fit in, how they will develop character, theme and plot. They must ensure their chapters are also consistent in both language and tone.

The current state of curriculum planning in some schools and colleges reminds of an old parlour game called Consequences whereby the first player writes a word or a sentence, folds the page (if it's a single word, they follow guidelines such as 'write an adjective to describe a man' followed by 'write the name of a man' and so on; if it's a sentence, they usually write freely but leave the last word or so of their sentence visible for the next player to see, onto which they can adjoin their sentence) and passes it on to the next player who adds a sentence of their own, folds the page and passes it on to the third player and so on. At the end, the paper is unfolded, and someone reads the story aloud. Invariably, it is nonsensical but amusing. Our curriculum is in danger of being nonsensical if we do not do more to remove the creases and ensure greater continuity – and there is nothing amusing about that.

How the subject curriculum is sequenced so that new knowledge and skills builds towards defined end points

In Book One in this series, I articulated a six-step process of curriculum design. Having articulated the broad vision and purpose of each subject curriculum, the process began by setting the destination. In other words, the act of planning a curriculum begins at the end. What do you want pupils to know and be able to do at the end that they didn't know and couldn't do at the beginning?

Where you plant the flag is up to you, but the key is starting with the destination in mind rather than starting from where pupils are now. Why? Because starting from where pupils are now might encourage you to dumb down or lower your expectations. Starting at the end, with 'the best that has been thought and said' in your subject discipline, ensures you have high expectations and aspirations and set pupils on a journey towards excellence.

As such, planning and sequencing a subject curriculum means building towards a defined destination, the clear end points or body of knowledge you have agreed upon as a department. Curriculum continuity, therefore, is not simply about building upon what went before, it is also about building towards a shared destination, an aspirational goal.

In further education and skills setting, implementation is also about...

How learners apply vocational and technical skills fluently and independently

Here, we need to recognise that the application of some practical skills can be observed and assessed. We also need to be mindful of the fact that some vocational qualifications are not built to support teaching for long-term learning. For example, some qualifications allow you to teach something, assess it, then move on and never return to it.

Here, I would caution against using the qualification specification as your guiding star. Of course, we need to teach the specification to enable learners to gain good qualifications that will open doors to future success, but the qualification is not the be-all and end-all of an FE college education. Rather, we need to do what is in the best interests of our learners and prepare them for the next stage of their training, employment and lives. This means keeping all the plates spinning throughout the course regardless of whether those plates will be assessed again as part of the qualification. If something was worth teaching and worth learning in the first place, then it must not be allowed to gather dust in our learners' long-term memories; rather, it must be kept alive and accessible so that our learners can apply that learning in college, in work and in life.

CHAPTER FOUR:
THE OFSTED CONTEXT

In the previous chapter I explained that Ofsted, the schools and college inspectorate in England, published a new education inspection framework which came into effect in September 2019.

The purpose of this new framework, Ofsted says, is to discourage schools from narrowing their curriculum offer – perhaps in the form of running a three-year GCSE or closing down certain subjects.

The EIF is also intended to end practices such as teaching to the test – being blinkered by what Amanda Spielman calls the 'stickers and badges' of qualification outcomes at the expense of a more rounded education that better prepares pupils for the next stages of their education, employment and lives.

Finally, the EIF aims to tackle social justice issues, ending educational disadvantage and affording every child, no matter their starting point and background, an equal opportunity to access an ambitious curriculum and to succeed in school and college. This final aim is, in part, achieved by providing disadvantaged children with the knowledge and cultural capital they need to succeed in life.

So, before we progress further along our own curriculum implementation journey, let us take a short pitstop to consider the Ofsted context...

The new key inspection judgments

Matt Bromley

There are four key judgment areas in the new EIF:

1. Quality of education
2. Behaviour and attitudes
3. Personal development, and
4. Leadership and management

In addition, as before, schools will receive an 'overall effectiveness' grade.

The old judgment pertaining to 'outcomes for pupils' has therefore been scrapped, making clear that test and/or exam results are no longer paramount and that schools in difficult circumstances which might not achieve good headline outcomes can nevertheless provide a good quality of education and serve their pupils well.

The 'teaching, learning and assessment' judgment has also gone. This implies that the focus will be on a whole school's provision – its curriculum – and how that curriculum is delivered and assessed, not so much on an individual teacher's classroom practice.

Both 'outcomes for pupils' and 'teaching, learning and assessment' have been subsumed within a new judgment called 'quality of education' which places the quality of the school curriculum centre-stage.

For the purposes of this series of books, we are focusing on the 'quality of education' judgment and its definition of curriculum according to its **intent, implementation** and **impact**...

Intent is "a framework for setting out the aims of a programme of education, including the knowledge and understanding to be gained at each stage".

Implementation is a means of "translating that framework over time into a structure and narrative within an institutional context".

Impact is the means of "evaluating what knowledge and understanding pupils have gained against expectations.

We might therefore conclude that:

- Intent is concerned with *curriculum design* and provision, the emphasis being on providing a broad and balanced curriculum for all pupils;
- Implementation, meanwhile, is about *curriculum delivery*, in other words on teaching, assessment and feedback, crucially that which leads to long-term learning; and
- Impact is about *pupil progress and achievement* as assessed by external test and/or exam results and by using progression and destinations data, recognising that good outcomes are not just measured in qualifications but in how well pupils are developed as rounded citizens of the world.

Earlier, I went even further and defined the 3I's simply as:

- Intent = *why and what?*
- Implementation = *how?*
- Impact = *how successfully?*

Each of the 3I's, Ofsted says, will not be graded separately but evidence for each will be aggregated into an overall grade for the 'quality of education'.

It is worth noting that 'quality of education' is considered a leading judgment – in other words, it will form the bulk of inspection activity, provide the majority of the evidence used to grade a school, and as such – put simply - if the quality of education is not judged to be 'good' then every other judgment and indeed 'overall effectiveness' are unlikely to be, though of course it's not impossible.

Before we home in on what more Ofsted has to say about the curriculum, let's examine some of the mechanics of inspection...

Preparation for Inspection

In the draft handbook, Ofsted proposed that, for section 5 (I.e. full) inspections, inspectors would arrive on site the day before inspection activity began in order to prepare. But, following feedback from senior leaders, Ofsted has said that, rather than be on site, all preparation will continue to be carried out off site and the notice of inspection will remain at half a day.

However, Ofsted also said that the pilot inspections convinced them that inspectors could enhance the way that they prepared for inspection. Accordingly, under the 2019 EIF inspectors will increase considerably the amount of time they spend speaking to leaders about the education provided by the school or college during the normal pre-inspection telephone call.

Indeed, this phone call – which will take place in the afternoon before an inspection, after '*the* call' (I.e. the one giving notice) has been made, will now last for approximately ninety minutes.

Inspectors will use this conversation to understand:

- the school or college's context, and the progress that's made since the previous inspection, including any specific progress made on areas for improvement identified at previous inspections
- the headteacher's or college quality nominee's assessment of the school's or college's current strengths and weaknesses, particularly in relation to the curriculum, the way teaching supports pupils to learn the curriculum, the standards that pupils achieve, pupils' behaviour and attitudes, and personal development
- the extent to which all pupils have access to the school's or college's full curriculum
- a discussion of specific areas of the school (subjects, year groups, and so on; and in the case of FE colleges, the types of provision on offer) that will be a focus of attention during inspection.

This call will, Ofsted says, give inspectors and headteachers/nominees a shared understanding of the starting point of the inspection. It will also help inspectors to form an initial understanding of leaders' view of the school's progress and to shape the inspection plan.

The method of inspection

In tandem with the final EIF, Ofsted outlined its methodology for inspection. Inspection activity will, it said, take three forms:

1. **Top-level view**: inspectors and leaders will start with a top-level view of the school's curriculum, exploring what is on offer, to whom and when, leaders' understanding of curriculum intent and sequencing, and why these choices were made.

2. **Deep dive**: next, they will be a 'deep dive' which will involve gathering evidence on the curriculum intent, implementation and impact over a sample of subjects, topics or aspects. This, Ofsted says, will be done in collaboration with leaders, teachers and pupils. The intent of the deep dive is to seek to interrogate and establish a coherent evidence base on the quality of education.

3. **Bringing it together:** finally, inspectors will bring the evidence together to widen coverage and to test whether any issues identified during the deep dives are systemic. This will usually lead to school leaders bringing forward further evidence and inspectors gathering additional evidence.

Top level view

This will largely take place during the initial 90-minute phone call between the lead inspector and headteacher/nominee and, as I say above, will focus on the school's context, the headteacher's assessment of the school's current strengths and weaknesses, the extent to which all pupils have access to the full curriculum, and specific areas of the school (subjects, year groups, aspects of provision, and so on) that will be a focus of attention during inspection.

Deep dive

The deep dive, meanwhile, will take place throughout the inspection visit and will include the following elements:

- an evaluation of senior leaders' intent for the curriculum in any given subject or area, and their understanding of its implementation and impact
- an evaluation of curriculum leaders' long- and medium-term thinking and planning, including the rationale for content choices and curriculum sequencing
- visits to a deliberately and explicitly connected sample of lessons
- the work scrutiny of books or other kinds of work produced by pupils who are part of classes that have also been (or will also be) observed by inspectors
- a discussion with teachers to understand how the curriculum informs their choices about content and sequencing to support effective learning
- a discussion with a group of pupils from the lessons observed.

Ofsted says that, during deep dives, context will matter. Carrying out lesson visits or work scrutiny without context will, they accept, limit the validity of their judgements.

It is important that, in order to make lesson visits and work scrutiny more accurate, inspectors know the purpose of the lesson (or the task in a workbook), how it fits into a sequence of lessons over time, and what pupils already knew and understood before the lesson began. Conversations with teachers and subject leads will, they say, provide this contextual information.

Ofsted also says that a sequence of lessons, not an individual lesson, will be their unit of assessment – accordingly, inspectors will need to evaluate where a lesson sits in a sequence, and leaders'/teachers' understanding of this.

As has been the case for some years – though perhaps not as widely known as some of us would like – inspectors will not grade individual lessons or teachers.

Ofsted says that work scrutiny will form a part of the evidence inspectors will use to judge whether or not the intended curriculum is being enacted. They'll ask: Do the pupils' books support other evidence that what the school set out to teach has, indeed, been covered?

Work scrutiny activities, Ofsted says, can provide part of the evidence to show whether pupils know more, remember more and can do more, but only as one component of the deep dive which includes lesson visits and conversations with leaders, teachers and pupils.

Coverage is a prerequisite for learning, Ofsted says; but simply having covered a part of the curriculum does not in itself indicate that pupils know or remember more.

Work scrutiny activities cannot be used to demonstrate that an individual pupil is working 'at the expected standard' or similar, and it is not always valid – Ofsted admits – to attempt to judge an individual pupil's individual progress by comparing books from that pupil at two points in time.

Ofsted says that inspectors can make appropriately secure judgments on curriculum, teaching and behaviour across a particular deep dive when four to six lessons are visited, and inspectors have spoken to the curriculum lead and teachers to understand where each lesson sits in the sequence of lessons.

The greater the number of visits, therefore, the more that inspectors can see the variation in practice across a deep dive. However, there is a point after which additional visits do little to enhance the validity of evidence. Since an inspection evidence base will include multiple deep dives, the total number of lessons visited over the course of the inspection will substantially exceed four to six.

Ofsted says that inspectors should review a minimum of six workbooks (or pieces of work) per subject per year group and scrutinise work from at least two-year groups in order to ensure that evidence is not excessively dependent on a single cohort. Normally, inspectors will repeat this exercise across each of the deep dives, subjects, key stages or year groups in which they carry out lesson visits.

In a research paper published in June 2019, Ofsted admitted to concerns with regards the reliability and validity of some of its proposed methods of inspection including lesson observations and work scrutiny, particularly in secondary schools and in FE. We can expect, therefore, further revisions or clarifications on their approach in the future and particularly in light of the negative response to the EIF from some lobby groups including the Headteacher's Roundtable and the largest teachers' professional association, the NEU.

Bringing it together

At the end of day one, the inspection team will meet to begin to bring the evidence together. The purpose of this important meeting is to:

- share the evidence gathered so far to continue to build a picture of the quality of education, identifying which features appear to be systemic and which are isolated to a single aspect
- allow the lead inspector to quality assure the evidence, and especially its 'connectedness'
- establish which inspection activities are most appropriate and valid on day 2 to come to conclusions about which features are systemic
- bring together evidence about personal development, behaviour and attitudes, safeguarding, wider leadership findings, and so on, in order to establish what further inspection activity needs to be done on day 2 to come to the key judgements.

Inspecting the curriculum

According to the inspection handbooks, inspectors will take a range of evidence, including that held in electronic form, into account when making judgments.

This, Ofsted says, will include official national data, discussions with leaders, staff and pupils, questionnaire responses and work in pupils' books and folders.

Gathering evidence

Before we consider what inspectors will want to do and see both before and during an inspection, I think it equally valuable to clarify what inspectors will not do and see because this can bust some unhelpful myths...

What Ofsted does NOT want

Ofsted makes clear that inspectors will not grade individual lessons, create unnecessary workload for teachers, routinely check personnel files (although inspectors may look at a small sample), or advocate a particular method of planning, teaching or assessment.

Likewise, Ofsted will not require schools to provide any written record of teachers' verbal feedback to pupils, individual lesson plans, predictions of attainment and progress scores, assessment or self-evaluation (other than that which is already part the school's business processes).

Ofsted will not require performance and pupil-tracking information, monitoring of teaching and learning and its link to teachers' professional development and the teachers' standards (other than that which is already part of the school's normal activity), specific details of the pay grade of individual teachers who are observed during inspection, or processes for the performance management arrangements for school leaders and staff.

What's more, Ofsted does not expect schools to carry out a specified amount of lesson observations, use the Ofsted evaluation schedule to grade teaching or individual lessons, ensure a particular frequency or quantity of work in pupils' books or folders, take any specific steps with regard to site security (in particular, inspectors do not have a view about the need for perimeter fences), or carry out assessments or record pupils' achievements in any subject, including foundation subjects in primary schools, in a specific way, format or time.

Ofsted does not expect secondary schools to be at similar stages of EBacc implementation as any other schools. They do not expect any schools or colleges to provide additional information outside of their normal curriculum planning, or to produce a self-evaluation document or summary in any particular format.

Ofsted does not specify that tutor groups/form time must include literacy, numeracy or other learning sessions, nor does it dictate the frequency, type or volume of marking and feedback, or the content of, or approach to, headteacher/principal and staff performance management.

So far so pragmatic. It is, I think, helpful that Ofsted has set out – and so explicitly – what it does not want or expect to see in order to dispel myths and prevent unhelpful leadership practices from emerging.

What Ofsted does want

As well as any publicly available information about the school, inspectors will look at a summary of any school self-evaluations (or, in FE settings, the self-assessment report or SAR) and the current school improvement plan including any planning that sets out the longer-term vision for the school, such as the school or the trust's strategy (or, in FE settings, the college strategy and quality improvement plan or QIP).

They will expect schools and colleges to have to hand at the start of an inspection the single central record, a list of staff and whether any relevant staff are absent, whether any teachers cannot be observed for any reason (for example, where they are subject to capability procedures), whether there is anyone working on site who is normally employed elsewhere (such as at a different school in a MAT or on a different site of a merged college group), and maps and other practical information.

They'll also want copies of the school's timetable, a current staff list and times for the school day, the Pupil Premium strategy, any information about previously planned interruptions to normal school routines during the period of inspection, records and analysis of exclusions, pupils taken off roll, incidents of poor behaviour and any use of internal isolation, records and analysis of bullying, discriminatory and prejudiced behaviour, either directly or indirectly, including racist, sexist, disability and homophobic/bi-phobic/transphobic bullying, use of derogatory language and racist incidents.

Ofsted also wants a list of referrals made to the designated person for safeguarding in the school or college and those who were subsequently referred to the local authority, along with brief details of the resolution, a list of all pupils who have open cases with children's services/social care and for whom there is a multi-agency plan, up-to-date attendance analysis for all groups of pupils, documented evidence of the work of those responsible for governance and their priorities, including any written scheme of delegation for an academy in a MAT and details of governance within a merged college group, and any reports from external evaluation of the school or college.

What Ofsted will do

During an inspection, inspectors will gather further evidence by observing lessons, scrutinising pupils' work, talking to pupils about their work, gauging both their understanding and their engagement in learning, and obtaining pupils' perceptions of the typical quality of education in a range of subjects.

Discussions with pupils and staff will also be used as evidence (as will – in primary schools – listening to pupils read), and inspectors will look at examples of pupils' work for evidence of progress in knowledge, understanding and skills towards defined endpoints.

The lead inspector will invite the headteacher or nominee, curriculum leaders and other leaders to take part in joint observations of lessons. Inspectors will not take a random sample of lesson observations. Instead, they will connect lesson observation to other evidence. Lesson observation will be used for gathering evidence about 'implementation' and how lessons contribute to the quality of education. And observations will provide direct evidence about how behaviour is managed within individual classrooms.

The lead inspector will also invite curriculum leaders and teachers to take part in joint scrutiny of pupils' work. Inspectors will not evaluate individual workbooks or teachers. Inspectors will connect work scrutiny to lesson observation and, where possible, conversations with pupils and staff. Work scrutiny will be used for gathering evidence about the 'impact' of the quality of education. Inspectors may also use work scrutiny to evaluate pupils' progression through the curriculum.

Those are the mechanics of inspection under the 2019 EIF. Now let's focus on the role that the curriculum will play in inspections...

What Ofsted say about curriculum design

As I said earlier, Ofsted defines curriculum in terms of its intent, implementation and impact. Let's take a closer look at each of the '3I's' in turn...

1. *Intent*

When inspecting 'intent' in <u>schools</u>, inspectors will look to see whether or not the curriculum builds towards **clear 'end points'**. In other words, they will want to see clear evidence of what pupils will be expected to know and do by each of these end points, be they the end of a year, key stage or phase.

In <u>FE</u> settings, rather than clear end-points, inspectors will look to see if curriculum managers and teachers have identified the **'body of knowledge'** students will be expected to acquire. Ofsted defines this 'body of knowledge' as the technical, vocational and life skills that a learner needs so that they will thrive in the future and not be left behind. It's worth a college considering how this body of knowledge has been influenced by the provider's local context and by the typical gaps in learners' knowledge and skills. It's also worth considering the extent to which the college takes account of the knowledge, skills and behaviours that learners bring with them.

Inspectors will also want to see evidence that a school's or college's curriculum is **planned and sequenced** so that new knowledge and skills build on what has been taught before, and towards those defined end points.

As well as being clearly sequenced and building towards a clear end-point, Ofsted says that a curriculum should also **reflect the provider's local context** by addressing typical gaps in pupils' and students' knowledge and skills.

The curriculum should remain as broad as possible for as long as possible, too, and, in schools, pupils should be afforded the opportunity to study a strong academic core of subjects, such as those offered by the English Baccalaureate (EBacc). In colleges, we might assume that inspectors will want to see that students are afforded the opportunity to study a well-rounded study programme which includes English and maths, employability and enrichment opportunities.

In schools, inspectors will want to see evidence that there are **high ambitions for all pupils**, whether they be academic, vocational or technical in nature. And Ofsted will want to see that the school does not offer disadvantaged pupils or pupils with SEND a reduced curriculum.

In FE settings, meanwhile, inspectors will seek to assure themselves that the provider intends to **include all its learners in its high academic, technical and vocational ambitions**. They will also seek to assure themselves that the provider offers disadvantaged learners or those with SEND, including those who are eligible for High Needs funding, a curriculum that remains ambitious and meets their needs.

In FE, it is also expected that the provider's curriculum intent will have regard to the needs of learners, employers, and the local, regional and national economy as necessary.

Curriculum narrowing

Talking of a reduced curriculum, inspectors will be particularly alert to signs of narrowing in the key stages 2 and 3 curriculums in primary and secondary schools respectively. In other words, if a school has shortened key stage 3, inspectors will look to see that the school has made provision to ensure that pupils still have the opportunity to study a broad range of subjects in Years 7 to 9.

At the heart of an effective key stage 4 curriculum, Ofsted says, is a strong academic core: the EBacc. On this point, the schools' inspection handbook invites contention. It restates the government's response to its EBacc consultation, published in July 2017, which was a commitment that a large majority of pupils should be expected to study the EBacc. Indeed, it is therefore the government's ambition that 75% of

Year 10 pupils in state-funded mainstream schools should be starting to study EBacc GCSE courses nationally by 2022, rising to 90% by 2025. Including this information in the handbook implies that Ofsted will expect schools to be working towards these goals and will have some explaining to do if they fall short. However, as I said above, Ofsted will not expect all schools to be at similar stages of implementation.

Cultural capital

There are several explicit mentions of 'cultural capital' in the schools' inspection handbook. Ofsted says that inspectors will judge the extent to which schools and colleges are equipping pupils with the knowledge and cultural capital they need to succeed in life. Ofsted's definition of this knowledge and cultural capital matches that found in the aims of the national curriculum: namely, that it is "the essential knowledge that pupils need to be educated citizens, introducing them to the best that has been thought and said and helping to engender an appreciation of human creativity and achievement".

In FE settings, Ofsted argues that the curriculum is a powerful means to address social disadvantage, giving learners access to the highest levels of knowledge, skills and experience. As such, the curriculum should be based on a firm agreement about what education and training should be provided for each learner.

We will return to cultural capital in more detail in Chapter Twenty-Three.

2. Implementation

As I explained in Chapter Three above, under curriculum implementation, inspectors will seek evidence of how the school curriculum is taught at subject and classroom level. They will want to see how teachers enable pupils to understand key concepts, presenting information clearly and promoting appropriate discussion, how teachers check pupils' understanding effectively, identifying and correcting misunderstandings, and how teachers ensure that **pupils embed key concepts in their long-term memory** and apply them fluently.

Further, they will want to see if the subject curriculum that classes follow is designed and delivered in a way that allows pupils to transfer key knowledge to long-term memory and it is sequenced so that **new knowledge and skills build on what has been taught before** and towards defined end points.

In FE settings, Ofsted argues that teachers need sufficient subject knowledge, pedagogical knowledge and pedagogical content knowledge to be able teach learners effectively. Ofsted recognises that there will be areas in which staff are not yet experts, so inspectors will explore what leaders are doing to support staff to ensure that no learner receives poor teaching.

Effective teaching and training should, Ofsted argues, ensure that learners in FE settings **know more and remember what they have learned** within the context of the approach that teachers have selected to serve the aims of their curriculum. Consequently, learners will be able to apply vocational and technical skills fluently and independently.

In both schools and FE settings, inspectors will want to see evidence that teachers use assessment to check pupils' understanding, and they will evaluate how assessment is used in the school or college to support the teaching of the curriculum, but – crucially – not in a way that substantially increases teachers' workloads. By including reference to the report of the Teacher Workload Advisory Group, 'Making data work', which recommends that school leaders should not have more than two or three data collection points a year, Ofsted rather implies – I think – that it will expect schools to follow this advice or have a solid rationale for not doing so.

In practice, as I said in Chapter Three, effective implementation involves high quality teaching that leads to long-term learning.

We will explore long-term learning in detail in Part Three of this book. For now, suffice to say that one of the central tenets of a quality curriculum is the provision of long-term – or deep – learning.

John Sweller's 'Cognitive Load Theory' (2011) posits that, "If nothing has altered in long-term memory nothing has been learned." The educational psychologist Paul Kirschner, meanwhile, defines learning as a change in long-term memory.

For its part, Ofsted argues that:

- Progress means knowing more and remembering more
- Knowledge is generative (or 'sticky'), i.e. the more you know, the easier it is to learn
- Knowledge is connected in webs or schemata
- Knowledge is when humans makes connections between the new and what has already been learned

We might, therefore, meaningfully define long-term learning as the acquisition of new information (knowledge, skills and understanding) and the application of that information at a later time and in a range of contexts. The theory being this: for pupils to succeed, particularly on linear courses with terminal assessments after a year or two, they must be able to retain information over the long-term. They must also be able to apply what they've learnt in one context to other contexts such as in an exam, in the workplace and in life.

Now let's turn to the third and final 'I' of the Ofsted framework...

3. Impact

Under impact, inspectors will gather evidence to help them judge whether the most disadvantaged pupils in a school or college – as well as pupils with SEND or those eligible for High Needs funding – are given the knowledge and cultural capital they need to succeed in life.

Ofsted says that national assessments and examinations are useful indicators of the outcomes pupils in the school achieve, but that they only represent a sample of what pupils have learned. As such, inspectors will balance these with their assessment of the standard of pupils' work from the first-hand evidence they gather on inspection.

Ofsted says that learning in schools must build towards a goal. As such, at each stage of pupils' education, they will want to see evidence that they're being prepared for the next stage of education, training or employment, and will consider whether pupils are ready for that next stage.

In FE settings, inspectors will make clear that there need be no conflict between teaching a broad, rich curriculum and achieving success in examinations and tests. A well-constructed, well-taught curriculum will lead to good results because those results will reflect what students have learned.

In FE, as in schools, national tests and examinations are therefore a useful indicator of the outcomes learners achieve, and inspectors will balance these with their assessment of the achievement of learners drawn from the first-hand evidence they gather on inspection about non-qualification activity and the progress that learners make from starting points.

As in schools, Ofsted says that learning in further education settings must build towards a goal. At each stage of learners' education, they are being prepared for the next stage of education, training or employment or independence. Inspectors of FE provision will consider whether learners are ready for the next stage by the time they leave the provider or provision that they attend. Inspectors in FE will also consider whether learners are ready for the next stage and are going to appropriate, high-quality destinations.

If, having read the last few paragraphs, you're getting a strange sense of déjà vu, then you should: Ofsted, like me, believe schools and FE have more in common than that which divides them, and so apply the same rationale and indeed the same high standards to all phases of education – hence the eerily similar language used in both inspection handbooks.

We will explore assessment in more detail in Book Three of this series.

Measuring outcomes

In terms of the evidence of impact, inspectors say they will use nationally-generated performance information about pupil progress and attainment – that which is available in the IDSR – as well as first-hand evidence of how pupils are doing, drawing together evidence from the interviews, observations, work scrutinies and documentary review described above. They will use nationally-published information about the destinations to which its pupils and students progress when they leave the school or college, and – in primary schools – they will listen to a range of pupils read.

Ofsted will not want to see internal assessment data such as that used to track progress in-year. Ofsted says that this is because inspectors do not want to add to school leaders' and teachers' workload by having them produce lots of data for the purposes of inspection. Unsaid but also a probable factor in this decision, is the belief that some schools and colleges will present 'massaged' data that isn't accurate or helpful.

In the final version of the inspection framework and handbooks, Ofsted softened its position with regards a school's and college's internal data. They clarified that they would be interested in hearing the conclusions headteachers/principals and school and college leaders had drawn from their own data but would not want to see the data itself.

As such, it's recommended that senior leaders extrapolate their own data and have clear findings to share.

What has Ofsted previously opined about curriculum?

Before we move away from Ofsted and begin our deeper exploration of curriculum implementation, I think it worthwhile mining some recent inspection evidence because this might prove useful when considering what Ofsted regards as strengths and weaknesses of school and college curriculums...

Evaluations of inspection reports show that, in the past, Ofsted has regarded the following – which I have taken the liberty of paraphrasing - as strengths:

- Leaders review the curriculum regularly and check the impact on outcomes for all pupils, then remodel it to help all pupils perform well
- Leaders are attuned to research findings, as well as reforms to national curriculum and qualifications, and use this to inform how their local curriculum is developed to improve outcomes and pupils' personal development
- CEIAG is integral to the curriculum and pupils' progression, and the curriculum helps pupils to experience and learn about their options for their future
- There is a recognition that challenge is for all not just the most able pupils.

Conversely, Ofsted has noted the following – which, again, I have paraphrased - as weaknesses:

- Coordination of numeracy and literacy across the curriculum is poor and, as such, pupils struggle to read and access learning
- Support from middle leaders to develop pedagogy is poor – notably in mixed ability classes in Key Stage 3

- Pupils in Key Stage 3 repeat work from primary school which leaves them bored and frustrated by the lack of challenge
- There is a lack of understanding and coherence in assessment, and a lack of oversight
- Expectations of pupils are low
- The timetable is fragmented and poorly planned, leading to a lack of coherence across the curriculum
- Leaders are slow to tackle issues as a result of teacher vacancies and lack innovation to sustain a good curriculum despite teacher shortages.

PART TWO:

EVIDENCE INFORMED EDUCATION

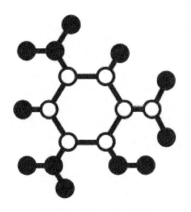

CHAPTER FIVE:
AN EVIDENCE-INFORMED PROFESSION

When I started teaching, we were not what you would call an evidence-informed profession. We did what teachers had been doing for decades, what our teacher-training lecturers told us to do and what our own teachers had done to us when we were at school. And we did these things irrespective of whether they were the best things, or the right things, to do.

Truth was, we simply didn't know what the best or right things to do were because no one really analysed teachers' methods or sought to compare one approach with another.

Of course, we had eyes and ears and could see and hear when an approach we'd taken was working and, conversely, when it was not. We knew when pupils were bored or stuck, when they appeared to be making progress and when they did not.

We improved our teaching by a process of trial and error, but it often felt like we were navigating the darkness. We learnt through practice and, even then, we could not be certain whether our approach, though appearing to work, was the best approach in the circumstances. We taught one way and if that didn't get results, we tried another. Or - in some cases - we kept teaching in the same way year after year irrespective of the outcomes.

Formative assessment, including in the form of Black and Wiliam's Inside the Black Box, signalled - for me, at least - the beginning of a paradigm shift, a change in the mindset of the educational establishment.

The National Curriculum - first introduced in 1988, brought greater continuity to *what* was taught in England's state schools; assessment for learning, and the government's interpretation of it in the form of the National Strategies - introduced a decade later in 1998 - brought greater continuity to *how* the curriculum was taught.

Suddenly, we were encouraged to hand aspects of teaching and learning over to our pupils, to share learning objectives and assessment criteria, and to get our pupils to self- and peer-assess their work.

It was as if, until then, teaching was what teachers did and it was none of our pupils' business; we kept all the mechanics of our profession hidden beneath the bonnet. Pupils simply had to guess at what they were learning, why they were learning it and how they were going to learn it. And little thought had been given to what they would do with that learning later, or so it seemed. Pupils also had to guess at how their work would be assessed, or in many cases simply wait until it was handed back to find out.

Too much of my time - I realise with hindsight - was dedicated to devising fun activities, things to do which would fill my timetable and entertain my pupils. My lesson planning would often start with the question, 'What will pupils do in this lesson?' As such, not enough of my time - and not enough of my pupils' attention - was focused on curriculum content, on what I needed them to think about and know. In retrospect, I know that my lesson planning should have started with the question, 'What will pupils think about this lesson?' Or, more accurately, 'in this series of lessons' because teaching and learning does not take place in one-hour chunks, artificially demarcated on a timetable, but over a much longer period of time.

These days, however, there's a surfeit of research evidence about what works and what doesn't. From the darkness there is light.

But which evidence should we use when implementing our curriculum in a way that leads to long-term learning?

Over the course of the next few chapters I will focus on the Education Endowment Foundation's (EEF) teaching and learning toolkit - though, as they say on TV, other sources of evidence are available.

I will analyse what the EEF claim works and try to put this into context, turning the theory into tangible classroom practice.

Before we delve into the detail, however, let's first explore who the EEF are and how their toolkit works...

Who are the EEF and how does their toolkit work?

The EEF was founded in 2011 – with help from a £125 million grant from the Department for Education - by The Sutton Trust, in partnership with the Impetus–Private Equity Foundation, although it began life in November 2010 when the then Education Secretary, Michael Gove, announced plans to establish a foundation intended to help raise standards in challenging schools, an idea inspired by Barack Obama's *Race to the Top* initiative in the US.

In 2012, the EEF was awarded a further £10 million by the DfE to identify and evaluate high-potential programmes focused on improving literacy for 10- and 11-year-olds. In March 2013, the EEF and Sutton Trust were jointly designated as the *What Works* centre for education, which set out to summarise and share research.

In 2016, the EEF launched the Research Schools network, in partnership with the Institute for Effective Education, aimed at fostering a network of schools who will support the use of evidence to improve teaching practice. In 2017, the EEF began publishing a series of guidance reports providing actionable recommendations for teachers and senior leaders.

What are meta-analyses and are they reliable?

One criticism aimed at the EEF concerns the way in which it conducts its meta-analyses in order to rank strategies by effect size and months of extra progress...

The teaching and learning toolkit, much like John Hattie's Visible Learning, is based on meta-analyses of other studies. A meta-analysis is a way of collating the outcomes of similar studies and converting the data into a common metric, then combining those in order to report an estimate which represents the impact or influence of interventions in that given area.

There are a number of advantages of meta-analyses when conducted as part of a systematic review. For example, they allow large amounts of information to be assimilated quickly. They also help reduce the delay between research 'discoveries' and the implementation of effective strategies. Meta-analyses enable the results of different studies to be compared, and in so doing highlight the reasons for any inconsistencies between similar studies.

However, meta-analyses are not without their problems...

Firstly, it is a misconception that larger effect sizes are associated with greater educational significance.

Secondly, it is a misconception that two or more different studies on the same interventions can have their effect sizes combined to give a meaningful estimate of the intervention's educational importance.

Why?

Because original studies that used different types of 'control group' cannot be accurately combined to create an effect size (not least because what constitutes 'business as usual' in each control group will be different).

Likewise, unless the studies used the same range of pupils, the combined effect size is unlikely to be an accurate estimate of the 'true' effect size of a particular strategy.

Also, the way in which researchers measure the effect can influence the effect size. For example, if you undertake an intervention to improve pupils' ability to, say, decode words, you could choose to use a measure specifically designed to 'measure' decoding, or you could use a measure of general reading competence that includes an element of decoding. The effect size of the former will be greater than the latter, due to the precision of the measure used.

Put simply, whenever we have two or more numbers, we can always calculate an average. However, if those two numbers are effect sizes taken from experiments that use significantly different outcomes measures, then the 'average' could, and probably will, be meaningless. The original effect sizes we combine to calculate an average (or meta-analysis), in order to be meaningful, must relate to the same outcomes and similar conditions and pupils, including in the control groups.

What's more, increasing the number of test items can influence the effect size. If the number of questions used to measure the effectiveness of an intervention is increased, this may significantly increase the effect size.

Finally, trials are often carried out without first analysing and understanding the barriers that pupils face. When random controlled trials (RCTs) are used in medicine, they only take place *after* intensive theorisation. In education, the process often begins with the trial and subsequent measurements. For example, if it is identified that pupils eligible for the Pupil Premium are not doing as well as their peers in literacy, then a trial is launched to test an intervention, the outcome is measured, and an intervention is recommended for all to use. However, there is rarely any theorising first about why some pupils are not doing as well as their peers and rarely any detailed analysis of the actual barriers some of these pupils will face in school. For example, for some pupils it may be that English is an additional language or it may be that their attendance is low. The intervention may work for some pupils but not all, and the meta-analysis may mask the complexity of the issue and send us down the wrong path.

Should we use the EEF toolkit and other meta-analyses?

So, should we ignore meta-analyses, effect sizes and the EEF toolkit altogether and go back to doing what we've always done? Of course not. As I say above, we are finally becoming an evidence-informed profession that uses data to ensure we get better at what we do and, ultimately, improve pupils' life chances. But, as I also say above, we should always exercise caution. We should not regard the data as an oracle; rather, we should contest it and balance what the evidence suggests works with what we know from our own experiences.

We should also dig beneath the meta-analyses and analyse the original studies on which the effect sizes are based because the averages may hide huge variations depending on the nature of the intervention and the context in which it was used.

In conclusion, curriculum implementation is a highly complex, nuanced art-form and we would do well not to reduce it to basic statistics or league tables of 'what works' for only madness lies that way.

CHAPTER SIX:
NOT WORTH IT?

In Chapter Five I explained how we must exercise caution when applying the findings of the EEF toolkit – or indeed any other meta-analyses of research in education – to our own school or college contexts and not act solely on the research findings but rather weigh these against what we know works.

Caution is needed the most, I would contend, when looking at the bottom of the EEF 'league table'...

In the relegation zone?

Teaching assistants (TAs) / additional learning support (ALS)

According to the first iteration of the EEF toolkit, teaching assistants are 'not worth it' because they are costly and have little demonstrable impact on pupil progress. As a result, many schools began cutting TA posts in a bid to tackle budget cuts.

However, delve beneath the headlines and you'll find the picture is a little more nuanced...

Firstly, although the positive effects of teaching assistants on pupils' academic learning are small, there is strong evidence that when teachers delegate routine administrative tasks to TAs it allows them to focus more time on teaching, planning, and assessment tasks. TAs have also proven beneficial in terms of reducing teacher workload and improving teachers' job satisfaction.

Those teachers featured in the EEF evidence base were also positive about the contribution TAs make in their classrooms. They said the presence of additional adults in the room helped increase pupils' attention and supported the learning of pupils who struggled most. Results from observations made as part of the DISS project also suggested that TAs had a positive effect in terms of reducing disruptions and therefore afforded teachers more time to teach.

Secondly, the poor effects related to the use of TAs tended to derive from situations where the TA had been used poorly or not at all. Naturally, if not well utilised TAs will have little positive impact on pupil progress.

In short, we must not take at face value claims that certain interventions are 'not worth it' and immediately stop doing them. We should consider what we know of our contexts and take a long-term, pragmatic, nuanced view. We should also consider the wider effects of certain strategies and look beyond hard outcomes data, for example, the EEF toolkit also claims reducing class sizes is 'not worth it'. However, although the direct impact on pupil outcomes may not be overwhelming, that doesn't mean that smaller classes do not have positive impacts in other ways...

Class sizes

The toolkit says that, overall, the evidence does not show particularly large or clear effects until class size is reduced substantially to fewer than 20 or even 15 pupils. It appears to be very hard to achieve improvements from modest reductions in class size to numbers above 20, for example from 30 to 25.

In short, the evidence does not show particularly large or clear effects, until class size is reduced substantially.

However, as the size of a class gets smaller, the amount of attention the teacher can afford each pupil will increase. Reducing class size should also increase the amount of high-quality feedback or one to one attention pupils receive.

Moreover, reducing class sizes means that the teacher's marking load reduces, and this should lead to improvements in work life balance which, in turn, should lead to increases in teacher retention, ensuring pupils receive a better quality of education and a more stable school environment. Certainly, all the evidence about why teachers quit the profession points to workload as the main driver and so reducing class sizes is bound to positively impact on this.

In short, the positive impact of reducing class sizes is likely to be long-term rather than lead to immediate improvements on pupil outcomes. Those positive impacts are more likely to be felt if class sizes are reduced sufficiently to allow teachers to teach differently and if those teachers are given professional development to help them adjust. This includes, though is not limited to, changes in the way teachers assess and give feedback.

Five top tips for TAs

Returning to TAs, if we take a more nuanced approach and continue to employ them, what do we know works best? Here are five tips...

1. Teachers need to spend at least as much time working with lower-performing pupils as they spend with other pupils which means that TAs should also work with a range of pupils within the class rather than work exclusively with lower-performing pupils. What's more, TAs should sometimes provide whole-class instruction from the front of the room whilst the teacher supports targeted pupils or engages in one-to-one feedback.

2. Teachers and TAs need to work together and communicate with each other effectively and frequently. Teachers may need training on how to manage, organise and work with TAs. Teachers and TAs may need to set aside time to plan and review lessons together and to feed back on pupils' learning. TAs need to approach lessons with a clear understanding of the concepts and information that will be taught, and they need to know the intended learning outcomes of the lesson and be aware of any specific learning needs of pupils they work with.

3. TAs should ensure pupils retain ownership of their learning and responsibility for their work. This means offering the least amount of support possible and allowing pupils to become increasingly independent. TAs should provide a healthy mix of support and challenge but allow the weighing scales to tilt away from support and towards challenge as time progresses.

4. When asking questions, TAs should afford sufficient wait time for pupils to think about and articulate their responses rather than proffer an answer themselves after just a few seconds, tempting though that may be.

5. When delivering intervention sessions outside the lesson, TAs should ensure these are well-structured, and that they explicitly consolidate and extend pupils' classroom-based learning. Intervention sessions should be kept brief (certainly no longer than 30 minutes), and they should be regular and sustained. Each session should have a clear objective, and they should be well-paced, well-resourced and carefully timetabled to minimise the time spent away from other lessons or activities. There needs to be planned opportunities for teachers and TAs to discuss the intervention sessions in order to ensure that they are focused and impactful, and that they remain closely aligned to classroom teaching.

To facilitate these five practices, it may be necessary to adjust TAs' working hours, for example to enable them to start early and finish early or start late and finish late in order to run before- and after-school interventions. It may be necessary to timetable free time for TAs that coincides with teachers' PPA time. It may be necessary to pay TAs to attend CPD days or events in order to train them in delivering interventions and in order to ensure they have the requisite knowledge and skills to support the teaching of the lessons in which they provide support.

Pupils can become over-reliant on TAs, particularly if they regularly work one-to-one with an adult, and this can lead to learned helplessness. It's important, therefore, that TAs slowly remove the scaffolds, provide less support and more challenge, and enable pupils to become increasing independent. Here are some strategies – adapted from 'The teaching assistant's guide to effective interaction: How to maximise your practice' (2016) by Bosanquet, P., Radford, J. and Webster, R. - that TAs can use to help pupils take greater ownership of their learning and progress:

- Correcting – here, the TA provides pupils with the answers when they get stuck. Pupils do not work independently and rely on the TA.

- Modelling – here, TAs show pupils how to complete a task by producing an exemplar and thinking aloud. Pupils observe the TA then produce a model of their own. Pupils become more independent through practice but still rely on the TA to model the process first.

- Clueing – here, TAs ask questions that provide cues to information stored in pupils' long-term memories. This is based on the notion that pupils know the answer but cannot actively recall the information from memory. The TA provides a cue that helps the pupil retrieve the correct information and relieve a bottle-jam in their thinking. Pupils are more independent and have to think for themselves.

- Prompting – here, TAs provide prompts (less detailed then clues and thereby encouraging pupils to think for themselves) to pupils that encourage them to use their own knowledge to solve a problem. This is similar to coaching whereby the TA encourages pupils to find the answers from within themselves by challenging their thinking, posing questions, and providing hints, but does not provide the answers or do the work for them.

- Self-scaffolding – here, TAs observe pupils and afford them sufficient time to process, think and articulate their understanding. Pupils are at their most independent at this stage.

In conclusion, if teaching assistants are to be used effectively to aid differentiation, then they must not be used as an informal teaching resource for lower-performing pupils, thus replacing the teacher and encouraging learned helplessness. Rather, TAs should be used to add value to the teacher and not to replace them. Indeed, under-performing pupils need as much access to the teacher as any other, perhaps more.

TAs can also be used effectively to help pupils develop metacognition and self-regulation so that pupils become increasingly independent and need less support over time.

Where additional interventions are used to support lower-performing pupils outside of lessons, these should be highly structured and have close links to what's happening in the lesson.

They should consolidate and extend classroom-based learning and this requires close communication between the teacher and the TA. Intervention sessions should be brief (up to 30 minutes), often (several times a week) and sustained over the long-term (at least a half-term, ideally a term or two). TAs should be trained to deliver interventions and be afforded time to plan them and to review them with the teacher. Interventions should be subject to regular monitoring, not just reviewed at the end but evaluated as often as possible to ensure they are having the desired effect – which, in turn, means that they should have a clear objective.

CHAPTER SEVEN:
FEEDBACK

So far in Part Two of this book we've established some health warnings with regards using research evidence to determine which curriculum implementation strategies work best and we've discussed the strategies that languish at the bottom of EEF's league table of 'what works'. But what do the EEF say are the most impactful teaching strategies?

Top of the table?

Feedback tops the EEF chart as the most impactful strategy at a teacher's disposal and so it would follow that schools should invest time and money in improving the effectiveness of feedback...

However, caution should be exercised because the term 'feedback' is a somewhat slippery one and it can mean many different things. So, before we continue, let's be clear how the EEF define feedback...

What is feedback?

The EEF say that feedback is "information given to the learner or teacher about the learner's performance relative to learning goals or outcomes. It should aim towards (and be capable of producing) improvement in students' learning. Feedback redirects or refocuses either the teacher's or the learner's actions to achieve a goal, by aligning effort and activity with an outcome."

Feedback, say the EEF, can be about "the output of the activity, the process of the activity, the student's management of their learning or self-regulation, or them as individuals (which tends to be the least effective)."

Likewise, this feedback can be "verbal or written, or can be given through tests or via digital technology. It can come from a teacher or someone taking a teaching role, or from peers."

Is feedback effective?

According to the EEF, studies tend to show very high effects of feedback on learning. However, some studies show that feedback can have negative effects and make things worse. It is therefore important, the EEF say, to understand the potential benefits and the possible limitations of feedback as a teaching and learning approach. In general, research-based approaches that explicitly aim to provide feedback to learners, such as Bloom's 'mastery learning', tend to have a positive impact.

What does effective feedback look like in practice?

The first thing to note is that, just because the EEF toolkit says that feedback is good does not imply that teachers should do lots more of it. It does mean that, when done well, it can really benefit pupils and so feedback should be done better, which is to say that feedback should be meaningful and helpful to pupils.

In practice, according to the EEF, effective feedback tends to:

- be specific, accurate and clear (e.g. "It was good because you..." rather than just "correct");
- compare what a learner is doing right now with what they have done wrong before (e.g. "I can see you were focused on improving X as it is much better than last time's Y...");
- encourage and support further effort;
- be given sparingly so that it is meaningful;
- provide specific guidance on how to improve and not just tell students when they are wrong; and
- be supported with effective professional development for teachers.

Broader research suggests that feedback should be about complex or challenging tasks or goals as this is likely to emphasise the importance of effort and perseverance as well as be more valued by the pupils.

It's also worth remembering that feedback can come from peers as well as adults.

The beast of burden

Marking and feedback are perhaps the most time-consuming activities in which teachers regularly engage outside of actual classroom teaching. There is a danger, therefore, that if school and college leaders see 'feedback' topping the EEF table, as indeed Hattie's list, they might interpret this as being a case of 'feedback is good therefore let's do more feedback'. However, effective feedback is about doing less of it but doing it better and ensuring it leads to improvement by planning opportunities in class for pupils to act on it.

In their 2016 report, 'Eliminating unnecessary workload around marking', the Independent Teacher Workload Review Group said, "Written feedback has become disproportionately valued by schools and has become unnecessarily burdensome for teachers."

The group argued that quantity should not be confused with quality. "The quality of the feedback, however given, will be seen in how a pupil is able to tackle subsequent work."

The group recommended that all marking should be meaningful, manageable and motivating... but what might this look like in practice?

1. Meaningful

To my mind, marking and feedback have but one purpose: to help pupils make better progress and achieve good outcomes. Feedback might do this directly by providing cues to the pupil about what to improve, and it might do it indirectly by providing assessment information to the teacher to guide their planning.

Marking and feedback carried out for any other purpose are not meaningful activities and - as well as being a waste of a teacher's precious time - can distract and indeed detract from this important goal.

The best person to decide which type of marking and feedback to use and when to use it is, of course, the teacher because it is the teacher who will use the assessment information to aid her planning and to support her pupils to make progress. Accordingly, the teacher should be allowed the freedom to determine whether to give written or verbal feedback, and whether to do so in class or in pupils' books.

Although a school's assessment policy may set broad guidelines about how often pupils' work should be marked in order to ensure that no pupil falls through the net, it also needs to build in sufficient flexibility so that teachers can decide how to do it.

Consistency is important but this does not necessarily mean unvarying practice. Whilst having a set of shared expectations regarding marking and feedback will help everybody to be clear about what is required of them, each curriculum subject should be allowed to determine the detail of the policy for their areas, responding to the different workload demands of their subject and to the differences inherent in each phase and key stage of education.

The nature and volume of marking and feedback necessarily varies by age group, subject, and what works best for the individual pupil and for the particular piece of work being assessed. As such, teachers should be encouraged to be pragmatic, adjusting their approach according to context. This involves trust and, as Henry L Stimson once said, the only way to make someone trustworthy is to trust them. School and college leaders will soon know if a teacher's practice is ineffective - they don't need to straitjacket all their staff in order to ensure consistency and quality.

In practice, this means that school and college leaders need to avoid asking teachers to mark at set times of the year because those times might not always be the best times for that subject and that teacher. Instead, schools and colleges should ask that teachers mark a set number of times through the year but allow them or their departments to choose precisely when this would be. In so doing, schools and colleges can ensure that marking is less frequent but more meaningful.

Schools and colleges should also be aware that marking looks very different in some subjects and vocations compared with others. As such, subject disciplines should be allowed to decide what effective marking and feedback should look like for them. Each area may collate examples of best practice to help new staff and to reinforce expectations for existing teachers. But these examples should not be regarded as 'the only way' to do things and should not acquire mythic status. Rather, they should continue to evolve over time, and to be challenged.

2. Manageable

A teacher's job is a complex one and it would be possible to work twenty-four hours a day and seven days a week and still not feel that the job is done. And yet there are only so many hours in the day. It is important that, whatever approach schools take to marking and feedback, they ensure they protect teachers' work life balances because tired teachers do not perform as well and burn-out can lead to issues with teacher retention and we all know teacher absences and staff shortages seriously impede pupils' progress.

Marking and feedback should, therefore, be proportionate. Here we should consider my 'energy versus impact' equation: we want to ensure maximum impact for pupils from the minimum amount of energy teachers expend. Any expectation on the frequency of marking should take into account the complexity of marking and the volume of marking required in any given subject, vocation, qualification type, and phase and key stage of education.

As I've said before, there is no doubt that feedback is valuable, but we need to decide which one of all the valuable things teachers do is more worthwhile than the others and focus on the areas of biggest impact for the smallest investment of teacher time and energy.

Put simply, if teachers are spending more time marking and giving feedback than pupils are spending on a piece of work then your priorities are wrong and should be changed.

Once a policy is in place, it's important that it is frequently reviewed because marking practices change, particularly in light of reforms to national curricula and qualifications, as well as in response to new research. It may have been tempting to assume that the removal of coursework at GCSE lightened the teacher marking load but in many cases the load simply got heavier as schools introduced more mock exams and other assessment heavy preparations for terminal tests.

In practice, school and college leaders need to ensure that teachers are selective in what they mark, rather than expecting them to mark every piece of work a pupil produces and 'tick and flick' every page of their exercise books or portfolios. Marking everything is time-consuming and counterproductive. Feedback becomes like a grain of sand on a beach, ignored by the pupil because of its sheer ubiquity.

Subject areas and teachers should identify the best assessment opportunities in each topic, module or scheme of work - this might be a synoptic piece that demonstrates pupils' knowledge and understanding across a range of areas, or it might be the exam questions that garner the most marks (for example, the teacher may only assess the 6+ mark questions, whilst pupils and their peers assess the 1 - 5 mark questions).

If nothing else, schools should end the pointless practice of 'tick and flick'.

3. Motivating

Marking should help to motivate pupils to progress. In this regard, short verbal feedback is often more motivational than long written comments on pupils' work.

Indeed, some pupils find written comments demotivating because they ruin the presentation of their work and are confusing or overwhelming. Once again there's a simple rule to obey here: if the teacher is doing more work than their pupils, they need to stop. Not only is it harmful to teacher workload, it can become a disincentive for pupils because there is too much feedback on which to focus and respond, and/or they do not think they have to take responsibility for improving their work - particularly if they had not sufficiently checked their own work before receiving feedback - because the teacher is spoon-feeding them.

What's more, too much feedback can reduce a pupil's long-term retention and harm resilience. To build retention and resilience, pupils need to be taught to check their own work and make improvements before the teacher marks it and gives feedback. The feedback should also prompt further thinking and drafting, perhaps by posing questions on which the pupil has to ruminate and act, as opposed to ready-made suggestions and solutions.

In practice, schools and colleges need to liaise with pupils on what kind of feedback motivates them best. Evidence suggests that rewarding pupils for their attainment rather than their effort is harmful and counterproductive. Many pupils, when surveyed, say they don't want summative comments, they just want to know how to improve. What's more, many pupils say they don't want praise. They don't need a written affirmation that they're working hard. In fact, many pupils simply ignore the praise when it's given.

However, what applies to written feedback does not always apply to verbal feedback - in fact, the only time to offer praise, in my opinion, is when giving verbal feedback. Positive verbal feedback can be motivating and certainly improves the learning environment. Written feedback, meanwhile, should focus on what needs to happen next.

CHAPTER EIGHT: METACOGNITION

Metacognition and self-regulation take equal top-billing on the EEF toolkit and, like feedback, are said to add an extra eight months of learning per year.

Also akin to feedback, metacognition can mean different things to different people. So, before we continue, let's be clear how the EEF define it...

What is metacognition?

The EEF say that metacognitive approaches aim to help pupils think about their own learning more explicitly, often by teaching them specific strategies for planning, monitoring and evaluating their learning.

Metacognition gifts pupils a repertoire of strategies to choose from and the skills to select the most suitable strategy for any given learning task.

Is metacognition effective?

The EEF say that metacognition and self-regulation approaches have consistently high levels of impact. These strategies are usually more effective when taught in collaborative groups so that pupils can support each other and make their thinking explicit through discussion.

The potential impact of these approaches is high but can be difficult to achieve in practice as they require pupils to take greater responsibility for their learning and develop their understanding of what is required to succeed. The evidence indicates that teaching these strategies can be particularly effective for low achieving and older pupils.

When seeking to develop pupils' metacognitive abilities, say the EEF, teachers should consider which explicit strategies they can teach pupils to help them plan, monitor, and evaluate specific aspects of their learning. Teachers should also consider how to give pupils opportunities to use these strategies with support, and then independently, and ensure they set an appropriate level of challenge to develop pupils' self-regulation and metacognition in relation to specific learning tasks.

In the classroom, teachers should consider how they can promote and develop metacognitive talk related to lesson objectives, and what professional development is needed to develop teachers' knowledge and understanding of these approaches.

Metacognition in the classroom

Before we answer the all-important question 'What does metacognition look like in the classroom?' I think it helpful to state what it does not look like...

Firstly, metacognition is not simply 'thinking about thinking', despite the morphology of the word. Although metacognition does indeed involve thinking about one's thinking, it is much more complex than this; rather, metacognition is actively monitoring one's own learning and, based on this monitoring, making changes to one's own learning behaviours and strategies.

Secondly, not every strategy used whilst performing a cognitive task can be described as metacognitive. Indeed, Flavell (1981) made a useful distinction. He said that strategies used to make cognitive progress are 'cognitive strategies'; strategies used to monitor cognitive progress, meanwhile, are 'metacognitive strategies'.

Thirdly, metacognition is not solely in the domain of the learner and not solely for the benefit of older learners. Although it's true that a metacognitive approach typically focuses on allowing the learner rather than the teacher to take control of their own learning, this is not to say that the teacher has no role to play. Indeed, the teacher is integral to the development of their learners' metacognitive skills. For example, in order for pupils to become metacognitive, self-regulated learners, the teacher must first set clear learning objectives, then demonstrate and monitor pupils' metacognitive strategies, and prompt and encourage their learners along the way. And metacognitive skills can be developed from an early age, certainly whilst pupils are at primary school; it is not something to be reserved for secondary pupils or FE learners.

What does metacognition look like in the classroom?

Metacognition describes the processes involved when learners plan, monitor, evaluate and make changes to their own learning behaviours. Metacognition is often considered to have two dimensions:

- Metacognitive knowledge, and
- Self-regulation.

Metacognitive knowledge refers to what learners <u>know</u> about learning. This includes:

- The learner's knowledge of their own cognitive abilities (e.g. 'I have trouble remembering key dates in this period of history')
- The learner's knowledge of particular tasks (e.g. 'The politics in this period of history are complex')
- The learner's knowledge of the different strategies that are available to them and when they are appropriate to the task (e.g. 'If I create a timeline first it will help me to understand this period of history').

Self-regulation, meanwhile, refers to what learners <u>do</u> about learning. It describes how learners monitor and control their cognitive processes. For example, a learner might realise that a particular strategy is not yielding the results they expected so they decide to try a different strategy.

Put another way, self-regulated learners are aware of their strengths and weaknesses, and can motivate themselves to engage in, and improve, their learning.

According to the EEF, we approach any learning task or opportunity with some metacognitive knowledge about:

- our own abilities and attitudes (knowledge of ourselves as a learner);
- what strategies are effective and available (knowledge of strategies); and
- this particular type of activity (knowledge of the task).

When undertaking a learning task, we start with this knowledge, then apply and adapt it. This, the EEF say, is metacognitive regulation. It is about "planning how to undertake a task, working on it while monitoring the strategy to check progress, then evaluating the overall success".

A metacognitive cycle

Metacognition and self-regulation might take the following form:

1. *The planning stage:*
During the planning stage, learners think about the learning goal the teacher has set and consider how they will approach the task and which strategies they will use. At this stage, it is helpful for learners to ask themselves:

- 'What am I being asked to do?'
- 'Which strategies will I use?'
- 'Are there any strategies that I have used before that might be useful?'

2. *The monitoring stage:*
During the monitoring stage, learners implement their plan and monitor the progress they are making towards their learning goal. Pupils might decide to make changes to the strategies they are using if these are not working. As pupils work through the task, it is helpful to ask themselves:

- 'Is the strategy that I am using working?'
- 'Do I need to try something different?'

3. The evaluation stage:

During the evaluation stage, pupils determine how successful the strategy they've used has been in terms of helping them to achieve their learning goal. To promote evaluation, it is helpful for pupils to ask themselves:

- 'How well did I do?'
- 'What didn't go well?' 'What could I do differently next time?'
- 'What went well?' 'What other types of problem can I use this strategy for?'

4. The reflection stage:

Reflection is an integral part of the whole process. Encouraging learners to self-question throughout the process is therefore crucial.

The EEF offer a slightly different version of this process which they call the *metacognitive regulation cycle*. Helpfully, they posit some concrete examples...

In one example, the EEF introduce us to John who is set a maths question to answer. John starts with some knowledge of the task (word problems in maths are often solved by expressing them as equations) and of strategies (how to turn sentences into an equation). His knowledge of the task then develops as it emerges from being a word problem into a simultaneous equation. He would then continue through this cycle if he has the strategies for solving simultaneous equations. He could then evaluate his overall success by substituting his answers into the word problem and checking they are correct. If this was wrong, he could attempt other strategies and once more update his metacognitive knowledge.

In another example, Amy's geography teacher asks the class to prepare a short presentation about rainforest ecosystems. To plan this, Amy reflects on how she learned best on the last topic (using the school textbooks) and decides to read the relevant chapter before drafting her presentation. However, when reading it she decides that the chapter does not really improve her understanding. She starts to panic as she was relying on this. Then Amy remembers a geography website her teacher mentioned. She adapts her strategy and searches the website. This provides a more useful overview and she uses the information to summarise some interesting facts. She reflects on the experience and decides that next time she will gather a range of resources before starting to research a topic rather than relying on one source.

Most learners, say the EEF, go through many of these thinking processes to some extent when trying to solve a problem or tackle a task in the classroom. The most effective learners, however, will have developed a repertoire of different cognitive and metacognitive strategies and be able to effectively use and apply these in a timely fashion. They will, in other words, self-regulate and find ways to motivate themselves when they get stuck. Over time, this can further increase their motivation as they become more confident in undertaking new tasks and challenges.

Teaching metacognition

The EEF argue that metacognition and self-regulation must be explicitly taught. This might look as follows:

1. *The planning stage:*
The teacher encourages pupils to think about the goal of their learning (set by the teacher, or themselves) and to consider how they will approach the task. This might include:

- ensuring they understand the goal,
- activating relevant prior knowledge about the task,
- selecting appropriate strategies, and
- considering how to allocate their effort.

2. *The monitoring stage:*
Here, the teacher emphasises the need for pupils to assess their own progress. This might include self-testing and self-questioning, as well as making changes to their chosen strategies. Teachers can explicitly teach these skills by prompting pupils with examples of the things they should be considering at each stage of a learning task.

The EEF use the example of pupils drawing or painting a self-portrait in art. Effective teacher questioning while modelling a self-portrait, they say, can aid the development of metacognitive reflection as follows:

Planning:
- 'What resources do I need to carry out a self-portrait?'
- 'Have I done a self-portrait before and was it successful?'
- 'What have I learned from the examples we looked at earlier?'
- 'Where do I start and what viewpoint will I use?'
- 'Do I need a line guide to keep my features in proportion?'

Monitoring:
- 'Am I doing well?'
- 'Do I need any different techniques to improve my self-portrait?
- 'Are all of my facial features in proportion?'
- 'Am I finding this challenging?'
- 'Is there anything I need to stop and change to improve my self-portrait?'

Evaluation:
- 'How did I do?'
- 'Did my line guide strategy work?'
- 'Was it the right viewpoint to choose?'
- 'How would I do a better self-portrait next time?'
- 'Are there other perspectives, viewpoints or techniques I would like to try?'

Some of the above 'planning' questions activate prior knowledge (resources, previous exemplars) whereas others model the use of the best cognitive strategies (viewpoint, line guides). The 'monitoring' questions, meanwhile, emphasise both general progress (proportion, editing) alongside checking general motivation (meeting goals and dealing with challenge). The 'evaluation' questions concentrate on assessing the relative success of the cognitive strategies used (line guide, viewpoint, comparison with other techniques) and on what can be learnt from the experience.

The EEF suggest that these prompts are accompanied by explicit instruction in the relevant cognitive strategies. In the self-portrait example, for instance, pupils will only be able to consider these questions and approaches if they understand the importance of perspective and the different techniques.

The EEF proffers a handy 7-step guide to teaching metacognitive strategies, as follows:

1. ***Activating prior knowledge*** – here, the teacher discusses with pupils the different causes that led to World War One while making notes on the whiteboard.

2. ***Explicit strategy instruction*** – here, the teacher explains how a 'fishbone' diagram will help organise their ideas, with the emphasis on the cognitive strategy of using a 'cause and effect model' in history that will help them to organise and plan a better written response.

3. ***Modelling of learned strategy*** – next, the teacher uses the initial notes on the causes of the war to model one part of the fishbone diagram.

4. ***Memorisation of learned strategy*** – here, the teacher tests if pupils have understood and memorised the key aspects of the fishbone strategy, and its main purpose, through questions and discussion.

5. ***Guided practice*** – next, the teacher models one further fishbone cause with the whole group, with pupils verbally contributing their ideas.

6. ***Independent practice*** follows whereby pupils complete their own fishbone diagram analysis.

7. Finally, in ***structured reflection*** the teacher encourages pupils to reflect on how appropriate the model was, how successfully they applied it, and how they might use it in the future.

CHAPTER NINE:
BEST OF THE REST

So far on this section of the book on evidence-informed education, we have focused on the teaching strategies at the top of the EEF hit parade as well as those languishing at the very bottom of the charts. Now let's take a brief look at some of those in between. We will focus on the following three strategies:

1. The teaching of reading
2. Homework
3. Parental engagement

The teaching of reading

What is it?

Pupils are taught a range of techniques which enable them to comprehend the meaning of what they read. These techniques can include:

- inferring meaning from context;
- summarising or identifying key points;
- using graphic or semantic organisers;
- developing questioning strategies; and
- monitoring their own comprehension and identifying difficulties themselves.

Is it effective?

On average, say the EEF, reading comprehension strategies deliver an additional six months of progress. The most impactful reading comprehension approaches allow activities to be carefully tailored to pupils' reading capabilities, and involve activities and texts that provide an effective, but not overwhelming, challenge.

More info

The EEF report 'Preparing for Literacy: Improving Communication, Language and Literacy in the Early Years' (2018), says that approaches that emphasise spoken language and verbal interaction can support the development of communication and language. In turn, communication and language provide the foundations for learning and thinking and underpin the development of later literacy skills.

The EEF say that focusing on language and communication is especially important for young children and will support the development of a range of early literacy skills as well as their wider knowledge and understanding.

In addition, developing communication and language is linked to other important outcomes including pupils' self-regulation, socio-emotional development, and reasoning.

A wide range of activities can be used to develop communication and language including shared reading, storytelling, and explicitly extending pupils' vocabulary. The EEF say that these activities should be embedded within a curriculum of rich and varied experiences.

The EEF report concludes that there is relatively limited evidence about how best to improve vocabulary, but argue the existing evidence suggests that schools should consider the following approaches:

- providing children with a rich language environment (implicit approaches) as well as directly extending children's vocabulary (explicit approaches);
- carefully selecting high-frequency words for explicit teaching;
- developing the number of words children know (breadth) and their understanding of relationships between words and the contexts in which words can be used (depth); and

- providing multiple opportunities to hear and use new vocabulary.

We'll return to the subject of vocabulary instruction later in this book. But let's stick with reading comprehension for now...

The EEF report also introduces the PEER framework which is a sequence to support shared reading. The idea is this: when reading with a pupil, teachers can pause and:

- **P**rompt the child to say something about the book;
- **E**valuate their response;
- **E**xpand their response by rephrasing or adding information to it; and
- **R**epeat the prompt to help them learn from the expansion.

The prompts that make up the P of PEER can be remembered using the acronym CROWD:

- **C**ompletion—leave a blank at the end of a sentence for children to complete
- **R**ecall—ask children about something they have already read
- **O**pen-ended—often with a focus on pictures in books
- **W**h—prompts that begin with 'who', 'what', 'where', 'why', and 'when'
- **D**istancing—connects the book to children's own life experiences and provides an opportunity for high quality discussion.

Putting the evidence into practice

One of the most important reading comprehension skills in any subject is fluency. Allow me to explain...

A few years ago, I discovered Instapaper, an app which collates reading material – newspaper articles and webpages, say – and converts them into audio so that I can listen to them on my daily dog walks. There's never enough time in the day. My backlog of reading material just gets longer and longer, and my sense of guilt bigger and bigger. But text-to-speech technology like Instapaper (other apps are available!) allows me to 'read' articles, research papers and blogs whilst on the move, thus helping me to catch up on the backlog and ease my guilt somewhat.

But there's a problem.

Like all text-to-speech programmes, the speaking voice in Instapaper is somewhat stilted and robotic (think Stephen Hawking) and is unable to detect nuance. Of course, it might be argued that most written texts lack nuance because it's difficult to discern – accurately and with any surety – the writer's mood and intended tone of voice.

Short-form texts, and transactional texts which are ephemeral, contemporaneous and written hastily – such as SMS messages, tweets and emails – are particularly difficult to 'read' for 'voice'. It's difficult to identify sarcasm, for example; and often a tongue-in-cheek 'joke' is interpreted as rude or offensive.

Try saying ' Shut up' in as many tones of voice as possible. Say it as if you're really angry. Now as if you're embarrassed. And scared. And irritated. Bored, even. Tired. And so on. Tone matters.

But with text-to-speech, this difficulty to discern tone is writ particularly large.

What is lacking from Instapaper's robotic voice is comprehension or, more accurately, fluency. The automated voice merely sounds out letters and letter combinations without any sense of meaning. The robot doesn't know, for example, whether the word 'read' should be pronounced as 'red' or 'reed'. And it certainly doesn't know if words should be read in a happy or sad tone.

So, what is fluency and why is it important?

Fluency is the ability to read text quickly and accurately, adopting the appropriate intonation. Fluency requires some background knowledge about the text, as well as an ability to rapidly retrieve the requisite vocabulary. Fluency also requires a knowledge of syntax and grammar in order to predict the words that are likely to appear next. Let me illustrate...

Read the following sentence quickly, instinctively (i.e. without looking ahead):

He could lead if he would get the lead out.

How about this one:

The dump was so full that it had to refuse more refuse.

And:

The bandage was wound around the wound.

The ability to adapt one's vocabulary and intonation according to a text's syntax and grammar, and the ability to read ahead, helps with both speed and accuracy.

English is not easy, of course. Just think of the number of ways in which *-ough* can be pronounced:

A rough-coated, dough-faced, thoughtful ploughman strode through the streets of Scarborough; after falling into a slough, he coughed and hiccoughed.

Experienced readers integrate these processes so that reading becomes automatic which allows their cognitive energy to be focused on the task of discerning meaning.

A useful analogy and one to which I will return later is learning to tie your shoelaces. When you first learn to tie your laces, because it is an unfamiliar task, you have to dedicate all your attention to it, utilising your working memory. You have to really think about how to tie your laces, what goes where and in what order, and so cannot concentrate on anything else at the same time. To do so would be to reach cognitive overload whereby thinking and doing fails. When you are first learning to tie your shoelaces, it is difficult – if not impossible – to do so whilst engaging in a conversation, for example.

However, once you've mastered the art of lace-tying – through repeated exposure to the task – you reach the point of automaticity, thus you can do it through habit without having to think about it. This frees up valuable space in your working memory to dedicate to other tasks, such as holding a conversation.

Reading is just the same. Through repeated exposure to reading, to decoding words and their meanings, you come to do it automatically which frees up cognitive capacity for you to read ahead, to think about syntax and grammar, and to discern meaning and tone, context and connotation, bias and allusion. All of this enables you to truly understand a text.

In other words, there is a strong correlation between fluency and reading comprehension; indeed, it is such a strong link that fluency and comprehension can be regarded as interdependent. After all, fluency only occurs when a reader understands the text; if reading is hesitant and disjointed, all sense of meaning is lost.

It is impossible to be a fluent reader if you have to keep stopping to work out what a word is. To be fluent you have to move beyond the decoding stage to accurately read whole words.

A fluent reader has ready access to a vast bank of words which can be used in different contexts.

The words to which a reader has immediate access are called their 'sight vocabulary'. Even complex words that originally had to be decoded – like 'originally' and 'decoded' rather than monosyllabic functional words like 'that' and 'had' – but which can now be recognised on sight, become a part of the fluent reader's lexicon.

But recognition is not enough to achieve fluency. As well as being in the reader's sight vocabulary, words must also be stored in their 'receptive vocabulary' – that is to say, words which the reader knows the meaning of.

The larger the bank of words that are both recognised and understood on sight, then the broader the range of texts which are accessible. For this reason, developing sight vocabularies and receptive vocabularies are the most effective ways of developing both fluency and reading comprehension.

Once your pupils' sight and receptive vocabularies have been developed, you must make sure that the texts to which you expose pupils are appropriate to their age and reading ability so that they do not contain unfamiliar or technical words that are outside pupils' knowledge base.

This is why early readers need simple texts to help them develop both speed and confidence.

Although it's sometimes tempting to give pupils 'harder books' as a way of challenging them, this is not always the best approach.

Texts within a pupils' knowledge base provide them with opportunities to practise their vocabulary, develop appropriate expression, and build confidence and belief in themselves as readers.

Once you've developed accuracy, you need to develop speed, increasing the rate at which your pupils can access texts.

Reading speed is also strongly linked with reading comprehension. When a reader is both accurate and quick, word identification becomes automated and they no longer require cognitive energy or attention, thus freeing up precious space in the working memory for higher order comprehension.

Reading speed is not the same as reading fast. People who read too quickly and therefore show no regard for punctuation, intonation or comprehension are not fluent readers. Reading speed is about being able to process texts quickly whilst understanding the text and taking account of punctuation and adopting an appropriate intonation. In short, improving pupils' reading speed is important but it must not be at the expense of comprehension.

As a 'back of an envelope' calculation, the average reading speed in the primary phase is as follows:

- by the end of Year 1 = 60 words per minute
- by the end of Year 2 = 90/100 words per minute
- in Years 3 to 6 = 100–120 words per minute with fewer than 3 errors

After accuracy and speed, prosody – that is to say, reading with expression – is the third component of reading fluently.

Prosody is more difficult to achieve than accuracy and speed because it involves developing stress, pitch, and rhythm. However, Prosody is essential in rendering reading aloud meaningful.

Poor prosody can cause confusion and has an impact on readers' interest and motivation to read. Good prosody, meanwhile, makes reading aloud come alive and reflects the author's message more accurately and more meaningfully.

So, how can we help our pupils to develop fluency? Here are nine top tips to consider...

1. One of the best ways for teachers to help pupils develop fluency is to read aloud to them in an engaging and motivating way in order to model fluency for them. Doing all the voices, adding sound effects and dramatic pauses, heightens pupils' engagement.

2. Using 'fluency cards' which contain lines of single letters and common letter combinations can also help pupils to develop fluency because fluency is achieved through automatic recognition of words and parts of words including letter sounds.

3. Another way of increasing pupils' fluency is to display high frequency irregular words. Word walls – when they are referred to and used in competitions or quizzes – help build pupils' automatic recognition of words.

4. Pupils may also need direct instruction in how to read punctuation. Most pupils, although they know how to punctuate their writing, have no idea how to read punctuation.

5. Whole class reading of short pieces of dialogue is a low risk activity – particularly when the teacher reads the passage first then pupils repeat it – to build fluency in lower ability readers.

6. Repeatedly reading a text provides the practice needed to develop accuracy, speed and confidence. A typical strategy is to pair pupils up and for the more fluent reader in the pair to model the appropriate rate and intonation for the less fluent reader who then repeats the passage.

Alternatively, both pupils could read simultaneously. The more fluent reader in the pair is likely to start fractionally ahead of the less fluent reader, modelling accuracy, rate and intonation, but as the less fluent reader gains in confidence, the two pupils will blend together.

7. Reading lots of poetry – as well as being enjoyable in itself – helps develop reading fluency because poetry tends to have a natural rhythm when it is read aloud.

8. Get pupils reading aloud from a script, say a monologue or short scene. The focus is not on dramatic kinaesthetic performance but on interpreting the text using only the voice. Pupils are encouraged to bring the plot to life

9. Listen to audio books or ask older volunteers (parents, local people, sixth formers) to record their favourite stories to play to the class.

Homework

What is it?

The EFF says that homework refers to tasks given to pupils by their teachers to be completed outside of usual lessons. Common homework activities in secondary schools, for example, include completing tasks assigned in lessons, preparing for tasks in future lessons, routine coursework, and revision for tests and examinations. Their definition also includes activities such as 'homework clubs' where pupils have the opportunity to complete homework in school but outside normal school hours, and 'flipped learning' models, where pupils prepare at home for classroom discussion and application tasks.

How effective is it?

EEF's meta-analyses show that the impact of homework, on average, is five months' additional progress. However, beneath this average there is a wide variation in potential impact, suggesting that how homework is set is likely to be very important.

More info

There is some evidence that homework is most effective when used as a short and focused intervention (e.g. in the form of a project or specific target connected with a particular element of learning) with some exceptional studies showing up to eight additional months' positive impact on attainment. Benefits are likely to be more modest, up to two to three months' progress on average, if homework is more routinely set (e.g. learning vocabulary or completing practice tasks in mathematics every day).

Evidence also suggests that how homework relates to learning during normal school time is important. In the most effective examples, homework was an integral part of learning, rather than an add-on. To maximise impact, the EEF days it's also important that pupils are provided with high quality feedback on their work.

Some studies indicate that there may be an optimum amount of homework of between one and two hours per school day (slightly longer for older pupils), with effects diminishing as the time that pupils spend on homework increases.

Putting the evidence into practice

I'm going to look beyond the EEF to provide some more practical advice on homework. Let's start by considering why we want pupils to do homework...

What's the point of homework?

Homework has had a rough ride in recent years with many teachers and parents calling for it to be scrapped. Those who fail to see the merits of homework tend to cite Professor John Hattie's book Visible Learning which gives homework an effect size of 0.26, meaning there's only a 21 per cent chance that homework will make a positive difference to a pupil's levels of progress.

One prominent advocate of scrapping homework is Tim Lott who once asked in a *Guardian* article: "Why do we torment kids in this way?"

He wrote: "I had no homework during my primary school years and very little during the first years of grammar school. This was the norm in the 1960s and 70s. At some point since, the work 'ethic' that has infected national life generally – not that it's particularly ethical – insists that if you're not working, you're doing something faintly dissolute or purposeless, even if you're six.

"Nothing is more precious than those islands of childhood that are left untouched by invading adults and their fund of schemes for the future when you finally make it as a 'worthy citizen'. Let children drift and dream and make up games ... but this makes evangelists for the work society uneasy."

Homework generates conflict with parents, Lott said, and, worse still, parents are required to help. The problem is, most parents are not trained teachers and are often impatient and ineffective.

The end result of homework, according to Lott and many others, is that study becomes associated in the young mind with conflict and unhappiness.

However, the facts are a little more nuanced. It is probably true that too much homework – particularly if it's meaningless "fluff" – for Lott's 10-year-old daughter is pointless, counterproductive and switches her and her parents off education.

But that's not the whole story. The benefits of homework vary by age; the older the pupil, the greater the benefit. Indeed, if you look in detail at what Hattie says in Visible Learning, you'll see that behind the headline figure of 0.26 are two separate figures, one for primary and one for secondary and those two figures are startlingly different.

But first let's look at effect sizes in general. An effect size of 0.2 is considered small. An effect size of 0.4 is considered medium. An effect size of 0.6 is considered large. Anything greater than 0.4 is therefore above average and anything above 0.6 is classified excellent.

Hattie says that the effect of homework on pupil outcomes is 0.26 overall but is 0.15 at primary and 0.64 at secondary. Therefore, it is small at primary but large at secondary.

In other words, the effect of homework on pupil outcomes in the primary phase is, as Lott and others rightly argue, negligible and could do more harm than good if it's not managed well. But the effect of homework on pupil outcomes in the secondary phase of education is excellent and therefore well worth persevering with, albeit improving. Homework, then, is not to be disregarded quite so quickly.

Hattie also goes into some detail about the kinds of homework that work best. The highest effects, he says, are associated with practice and rehearsal tasks. And short, frequent homework tasks that are closely monitored by the teacher have the most impact on pupil progress.

The optimal time per-night for pupils to spend on homework also varies by age; the older the pupil, the more time they should spend on homework. This is an imperfect science but, roughly, I would argue that the following is a good guide: pupils in the primary phase should do no more than about 20 minutes a night, pupils in key stage 3 should do about 40 minutes, pupils in key stage 4 should do about 60 minutes, and pupils in key stage 5 should do about 90 minutes a night.

What homework works best?

In my experience, homework – like all forms of assignments – works best when you give pupils a clear picture of the final product and a real audience for their work. Homework also works best when you allow a certain degree of autonomy, whereby pupils can make choices about which tasks they carry out, how they carry them out and how they will be assessed on the final product. And homework also works best when you incorporate cultural products into it such as television, film, magazines, food, and sports – to name but five examples – in order to engage pupils' personal interests and awaken prior knowledge.

Naturally, it is always best to avoid "fluff" assignments – homework tasks which bear no relation to what is being learnt and which simply waste pupils' time.

When she was in Year 11, for homework, my daughter baked a cake in the shape of a wind turbine for a science project. It took her five hours. Needless to say, I was less than impressed. What aspect of science did she practise, rehearse or consolidate during those five hours, I asked her. She struggled for an answer. "But I like baking," came her eventual reply.

Homework must have genuine purpose and the "doing" must be linked to the "learning" because pupils remember what they are asked to do more than what they are asked to think about.

It is also wise to vary the language of homework tasks, perhaps by using Bloom's Taxonomy. Rather than always asking pupils simple comprehension questions or to summarise a text, try to move up and down the taxonomy by asking them to: define, recall, describe, label, identify, match, name, or state (knowledge); translate, predict, explain, summarise, describe, compare, or classify (comprehension); demonstrate how, solve, use, interpret, relate, or apply (application); analyse, explain, infer, break-down, prioritise, reason logically, or draw conclusions (analysis); design, create, compose, combine, reorganise, reflect, predict, speculate, hypothesise, or summarise (synthesis); assess, judge, compare/contrast, or evaluate (evaluation).

Homework, if it is to be taken seriously, should be non-negotiable like class-work. As such, you should not allow "passes" whereby pupils can be excused from handing homework in and you should require everyone to "turn in a paper", so even when someone has forgotten to bring their homework in on the due-date they should be required to write their name on a piece of paper and the reason they haven't got their homework and submit that instead.

Then, crucially, at the bottom of the page they should add a parent/carer's name and daytime phone number. That way you have a paper from everyone, a record of who hasn't handed their homework in on time and a way of contacting parents to make them aware of their child's failure to comply with the rules. I'm sure you will find that the tactic of requiring pupils to submit phone numbers will quickly have the desired effect.

Occasionally, homework could be integrated with other subjects, becoming cross-curricular and thematic, enabling pupils to see the natural links that exist between subjects and the transferability of key skills, as well as to provide variety. This could occur once every half-term as an extended project.

Types of homework

Broadly speaking there are four types of homework task: practice, preparation, study, extend/elaborate.

Of these, practice is the most valuable in terms of producing measurable academic gains because practice builds proficiency and mastery. Practice can be single skill or cumulative. Cumulative practice is where a new skill is practised alongside a previously learnt skill.

A pupil must have demonstrated competence in the skill being practised before being asked to do it for homework. Homework should not – except in the case of flipped learning – introduce new concepts or information. There are three forms of practice worth considering for homework tasks:

1 Spaced repetition

This is where information is learnt initially then repeated again several times at increasingly long intervals so that pupils get to the point of almost forgetting what they have learnt and have to delve into their long-term memories to retrieve their prior knowledge, thus strengthening those memories. As well as returning to prior learning following an interval, we should explore that information in a new way because making new associations further strengthens our memories, hence homework task number two...

2 Retrieval practice

This is testing or quizzing (such as multiple-choice) used not for the purposes of assessment but for reinforcement and to provide pupils with feedback information on what they know and don't yet know so that they can better focus their future studies.

The number of different connections we make influences the number of times memories are revisited, which in turn influences the length of time we retain a memory. When we connect different pieces of information with each other, we retain them for longer, because we retrieve them more often. It follows, then, that the more often we connect what we are teaching today to what we taught previously, the better the information will be learnt.

If we retrieve a memory in order to connect prior knowledge to new information, the memory is strengthened even further, so using quizzes in which the information is presented in new ways helps pupils to improve their learning. We could also plan opportunities for our pupils to reorganise the information they have learnt by writing or talking about it.

3 Cognitive disfluencies

This is otherwise known as desirable difficulties. This is a memory technique that makes learning stick by placing artificial barriers in the way of pupils' learning. Doing this means that the process of encoding (initial learning) is made harder so that the process of retrieval (recalling that learning later, say in a test) is made easier.

One example of a desirable difficulty is making learning materials less easy to read, perhaps by using a difficult to decipher font, in order to make pupils think harder about the content. Another example is to use more complex language when forming questions and tasks so that pupils have to think harder about what is being asked of them before tackling the work.

General advice

Let's conclude this exploration of homework with some general dos and don'ts:

- Don't use a one-size-fits-all approach: homework should be differentiated to meet individual pupil needs.
- Don't set homework that contains new information – it should be used to practise taught skills.

- Don't set homework too quickly at the end of a lesson – time needs to be spent explaining it.
- Don't collect homework in but not review it – it needs to be assessed and feedback given.
- Don't give out homework that has no purpose or objective
- Do give less homework but more often.
- Do have a specific purpose for every homework task you set; don't set "busy work".
- Do ensure that homework is engaging.
- Do allot sufficient time in the lesson to present and explain the homework.
- Do answer pupils' questions about the homework and check their understanding.
- Do articulate the rationale for the homework and how it will be assessed.
- Do provide timely feedback on what has been mastered and what still needs to be practised.
- Do provide choices about the homework task, format and presentation.

Parental engagement

What is it?

The EEF define parental engagement, sensibly enough, as the involvement of parents in supporting their children's academic learning. It includes:

- approaches and programmes which aim to develop parental skills such as literacy or IT skills;
- general approaches which encourage parents to support their children with, for example reading or homework;
- the involvement of parents in their children's learning activities; and
- more intensive programmes for families in crisis.

How effective is it?

The EEF say that, although parental engagement is consistently associated with pupils' success at school, the evidence about how to improve attainment by increasing parental engagement is mixed and much less conclusive, particularly for disadvantaged families.

More info

Two recent meta-analyses from the USA suggested that increasing parental engagement in primary and secondary schools had on average two to three months' positive impact. There is some evidence that supporting parents with their first child will have benefits for siblings. However, there are also examples where combining parental engagement strategies with other interventions, such as extended early years provision, has not been associated with any additional educational benefit. This suggests that developing effective parental engagement to improve attainment is challenging and needs careful monitoring and evaluation.

Parents' aspirations also appear to be important for pupil outcomes, although there is limited evidence to show that intervening to change parents' aspirations will raise their children's aspirations and achievement over the longer term.

Putting the evidence into practice

I will return to the subject of parental engagement in more detail in Book Three of this series about School and College Curriculum Design when we turn our attentions to 'impact'. But, for our current purposes, permit me to share what I consider useful starting principles for effective parental engagement...

Firstly, **parental communication needs to start early** and continue throughout a pupil's journey through school and, where applicable, college. The parents of pupils moving from nursery to primary school, or from primary to secondary, and indeed from secondary to FE, will not want to receive information halfway through the summer holiday at which point it will be deemed too late. Schools need to engage with parents early and clearly set out their expectations and requirements.

Secondly, **parental communication needs to be a two-way process**: as well as the school staying in touch with parents, parents also need a means of keeping in contact with the school. One way to do this is to create a frequently asked questions (FAQ) page, as well as a Q&A facility and a parents' forum on the school's website. This will need to be monitored carefully, of course, or perhaps pass through a 'gatekeeper' in order to be vetted before comments are made 'live', and a set of guidelines about what is acceptable and what it not will need to be published. In order for it to be viewed as worthwhile, the school will also need to communicate its response to parental comments and suggestions, perhaps through a 'You Said, We Did' page.

Thirdly, **parental communications need to be appropriately timed, relevant and useful** and one way to do this is to utilise the experience and expertise of pupils and their parents. For example, the parents of current Reception or Year 7 pupils, as well as those in their first year of college, will be able to share their thoughts on what information they needed when they went through the transition process with their son or daughter not so long ago, as well as when they needed it most, whilst current Reception or Year 7 pupils and first year learners will be able to offer their advice about how to prepare for primary or secondary school, or college by, to give but two examples, providing a reading list for the summer and sharing their advice on how to get ready for the first day of school.

Fourthly, **parental communication should take many forms and embrace new and emerging technologies**. The use of technologies such as email, texting, websites, electronic portfolios and online assessment and reporting tools have - accordingly to Merkley, Schmidt, Dirksen and Fuhler (2006) - made communication between parents and teachers more timely, efficient, productive and satisfying.

Of course, doing all of this well takes time and yet it is important to balance the needs of parents with those of hard-working teachers. You do not want the unintended consequence of adding to teachers' workloads. So, how can you ensure you remain mindful of workload concerns whilst meeting the needs of parents?

The DfE advises that schools do the following:

- Consider why you are communicating. Think about all the communications you make in the day and review if they are making a difference – if not, stop.
- Establish and publish a communications policy or protocol planned around pinch points in the year.

- Start small with little activities that chip away at the time in a working day. Find out which areas of the school generate the most paper, slips or forms and consider if they are necessary, or if alternative systems can be used.
- Consider running a communications workshop.
- Review staff meetings. Reduce meeting times. Have clear start and end times with timed agenda items. Consider the number of meetings in place each week and provide flexibility. Have a nominated person look over departmental/phase/staff meeting agendas and reject them if they are not focused on pedagogy. Consider using tools like Google Forms to book meetings online.
- Use a variety of communication channels with parents and carers. Add frequently asked questions or 'decision tree' options to the school website to direct users, e.g. a short email may be as appropriate as a phone call, or a phone/video call could replace a face to face meeting.
- Apps and software can be used to send letters and reminders home, as well as collecting forms, making payments and booking appointments.
- Consider use of email. Set out times after which staff should not check, send or reply to work emails (whilst being mindful of urgent needs, for example, in relation to safeguarding).
- Use distribution lists and functions such as out of office messages and delayed delivery. All emails should have a descriptive heading with a status assigned to it to signify its urgency.
- Consider a daily/weekly bulletin using cloud services, and alternative messaging tools to reduce emails or categorise messages.
- Review the number and effectiveness of parental events. Consider the impact on pupil progress of each event as well as attendance from parents and balance the range of events on offer. Monitor staffing at events – decide on the supervision required and create a rota to reduce the number of events that staff are required to attend.
- Agree with staff what is a reasonable number of out-of-hours events (taking into account directed time) and prioritise your programme around the capacity you have.
- Review your approach to written reports. Assess the time and impact of current practice. Explore alternatives to written reports. Compare your current approach with the requirements for reporting to parents and the considerations in the Making

Data Work report. Consider how reports could be made more succinct (e.g. limiting the word count) and meaningful (e.g. focusing on key strengths and areas for development), as well as how the right technology can help to automate reporting where possible.

CHAPTER TEN:
CREATING A PHYSICAL LEARNING ENVIRONMENT

Before we embark on the three-step process of teaching for long-term learning and consider ways to translate our curriculum plans into classroom practice, I'd like to explore the role of the learning environment in curriculum implementation. In order to do so, permit me a brief anecdote...

I infuriate family and friends whenever we eat out because I insist on sitting in a corner of the restaurant where I can see the room and, crucially, the exit. This often involves a mirthless game of musical chairs. I'm not sure why – I don't recall a related childhood trauma and I've never had to make a quick escape from the clutches of an enemy – all I know is I feel a creeping sense of unease whenever I have my back to a room.

In a similar vein, I'm forever fighting over the thermostat in my house to ensure my ideal temperature is achieved (some like it hot, but not me). Likewise, I'm uncomfortable when the house lights are up because I prefer gloominess to the full glare of an interrogation cell. I don't like too much noise and work best in complete silence whereas, I know, others prefer background music or like the TV conversing in the corner even if no one is watching it.

I know what I'm describing sounds like diva-esque behaviour (I'm quite easy-going really) but I'm sure each of us has a set of personal preferences with regards our immediate environment. We are each of us comforted by certain conditions and discomforted by others - whether it's light, heat and noise, or more tangible features (some of us like order and organisation, perhaps to the point of sparsity; others like clutter and chaos and only feel safe when surrounded by their hordes).

And this is only the physical environment; there are also the social and emotional environments to consider. Some people like company; others solitude. Some people like a buoyant, busy atmosphere; others library-like quietude.

And what applies to the home also applies at school and college – so, what of the educational environment? What physical, social and emotional conditions are most conducive to learning? And what may distract pupils from their work?

The answer, I think, rather unhelpfully, is that it depends: it depends on the pupil and it depends on the context. You'll find no easy answers here, I'm afraid. However, what we do know with some degree of certainty is that the quality of the learning environment really does matter.

Pupils need to feel comfortable if they are to accept the challenge of hard work, and their basic needs must be met (think Maslow) if they are to attend to teacher instruction. And the environment must help ensure pupils focus on the curriculum content we need them to learn and avoid unhelpful distractions or detractions.

How we use our classroom space and the rules, routines and expectations we establish are therefore crucial considerations.

In this chapter and the one which follows, we'll wade through some best practice advice for creating the physical, social, and emotional learning environments that best support pupils' study and then, in Chapter Thirteen, we will explore those features of the classroom environment that are particularly conducive to long-term learning.

The physical environment

When I talk about the physical learning environment, I refer of course to those concrete aspects of our surroundings that stimulate or offend our senses – the quality of the school buildings, the attractiveness and usefulness of classroom walls, the quality of light and the temperature, and to how the physical space is utilised.

Research by the University of Salford suggests that pupils' emotional and physiological stability can directly impact on their understanding of the school curriculum and, therefore, affect the pace of their progress. Creating a physical environment that allows pupils to feel comfortable, content and focused, they argue, can help them to become more attentive to their teacher and more attuned to the content of the curriculum they are studying. In other words, pupils' conscious and subconscious attentions, and the development of their knowledge, skills and understandings are more effectively piqued when they study in a positive physical space.

So, what exactly is a "positive physical space"?

The University of Salford study suggests that a wide range of environmental factors can contribute towards the emotional and physiological effects of a classroom. For example, environmental factors including temperature, light, noise, classroom orientation, and even air quality have been shown – they say – to improve pupils' achievement.

Let's take a closer look at some of these physical attributes...

Temperature

Earlier I referenced in passing Abraham Maslow whose hierarchy of needs is widely known, and we can't ignore the importance of catering for our pupils' more basic needs because if they are uncomfortable they are less likely to concentrate in lessons. It's important to consider any individual needs such as those outlined on pupils' education health and care plans (EHCPs) as well as to refer to SEND law and best practice, particularly for pupils with sensory difficulties.

Lowe (1990) - as reported in a literature review by Buckley, Schneider, and Shang, 2004 - found that the best teachers in the US (winners of State Teachers of the Year awards) emphasised their ability to control classroom temperature as central to the performance of both teachers and pupils.

Lackney (1999), meanwhile, found that teachers believed thermal comfort affects both teaching quality and pupil achievement. A study by Corcoran et al. (1988) focused on how the physical condition of school facilities, including thermal factors, affected teacher morale and effectiveness.

Light

According to the research, classroom lighting also plays a critical role in both pupil performance and staff wellbeing (see Phillips 1997). Jago and Tanner (1999) cite results of seventeen studies from the mid- 1930s to 1997. The consensus of these studies is that appropriate lighting improves test scores, reduces off-task behaviour, and plays a significant role in the achievement of pupils.

Lemasters' (1997) synthesis of 53 studies pertaining to school facilities, pupil achievement, and behaviour, reports that daylight fosters higher pupil achievement. The study by the Heschong Mahone Group, covering more than 2000 classrooms in three US school districts, is perhaps the most cited evidence about the effects of daylight. The study indicated that pupils with the most classroom daylight progressed 20% faster in one year on maths tests and 26% faster on reading tests than those pupils who learned in environments that received the least amount of natural light.

Noise

Another physical condition that Buckley, Schneider and Shang note as being important to both pupil success and staff wellbeing pertains to noise levels...

The research linking acoustics to learning is consistent and convincing, they say: good acoustics are fundamental to good academic performance. Earthman and Lemasters (1997) report three key findings: that higher pupil achievement is associated with schools that have less external noise, that outside noise causes increased pupil dissatisfaction with their classrooms, and that excessive noise causes stress in students.

Teachers also attach importance to noise levels in classrooms and schools. Lackney (1999) found that teachers believe that noise impairs academic performance. Indeed, so say Buckley, Schneider and Shang, it appears that external noise causes more discomfort and lowered efficiency for teachers than for pupils.

Layout

Another physical factor to consider is classroom layout. It stands to reason that an intelligently designed physical environment with, for example, distinct and clear lines of communication can help promote dialogue between pupils and teachers. This, in turn, can help pupils to feel better integrated in the learning process which, in turn, helps promote wellbeing within the classroom.

There's often a lively debate on social media about whether or not pupils should be seated in rows, but my advice is: What works is what works. Sometimes it is best for pupils to be seated in rows facing the teacher and the board; other times, if it's logistically possible and not time-consuming, it may be best to deviate from this layout to facilitate discussion and debate or to allow safe movement around the classroom. My advice would be to obey the school's policy (if it has one) or choose whichever layout works for you and the context.

Seating in rows is regarded by its detractors as 'traditional' or old fashioned, only fit for the Victorian schoolhouse, but it has survived through the years for a reason – it focuses pupils on the teacher and whiteboard and therefore minimises distractions and low-level disruption. What's more, it enables the teacher to see every pupil at all times.

If and when you want to vary the layout, moving from rows to a horseshoe, or grouped tables for different activities, then I'd suggest you make sure you explicitly teach pupils how to do it safely and quickly and with minimum disruption – practise the routines to ensure smooth and speedy transitions.

Displays

When deciding how to organise wall displays, meanwhile, I think there's a balance to be struck. On the one hand, we do not want bare walls because such a stark environment is uninspiring and can be demotivating. But likewise, we do not want the walls to be so engaging as to distract pupils from the lesson or offend their eyes with a kaleidoscope of colour and shape. If we do have displays, we want them to be useful and useable, not mere wallpaper, and we want them to be up-to-date and relevant not formed of peeling and yellowed posters from yesteryear.

We should think carefully, therefore, about what would prove most useful to the majority of pupils who study in the room, what would provide cues for their learning and act as schemata (which we'll come back to later) or stimulants to thought. For example, we may want to display key words or concepts, perhaps threshold curriculum content or ideas from knowledge organisers.

In Chapter Eleven, we will continue our exploration of the learning environment and focus on the social and emotional aspects of an effective classroom space...

CHAPTER ELEVEN:
CREATING A SOCIAL AND EMOTIONAL
LEARNING ENVIRONMENT

In Chapter Ten we focused on the physical attributes of an effective learning environment, now let us turn to the social and emotional aspects...

The social environment

Once we've catered for our pupils' basic needs and created a physical learning environment in which they are comfortable and focused on learning, we need to consider the social learning environment...

An effective social learning environment, at least in part, equates to a whole school culture which promotes good behaviour and attitudes to learning, tackles poor behaviour including low-level disruption, and protects all staff and pupils from harassment and harm. One way to build such a social environment is to create a set of social norms that define good conduct.

In 'Promoting the conditions for positive behaviour' (2012), Philip Garner says, "It remains clear that [...] the promotion of good behaviour and learning can be firmly linked to effective leadership."

The SLT therefore have a crucial role to play in terms of consulting on, agreeing and articulating the features of their school's social environment and then ensuring that this is established and enforced by every adult working in the school.

I think the right social environment is best created in four stages, by:

1. **Creating** the social environment,
2. **Communicating** the social environment,
3. Making the social environment **concrete**, and
4. Making the social environment **continuous**.

Let's look at each of these stages in turn...

1. Creating the social environment

A key role of SLT is to articulate a detailed vision of what the social environment should look like for their school, focusing on pupil conduct. Expectations must be as high as possible, for all. Designing the social environment is about agreeing the social norms that you'd want to see reproduced throughout the school community. Here, I'd suggest, school leaders should ask, 'What would I like all pupils to do, routinely?' 'What do I want them to believe about themselves, their achievements, each other, the school?' Once these questions have been answered, SLT can then translate these aspirations into expectations.

2. Communicating the social environment

Social norms are found most clearly in the daily routines of the school. Any aspect of school behaviour that can be standardised because it is expected from all pupils at all times should be, for example walking on the left or right of the corridor, entering the class silently and in single file, entering assembly in year and form order, clearing tables after lunch. These routines should be communicated to, and practiced by, staff and pupils until they become automatic. This then frees up time, mental effort and energy towards more useful areas, such as study.

3. Making the social environment concrete

Next, school leaders need to make the social environment concrete with as much detail and clarity as possible. Staff and pupils need to know how to achieve this, and what the social environment looks like in practice from behaviour on buses, to corridor and canteen conduct. This means demonstrating it, communicating it thoroughly, and ensuring that every aspect of school life feed into and reinforce that culture.

One way to make the social environment concrete is to design routines that pupils and staff should follow. The school must have well-established and universally known and understood systems of behaviour, for example, pupil removal, consequences, and sanctions, corridor and classroom expectations, behaviour on trips, arrival, transition and departure behaviour and so on.

4. Making the social environment continuous

Once built, school systems require regular maintenance - school leaders must not assume that, once it has been created, communicated and made concrete, their social environment will flourish if left alone. Rather, school leaders need to continuously cultivate that social environment. In short, it requires their constant attention. Although it is reasonably straightforward to identify what a good social environment might look like, the difficulty lies in embedding and maintaining it. This includes staff training, effective use of consequences, data monitoring, staff and pupil surveys and so on.

In order to make the social environment continuous, school leaders need to establish the right conditions within which such a culture can flourish and – amongst other means - this can be done through the use of assemblies, displays, expectations around punctuality and appearance, and what happens if pupils do not come to class with the right equipment.

Let us now home in on perhaps the most crucial aspect of this social environment: pupil behaviour...

Pupil behaviour

In the 2014 report, 'Below the Radar', Ofsted found that only a third of teachers felt their school's behaviour policies were being applied consistently. Teachers said this inconsistency, and a lack of support from senior leaders, undermined their efforts to effectively manage behaviour.

Five years on, Ofsted decided to update what they know about managing challenging behaviour in schools, looking not just at low-level disruption as they did in 2014, but at more challenging forms of misbehaviour too.

They did so because pupils' behaviour and attitudes are a major concern for teachers. The NASUWT big question survey, the OECD TALIS study and Ofsted's study on teacher well-being all showed recently that teachers feel misbehaviour is common and is a major source of stress. The Ofsted well-being study found many teachers felt senior leaders provided insufficient support.

In Ofsted's latest study, published in September 2019, the inspectorate looked at what had changed since 'Below the Radar'. Ofsted's aim was to identify the strategies that schools use to pre-empt and manage challenging behaviour and persistent absence and promote good behaviour and attitudes.

Compared with 'Below the Radar', Ofsted's latest research found some positive developments. For instance, they found that teachers and leaders better understood the importance of consistency in the implementation of behaviour policies.

Most schools in the study favoured whole-school behaviour management approaches in which a set of consistent routines arc put into practice and rigorously and consistently applied.

Staff, particularly in secondary schools, emphasised the value of teaching desired behaviours and making them routine. This is especially the case for those behaviours that are repeated regularly throughout the school day and that ensure the safe movement of pupils around the school, the smooth running of lessons and the minimum loss of learning time to low-level disruption.

Ofsted concluded that, when pupils and staff have a shared understanding of the expectations for these common behaviours and both staff and pupils follow established routines, overall consistency is easier to achieve.

A whole-school approach to behaviour is, Ofsted say, much more than a set of policies or documents; it is about what everyone in the school does, how they behave, and what expectations are set and taught. It is also about the values and ethos of the school. Strong values underpin good behaviour.

In the best schools, the values underpinning the behaviour management policy are clear and explicit. Staff and pupils across the school know what the values are. In these schools, pupils know that good behaviour and attendance prepares them well for their future lives. Indeed, one way to improve attendance in particular is to make an explicit link between attendance and educational outcomes, and between educational outcomes and later success in life and work. Such a strategy can encourage pupils and their parents to appreciate the longer-term impact of absenteeism on their life chances and potential earnings.

In the best schools and colleges, leaders and teachers appreciate the need to build and maintain positive relationships with all pupils and students in order to ensure ongoing good behaviour. Through good relationships, staff are more able to spot potential concerns or behaviours that are out of character and may lead to low level disruption or absences and so can take preventative action.

Zero tolerance?

Before we move on, let's drag the elephant into the centre of the room...

There's a lot of debate via social media at the time of writing about whether or not zero tolerance approaches to behaviour management are appropriate. But one of the issues, I think, is that policies described as 'zero-tolerance' mean different things in different contexts.

Rather than talking about zero tolerance, the teachers and leaders in the Ofsted study spoke about the different types of behaviours they wanted to see in their pupils. Foundational behaviours, such as attending and being punctual to school and to lessons, are the baseline pupils need to meet to allow effective teaching and learning to happen.

As well as these foundations, pupils also need to show positive attitudes to learning, such as making a strong effort, a positive contribution in class, engaging in their learning and completing homework to a high standard.

Social behaviours, the ways in which pupils interact with each other and with adults, formed the third component.

These three types of behaviours are reflected in the new Education Inspection Framework under 'behaviour and attitudes'. In the framework, Ofsted state that – amongst other things – in order to be judged good the following standard needs to be reached: "Pupils have high attendance, come to school on time and are punctual to lessons. When this is not the case, the school takes appropriate, swift and effective action."

Of course, the opposite of zero tolerance is a potentially harmful leniency. For example, some schools, in seeking to re-engage with a persistent absentee, may agree a staggered return to school and/or a part-time timetable. But such strategies need to be carefully thought through because they can send a signal that attending school is optional and that missing some days and lessons is permitted.

The part parents should play

Creating an effective social environment in order to ensure good behaviour and attitudes is not solely the responsibility of school leaders and teachers, of course. Rather, parents also need to work positively with their son or daughter's school or college in order to support its policies and ensure compliance and conduct.

Parents reinforcing school policies makes it easier for staff to apply those policies and for pupils to accept the consequences.

Parental engagement is an important element of effective whole-school behaviour management. It gives parents a sense of involvement, provides a consistent message and helps their understanding of procedures and rules. Families are most likely to support a school's behaviour policies if they understand the reasons for a particular approach. To allow parents to do so, they need to be properly informed of the school's practices.

Parental engagement can be achieved in a number of ways. For example, some schools focus on improving behaviour and attendance at parents' evenings. Others find positive ways to re-engage with parents when their son or daughter has misbehaved and/or been absent. In the Ofsted report, many teachers mentioned the power of regular positive communication.

Conversely, in extreme cases where parents refuse to engage with the school in support of efforts to improve a child's behaviour and/or attendance, schools have legal powers to use parenting contracts, parenting orders and penalty notices to address poor attendance and behaviour in school.

Managing transitions

The features of an effective social environment – what good behaviour and attitudes look like in practice – need to be explicitly taught and reinforced as early as possible and expectations raised as pupils get older. Times of transition, from primary school to secondary, or from one school to another, as well as when students move from school to college, are therefore important here.

Leaders interviewed as part of Ofsted's 'Below the Radar' study talked about the value of managing transitions to make them as smooth as possible. For some pupils, going from a relatively small primary community, where you're known by everyone and where you have a close relationship with a small number of teachers, to a much larger secondary school with several teachers will be particularly challenging and can lead to instances of low-level disruption and/or absenteeism. Likewise, moving from school to college, where learners are expected to be much more independent and mature, can be challenging and lead to attendance or behaviour issues. Colleges would do well to remember that it is but six short weeks since their adult learners were school students used to routine and structure.

The schools in the Ofsted study felt that it was important to identify pupils who were particularly at risk of challenging behaviours and absenteeism *before* they started secondary school so that they could provide appropriate support and prepare them for 'big school'. Specific plans could then be put in place to minimise the risk of these children displaying challenging behaviours, being absent or late to school and lessons after transition.

There was agreement amongst the schools in the study that early identification should not result in secondary schools discouraging admission under the guise that the child 'would not fit in here'.

In the schools that had successfully improved transition arrangements, individual support plans, or an extended period of transition were two of their solutions. Some secondary schools said they had also had success when starting work with pupils in Year 5 or had run summer schools or literacy and numeracy catch-up sessions in Year 7 for pupils who were struggling at the end of primary school. Leaders explained that this was to prevent pupils falling further behind, which leads to absenteeism and displays of challenging behaviour as pupils struggle to access the curriculum.

In the schools that had improved transition, there was also effective training for all staff which included training for school leaders and those with pastoral responsibilities. These schools achieved consistency through regular training, mentoring and induction of new teachers. Many teachers also valued informal discussions with school leaders alongside clear monitoring systems and policies.

The emotional environment

As well as building a comfortable and engaging physical space and developing appropriate behaviour and attitudes – and indeed routines – towards learning, we want our pupils to feel safe and secure in school so that they willingly take risks and make mistakes from which they can learn.

The first few days spent in a new learning environment are perhaps the most pivotal in determining a pupil's academic progress. We need only look at the effects of a pupil's transition from primary to secondary school – whereby almost 40% of children fail to make expected progress – to see this. If a pupil does not feel emotionally safe and intellectually comfortable, it can prove difficult for them to make progress.

Below, then, are my five suggested strategies to help instil this willingness to take risks – what we might refer to as a 'growth mindset' or a positive emotional environment – in our classrooms...

1. Use frequent formative feedback

The first strategy to help develop the sort of emotional environment that encourages risk-taking is to provide pupils with frequent formative feedback. Dr Carol Dweck, in her book 'Mindset' (2013), argues that people with a fixed mindset "greatly mis-estimated their performance and their ability (while) people with the growth mindset were amazingly accurate". Why should this be? Because, as Dr Dweck says: "If, like those with the growth mindset, you believe you can develop yourself, then you're open to accurate information about your current abilities, even if it's unflattering. What's more, if you're oriented towards learning, as they are, you need accurate information about your current abilities in order to learn effectively."

TIP: We should, therefore, ensure that our pupils are acutely aware of their strengths and areas for development. We should frequently assess our pupils and give them formative feedback so that they know what they do well and what they can do better. We should dedicate quality time in our lessons for our pupils to act on this feedback, to redraft work in order to improve upon it.

2. High levels of challenge for every pupil

Everyone can improve with practice. Therefore, we must challenge our pupils to be the best they can be, we must have high expectations of all our pupils and must encourage them to take a leap of faith, even if that means falling over a few times. Appropriate challenge – and high expectations – are not just advisable, they are essential to the process of learning. If pupils are not given hard work to do which makes them think, they won't learn anything. Likewise, we know from the work of Rosenthal and Jacobson that having high expectations of pupils demonstrably improves their outcomes. Conversely, if we set the bar low, pupils are likely to underperform.

TIP: It's important, therefore, that our emotional environment is built on high expectations and the provision of stretch and challenge for all pupils.

3. Explicitly welcome mistakes

Another way of developing an emotional environment that encourages risk-taking is to actively encourage pupils to make mistakes, and to do this we must foster a safe and secure environment in which falling over is not only accepted without criticism or humiliation, but in which it is actively encouraged as evidence of effective learning and of getting better at something.

Every teacher knows that some pupils do not raise their hands in class to answer a question because they fear they will be criticised or made to feel embarrassed for being wrong. And yet the opposite should be true: pupils should be eager to raise their hands because to get an answer wrong is to learn from their mistakes; to get an answer wrong is to learn the correct answer. Equally, raising a hand to say, "I don't understand this ... can you help?" is not a sign of weakness or low intelligence, it is a means of increasing one's intelligence.

Of course, making a mistake – even if you have a positive mindset – can be a painful experience. But a mistake shouldn't define you; it's a problem to be faced and learnt from. We teach this by modelling it, by publicly making mistakes and by making explicit our own implicit learning.

TIP: An effective emotional environment, therefore, is one in which mistakes are welcomed and learned from. This means we have to model this in our words and actions, being honest when we too make mistakes, and reassuring pupils that their mistakes are helpful to us and to their learning journey.

4. Engaging in deliberate practice

People with a belief in the growth mindset and an eagerness to take risks and learn from mistakes, rather than valuing natural, effortless accomplishments, believe even geniuses have to work hard for their achievements and that there nothing heroic about having a gift.

Moving from novice to expert in any field requires practice. We should, therefore, provide our pupils with plenty of opportunities to practise and perfect their knowledge and skills.

Professor Daniel Willingham, in his book Why Don't Students Like School? (2010), says that deliberate practice "reinforces (the) basic skills required for more advanced skills, it protects against forgetting, and improves transfer". Professor Siegfried Engelmann says that students need "five times more practice than many teachers expect".

There are two kinds of practice proven to be the most effective: first, distributed or spaced practice which is "a schedule of practice that spreads out study activities over time", and second, interleaved practice which is "a schedule of practice that mixes different kinds of problems, or a schedule of study that mixes different kinds of material, within a single study session" (Dunlosky et al, 2013).

TIP: An effective emotional environment, therefore, is one which provides pupils with plentiful opportunities to engage in deliberate practice, both to activate prior learning and keep it accessible, and to ensure that pupils continue to improve.

5. Reward effort not attainment

Returning to Dr Dweck for a moment, she conducted research into the effects of rewards and concluded that praising pupils' abilities actually lowers their IQs whereas praising effort raises them.

Dweck also found that praising pupils' intelligence can harm their motivation because, although pupils love to be praised, especially for their talents, as soon as they hit a snag their confidence goes out of the window and their motivation hits rock bottom. If success means they're smart, then failure means they're dumb.

TIP: The above findings should not lead us to the conclusion that we shouldn't praise pupils, of course. But they do suggest that an effective emotional environment is one in which we use praise carefully, predominantly praise pupils for the "growth-oriented process – what they accomplished through practice, study, persistence, and good strategies", whilst avoiding the kind of praise that judges their intelligence or talent.

PART THREE:

TEACH FOR LONG-TERM LEARNING

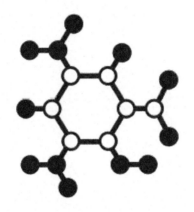

CHAPTER TWELVE:
AN INTRODUCTION TO THE 3 STEPS

When we talk about curriculum implementation or delivery, we often refer to it as teaching and learning. Teaching *and* learning; cause *and* effect. If we put good teaching in, we should get good learning out.

Curriculum implementation is more complex than this, of course.

There are myriad factors that determine a pupil's or student's academic or vocational success, not least their own hard work, diligence and, yes, innate intelligence. Environmental factors play their part, too, as does the amount of support and influence that a pupil receives from their community of friends and family.

I'd like to focus on factors that are within a school and college leader's or teacher's control, however. It is about what we put in so that we can maximise the chances of pupils getting 'learning' out.

So, what should a teacher put in when implementing the curriculum in a way that leads to long-term learning? In other words, if long-term learning is our desired effect, what is the cause?

What works is what works. Only, some things seem to work better than others.

As I explained in Part Two of this book, I like research evidence. When I started teaching there was very little of it around. Back then, as I explained earlier, we didn't know what the best or right things to do were because no one really analysed teachers' methods or sought to compare one approach with another.

When I started teaching, cognitive science was alien to educators. Spacing and interleaving, to give but two examples, were foreign terms. These days, there's a surfeit of research evidence about what works and what doesn't. Of course, evidence can only take us so far...

We need to be discerning in our diet of evidence; we need to regard external data as a starting point not a destination; evidence is not a tablet of stone handed down from a higher authority, it is to be questioned and disputed and weighed against our own professional judgment.

Indeed, I always advise colleagues to be influenced by the evidence of what works elsewhere, but to be informed by their experience and by their own context because they know their pupils and their classroom better than anyone else, and they know what works for them and for their pupils, and - of course - what doesn't.

Context matters. What works for one teacher with one class at one point in the week might not work, or work as well, for a different teacher and a different class, timetabled at a different time.

But my plea for pragmatism doesn't mean we ignore the evidence altogether. As I said earlier, research evidence should influence every teacher's thinking. The evidence should act as a route map. If, on the journey, a teacher encounters roadworks or delays, or knows the vicinity well so has a short-cut up their sleeve, then they should be willing and able to deviate from the route guidance and do what their own eyes and ears tell them is right.

Yes, we should be influenced by the evidence but informed by our experience.

Evidence might also provide us with the strategy but not the technique. For example, Hattie's meta-analyses tell us that giving pupils feedback can lead to some significant academic gains. The EEF toolkit, which I dissected earlier, suggests that feedback can add an extra eight months of progress every year. But what neither analysis really tells us is how that feedback should be carried out. So, evidence tells us we should give pupils frequent, formative feedback - I'd argue that common sense dictates the same, of course - but our experience and our knowledge of our unique context tells us how and how often this feedback should be given, and in what form it should be given in each instance.

I've taught a lot of lessons over the years and observed many more. I've been lucky enough to see countless excellent teachers toiling away at the chalkboard. And all this experience has taught me that there is no such thing as the right way of teaching or the wrong way of teaching. There is no checklist or blueprint. There is no secret formula.

Teaching is a highly complex, nuanced art form - and I use the term 'art form' advisedly because although I think we teachers can learn a lot from cognitive science about how pupils learn and therefore how to approach our teaching, I don't think teaching is in and of itself a science. I think, instead, it is about a human connection, an interaction between a teacher and a pupil and between one pupil and her peers (indeed, as Sarah Lawrence-Lightfoot said, good teaching is "ideas as conveyed through relationships" [Moyers, 1989]). And anything that operates at this level is an art not a science. What's more, anything complex and nuanced cannot be reduced to a single measurement for that is to ignore its complexity, to negate its nuance.

In the best lessons I've observed, the 'secret' has been simply this: the teacher has been sensitive to the needs of their pupils and has adjusted to the here and now circumstances of the classroom.

In other words, they have known about and cared about each and every one of their pupils. They have been well-attuned to the dynamics of their classroom, acutely aware if the pace has been too fast or too slow, and if pupils have become bored or stuck. And rather than sticking slavishly to a lesson plan, they have adjusted their teaching accordingly. They have been fluid and flexible in their delivery, human in their approach.

Of course, knowing your pupils is much easier said than done. It involves a lot of data - and data in the widest sense of the word, moving beyond a regiment of numbers on a spreadsheet to a detailed understanding of: each pupils' prior attainment; what they can do and cannot yet do, including outside of test conditions; what they have mastered and what they still need to practice; how they learn best and what motivates and demotivates them; how they like to be rewarded, and what interests them outside the classroom; what barriers they face both inside and outside of school; and so on.

Knowing your pupils involves ongoing formative assessment in all its forms, including using, say, hinge questions in class, as well as self- and peer-assessment, gallery critique and so on.

Caring about your pupils means having high expectations of each of them and supporting them to meet or exceed those expectations. It means taking an interest in them as a person not just as a name on the register or a mark in a spreadsheet.

It means showing resilience in the face of adversity - being patient when pupils are slow or reluctant to learn; being kind when they need it but tough when that's what's required.

Surveys of pupils' views on what makes a good teacher invariably proffer the following characteristics:

Firstly, pupils want a teacher who shows them respect - in order words, they want to be treated like a person and afforded dignity.

Secondly, they want a teacher who is knowledgeable in their subject - this is twofold: it means that the teacher knows not just their subject content but also how to teach that content in a way that makes sense to pupils; it means they can see their expertise through the eyes of a novice pupil, and thus pre-empt and resolve pupils' misconceptions and questions, foreseeing potential pitfalls and planning how best to overcome them.

Thirdly, pupils want a teacher who is approachable and willing to listen to them.

They also want a teacher who is positive and enthusiastic about their subject and about teaching that subject; and they want a teacher who doesn't take themselves too seriously, is willing to laugh at themselves, and admit to their mistakes and learn from them.

Finally, learner voice tells us that pupils want a teacher who encourages them to succeed and who sets work that is both interesting and challenging, engaging and difficult. They want a teacher who sets high expectations, builds relationships upon foundations made of trust, and deals with disruptions quickly and unobtrusively to ensure learning is not stymied.

This, I believe, is what great teaching is about. This is in the input. So, what, then, is the output? If this is great teaching, what is great learning?

And, perhaps more importantly, how can we ensure it happens in our classrooms...?

What is learning?

What is learning? It's a simple question, isn't it? And surely, as teachers, our understanding of what we do - the act of teaching - is contingent on having first developed a fundamental understanding of what we produce - learning.

After all, we wouldn't attempt to assemble a flat-packed cabinet without first looking at a picture of the finished product and without then following step-by-step instructions that take us from flat-pack to fully-assembled furniture in five easy moves.

In short, if pedagogy is a process whereby teaching is the input and learning is the output, then we need to know what the output (the product) looks like in order to decide what raw components we need and in which sequence we need to put them together.

As such, I'd like you to take a moment to answer that question. What is learning?

You might like to start by throwing all your initial thoughts and ideas at a piece of paper, then refine those thoughts into a dictionary-style, one-sentence definition, something succinct and pithy.

Whatever approach you take, don't read on until you have attempted an answer...

Done? Ok, let's continue...

So, what is learning? It is, as I say, a simple question but it's not so easy to answer, is it? I'll wager you're not wholly satisfied with your definition, that you struggled to do justice - in a sentence at least - to what is, in truth, a complex, nuanced process.

What's more, learning is often intangible, hard to pin down. Something happens in the brain but we're not sure exactly what and can't always see or know what's changed.

Don't be downbeat if your definition isn't perfect: after all, many great thinkers before you have tried and - in my opinion - failed this task...

John Hattie, for example, says that learning is "the process of developing sufficient surface knowledge to then move to deeper understanding such that one can appropriately transfer this learning to new tasks and situations".

I don't know about you, but I find this definition a little clumsy, too wordy, and perhaps even misleading in the way it seeks to distinguish surface knowledge from deep understanding.

Paul Kirschner, meanwhile, says learning is "a change in long-term memory".

There is, I think, very little with which to take issue in this surprisingly succinct sentence, but perhaps that's precisely because Kirschner's definition is too succinct, too simplistic, and therefore too vague?

Paul Black and Dylan Wiliam, for their part, believe that learning is "an increase, brought about by experience, in the capacities of an organism to react in valued ways in response to stimuli".

I find this definition too lofty because it focuses on the biology of learning (why 'organism'?) rather than on the behaviour of learning. It certainly seems far removed from the context in which most of us would operate and think - the classroom - and as such offers little help to a teacher seeking to understand what will make their pupils more successful at school.

And Nicholas Sonderstrom and Robert Bjork think that learning creates "relatively permanent changes in comprehension, understanding, and skills of the types that will support long-term retention and transfer".

This definition comes closest to my own current thinking but, as such, my tendency to favour it could simply be a case of confirmation bias. And just because this definition closely mirrors my own doesn't make it right or even better than the others. Indeed, I've already started to wonder - having at first agreed with Sonderstrom and Bjork - if 'transferability' is necessary for something to be considered 'learnt'. And what of long-term retention? Just because we can't recall something later doesn't mean we haven't learnt it. For example, I can't recall my home address from childhood but that doesn't mean I couldn't pick it out from a list of addresses, thus proving that the information was learnt and retained in my long-term memory, even if I couldn't actively recall it.

Learning, it seems, is even more complex and nuanced than first thought.

Although all these definitions contain a common thread - namely, that something must happen in the long-term memory - each has a slightly different take and yet none is, well, satisfactory.

Perhaps Dan Willingham is right when he says we "ought not to worry overmuch about definitions".

Willingham says that "the current status of learning is that it's defined (usually narrowly) in the context of specific theories or in the context of specific goals or projects. Kirschner et al were offering a definition in the context of their theory... Hattie was offering a definition of learning for his vision of the purpose of schooling... neither hoped to devise a definition that would serve a broader purpose."

I think Willingham is right. Learning can be a range of different things depending on its purpose and context, and can encompass different processes, procedures and indeed outcomes. For example, learning my telephone number (which, admittedly, I struggled with for longer than I care to admit) is not the same as learning to ride a bike which, in turn, is not the same as learning how to analyse a poem or interpret a set of raw data and present the findings in a graph.

It's true that practice - no matter whether we're practicing our golf swing or our times tables - has the same biological effect on the brain (namely, that it creates more layers of myelin around our nerve fibres - what we call 'muscle memory' but is, in fact, nothing to do with our muscles). But this doesn't mean that we follow the same process whether we're learning to swing a golf club or memorise our seven times table. And it doesn't mean that what we learn is stored and used in the same way, nor that it can be, or needs to be, demonstrated in the same way.

Learning is multi-faceted.

When I taught my daughter to ride a bike, for example, I could see that she'd learnt it immediately by observing her riding without my help and without the support of stabilisers. She cycled down the hill, turned around, and cycled back up it. She got off and back on again, and cycled some more. She was able to demonstrate her learning and I was able to observe it. I don't think anyone would suggest she was merely regurgitating, rote-like, something I'd just modelled for her and that therefore riding her bike was merely a 'performance' as opposed to genuine, deep 'learning'. Yes, her skill may erode over time if she doesn't keep practicing it (despite the fact we're told 'it's like riding a bike, you never forget'), but that doesn't mean she didn't learn it.

But not all types of learning are observable and not all learning is acquired immediately. For example, if I taught a pupil how to identify bias in a non-fiction text - let's say, oh I don't know, the Daily Mail - and they immediately identified an example of bias in the pages of the Mail in that lesson, I couldn't be certain they'd learnt the various interconnected skills of - to name but a few - skimming, scanning, and detecting inference, and were able to apply those skills to the pages of the Mail as well as to The Guardian and online in Wikipedia and on Facebook, and would then know to do so in History and Economics not just with me in English.

To be certain she had learnt all these skills and that they could be transferred, I would need to observe and assess her doing so later and in a range of different contexts.

The pupil's immediate demonstration could, in this case, have been a mere 'performance', the instant regurgitation of what I'd just modelled - mimicry rather than mastery.

A quick aside on the subject of 'performance' versus 'learning': performance is often an unreliable index of whether a pupil has made the longer-term changes that constitute learning. Improvements in performance can fail to yield any significant learning and can even make learning more difficult. What's more, and more confusing, is that it's possible for learning to take place even if we can see no discernible changes in a pupil's performance.

Mastery not mimicry

Our goal, then, is mastery not mimicry. There's nothing necessarily wrong with mimicry if it helps a pupil pass a test and get a qualification but, assuming we want to do more than 'teach to the test' and assuming we regard education as something meaningful and long-term, a life skill if you like, a way of becoming an engaged and active citizen, and an inquisitive, cultured adult, then surely, we must aim to move beyond mimicry and towards mastery. Surely, therefore, we need to consider how to move beyond performance towards genuine learning. And, if this is the case, then we must teach in such a way as to ensure our pupils not only acquire new knowledge and skills but can apply that knowledge and those skills later and in a range of different contexts.

With this in mind, to help us with our explanation of curriculum implementation, and as applied to the process of 'learning' more complex curriculum content within an academic or vocational setting, I will share my own definition. It, too, is far from perfect and changes daily but here it is nevertheless:

> *Learning is the acquisition of knowledge and skills, and their application at a later time and in a range of contexts.*

It is this definition which will guide the remainder of Part Three of the book. We will examine ways of achieving its aim: to ensure our pupils acquire knowledge and skills and are able to apply them at a later time and in a range of contexts.

I argued above that learning means different things in different contexts and one definition does not fit all. Learning can, sometimes, be observed and can, sometimes, be immediate. And just because we can't recall something we were once taught, that does not mean we did not learn it and that the information isn't still hidden away somewhere in the cluttered attic of our minds.

However, by definition, the opposite is also true: not all types of learning are observable and not all learning is accomplished immediately. Therefore, to be certain that a pupil had learnt something and was able to transfer that learning, we would need to observe and assess the pupil doing so later and in a range of different contexts. The pupil's immediate regurgitation of knowledge or their immediate demonstration of a skill could be mere 'performance', the instant repetition of what we'd just modelled - mimicry rather than mastery.

Although there's nothing necessarily wrong with mimicry, as I said earlier, if we want to do more than 'teach to the test' and if we regard education as something meaningful and long-term, then surely, we must aim to move beyond mimicry and towards mastery. And this is exactly the kind of learning I defined in Chapter Three, which closely mirrors Ofsted's own working definition of curriculum implementation.

Furthermore, this immediate regurgitation or mimicry is likely to take place in the working memory. In other words, the knowledge or skill is not encoded into long-term memory and is not, therefore, learnt in any meaningful sense of the word for it cannot be applied later and in a range of different contexts. Rather, it is ephemeral. There's also evidence to suggest that a pupil's performance can be misleading. Pupils who perform better tend to learn less; those who do not perform so well in lesson, tend to do better in later assessments.

Let's unpack my definition of learning...

First of all, learning, I said, is the acquisition of knowledge and skills...

The act of acquiring new knowledge and skills is the start of the learning process, it is what happens (or begins to happen) in the classroom when a teacher - the expert - imparts their knowledge or demonstrates their skills (perhaps through the artful use of explanations and modelling, of which more later) to their pupils - the novices.

Next, pupils store this new information in their long-term memories (via their working memories) where it can be recalled and used later.

The process of storing information in the long-term memory is called 'encoding'. The process of getting it back out again is called 'retrieval'.

Retrieval is concerned with the second half of my definition of learning: the application of knowledge and skills at a later time and in different contexts...

A pupil could demonstrate their immediate understanding of what they've been taught by repeating what the teacher has said or by demonstrating the skill they've just seen applied. But this immediate display is not 'learning'. Rather, it is 'performance'. It is a simple regurgitation of what they've just seen or heard and takes place in the working memory, without any need for information to be encoded in the long-term memory.

We can all repeat, rote-like, something someone else has just said or mimic a skill they've just demonstrated. But unless we can retain that knowledge or skill over time, we haven't really learnt it. And if we can't apply that knowledge or skill in a range of different situations, then - similarly - we haven't really learnt it, or at least not in any meaningful sense.

Let me give you an example...

We can, perhaps through direct instruction, teach pupils what 'alliteration' means.

Next, pupils can repeat the definition and can pick out an example of alliteration from four sentences in a multiple-choice quiz (which acts as a hinge question) like this one, for instance:

Which of these sentences is an example of alliteration?
A. A golden orb illuminated the sky.
B. The sun spun strips of silk across the sky.
C. The sun looked like a giant blood orange.
D. The sky was reddened by the low winter sun.

If most pupils identify B as an example of alliteration and can explain that it is thus because the initial consonant 's' is repeated (a type of alliteration known as 'sibilance' because it makes a hissing sound), then, great, we think, they must have successfully learnt alliteration, so we can now move on to the next thing.

But...

If we don't repeat that learning several times - at last three times but ideally much more often - then their memory of what alliteration is will inevitably fade. It will probably remain in their long-term memories somewhere (we forget very little) but like a box of childhood toys stowed in the attic the knowledge will grow dusty and get pushed to the back, hidden among the other items we heave through the hatch over time.

If we told pupils the definition again, chances are they would think 'oh yes, of course - I remember it now' but, unprompted, they would be unable to volunteer a definition or identify an example.

The more we repeat the information - the more often we ask pupils to tell us what alliteration is and identify an example of it within a text - the stronger the retrieval strength of that information will become, making its recall easier and more efficient.

But the act of recalling the information from their long-term memory and bringing it into their working memory will also increase the storage strength of that information. It will be returned to the attic dusted down and in an easy-to-reach location.

However, if we simply repeat the information over and again verbatim, we will only really improve pupils' surface knowledge of that information. They will more easily remember what alliteration means and be able to pick out an example from a list of four sentences. But they are unlikely to get any better at, say, writing alliterative sentences of their own. They're also unlikely to get any better at identifying why a writer has used alliteration, for what purpose, and what effect it has created.

There's a danger they may not be able to identify alliteration in other contexts, too. They may be attuned to its use in poetry if that's the context in which they were taught alliteration the first time. But they might not know to look for it in a novel or in non-fiction texts, such as in a newspaper headline, if they're not told to do so and made to see the connections.

To improve and deepen pupils' understanding of alliteration, we need to teach it in different contexts. We need to model examples of its use in a range of texts and contexts. We need to teach pupils how to use alliteration in their own writing and explain how, why and when to do so.

And when we repeat learning we should do so in different ways. For example, we could ask a hinge question which requires pupils to identify an example of alliteration from four sentences, then we could get them to write about that sentence, explaining what makes it alliterative, why the writer chose to use that device and what effect it creates. Then we could ask pupils to write a piece of fiction which uses alliteration, followed by a piece of non-fiction. Then we could get them to teach each other and/or test each other, perhaps by creating their own multiple-choice quizzes.

The more times we repeat the learning and the more we do so in different ways, requiring pupils to demonstrate their learning through various means, the stronger it will be stored, the more easily it will be retrieved, and the better pupils will be at transferring their learning to different contexts.

Learning, therefore, is being able to apply knowledge and/or skills long after we had first taught them and in several different situations, perhaps in an assessment as well as repeatedly over a period, or even a lifetime.

The 3 steps of long-term learning

The process of learning, then, is the interaction between one's sensory memory (sometimes referred to as our 'environment') and one's long-term memory.

Our sensory memory is made up of:

- What we see - this is called our **iconic** memory;
- What we hear - this is called our **echoic** memory; and
- What we touch - our **haptic** memory.

Our long-term memory is where new information is stored and from which it can be recalled when needed, but we cannot directly access the information stored in our long-term memory.

As such, the interaction that takes place between our sensory memory and our long-term memory occurs in our working memory, or short-term memory, which is where we think and do.

It might be helpful to think of our sensory memory as a haulage truck, our long-term memory as a warehouse, and our working memory as the holding bay where new deliveries are received, processed and labelled ready for stowing. The payload cannot be passed directly into the warehouse, it must first pass through the holding bay to be sorted. (In this paragraph, incidentally, I employ an analogy - relating the properties of our memory to a warehouse - to help you process potentially new information in the context of what you already know. This is a concept to which we'll return later.)

In order to stimulate pupils' sensory memories and thus engage the attention of their working memories and make them think, we need to create classroom conditions conducive to learning, conditions that stimulate pupils' iconic, echoic and haptic memories. In other words, we need to engage pupils' senses in order to gain their attention.

It might sound like common sense - indeed it is - to say that, for our pupils to learn, we must first gain their attention, but it's all too easy for learning to fail simply because we haven't stimulated our pupils' senses and therefore gained their attention, or because we have focused their attention on the wrong things.

I'm sure you've seen the video of the Dancing Gorilla Awareness Test before. In short, observers are asked to watch a video of a group of about eight people playing basketball and are told to count the number of passes made by the players in white, ignoring the players in black. In the middle of the game, a man in a gorilla suit dances across the scene, weaving his way through the players. Most observers count the passes correctly but utterly fail to spot the gorilla. Their attention is not grabbed by the gorilla because they don't expect to see such an incongruous thing and are only focused on the ball as it passes from one player in white to another.

It's just as easy to get pupils to focus on the wrong things. For example, if I wanted a class to research the origins of two online encyclopaedias, Wikipedia and Microsoft's Encarta, and find out why Wikipedia - with no money and a reliance on volunteers to act as contributors - proved more successful than the encyclopaedia backed by big business, boasting an army of well-paid, qualified staff including Bill Gates, and asked them to do so on the internet, there's a danger that they would focus their attention on the act of researching rather than on the topic they'd been asked to research.

In other words, if I didn't explicitly teach them the skills needed to carry out the task and learn about Wikipedia, they would use all their working memory capacity on acquiring and using these skills and none, or very little, on the content.

They'd have to think about where to search, what search terms to use, how to sift information and make decisions about what was relevant and what was not, what was reliable and what was not. However, if I'd explicitly taught them how to conduct independent research - such as the use of three independent sources, skimming and scanning for key facts and names and dates, how to use quotations, how to detect inference and bias, etc., then modelled the process and got them to practice the skills until they become automatic - they could have focused their attentions on the information they'd found out about Wikipedia (such as: In 2009, the year Encarta closed, only 1.27% of encyclopaedia searches in America were carried out using Encarta; Wikipedia meanwhile accounted for 97%).

In short, their attention could be focused on the right things.

This is important because if you don't think, you don't learn. We must gain pupils' attentions and make them think hard in order for information to be processed in their working memories and then be encoded in their long-term memories. And if we get them thinking hard about how to research, then they will process and encode this and learn nothing - or too little - about what they actually researched.

In short, stimulating pupils' sensory memories and focusing their attention on the right things, is essential if our pupils are to engage their working memories.

Talking of which...

In order to help pupils utilise their limited working memories (depending on which research paper you read, it's thought that we can only handle between five and nine concepts in working memory at any one time - see, for example, Miller 1956), we need to ensure they are made to think hard - are challenged with work that is difficult but achievable.

If the work is too easy, pupils will be able to complete it through habit without thinking - this is called 'automaticity'. For example, if I asked you to calculate 2 x 10, you would do so automatically, through habit, without having to think about it because you likely mastered your times tables many years ago.

If the work's too hard, pupils will be unable to complete it because they will overpower their limited working memories with too much information (what's called 'cognitive overload') and the learning process will fail. For example, if I asked you to calculate 367 x 2892 in your head in a minute, you wouldn't be able to do so. Chances are, you'd do one of two thins. Either you'd not attempt it because you'd quickly assess the task to be beyond your reach and therefore a pointless waste of energy. Or you'd attempt it but be unable to hold so much information in your working memory and so would fail. Either way, you would be demotivated by your failure and, more importantly, you'd not have learnt or practiced anything, so the task would have been pointless.

Like Goldilocks, you need to find the bowl of porridge that's neither too hot nor too cold but is just right. In other words, you need to pitch your lesson in the 'struggle zone', or what Robert Bjork calls the 'sweet spot' at the edge of pupils' current knowledge and abilities, albeit just within their reach. Lev Vygotsky defined this as the 'zone of proximal development' which is sandwiched between what pupils can do unaided and cannot yet do, in the area which is hard but achievable with time, effort and support.

But, in making pupils think hard, we also need to help them think efficiently. Thinking, as we have seen, will fail if pupils overload their working memories. As such, we need to help pupils cheat the limited space in their working memories (to mitigate cognitive overload) by learning new things in the context of what they already know (allowing them to 'chunk' information together to save space) and by teaching requisite knowledge and/or skills before they are applied because, as Dan Willingham puts it, "memory is the residue of thought".

Once pupils have been made to think hard but efficiently and have processed information in their working memories, we need to ensure they encode that information in their long-term memories and can easily retrieve the information at a later time.

In order to help pupils store information in their limitless long-term memories (long term memory is so big, it will take more than a lifetime to fill it), we need to plan opportunities for deliberate practice, and we need to use two teaching strategies called spacing and interleaving.

Only by repeating learning and by doing so in a range of contexts, will we increase the storage strength of the information in long term memory. The better the storage strength, the more readily available will be our knowledge and skills.

Repeating learning - the very act of recalling prior knowledge and skills from long term memory - also improves their retrieval strength. The better the retrieval strength, the more easily, quickly and efficiently are knowledge and skills recalled from long term memory and brought into the working memory where they can be used.

The best form of repetition is purposeful practice which has well-defined, specific goals, is focused, involves feedback, and requires pupils to get out of their comfort zones because, if they don't push themselves beyond their comfort zones, they'll never improve. Getting out of their comfort zones means trying to do something that they couldn't do before. In this respect, the secret is not to "try harder" but rather to "try differently."

In summary, there are - to my mind - three steps to improve the process of teaching for long-term learning which I outline above, and these three steps will frame the rest of Part Three of this book. The steps are:

1. Stimulate pupils' senses to gain the attention of working memory

2. Make pupils think hard but efficiently to encode information into long-term memory

3. Embed deliberate practice to improve pupils' storage in and retrieval from long-term memory

In the remainder of Part Three of this book we'll take a closer look at each of the three steps in turn, starting with stimulating pupils' senses to gain the active attention of working memory.

So, without further ado, let's begin...

.

STEP ONE:

STIMULATE PUPILS' SENSES TO GAIN THE ATTENTION OF WORKING MEMORY

CHAPTER THIRTEEN:
COMFORTABLE WITH DISCOMFORT

In this chapter we will explore in greater depth how to create the kind of learning environment that stimulates sensory memory... by which I mean an environment in which pupils' senses are piqued so that they pay attention to the right things and are made to think hard but efficiently about curriculum content. I also mean an environment in which pupils are challenged by hard work but know that they are safe to take risks and make mistakes.

I do not mean an environment in which fun and laughter are paramount. There's nothing wrong with pupils enjoying themselves whilst they learn, and we certainly wouldn't want school to be a dull and boring place. However, fun is never the goal. Rather, as I have already said, we want pupils to think and work hard. If, along the way, they can have fun and enjoy learning, then all the better but fun is not necessary in order for pupils to learn and enjoyment is not an essential ingredient in the recipe for a positive learning environment.

In short, when we start the process of curriculum planning, we should start with the question 'What do I want pupils to think about?' not 'What do I want pupils to do?' Activities are secondary to instruction.

Having said this, we do want our learning environment to be one in which pupils are enthusiastic about learning for enthusiasm breeds intrinsic motivation.

So, what, if not necessarily fun, are the hallmarks of an effective learning environment?

To my mind, an effective learning environment – to begin with – is one in which all pupils:

- Feel welcomed,
- Feel valued,
- Are enthusiastic about learning,
- Are engaged in their learning,
- Are eager to experiment, and
- Feel rewarded for their hard work.

I could, of course, go on (and indeed I did explore other aspects of the learning environment – including the physical, social and emotional – earlier). I'm also certain you could add to my list with some important characteristics of your own.

You may even disagree with some of my suggestions and wish to replace them with your own.

But behind all these characteristics - and any more we care to mention - is a simple, albeit oxymoronic, aim: to ensure pupils are comfortable with discomfort.

In other words, we want our pupils to know that the work they'll be asked to do in our classrooms will be tough, that they will be challenged with hard work and made to think. We want our pupils to know that there will be no hiding place in our classrooms; they must ask and answer questions and attempt everything we ask of them.

However, in so doing, we want them to feel safe and protected, we want them to be eager for challenge, and to willingly attempt hard work because they know that we've strung a safety net beneath them: yes, they might falter but we will catch them if they fall.

We also want our pupils to know that taking risks and making mistakes is not just accepted in our classrooms but is positively and proactively welcomed as an essential part of the learning process. Indeed, the only people who don't make mistakes either never get any better at anything or have reached the point of automaticity - they have fully mastered something and so can now do it through habit.

Our pupils are not at the point of automaticity and so must make mistakes if they are to get better in our subject. If they don't make mistakes, they cannot receive feedback; if they don't receive feedback, they will not know how to improve; if they don't know how to improve, then they are unlikely to do so.

There are many ways of achieving an effective learning environment in which pupils are comfortable with discomfort: some are simple common sense; some are more complex...

Let's take each of the hallmarks I list above in turn and discuss some tangible ways of achieving them.

Firstly, I said an effective learning environment is one in which pupils feel welcomed. The best - and simplest - way of achieving this is to physically welcome them into our classrooms. For example, we could establish a habit of greeting pupils at the classroom door at the start of every lesson, and then do so with a smile and by greeting some pupils by name. For some pupils in some contexts, that might be the first time someone - an adult, at least - has acknowledged their existence. If we can't show our pupils that we are pleased to see them and eager to teach them, then can we really expect them to be pleased to be in our lesson?

Secondly, I said an effective learning environment is one in which pupils feel valued. We can achieve this by making sure we're on time and have a lesson planned and ready to go. We can also do this by creating a culture whereby everyone's contributions are welcomed and given the time and attention they deserve. This might involve explicitly teaching and repeatedly reinforcing, not to mention modelling, debating skills such as active listening. Valuing each pupil's contribution is not the same as agreeing with everything they say. Indeed, if a pupil gives a wrong answer then they need to know it's wrong and why it's wrong. But a pupil's response doesn't have to be right for it to be useful.

Thirdly, I said that we want pupils to be enthusiastic about learning. This is, in part, achieved by developing pupils' intrinsic motivation but this isn't always possible and is rarely easy. So, another tangible, teacher-led strategy for enthusing pupils is to model that enthusiasm by constantly articulating - through our words and actions - our joy at teaching our pupils and at teaching our subject. In this regard, sometimes a little over-acting goes a long way. It's better to be considered the kooky, eccentric teacher who's truly, madly, deeply in love with science, say, than the boring, staid one who never cracks a smile and only perseveres for the pension.

Fourthly, we want our pupils to be engaged in their learning. But what is 'engagement' and why does it matter? Let me return to the point with which I started this chapter: fun is never our goal as teachers; we don't need pupils to enjoy our lessons in order to learn. We need them to think about the right things. If they happen to enjoy what they do, then that's a bonus. But 'fun activities' are not our guiding star; rather, thinking hard but efficiently about curriculum content is.

So, when I talk about pupils being engaged in their learning I do not mean - or do not solely mean - that they are enjoying what they're doing. Instead, I mean that they are actively paying attention to the right things and are thinking hard. It's about being engaged (as in 'meaningfully occupied by or connected to') as distinct from enjoying (as in 'taking pleasure from').

It's understandable that we should want our pupils to enjoy our lessons and to be busy, but the emphasis should not be on enjoyment and it's not desirable to employ a strategy in which pupils are engaged by something that appears interesting but leads to little substantive learning or, at any rate, slows down the process of learning because this will prove ultimately demotivating. In other words, their initial interest and their investment of time and energy will gradually fade then disappear altogether because motivation can only be maintained if it is accompanied by positive results. Without positive results, demotivation - and indeed amotivation - quickly develops.

Our goal as teachers should therefore be to ensure our pupils learn in an effective, efficient, and enjoyable way (in that order).

Yes, we want pupils to be motivated and engaged but motivation and engagement are not appropriate substitutes for learning, nor can they be a proxy for learning.

In a paper in July 2017, Paul Kirschner said that he'd "long thought that one of the weakest proxy indicators of effective learning [was] engagement, and yet it's a term persistently used by school leaders (and some researchers) as one of the most important measures of quality. In fact, many of the things we've traditionally associated with effective teachers may not be indicative of students actually learning anything at all."

Kirschner urged "fellow researchers, teachers, trainers, instructional designers, and all other learning professionals" to "agree that motivation, engagement, fun, and many other positive emotions during learning are great to strive for but let's first go for learning."

After all, without learning, what's the point of pupils being motivated and engaged?

Fifthly, I said an effective learning environment was one in which pupils are eager to experiment. I have already said that taking risks and making mistakes is an essential part of the learning process; it is not just to be accepted but to be positively and proactively welcomed in our classrooms. But why? Why is taking risks and making mistakes so desirable?

In the next chapter I will explain all...

CHAPTER FOURTEEN:
LEARNING TO FAIL

In the previous chapter I explained that, amongst other things, an effective learning environment is one in which all pupils:

- Feel welcomed,
- Feel valued,
- Are enthusiastic about learning,
- Are engaged in their learning,
- Are eager to experiment, and
- Feel rewarded for their hard work.

So far, we have examined what it means to make pupils feel valued and welcomed, and to be enthusiastic about - and engaged in - their learning. Now let's delve somewhat deeper into the final two hallmarks of an effective learning environment: to be eager to experiment and to feel rewarded for hard work...

Taking risks and making mistakes is an essential part of the learning process; it should not simply be accepted, rather we must positively and proactively encourage it. But why is taking risks and making mistakes so desirable?

Allow me to explain...

Matthew Syed is three-time Commonwealth table-tennis champion. In 1995 at the tender age of 25, he became the

British number one. To put that into perspective, there are 2.4 million players in Britain, 30,000 paid up members of the governing body and thousands of teams. So, what marked Syed out for excellence? Was it his speed, guile, mental strength, agility and reflexes? There was certainly no silver spoon, no nepotism. He came from an ordinary family in an ordinary suburb of an ordinary town in south-east England.

In his book, Bounce, Syed argues that "we like to think that sport is a meritocracy - where achievement is driven by ability and hard work - but it is nothing of the sort". He goes on to say that, "Practically every man and woman who triumphs against the odds is, on closer inspection, a beneficiary of unusual circumstances. The delusion lies in focusing on the individuality of their triumph without perceiving - or bothering to look for - the powerful opportunities stacked in their favour."

Syed says his was not a triumph of individuality, a personal odyssey of success, or a triumph against the odds; it was the result of a fortunate set of circumstances. His parents bought him a table-tennis table and they were lucky enough to have a garage big enough to house it. He had a brother who loved table-tennis as much as he did and with whom he could practice daily. He had a teacher who just happened to be the nation's top coach and a senior figure in the Table Tennis Association. His local club, Omega, was open 24 hours a day and gave out keys to its select group of members so that they could practice endlessly at any time of day and night.

Because of these circumstances, the local area produced several top players not just Syed. His brother won three national titles; one of the top female players of her generation lived in the house opposite and won countless junior titles and a national senior title; in-between their two houses lived another successful player who went on to win a series of doubles titles. There were other outstanding players in the neighbourhood, too, which meant that this one ordinary street in Reading produced more outstanding table tennis players than the rest of the country put together.

This supports the famous claim made by Malcolm Gladwell in his book, Outliers, that outstanding performance is not about 'who you are' but rather 'what you do' and 'where you come from'.

So, what, then, is talent? Anders Ericsson, a psychologist at Florida State University, investigated the causes of outstanding performance. His subjects were violinists from the Music Academy of West Berlin. He divided his subjects into three groups: the first group were the outstanding violinists who were expected to become soloists; the second group were very good (though not as accomplished as the first group) and were expected to join the world's top orchestras; the third group were good but the least able and were expected to become music teachers (no offence to any music teachers reading this). The 'setting' of the three groups was based on assessment conducted by the academy's professors and on the level of success the pupils had enjoyed in open competitions.

The biographical details of all the pupils were very similar with no systematic differences: they each began playing the violin when they were aged 8; they each decided to become musicians when they were 14; they each had the same number of music teachers and had studied the same number of musical instruments beyond the violin. In fact, there was only one difference, but it was quite a striking one: the number of hours they had devoted to practice.

By the age of twenty, the pupils in the first group had practiced an average of ten thousand hours which is over two thousand hours more than the second group and over six thousand hours more than the third group. Ericsson found that there were no exceptions to this pattern: nobody in the first group who had reached the top of their game had done so without copious amounts of practice; and nobody who had worked so hard had failed to excel. The only distinguishing feature between the best and the rest was purposeful practice: the best people were eager to experiment; the best people took risks and made mistakes.

Jack Nicklaus, the most successful golfer of all time, has said the same thing: "Nobody - but nobody - has ever become really proficient at golf without practice, without doing a lot of thinking and then hitting a lot of shots. It isn't so much a lack of talent; it's a lack of being able to repeat good shots consistently that frustrates most players. And the only answer to that is practice."

Syed quantifies the amount of 'purposeful practice' that is required to achieve excellence. He points out that extensive research has come up with a specific answer: "from art to science and from board games to tennis, it has been found that a minimum of ten years is required to reach world-class status in any complex task". Malcolm Gladwell, meanwhile, asserts that most top performers practice for around one thousand hours per year.

There is a logic here: if someone believes that attaining excellence relies solely on talent, they are more likely to give up if they do not show early promise. However, if they believe that talent is not a (or is not the only) factor in achieving excellence then they are more likely to persevere.

Anders Ericsson calls talent the 'iceberg illusion'. In other words, when we witness excellence, we are witnessing the end product of a process that took years to realise. The countless hours of practice that have gone into this end result of excellence are invisible to us - they are submerged beneath the icy waters leaving only the tip of excellence visible.

Syed says that "world class performance comes by striving for a target just out of reach, but with a vivid awareness of how the gap might be breached". This is why great teachers do not 'dumb down' but provide real challenge for their pupils.

Syed says that "ten thousand hours of purposeful practice" is required to achieve excellence. By 'purposeful' he means "concentration and dedication" but also having "access to the right training system, and that sometimes means living in the right town or having the right coach".

When we transfer the idea of excellence to our own schools and colleges, having the right training system or method is easier to realise and less concerned with good fortune. It is about leaders and teachers creating the right conditions in their institutions and classrooms for learning to take place. It is about providing challenge, not 'dumbing down'; it is about providing a safe and secure atmosphere in which it is not only acceptable to make mistakes, but it is positively encouraged because to make mistakes is to learn.

Syed cites the Olympic figure-skater Shizuka Arakawa as an example of the importance of making mistakes. Arakawa fell down more than twenty thousand times in her pursuit of excellence. Syed says, "When examining [Shizuka's] story, the one question...to ask was: Why would anyone endure all that? Why would she keep striving in the teeth of constant failure? Why not give up and try something else?... It is because she did not interpret falling down as failure. Armed with a growth mindset, she interpreted falling down not merely as a means of improving, but as evidence that she was improving. Failure was not something that sapped her energy and vitality, but something that provided her with an opportunity to learn, develop, and adapt."

If this seems odd, Syed reminds us that in an advert for Nike, Michael Jordan declared: "I've missed more than nine thousand shots. I've lost almost three hundred games. Twenty-six times I've been trusted to take the game-winning shot and missed." In other words, in order to become the greatest basketball player of all time, Jordan had first to embrace failure. Jordan has said that "mental toughness and heart are a lot stronger than some of the physical advantages you might have." Thomas Edison said the same thing: "If I find 10,000 ways something won't work, I haven't failed. I am not discouraged, because every wrong attempt discarded is another step forward."

In Bounce, Syed asks us to think of life having two paths: one leading to mediocrity, the other to excellence. The path to mediocrity, he says, is "flat and straight [and] it is possible to cruise along on autopilot with a nice, smooth, steady, almost effortless progression [and] you can reach your destination without stumbling and falling over". The path to excellence, meanwhile, "could not be more different...it is steep, gruelling, and arduous. It is inordinately lengthy, requiring a minimum of ten thousand hours of lung-busting effort to get to the summit [and] it forces voyagers to stumble and fall on every single stretch of the journey."

Excellence, after all, is about "striving for what is just out of reach and not quite making it; it is about grappling with tasks beyond current limitations and falling short again and again." In short, excellence is about experimenting, taking risks and making mistakes, and learning from those mistakes in order to move, incrementally, towards automaticity.

A recap: so far, we have explored the importance of pupils feeling welcomed and valued, enthusiastic and engaged, and eager to experiment. The final feature of our learning environment, I said, was that pupils feel rewarded for their hard work...

Rewarding hard work and effort not only creates a level playing field on which every pupil has equal chance of scoring a goal (because everyone can try hard, after all), it also makes explicit the progress each pupil is making from their individual starting point. Not every pupil can achieve a grade 9 or a distinction, but every pupil can improve to beat their previous score.

In the next chapter we will take a closer look at the use - and mis-use - of rewards...

Matt Bromley

CHAPTER FIFTEEN:
EXTRINSIC MOTIVATION

Human beings have a biological drive that includes hunger, thirst and sex. But we also have another long-recognised drive: the drive that responds to rewards and punishments.

However, in his book Drive, Daniel Pink argues that rewards don't work; instead, they "encourage unethical behaviour, create addictions, and foster short-term thinking".

Pink calls this type of behaviour - the drive that responds to rewards and punishments - Type X behaviour. He says Type X behaviour is "fuelled more by extrinsic desires than intrinsic ones and concerned less with the inherent satisfaction of an activity and more with the external rewards to which an activity leads"

Not only does Type X behaviour lead to unethical acts, it also has a short shelf-life. People do not remain motivated for long. They lose interest in the thing they're doing. They are only interested in the rewards that the task brings. And their performance suffers. They stop getting better at it. They stop learning.

In Drive, Daniel Pink recounts experiments conducted by Harry Harlow and Edward Deci. Harlow was a professor of psychology at the University of Wisconsin and studied primate behaviour in the 1940s. In 1949 Harlow and two colleagues carried out a two-week experiment on eight rhesus monkeys. They devised a simple mechanical puzzle which could be solved by pulling out a vertical pin, undoing a hook and lifting a hinged door. The researchers placed the puzzles in the monkeys' cages in order to observe how they reacted. Almost immediately, and without any prompting, the monkeys began playing with the puzzles with what Harlow described as focus, determination and enjoyment.

Relatively quickly, the monkeys began figuring the mechanism out. By days thirteen and fourteen, the monkeys had become adept: they could solve the puzzles quickly; indeed, two-thirds of them did so in less than a minute. Nobody had taught the monkeys how to do it and they had received no reward for doing so.

This behaviour was contrary to what we know of primates. As I have said, there are two drives that power our behaviour: a biological drive such as the need for food, water and copulation to satiate hunger, quench thirst and satisfy carnal needs - in other words, the internal drive; and the external drive in which we behave in certain ways to be rewarded or to avoid punishments. If people knew they would be paid for doing something, or they would be fined for not doing it, they would be more motivated to do it.

However, in this experiment the "solution did not lead to food, water or sex gratification" as Harlow explained. Nor did it lead to rewards, not even affection or a round of applause. Harlow was perplexed. He wrote, "The behaviour obtained in this investigation poses some interesting questions for motivation theory, since significant learning was attained, and efficient performance maintained without resort to special or extrinsic incentives".

To try to explain this anomaly, Harlow offered a new theory: he proposed a third drive. "The performance of the task provided intrinsic reward." In other words, the monkeys solved the puzzles and got better and quicker at solving them simply because they enjoyed doing so, they found it gratifying.

The task was its own reward. Harlow eventually called this 'intrinsic motivation'.

Harlow wanted to know whether their performance would improve further if rewards were introduced. When he tested the theory, he found something astonishing: the monkeys actually made more errors and solved the puzzles slower and less frequently when rewards were at stake. "The introduction of food in the present experiment served to disrupt performance," he said.

Harlow concluded that this third drive, intrinsic motivation, "may be as basic and strong as the [biological drive and the drive powered by rewards and punishments]. Furthermore, there is some reason to believe that [the third drive] can be as efficient in facilitating learning."

Twenty years later, in 1969, a Carnegie Mellon University psychology graduate, Edward Deci, studied the notion of intrinsic motivation for his dissertation using a group of male and female university students. He chose a Soma puzzle cube which consisted of seven plastic pieces, six with four one-inch cubes and one with three one-inch cubes. The pieces could be arranged into several million combinations. Deci divided his participants into Group A - an experimental group, and Group B - a control group. Each group took part in three hour-long sessions on consecutive days. Each participant was given seven Soma puzzle pieces, illustrations depicting three puzzle combinations and a copy of Time magazine, The New Yorker and Playboy. Deci explained the instructions and timed the students using a stopwatch.

In the first session, participants in Groups A and B had to assemble their pieces into the combinations shown in the illustrations. In the second session, they did the same thing with different illustrations, but this time Deci told Group A they'd be paid $1 for everyone they got right. Group B were not paid. In the third session, both groups received new illustrations and neither group was paid.

Halfway through each session, Deci stopped the participants after they had assembled two of the three combinations and gave them a fourth drawing. In order to choose the right combination, he said, he had to feed the results into a computer which would take several minutes. Deci left the room ostensibly to use the computer but actually observed the participants from behind a two-way mirror. He told them as he was leaving, "I shall be gone only a few minutes, you may do whatever you like while I'm gone". He watched them for exactly eight minutes.

In the first session there was little difference between Group A and Group B: both sets of participants continued playing with the puzzles for about three to four minutes. After which time, presumably, they would flick through the magazines or sit idle. In the second session, when Group A was being paid to complete the puzzles and Group B was not, Group B continued to behave as they had the previous day - they played with the puzzles for about half their free time. But Group A spent more time playing with the puzzles, about five minutes on average. So far so predictable. When being paid, the participants wanted to get a head-start so that they earned more money. This proved the second drive: reward someone and they will be motivated to work harder.

In the third session, however, something strange happened. Group A and B were now unpaid - Group A were told there wasn't enough money to pay them for a second day. When left alone for eight minutes, Group B played with the puzzles for a little longer than they had previously, suggesting that, over time, they were becoming more engaged in the task. But Group A now spent significantly less time playing with the puzzles, on average two minutes less than they had previously when being paid, suggesting they now enjoyed the task less.

This experiment echoed what Harlow had discovered twenty years earlier: "When money is used as an external reward for some activity, the subjects lose intrinsic interest for the activity," wrote Deci. Rewards encouraged short-term increases in productivity, but the effect wore off and eventually reduced the person's motivation for the task. Deci concluded that we have an "inherent tendency to seek out novelty and challenges, to extend and exercise [our] capacities, to explore, and to learn".

We will return to Daniel Pink's Drive in the next chapter and explore the idea of autonomy - the desire to direct our own lives; mastery - the urge to get better and better at something that matters; and purpose - the yearning to do what we do in the service of something larger than ourselves...

Matt Bromley

CHAPTER SIXTEEN:
INTRINSIC MOTIVATION

Returning to Drive, Daniel Pink says that Type I behaviour (unlike Type X which - as I have already said - is "fuelled more by extrinsic desires than intrinsic ones and concerned less with the inherent satisfaction of an activity and more with the external rewards to which an activity leads") is concerned "more with the inherent satisfaction of the activity itself". This third drive, or intrinsic motivation, is - according to Pink - three-fold:

1. **Autonomy** - the desire to direct our own lives
2. **Mastery** - the urge to get better and better at something that matters
3. **Purpose** - the yearning to do what we do in the service of something larger than ourselves

Let's look at what each of these aspects of intrinsic motivation means...

Autonomy: Pink says that "people need autonomy over task (what they do), time (when they do it), team (who they do it with), and technique (how they do it)". The theory being this: if someone is in control of their activities, they are more likely to be motivated by them and more likely to excel at them.

Mastery: Pink says that "only engagement can produce mastery - becoming better at something that matters". He goes on to say that "mastery begins with 'flow' - optimal experiences when the challenges we face are exquisitely matched to our abilities - [and] requires the capacity to see your abilities not as finite, but as infinitely improvable." Again, this is about the desire to improve, to want to get better and better at something. People are only motivated to get better at something they are engaged in and enjoy. Pink goes on to say that "Mastery is a pain: it demands effort, grit and deliberate practice. And mastery is asymptote: it's impossible to fully realise, which makes it simultaneously frustrating and alluring."

Purpose: Humans seek purpose, "a cause greater and more enduring than themselves". This is to say that people need to feel that what they are doing will have a long-term purpose and meaning in the world. It's the desire to leave your mark on the world, to do something worthwhile and with impact.

Earlier, I alluded to one famous example of the power of autonomy, mastery and purpose in action: the battle between Wikipedia and Microsoft's Encarta. Here's a bit more detail...

In 1995 there were two organisations concerned with developing a new encyclopaedia: the first model comes from Microsoft, a multi-million-pound global organisation; the other is the result of a not-for-profit 'hobby'. Microsoft's encyclopaedia involves a band of paid professional writers and editors working for well-paid managers who oversee a project which is delivered on time and on budget. Microsoft sell the encyclopaedia on CD-ROMs and online. The hobbyists, meanwhile, do not belong to a company and are not paid. Instead, tens of thousands of people write and edit entries in the encyclopaedia just for fun. Contributors offer their time and expertise for nothing and the encyclopaedia itself is offered free of charge to anyone who wants it via the internet.

Everyone expected the encyclopaedia funded by Microsoft to thrive and Wikipedia to falter. But, by 2009, Microsoft had discontinued 'Encarta' whilst 'Wikipedia' continued to thrive

- with 13 million entries in 260 languages, it had become the largest and most popular encyclopaedia in the world.

In short, the business model that relied on traditional rewards to motivate its employees and customers failed; the one that relied on intrinsic motivation (doing something simply for the fun of it) succeeded; in the battle for supremacy, money had lost to the love of learning.

Let us now take Pink's notion of Type X behaviour a step further in order to consider how damaging praise might be...

Pink says that being motivated by extrinsic desires leads, at best, to short-termism whereby someone loses interest in what they are doing because they are doing it, not for the enjoyment and interest of the thing itself, but for other rewards.

Carol Dweck goes further in her cautionary assessment of the dangers of rewards. You may recall that I briefly alluded to this earlier when exploring ways to create the right emotional learning environment but I will expand on it here...

Dweck conducted research with hundreds of pupils, mostly early adolescents. She gave each pupil a set of ten fairly different problems to solve from a non-verbal IQ test.

Most of the pupils did pretty well and when they'd finished, she praised them. She praised some of the pupils for their ability (e.g., 'You got such a high score, you must be really smart'); she praised the others for their effort (e.g., 'You got such a high score, you must have worked really hard'). Both groups were exactly equal to begin with. But after receiving praise, they began to differ...

The pupils whose ability was praised were pushed into what she termed 'the fixed mindset'. When they were given a choice, they rejected a challenging new task that they could learn from, favouring more of the same instead. Why?

Because they didn't want to do anything which would expose flaws in their intelligence and bring their talent into question.

In contrast, 90% of the pupils whose effort was praised wanted to try the challenging new task precisely because they could learn from it.

All the pupils were given new challenging tasks to do. None of the pupils did particularly well. Those who were praised for their ability now thought they weren't very smart because, if success means they are intelligent, then failure must mean they're deficient. Those praised for effort, on the other hand, didn't see it as failure. They believed it meant they had to try harder. As for the pupils' enjoyment of the task, all pupils enjoyed the first task but those praised for ability did not enjoy the harder task because it isn't fun when your talent is called into question. Those praised for effort, however, said they still enjoyed it and indeed some felt the harder task was more fun because they had to exert more effort in order to try to complete it.

As the tests were IQ tests, Dweck concluded that praising ability actually lowered pupils' IQs whereas praising effort raised them. Dweck also states that praising children's intelligence harms their motivation and harms their performance. Why? Because although children love to be praised, especially for their talents, as soon as they hit a snag their confidence goes out of the window and their motivation hits rock bottom. If success means they're smart, then failure means they're dumb.

Dweck talks about hidden messages in the praise we give our pupils. The statement, 'You learned that so quickly, you must be really smart' can be translated in a child's mind to: 'If I don't learn something quickly, I'm not smart'. Similarly, the statement 'You're so brilliant, you got an A without even trying' can be translated in a child's mind to: 'I'd better quit whilst I'm ahead or they won't think I'm smart anymore'.

This doesn't mean we shouldn't praise pupils, Dweck argues. But it does mean we should only use a certain type of praise. We can praise our pupils as much as we want for the "growth-oriented process - what they accomplished through practice, study, persistence, and good strategies". But we should avoid the kind of praise that judges their intelligence or talent, and we should avoid the kind of praise that implies "we're proud of them for their intelligence or talent rather than for the work they put in".

CHAPTER SEVENTEEN:
LEARNING OUTCOMES

So far in Part Three of this book on teaching for long-term learning, we have said that the process of learning is an interaction between our sensory memory and our long-term memory.

Our sensory memory, we said, is made up of: What we see - this is called our iconic memory; what we hear - this is called our echoic memory; and what we touch - our haptic memory.

Our long-term memory, meanwhile, is where new information is stored and from which it can be recalled when needed, but we cannot directly access the information stored in our long-term memory.

As such, this interaction takes place in our working memory, or short-term memory, which is the only place where we can think and do.

In short, therefore, there are three steps to improving the learning process. They are:

1. Stimulate pupils' senses to gain the attention of working memory
2. Make pupils think hard but efficiently to encode information into long-term memory
3. Embed deliberate practice to improve pupils' storage in and retrieval from long-term memory

In this section of Part Three of the book, we are focusing on the first of these three steps: stimulating pupils' senses to gain the attention of working memory.

In order to stimulate our pupils' sensory memories and thus engage the attention of their working memories, we need to create classroom conditions conducive to learning, conditions that stimulate their iconic, echoic and haptic memories. In other words, we need to engage our pupils' senses in order to gain their attention.

In the previous chapters we looked at ways of making our pupils feel welcomed and valued, enthusiastic about - and engaged in - their learning, eager to experiment, and rewarded for their hard work.

In this chapter we will examine what happens next...

Occasionally, on my teacher-training courses and when the mood takes me, I ask colleagues to draw a picture of something familiar, something a child might doodle. A boat. A car. An island. A house.

I give them five minutes and ask them to work alone and in silence. When the five minutes are up, I ask them to swap their drawings with the person sitting next to them so that they can peer-assess their artwork. At this point I reveal the assessment criteria.

If I had asked colleagues to draw a house, say, I might inform them that if they have included a front door, their neighbour can award them five points. If they have drawn a path leading up to that front door, they can have a further five points. If they have five or more windows, each with curtains, they can add another five marks. A chimney with two chimney pots gets them another five; a garage, five points; a driveway with a car parked on it, five points; and so on.

Trainees then calculate their partner's total score and equate this to a grade before handing it back. It is rare – unheard of, in fact – for anyone to get an A or a B. More often than not, colleagues get an E or an F.

Having shared the group's grades – in a deliberately public, humiliating manner – we discuss how this makes people feel and, invariably, trainees tell me they feel upset that their hard work and creativity has not been recognised.

Some say they feel angry and cheated because they were given a vague task and yet the criteria against which their work was assessed was specific and arbitrary. Others say they feel dejected and demotivated, unwilling now to dedicate any real effort to the next task because of the unfairness of the first. This inevitably leads us to the following conclusions...

We agree that learning outcomes and task instructions must be specific and that the outcomes and the assessment criteria must correspond.

We also agree that the assessment criteria must be shared with pupils before they embark on the task and that, ideally, pupils should be involved in agreeing that success criteria.

For this task, for example, I could have engaged colleagues in a discussion about the features they would expect to find on an excellent drawing of a house.

Such a discussion would not only have made it clearer how pupils would eventually be judged – therefore, ensuring greater chances of success and mitigating their feelings of unfairness and arbitrariness – but would also have ensured that pupils took ownership of the task and had a vested interest in completing it to the best of their abilities.

We also agree that the assessment criteria should allow for a degree of creativity and flair, and not be too prescriptive.

And, finally, we agree that feedback should be formative, focused on what pupils need to do to improve ("Your drawing was creative and had many good features but, next time, consider including..." for example); rather than summative and final ("You got 20 out of 40, that's a grade E which isn't very good").

In short, we decide that it is important to share the "bigger picture" with pupils, to make explicit what they are learning, why they are learning it, and what success looks like.

Surely, an effective learning environment - one that is conducive to learning - is built upon these basic foundations: pupils must first know what they are expected to learn, how that learning fits in the wider context, and how that learning will be assessed.

However, here's an important caveat: sharing learning outcomes and assessment criteria does not mean that every lesson must start with a set of objectives on the board which pupils have to copy down. Lessons are artificial blocks of study not a complete learning sequence. Not every lesson, therefore, needs to start with objectives and there is never anything to be gained by getting pupils to copy them down. Rather, the direction of travel should be shared with pupils when you begin a new topic or module.

Before we move on, let's consider how to write learning outcomes and what we should do them once written...

Learning outcomes should be measurable statements that articulate what pupils should know and/or be able to do by the end of a lesson or sequence of lessons. The best learning outcomes are pupil-centred rather than teacher-centred, and are specific, and measurable, thus providing a means of determining the content, organisation, and assessment of the lesson or topic.

Learning outcomes can help pupils to acquire foundational knowledge and can improve their short-term retention, as well as improve higher-order cognitive processing such as the application of knowledge and the transferability of knowledge.

The best learning outcomes actually shape what pupils learn because when pupils know what they're expected to learn they can direct their attention towards those ideas or concepts.

The best learning outcomes are closely aligned to assessments.

As I explained in Book One of this series, we can use the 'clear end points' or 'body of knowledge' we articulated in our curriculum plans, as well as the 'threshold concepts' that act as waypoints towards those destinations, as our learning outcomes.

Once you've written your learning outcomes, you can check their validity by asking yourself the following questions:

- Does this learning outcome identify what pupils will be able to do after the lesson?
- Does it focus on specific and concrete actions?
- Will I be able to observe that pupils have achieved the outcome and is it clear to me how a pupil's achievement of the outcome will be measured?
- Does the outcome align with the level of knowledge expected of pupils and have a clear meaning to the teacher and pupils?
- Is the outcome relevant and useful to pupils and does it align with the tasks and assessments I have planned?

Sharing the learning outcomes at the start of a sequence of lessons on a particular topic is an important element of direct instruction (which is proven to be a more effective strategy than less-structured approaches such as enquiry-based learning, particularly for novice learners) because knowing the learning outcomes in advance helps pupils to practice their metacognitive skills and to become more self-regulated.

Having clear learning outcomes helps pupils to narrow their focus to the most important knowledge and skills, and they can help pupils to organise their notes, track their progress towards meeting the outcomes, and improve their self-study.

Sharing learning outcomes prior to studying a topic can also increase pupils' levels of motivation and engagement because learning outcomes give pupils a clearer sense of purpose.

When pupils understand what is expected of them, they are more likely to feel confident that they can meet those expectations.

Perhaps the most important part of sharing learning outcomes is checking that pupils understand them. To be certain of this, it's important to engage pupils in a discussion. For example, you may ask pupils what - in their own words - they think the learning outcomes mean. You may ask how they will know that they've achieved the learning outcomes, and why they think it's important to do so. You may also ask pupils how the learning outcomes relate to what they've previously learnt and how they think achieving the learning outcomes will help them with their future learning.

To summarise the argument so far...

First, we need our pupils to feel welcomed into our classrooms and to feel that their contributions are valued. We need them to arrive at our lessons feeling enthusiastic about - and ready to be engaged in - their learning. And we need them to be ready and eager to experiment, to take risks and make mistakes, and then to feel rewarded for their hard work and effort.

Second, we need our pupils to know what they are expected to learn - we need to explicitly direct their attention to what they need to think about - and how that learning consolidates and builds upon their prior learning and how it will be extended and utilised in the future. And we need pupils to know how their work will be assessed and what excellence looks like.

Once we have created these conditions, we need to provide opportunities for pupils to apply and practice their learning, receive feedback and act upon that feedback in order to improve. This is sometimes called 'the open loop'...

CHAPTER EIGHTEEN:
USING FEEDBACK TO DIRECT LEARNING

Think of something you're good at.

How did you become good at it? How do you know you're good at it - on what evidence is your judgment based?

Now think of something you're not very good at and consider why - what went wrong when you were trying to learn this thing and who, if anyone, was to blame?

Next, think about something you are good at now but didn't initially want to learn. What kept you going in lieu of motivation?

Finally, think of a time you've helped someone - ideally not a pupil in a school setting, but perhaps a friend or family member - to learn something. To what extent did you understand the subject better once you'd taught it to someone else?

Now, just like Derren Brown, I'll read your mind and reveal your answers...

I'm confident you said you became good at something through practice, by learning from your mistakes, by experimenting. You also learnt best when you engaged in a process of trial and error and when you repeated your actions several times, making incremental improvements each time. As the Danish nuclear physicist Niels Bohr once said, "[An expert is] someone who has made all the mistakes which it is possible to make in a very narrow field".

I'm also confident that you knew you were good at something because of the evidence given to you in the form of feedback, particularly praise, and as a result of receiving a reward for doing well. You might also have known that you were good at something because you were asked to help others achieve the same end-goal and because you saw the results of your labours for yourself.

I'll wager that, when learning failed for you, it was because you didn't engage in a sufficient amount of practice, didn't work hard enough or lacked focus. Perhaps the feedback you received was poor or else you did not act upon it, or at any rate did not act upon it in a timely manner. Perhaps the communication between you and your teacher was poor.

Often, though, when learning failed for you it was because you lacked sufficient motivation, you simply weren't interested in learning the thing being taught because it wasn't personally meaningful to you.

So, what, in the absence of motivation - when you didn't have the *want* to learn - kept you going until you succeeded?

I'll bet it was the *need* to learn - having a rationale, a necessity to learn, and therefore taking ownership of the learning - that kept you going and helped you overcome your lack of motivation to succeed.

Finally, I bet that by teaching something to a third party you learnt more about it yourself because the act of teaching enabled you to gain feedback and make better sense of a topic. Teaching is also a form of learning by doing, of learning through practice. And the fact you had to teach something to someone else addressed the *need* to learn it (you had to learn it in order to teach it to someone else, after all).

So, what does all this have to do with 'the open loop'?

In order that our pupils learn, we need to provide them with opportunities to practice, receive feedback and act upon that feedback.

Practice builds proficiency and mastery. As I explained earlier when sharing some features of effective homework, the three forms of practice that work best are:

1. Spaced repetition.

This is where information is learnt initially then repeated several times at increasingly long intervals so that pupils get to the point of almost forgetting what they've learned and must delve into their long-term memories to retrieve their prior knowledge, thus strengthening those memories.

2. Retrieval practice.

This is low-stakes testing (such as multiple choice quizzes) used not for the purposes of assessment but for reinforcement and to provide pupils with feedback information on what they know and can do and what they don't yet know and cannot yet do so that they can better focus their future studies.

3. Cognitive disfluency (otherwise known as desirable difficulties).

This is a memory technique that makes learning 'stick' by placing artificial barriers in the way of pupils' initial study. Doing this means that the process of encoding (learning something for the first time) is made harder so that the process of retrieval (recalling that learning later, say in a test) is made quicker and easier.

The power of practice - of learning by doing through a process of trial and error - has a foundation in neurochemistry...

Whenever we do something – think, move, read this book – our brain sends a signal (like an electric charge) along the neurones in our brains and through our nerve fibres to our muscles. In other words, every skill we possess – swinging a golf club, writing great fiction, playing the piano – is created by chains of nerve fibres carrying small electrical impulses like the signals travelling through a circuit. Each time we practise something, a different highly specific circuit is illuminated in our heads and it is these circuits that control our thoughts and movements. Indeed, the circuit is the movement because it dictates the content of each thought and the timing and strength of each muscle contraction.

More importantly, each time we practise something – be it a mental or physical skill – our nerve fibres are coated in a layer of insulating material called myelin which acts in much the same way as the rubber insulation that coats a copper wire: it makes the electrical impulses stronger and faster by preventing the signals from leaking out.

Each time we practice a skill, a new layer of myelin is added to the neurone and the thicker the myelin gets, the better it insulates our nerve fibres and, therefore, the faster our movements and thoughts become. But that's not all...

As well as getting faster, our thoughts and movements also become more accurate as we add more and more layers of myelin. Why should this be? Because myelin regulates the velocity with which those electrical impulses travel through our nerve fibres, speeding up or slowing down the signals so that they hit our synapses at exactly the right moment. And timing is all important because neurones are binary: either they fire, or they don't. Whether or not they fire is dependent on whether the incoming impulse is big enough to exceed their so-called "threshold of activation".

Neurochemistry teaches us, therefore, that every skill can be improved and perfected by performing it repeatedly because this helps us to hone our neural circuitry. But not all forms of practice are equal. We create myelin most effectively when we engage in *deliberate* practice.

Deliberate practice is about struggling in certain targeted ways – placing artificial barriers in the way of our success in order to make it harder to learn something. In other words, you slow your learning down and force yourself to make mistakes. This is what Robert Bjork calls "desirable difficulties" which we will explore in Step 2 on working memory. For now, suffice to say, the act of slowing down and making mistakes ensures we are operating at the edges of our ability.

So, the best form of practice – and therefore the best way to create more myelin – is to set yourself a target just beyond your current ability but within your reach. This is what Lev Vygotsky calls the "zone of proximal development" and what Robert Bjork calls "the sweet spot". This spot is the optimal gap between what we know and what we're trying to do and, Bjork says, when we find that sweet spot, "learning takes off".

CHAPTER NINETEEN:
USING FEEDBACK TO INFORM PLANNING

Once pupils have practiced their learning, we need to ensure they receive - and produce - information about what they have mastered and what they still need to practice.

Feedback should redirect the pupil's and the teacher's actions to help the pupil achieve their target. In my experience, the most effective feedback:

- Addresses faulty interpretations;
- Comments on rather than grades work;
- Provides cues or prompts for further work;
- Is timely, specific and clear; and
- Is focused on task and process rather than on praising.

Feedback works best when it is explicit about the marking criteria, offers suggestions for improvement, and is focused on how pupils can close the gap between their current and their desired performance. Feedback does not work when it focuses on presentation or quantity of work.

Feedback can promote the growth mindset if it: is as specific as possible; focuses on factors within pupils' control; focuses on factors which are dependent on effort not ability; and motivates rather than frustrates pupils.

Self- and peer-assessment can often prove effective strategies - particularly as we want our pupils to become increasingly metacognitive in their approach to learning - because these strategies: give pupils greater responsibility for their learning; allow pupils to help and be helped by each other; encourage collaboration and reflection; enable pupils to see their progress; and help pupils to see for themselves how to improve.

But self- and peer-assessment need to be used wisely and pupils need to be helped to develop the necessary skills and knowledge to be able to assess and give feedback because research suggests eighty per cent of the feedback pupils give each other is wrong. It is, therefore, well worth investing lesson time to help pupils improve their self-assessment skills because research suggests that when it's done well it can increase pupils' achievement.

Ultimately, though, the only useful feedback is that which is acted upon – it is crucial, therefore, that the teacher knows the pupil and knows when and what kind of feedback to give, then plans time for pupils to act on the feedback they receive. For example, DIRT - 'directed improvement and reflection time' - is a great use of lesson time and helps to condition pupils in the drafting and re-drafting process, as well as getting them used to responding positively to feedback, to learning from their mistakes, and to improving through a process of trial and error.

According to Professor Dylan Wiliam, feedback after a test that includes the correct answer increases pupils' capacity to learn because it enables them to correct any errors in their work. The critical mechanism in learning from tests, Wiliam argues, is successful retrieval. However, if pupils do not retrieve the correct response after taking the test and have no recourse to learn it, then the benefits of testing can be limited or indeed absent altogether.

As such, providing feedback after a retrieval attempt, regardless of whether the attempt was successful or unsuccessful, will help to ensure that retrieval is successful in the future.

Feedback is important after any type of test, but it is particularly important after pupils have taken a recognition test such as a multiple-choice quiz and a true/false question because pupils are exposed to incorrect information in the form of false options.

Another important consideration, according to Wiliam, is *when* to give feedback. Conventional wisdom - supported by studies in behavioural psychology - suggests that providing immediate feedback is best. However, experimental results have shown that delaying feedback might be more powerful.

In one study, for example, pupils read a text and then either took or did not take a multiple-choice quiz. One group of pupils who took the quiz received correct answer feedback immediately after making each response (immediate feedback); another group who took the quiz received the correct answers for all the questions after completing the entire test (delayed feedback). One week after the initial session, pupils took a final test in which they had to produce a response to the question that had formed the stem of the multiple-choice question (in other words, they had to produce an answer of their own rather than selecting one from among several alternatives). The final test consisted of the same questions from the initial multiple-choice quiz and comparable questions that had not been tested.

The study found that taking an initial quiz (even without feedback) tripled final recall relative to only studying the material. When correct answer feedback was given immediately after each question in the initial quiz, performance increased by another 10%. However, when the feedback was given after the entire test had been completed, it boosted final performance even more. In short, the study concluded that delayed feedback led to better retention than immediate feedback.

Although giving the answers to questions straight after a test is still relatively immediate feedback, the benefits of delayed feedback might represent a type of spacing effect. In other words, the phenomenon whereby two presentations of material are given with spacing between them leads to better retention than so-called 'massed' practice.

However, here's a note of caution regarding delayed feedback...

Kulik and Kulik (1988) and many other studies have found that pupils perform better when feedback is given immediately. Kulik and Kulik's conclusion - based on fifty-three meta-analyses - was that although delayed feedback was often found to produce better results in laboratory studies, immediate feedback resulted in better performances in applied studies in actual classrooms.

Ultimately, we should be influenced by the research but informed by our own context. In other words, we should try different methods with our own pupils and do what we find works best for us.

As well as providing pupils with time to respond to feedback, they also need time to reflect on their learning. Reflection might involve pupils rethinking their understanding of important ideas, perhaps with the teacher's guidance. It might involve pupils improving their work through revision based on self-assessment and feedback. It might involve pupils reflecting on their learning and performance.
With big ideas and questions being central to our well-planned lessons, it stands to reason that taking a linear path through the curriculum content (teaching it once then moving on) is a mistake. After all, how can pupils master complex ideas and tasks if they encounter them only once? Therefore, the flow of a sequence of lessons must be iterative, pupils must

be made fully aware of the need to rethink and revise in light of current learning, and the work must follow the trail back to the original big idea and learning outcome.

Let's take an example: in a key stage 3 humanities lesson pupils might explore the big question "What is democracy?" by discussing their experiences and by reading various texts about democracy. Pupils might then develop a theory of democracy and create a concept map for the topic. The teacher might then encourage them to rethink their initial ideas by raising a second big question, using an appropriate example: "What is representative democracy and majority rule – and how does it work?"

The pupils might then modify their concept of democracy as they come to understand that democracy can sometimes feel disenfranchising and unfair if the majority of voters do not share your own beliefs and values and if your own MP votes against constituents' wishes.

In-built rethinking and reflection are critical and deliberate elements of well-planned lessons; they are central to learning for understanding. We must, therefore, plan to make pupils constantly reconsider earlier understandings of the big ideas if they are ever to get beyond simplistic thinking and to the heart of deep understanding.

Once pupils have received feedback on their work and rethought their ideas, we need them to engage in metacognition - in other words, we need them to take ownership of their own learning, making improvements but also reflecting on how successfully they have learnt and what skills they need to practice further. This means developing the capacity to self-monitor and self-adjust as needed; to proactively consider what is working, what isn't, and what might be done better. In order to achieve this, we need pupils to engage in some form of self-evaluation, which means teaching them how to take stock of what they have learned and what needs further inquiry or refinement.

In practice, this means that pupils need opportunities in lessons to self-monitor, self-assess, and self-adjust their work, individually and collectively, as the work progresses. We can do this by:

- Allocating five minutes in the middle and at the end of a lesson in order to consider 'What have we found out? What remains unresolved or unanswered?

- Asking pupils to attach a self-assessment form to every formal piece of work they hand in

- Including a one-minute essay at the end of an instruction-based lesson in which pupils summarise the two or three main points and the questions that still remain for them (and, thus, next time, for the teacher)

- Asking pupils to attach a note to any formal piece of work in which they are honest about what they do and do not understand

- Teaching pupils to evaluate work in the same way that teachers do so that pupils become more accurate as peer reviewers and self-assessors, and more inclined to "think like teachers" in their work.

- Starting lessons with a survey of the most burning questions pupils may have. Then, as part of the final plenary, judge how well the questions were addressed, which ones remain, and what new ones emerged.

- Leaving the second half of a unit deliberately 'open' to allow pupils to frame and pursue the inquiry (rather than be directed by the teacher) based on the key questions that remain and clues that emerge at the end of the first half

- Getting pupils to develop a self-profile of their strengths and weaknesses as learners at the start of the year whereby they consider how they learn best, what strategies work well for them, what type of learning is most difficult, and what they wish to improve upon. Then, structure periodic opportunities for pupils to monitor their efforts and reflect on their struggles, and successes, and possible edits to their own profiles.

Earlier, I talked about the importance of sharing learning outcomes and success criteria with pupils so that they know what they're learning, how that learning fits into the 'bigger picture' and how they will be assessed. Sharing the big picture in this way is about connecting the learning, too; and making explicit the purpose of learning - articulating why pupils need to achieve the learning goals we're setting for them and of what use their learning will be to them in the future.

Connecting the learning in this way is also about sharing pupils' starting points – understanding, through diagnostic tests perhaps, what prior knowledge and skills (as well as misunderstandings) pupils bring with them to the classroom, and what their interests and talents are and how these might influence the way in which they learn.

Let's explore these ideas in greater depth...

Pupils need clear goals – they need to know what the performance you desire of them looks like and they need to know against what criteria that performance will be assessed.

Pupils also need to understand the general direction of travel – what can they expect in the scheme of work in relation to the key questions, tasks, tests, assignments, assessment criteria, and expected standards of work? In other words, the final outcome must be made transparent to pupils at the beginning of a sequence of lessons on a particular topic.

Once the learning goals have been articulated, pupils should be able to answer the following questions:

• What do I have to understand by the end of this unit?
• What am I expected to produce at the end of this unit in order to demonstrate my understanding? What will my understanding look like in practice?
• What knowledge and skills should I currently possess, or will I need to acquire, in order to meet the assessment criteria and, therefore, demonstrate my understanding?
• What resources and assistance will be available to help me learn?

- How does the work I am doing today relate to what we did previously?
- How will the work I am doing today help me to meet the final assessment criteria?
- What aspects of today's and future work demands the most attention?
- What are the strengths and weaknesses in my current performance? What can I do to improve?
- How will my final work be assessed?

Pupils need to know that the work they are being asked to do is purposeful. In other words, in order for them to invest time and energy into producing high-quality work, pupils need to know why they are being asked to do what they are being asked to do: what's the rationale, what's the benefit?

Where work is abstract, it is important to transform the learning goals into intelligible, practical tasks and criteria that pupils can understand.

For example, if teaching An Inspector Calls, an English teacher might begin by articulating a performance challenge and by posing a big question in order to signal where the unit is headed, how studying the play will be tackled, and how pupils' final performance will be assessed. The teacher might say to the class:

"At the end of a close study of An Inspector Calls, you will act as the jury in the case against the Birling family in the matter of Eva Smith's death. Using testimony from the Inspector, the Birling family and Gerald Croft, as well as diary extracts from Eva, you will decide which member of the Birling family is most responsible for Eva's death and why.

"You will write a diagnostic report for the coroner and a prescriptive letter to Eva's executor explaining what happened to Eva (the assessment criteria for the letter will also be distributed at this point).

"You will be given daily quizzes on your reading and a writing excrcise in which you will describe Eva from the perspective of two different characters. Following each reading assignment and before the next lesson, you will respond in your exercise book to two questions: what is the most important thing you learn about Eva in this section of the play? What is the most important unanswered question about Eva at this point in the play? Your responses to these questions will begin and end our classroom discussions.

"At the end of the unit, you will be asked to reflect on your emerging understanding of the play, as chronicled in the daily entries you make in your exercise book. On the last day of this unit, you will answer the following three questions: what changed about the way you saw Eva as the play progressed? What were your misunderstandings at any point during this unit? If you were to teach this play to next year's Year 10, what would you do in order to ensure that they truly understand the play as opposed to just knowing some facts about it?"

What this approach does is give pupils a purpose and a context for their studies, along with a challenge. From the first lesson in the unit, pupils know what is expected of them and how they will be assessed – which is to say in myriad different ways, including via a written response which will provide the teacher with evidence of pupils' comprehension and engage pupils in becoming effective readers by summarising the text and posing questions.

Signalling the essential questions for this unit to pupils from day one is also an effective means of articulating learning priorities – by knowing the essential questions and that those questions frame the main assessment tasks, pupils can study, do research, take notes, and ask questions with far greater clarity and confidence.

Another aspect of connecting the learning is to consider pupils' starting points: what prior knowledge do they bring to this unit? What misconceptions do they have? And what are their interests and talents (in as far as these may influence the way they learn and the way you teach)?

Once the answers to these questions have been ascertained, we need to use the information as rich diagnostic data in order to determine – or at least influence – the way in which we plan the unit.

One common diagnostic technique and a means of acquiring data on pupils' starting points is asking pupils at the beginning of a new topic to identify what they already know (or think they know) about the topic they are about to study.

Their responses are then listed in a table or graphic organiser. The contents of the first column provide teachers with a sense of pupils' prior knowledge, while also unmasking any misconceptions that may exist and therefore may need to be addressed.

Next, the teacher asks pupils to identify "what I want to learn" about the topic and asks them to raise any questions they may have about the topic at this early stage. These responses are recorded in the second column and serve as indicators of areas of interest.

As the unit unfolds, the knowledge and skills that pupils begin to acquire are recorded in the third column of the table, providing a record for pupils of "what I have learned".

An alternative to this is to begin the topic with an initial assessment, perhaps a low-stakes, non-graded multiple-choice quiz. The results of these pre-tests can yield invaluable evidence about pupils' prior knowledge and misconceptions and, when repeated at various stages of the scheme, can provide evidence of pupils' growing knowledge and understanding.

Regardless of the approach taken, information from diagnostic assessments can guide teachers in their planning so that lessons are more responsive to pupils' needs and their existing knowledge base.

An important practical implication, of course, is that teachers must remember to plan opportunities in their scheme for the assessments and allow sufficient wriggle room to adjust based on the feedback garnered by the assessments.

In-built flexibility like this is not just advisable, it is a key aspect of effective planning because it enables learning to be personalised to match the needs and pace of pupils' learning. It ensures that gaps in pupils' learning are identified and filled, which in turn avoids an off-the-peg, one-size-fits-all approach to lesson-planning and enables good progress to be made by all.

Once we've connected the learning, we need to consider how pupils will be engaged in exploring the big ideas and questions around which we have framed our scheme of work. We also need to consider what approaches, including direct instruction, will support and equip our pupils for their final assessment. And we need to consider what homework and additional interventions may be needed in order to enable pupils to develop and deepen their understanding of important ideas.

Often teachers don't fully consider the gaps in pupils' experiences and skills and falsely think that what they need to do in order to rectify this is teach more knowledge, cover more curriculum content. But understanding requires an iterative mix of experiences, reflections on those experiences, and targeted instruction in light of those experiences. Good curriculum design involves the provision of sufficient real or simulated experiences in order to enable pupils' understanding to develop.

It is the teacher's job to equip and enable pupils to eventually perform with understanding and increasing autonomy. That is very different from preparing them for a test. In order to do this, teachers should ask themselves, 'What kinds of knowledge, skill and routines are prerequisites for a successful pupil outcome?' and 'What kinds of tasks and activities will help pupils develop and deepen their understanding of key ideas?'

Teachers often complain that pupils cannot transfer what they have been taught into new problems and tasks – a concept we'll explore in more detail later. Yet, when you ask teachers to carefully consider all the prerequisites related to gaining an ability to transfer, they generally make no mention of their plan to help pupils learn how to transfer knowledge to different situations. The problem is typically regarded as a pupil deficit rather than an additional teaching need.

However, attempts to cover too many topics too quickly can hinder pupils' learning and subsequent transfer, because either pupils learn only isolated sets of facts that are not organised and connected, or pupils are introduced to organising principles that they cannot possibly grasp because they lack sufficient and specific background knowledge to make the information meaningful.

Therefore, providing pupils with opportunities to engage with sufficient, specific information that is relevant to the topic they are learning creates "time for telling" that enables them to learn much more than pupils who do not have these opportunities.

Also, providing pupils with time to learn includes providing enough time for them to process information. Pezdek and Miceli (1982) found that on one task it took third grade pupils in the US fifteen seconds to integrate pictorial and verbal information. When given only eight seconds, they couldn't mentally integrate the information, probably because of the limitations of short-term memory.

In other words, learning cannot be rushed; the complex cognitive activity involved in integrating information takes time. According to Klausmeier (1985), pupils, especially in school settings, are often faced with tasks that do not have apparent meaning or logic. It can be difficult for them to learn with understanding at the start; they may need to take time to explore underlying concepts and to generate connections to other information they possess.

And so, when planning lessons in a way that will help create a positive learning environment, we should aim to cover less curriculum content but to cover that content in greater depth. We should provide opportunities for pupils to explore the subject matter from a range of perspectives and to provide sufficient experience and context.

Finally, teaching less and learning more means repeating learning several times so that it penetrates pupils' long-term memories. Tests are a good way of "interrupting forgetting" and revealing what's been learnt as well as what gaps exist. Accordingly, we should run pre-tests at the start of every unit – perhaps as a multiple-choice quiz – which will provide cues and improve subsequent learning. Retrieval activities like this also help pupils to prepare for exams.

Matt Bromley

CHAPTER TWENTY:
STIMULATING PUPILS' SENSES

So far in Step 1 of our 3-step process of teaching for long-term learning, we've got our pupils feeling welcomed and valued, enthusiastic and engaged, eager to experiment and rewarded for their hard work. We've made explicit what our pupils need to learn and how that learning fits into the 'bigger picture'. We've shared with them the assessment criteria and exemplars of what excellence looks like. We've then provided opportunities for pupils to practice their learning and to receive and act upon feedback.

But how do we engage the attention of their senses? After all, we said earlier that in order to fully engage pupils' sensory memories and gain the attention of their working memories, we should try to appeal to their iconic, echoic and haptic memories: sight, sound and touch.

First, a caveat: I said it earlier but will do so again - appealing to pupils' senses does not mean identifying a pupil's preferred or dominant sense (or learning style) and teaching in a way that appeals to that sense alone. Although some studies claim to show that changing one's approach to teaching to cater for pupils' learning styles leads to improvements in outcomes, other studies have found that forcing learners to learn in a style different from their preference improves outcomes still further (see, for example, Adey, Fairbrother, Wiliam, Johnson, & Jones, 1999).

The message to take from all the research on and debate about learning styles, or so it seems to me, is that our teaching approach should cater for a range of learning styles. In other words, we should utilise all of our pupils' senses to make use of their visual and verbal processing powers and thereby expand the capacity of their working memories.

I'll talk about the importance of appealing to all the senses in more detail in Chapter Twenty-One but for now let us consider ways of gaining the attention of their working memories...

First, pupils are more likely to want to learn – and to actually learn – if their interest is piqued by newness, by the extraordinary, by the unfamiliar.

You see, all pupils crave variety; they need lessons to surprise them, to excite them, to ignite new sparks and pose new questions. They need lessons to unsettle them, too; to discomfort and challenge them, not bore them with the feeling of déjà vu.

In short, we all grow tired of repetition, of the predictable and prosaic, of the monotonous and mundane, and we all need a frequent frisson of freshness in our lives. And the lessons we teach should be no exception.

I'm not suggesting that every lesson we teach should provide novelty value. And indeed, later I will argue in favour of taking a common approach to introducing pupils to new information using a four-step sequence and explain why classroom consistency is important in avoiding cognitive overload. But I am suggesting that, to make ideas stick, we need to make them concrete by grounding them in sensory reality. In fact, the more sensory hooks we use, the better ideas will stick.

Moreover, to ensure that ideas "stick" we need to make them tangible, because pupils find it hard to care about or understand abstract concepts. If we ground an abstract concept in sensory reality and thus engage our pupils' emotions, our pupils are made to care about something, they are made to feel something, and this is an important part of the learning process.

When we are exposed to new information, we process it and then attempt to connect it to existing information (in other words, we try to assimilate new knowledge with prior knowledge). The richer – sensorily and emotionally – the new information is, and the deeper the existing information is ingrained, the stronger we will encode the new information in our long-term memories.

Ensuring our lessons provide variety and novelty, therefore, helps to appeal to pupils' senses and engage their emotions – if nothing else, simply by piquing their interest in something out of the ordinary, we are making them think – and therefore the information we teach them is more likely to be retained over the long-term.

In practice, there are four ways to make ideas stick: to make them tangible; to make them satisfying; to make them concrete; and to make them clear. Allow me to explain...

1. Make it real

One way to make information tangible is to use metaphor. Metaphor is good at making ideas stick because it brings ideas to life, it draws connections between new knowledge and existing knowledge. For example, if you are trying to describe how electricity flows through a material, you'll need to explain the structure of atoms.

You might use a metaphor which describes atoms as "nature's building blocks" to help pupils understand an atom's function. You will then need to explain how each atom is comprised of protons, which are positively charged, neutrons, which have no charge, and electrons, which are negatively charged.

Then you would need to explain that, together, the protons and neutrons form the "nucleus" of the atom, and that the electrons travel around this nucleus. You might then use a metaphor which compares this "orbit" to the way the earth travels around the sun.

In each case, you are relating new information which pupils are unlikely to be able to process and therefore retain, with existing information (or prior knowledge) in order to help them imagine it, process it and retain it.

2. Make it satisfying

One way to make information satisfying is to pique pupils' curiosity. Teachers tend to focus on imparting facts, but unless pupils know why those facts are important, then they are unlikely to retain them. Therefore, before teaching your pupils facts, you could take the time to pique their curiosity and make them realise why they need those facts.

The secret to convincing pupils that they need the information you intend to teach them, according to Professor George Loewenstein, is to start by highlighting the knowledge they are missing. Another technique is to start a lesson by asking pupils to make a prediction.

3. Make it concrete

One way to make information concrete is to make it tangible. Pupils find it hard to care about or understand abstract concepts. Instead, try to make ideas concrete by grounding them in sensory reality. The more sensory "hooks" you use, the better the ideas will stick.

Take, for example, Jane Elliott's famous "blue-eyed/brown-eyed" experiment with third grade pupils the day after Martin Luther King had been assassinated in 1968. The purpose of the exercise was to teach her pupils the effects of belonging to a minority. First, Elliott had a class discussion about racism but said she "could see that [the pupils] weren't internalising a thing". Instead, "they were doing what white people do ... when white people sit down to discuss racism ... [they experience] shared ignorance".

Most of Elliott's pupils were, like her, born and raised in a small town in Iowa, and were not normally exposed to Black people. She felt that simply talking about racism would not allow her all-white class to fully comprehend its meaning and effects.

Accordingly, she divided the class into the brown-eyed and the blue-eyed children. She said the blue-eyed children were the superior group, provided brown fabric collars and asked the blue-eyed pupils to wrap them around the necks of their brown-eyed peers as a method of easily identifying the minority group.

She gave the blue-eyed children extra privileges, such as second helpings at lunch, access to the new jungle gym, and five extra minutes at recess. The blue-eyed children sat in the front of the classroom, and the brown-eyed children were sent to sit in the back rows.

The blue-eyed children were encouraged to play only with other blue-eyed children and to ignore those with brown eyes. Elliott often chastised the brown-eyed pupils when they did not follow the exercise's rules. At first, there was resistance among the pupils in the minority group to the idea that blue-eyed children were better, but eventually those who were deemed "superior" became arrogant, bossy and otherwise unpleasant to their "inferior" classmates.

Their grades also improved, doing mathematical and reading tasks that had seemed outside their ability before. The "inferior" classmates also transformed into timid and subservient children who even during recess isolated themselves, including those who had previously been dominant in the class. These children's academic performance suffered, even with tasks that had been simple before.

Once she had concluded the experiment, she asked the children to reflect by writing down what they had learned, and it became clear that her pupils had come to deeply understand racism because Elliot had made it feel real, she had grounded an abstract concept in sensory reality and thus engaged her pupils' emotions. As I said earlier, if pupils are made to care about something, they are made to feel something, and this is an important part of the learning process.

So, in short, we should obey the maxim "show don't tell" wherever possible. Telling pupils something means we do all the work for them; showing them means they must work for themselves.

4. Make it clear

One way to make information clear is to ensure you maximise your pupils' capacity for learning. In practice, this means reviewing your lessons to make sure they follow the inverted pyramid structure. In other words, you need to make sure that each of your lessons clearly articulates its "lead".

The cognitive scientist Daniel Willingham argues that lesson plans should be focused on what pupils will think about rather than what they will do. And, although we are not naturally good thinkers, we do enjoy problem-solving – so you should frame your key messages (or "lead") around a problem to be solved or an enquiry to be investigated and answered.

First, decide what the vital "take-away" messages are – rather than what will merely add hue and texture – then concentrate on writing questions rather than creating fun activities. Try to write a "big question" which forms the basis for the lesson. Alternatively, you could pose a hypothesis to be proven or disproven.

This is all made easier if you've engaged in the process of curriculum planning first, of course, and have identified clear end points or the body of knowledge to be learned. These end points, or indeed waypoints, can be used for formulate learning outcomes of intentions and these are the "take-away" messages on which your pupils must be made to ruminate.

To summarise...

In order to stimulate pupils' senses and gain the attention of their working memories, we need to make sure:

- Each lesson or sequence of lessons has a clear "lead", a take-away message that will make pupils think.
- Some lessons are built around a question, hypothesis or prediction to pique curiosity.
- Gaps in pupils' knowledge are opened before they are filled.
- New ideas are grounded in sensory reality to elicit an emotional response from pupils.
- New ideas are made concrete by using metaphor and analogy.
- New information is related to prior knowledge so that learning is sequenced.

CHAPTER TWENTY-ONE:
DUAL CODING

In the previous chapter I talked about the importance of appealing to pupils' senses because we need to engage pupils' sensory memories in order to gain the attention of their working memories and only once we've done this can pupils think and therefore learn.

I also said that there were four ways in particular of appealing to pupils' senses, namely: making information tangible; making information clear; making information satisfying; and making information concrete.

Not only does appealing to pupils' various senses help ideas to stick, it also helps to utilise the limited space in their working memories. This approach is often called 'dual coding'. Allow me to explain...

Dual coding is the combination of words and images. We have two specific yet connected cognitive subsystems: one specialises in representing and processing non-verbal objects or events; the other specialises in language. In other words, we process verbal and visual information separately and so can double the capacity of our working memory if we utilise both verbal and visual processing at the same time.

Written and spoken words only get coded once but images of words get coded twice: first visually and then verbally. In other words, images leave double the amount of traces in our brains.

To coin a phrase, let's look at the science...

Dual coding enables us to process the same information in two different ways, thus allowing us to access more working memory capacity. In other words, we access both visual and verbal memory capacity increasing our processing powers and cheating working memory.

By so doing, we not only boost the information traces in our long-term memory (two connected traces are stronger than a single trace), we also recognise or recall the information in two different ways.

So how does it work? Well, combining an image with a complementary word (written or – preferably – spoken), allows us to use both a verbal/semantic process (in other words, we decipher spoken/written words) and an iconic process (in other words, we decipher images).

Simone Herrlinger et al (2016) investigated whether - for children aged 9 to 11 - written learning materials for biology, when presented in combination with complementary images, facilitated learning. Herrlinger also studied the extent to which the modality of the text (whether it was written or spoken) influenced pupils' ability to learn.

The use of dual coding had a positive effect in general, however the effects were most striking when images were combined with spoken rather than written text. This finding is echoed by a 2004 meta-analysis by Paul Ginns who concluded that pupils learn best when images are combined with spoken - rather than written - texts.

What's more, the effect was greatest with younger pupils because reading a text by themselves whilst also 'reading' the images was beyond their cognitive capacities, and especially their visual channel.

In the case of the younger pupils, written text and images could not be integrated into one coherent mental model, and as such effective learning couldn't take place. This phenomenon is called the modality effect, or the modality principle, and it means that the visual modality gets overloaded because young pupils' reading skills are still developing and so they have to work harder to decode words.

However, as with all teaching strategies, dual coding only works when it's done well. Reading a text aloud in parallel with the same written text onscreen (such as reading text verbatim from a PowerPoint slide) is a bad combination because pupils are required to conduct one and the same verbal/semantic decoding process in two different ways - rather than splitting and therefore doubling working memory capacity, it requires pupils to process the same information twice using just one process, thus halving working memory capacity. As a result, working memory becomes overloaded in what's known as 'the redundancy effect'.

The best way to make use of dual coding therefore is to, for example, explain a visual (a diagram, graph, mind-map, etc) verbally, not through text on the visual. If there is writing on the visual, it's best not to explain it. Furthermore, we should present visuals and text at the same time so that pupils don't have to remember one part while processing the other.

And here's another caveat before we move on - a caveat emptor, if you like - that applies to most of the cognitive science in this book: dual coding theory is based on several assumptions. For example, we must assume that there are indeed two separate channels (auditory and visual) for processing information. We must also assume that there is limited channel capacity. And we must assume that learning is an active process of filtering, selecting, organising, and integrating information.

There is still so much we do not know about how our brains work and about how to acquire and process information. The advice in this chapter on dual coding - like much of the advice in this book - is based on our best guess and on research evidence.

CHAPTER TWENTY-TWO:
TRANSFERABILITY

I've talked about the 'transferability' of information a number of times – indeed, it formed part of my definition of learning in Chapter Twelve. I later said that the ability to transfer knowledge and skills was not innate, we must teach it. So how, exactly, do we teach this ability?

Bransford et al (2000) argue that several critical features of learning can affect a pupil's ability to transfer what they have learned. For example, one factor in the development of pupils' expertise and ability to transfer what they have learned is the amount of time spent learning something for the first time.

Attempts to cover too many topics too quickly may hinder pupils' learning and subsequent transfer because either:

- Pupils learn only isolated sets of facts that are not organised and connected, or
- Pupils are introduced to organising principles that they cannot possibly grasp because they lack sufficient and specific background knowledge to make the information meaningful.

Providing pupils with opportunities to engage with sufficient, specific information that is relevant to the topic they are learning creates what Bransford calls "time for telling", which enables them to learn much more than pupils who do not have these opportunities.

As I explained earlier, providing pupils with time to learn also includes providing enough time for them to process information. When pupils are faced with tasks that do not have apparent meaning or logic, it can be difficult for them to learn with understanding at the start and they may need to take time to explore underlying concepts and to generate connections to other information they possess.

So, the first piece of practical advice for developing pupils' ability to transfer is...

Give pupils enough time to explore underlying concepts.

However, returning to Bransford, as well as the amount of time spent learning something for the first time, there's another key factor in the development of pupils' expertise and ability to transfer knowledge: how that time is used. Having sufficient time to learn is not, in itself, enough. What pupils do with that time is just as important because different ways of using one's time have different effects on learning and transfer.

Bransford says that "while time on task is necessary for learning, it is not sufficient for effective learning. Time spent learning for understanding has different consequences for transfer than time spent simply memorising facts or procedures from textbooks or lectures".

In other words, simply learning facts by rote is more limiting than learning to understand what those facts mean and/or how they might be connected. I can vouch for this.

On one of my teacher-training courses, I asked delegates to memorise a list of word pairs in order to explore the different ways in which people learn and the relative benefits of each approach.

It is fascinating watching colleagues perform this task: their methods are always writ large upon their faces. Some people stare at the list for the full two minutes allocated to the task, reading and re-reading the words over and over again in the hope that simple repetition will strengthen their powers of recall.

Others spend perhaps half a minute reading the list then turn away or close their eyes for the remaining 90 seconds. Whatever they are doing behind closed eyes, it is clear that they are not simply spending more time on task by reading and re-reading the list; instead, they are applying what they have learned in a different context or making connections between the words.

Some delegates use the method of loci - also known as the "mind palace" technique made famous by Sherlock Holmes - in which visual cues are employed in order to memorise information in a particular sequence, perhaps by walking through a familiar location and using objects to trigger memories.

Others create a mnemonic with the words or try to visualise the actual list as if they have taken a photograph of it with their minds which they can refer to later when the actual list has been removed.

The second tactic – spending a short time learning then making connections between what they have learned rather than just repeating the task – always has more success than the first, because just dedicating time to learning isn't enough. If we are to help our pupils to develop the ability to transfer, we must think carefully about how our pupils will use that time.

In 1917, a young Columbia University psychologist called Arthur Gates studied how the act of recitation interacts with memory. For centuries, classics pupils had spent hours learning to recite epic poems and pieces of scripture from memory. Gates wanted to find out if there was an ideal ratio between reading (memorising) and reciting (rehearsal).

In other words, Gates wanted to calculate what proportion of time you should spend studying the text on a page and what proportion you should spend reciting it from memory or doing something different with the information.

To find out if such a ratio existed, Gates enlisted five classes from a local school, ranging from third to eighth grade, for an experiment. He assigned each pupil a number of Who's Who entries to memorise and recite. He gave them each nine minutes to study but each group of pupils was given a different set of instructions on how to use that time.

One group would spend a minute and 48 seconds memorising, and seven minutes and 12 seconds reciting. A second group would split its time exactly in half. And a third group would spend eight minutes of its time memorising, and only a minute rehearsing. So, what did he find?

"In general," Gates concluded, "the best results are obtained by introducing recitation after devoting about 40 per cent of the time to reading. Introducing recitation too early or too late leads to poorer results." In older pupils, the percentage was closer to a third. "The superiority of optimal reading and retention over reading alone is about 30 per cent," he added.

So, it is no surprise that my delegates performed better at remembering and reciting word pairs if they spent about a third of their time reading the list then turned away and spent the other two-thirds anchoring their learning in a particular context, or making connections between words in their mind. So, the second piece of practical advice for developing pupils' ability to transfer is...

Make sure pupils spend their time learning in a distributed way.

The memory technique known as distributed learning or, more commonly, spaced practice is one of the oldest learning techniques in cognitive science and yet is also one of the most powerful, reliable, and easy to use. It works to deepen the acquisition of knowledge or skills that call for rote-learning.

Put simply, pupils learn at least as much – and retain what they have learned for much longer – when they distribute or space their study time than when they concentrate (or cram) it. Scientists say that spaced learning can double the amount we remember later.

The spacing effect is especially useful for learning new material. Why spaced study sessions have such a big impact on learning is still a matter of some debate, but it is probably something to do with the fact that repeating the same task over and over – reading and re-reading a list of words, say – makes our brain progressively less interested in the material. It has just heard, and stored, a word so if the same word is repeated again, then a third time, the brain pays progressively less attention to it.

In other words, studying a new concept immediately after you have learned it does not deepen the memory very much, if at all. Studying it an hour later, or a day later, however, does.

So, if I tell you three times in quick succession that a rainbow created by the sun's rays reflecting off the moon is called a moonbow, you'd remember it for a while. But if I told you it three times at 10-minute intervals, you'd remember it for much longer.

This is because storage and retrieval are two different things. Just because you've studied (stored) the word "moonbow" doesn't mean it's retrievable when you read or hear about it later. To build fluency takes more than the time needed to store it. In the first scenario, you had maybe a minute to store the fact. In the second, you had over half an hour.

So, the third piece of practical advice for developing pupils' ability to transfer is...

Give pupils opportunities to engage in deliberate practice.

Learning is most effective when pupils engage in deliberate practice and when pupils actively monitor their own learning. As Ericsson et al (1993) say, monitoring one's own learning involves attempts to seek and use feedback about our progress. Feedback was identified as important for successful learning as long ago as 1913 (see Thorndike), but Chi et al (1989, 1994) argue that it should not be regarded as a unidimensional concept.

For example, feedback that signals progress in memorising facts and formulas is different from feedback that signals the state of the pupils' understanding. Pupils need feedback about the degree to which they know when, where, and how to use the knowledge they are learning.

So, the fourth piece of practical advice for developing pupils' ability to transfer is...

Ensure pupils are motivated to learn.

We have talked about the amount of time pupils need to spend learning something for the first time and how best to spend that time. But in order to secure pupils' time investment, they must first be motivated to learn, because a pupil's level of motivation can affect the amount of time they are willing to devote to learning.

As we've already seen, Daniel Pink explores what motivates people in his book, Drive. He argues that people tend to be motivated by autonomy – in other words, being accorded control over the way they work; mastery – being good at their jobs and getting better; and purpose – doing a job which is considered meaningful and worthy.

White (1959) says that people are motivated to learn if they know it will help improve their ability to solve problems – what White calls "competence motivation".

Dweck's work on the growth mindset has taught us that people work best for intrinsic rather than extrinsic rewards. In other words, working hard in order to learn something – not working in order to get a prize – is the best reward. But in order to do this, you need to be learning-oriented not performance-oriented, have a growth mindset not a fixed one.

Whatever they believe the real motivator to be, all these thinkers have one thing in common: they are convinced that, in order to be and remain motivated, pupils must be given work that provides an appropriate level of challenge – tasks must be difficult but not too difficult. Work that is too easy quickly becomes boring and is performed out of habit; work that is too hard quickly becomes frustrating and is not performed at all.

As well as being challenged by work, pupils – if they are to remain motivated and invest their time – must understand the purpose of learning. In other words, when they can see the usefulness of what they are learning (when and how they will be able to use that learning for their own and others' benefit), pupils will dedicate time to it.

So, the fifth piece of practical advice for developing pupils' ability to transfer is...

Give pupils work that provides an appropriate level of challenge.

Let's take stock: in order to develop transfer, we need to make sure our pupils are motivated to learn then provide them with sufficient time to learn in a distributed, deliberate way. But, as well as learning in a deep, distributed, and deliberate way, our pupils need to learn new information, not in isolation, but in a range of different contexts.

The context in which a pupil learns is important for promoting transfer. So once something has been learned for the first time in one context, it is important to teach it again in a different context because knowledge that is taught in only a single context, is not as likely to support flexible transfer at a later stage as knowledge that is taught in multiple contexts.

"With multiple contexts," Bransford et al say, "pupils are more likely to abstract the relevant features of concepts and develop a more flexible representation of knowledge." In other words, as well as learning what facts mean, it is important to understand what facts might mean in a range of different contexts – i.e. how context can affect meaning.

So, the sixth piece of practical advice for developing pupils' ability to transfer is...

Give pupils information in a variety of different contexts.

These different contexts might take one of two forms. First, we might give pupils a number of similar cases to study. Pupils can learn in one context but fail to transfer to other contexts. One way to deal with this lack of flexibility is to ask pupils to solve a specific case and then provide them with an additional, similar case. According to Gick and Holyoak (1983), this helps pupils to abstract general principles that lead to more flexible transfer.

A second way to improve flexibility is to let pupils learn in a specific context and then get them to engage in "what-if" type problem-solving activities that are designed to increase the flexibility of their understanding. A third way is to generalise the learning. For example, ask pupils to create a solution that applies not simply to a single problem, but to a whole group of similar problems.

Second, we might give pupils contrasting cases to study because the use of well-chosen contrasting cases can help pupils learn the conditions under which new knowledge is applicable. Gagné and Gibson, 1947; Garner, 1974; Gibson and Gibson, 1955 – in their work on perceptual learning – say that understanding when, where and why to use new knowledge can be enhanced by using "contrasting cases". In other words, appropriately arranged contrasts can help pupils notice new features that previously escaped their attention and can help them learn which features are relevant and irrelevant to a particular concept. Third, we might give pupils abstract representations of problems because this, too, can facilitate transfer.

The seventh and final strategy is to...

Teach pupils metacognition.

Transfer can also be improved by helping pupils to become more aware of themselves as learners, by helping pupils to actively monitor their learning strategies and resources and assess their readiness for particular tests and performances.

Palincsar and Brown (1984) argue that reciprocal teaching designed to increase reading comprehension can help pupils acquire specific knowledge and learn a set of strategies for explicating, elaborating, and monitoring the understanding necessary for independent learning and transfer. The three major components of reciprocal teaching, according to Palincsar and Brown, are:

- Instruction and practice with strategies that enable pupils to monitor their understanding.
- Provision, initially by a teacher, of an expert model of metacognitive processes.

- A social setting that enables joint negotiation for understanding.

Furthermore, it is important to understand – and respond to – how previous knowledge can help or hinder pupils' understanding of new information.

We can help pupils change their original conceptions by building in opportunities for them to make their thinking more visible so that misconceptions can be corrected and so that pupils can be encouraged to think beyond the specific problem in hand or to think about variations of that problem.

In short, a metacognitive approach to teaching can increase transfer by helping pupils learn about themselves as learners. One characteristic of being an expert is the ability to monitor and regulate your own understanding in ways that allow you to keep learning adaptive expertise. For pupils to be able to do this, they need feedback from their teacher. Indeed, frequent formative feedback is critical if our pupils are to gain an insight into their learning and understanding.

In conclusion, initial learning is necessary for transfer, and a considerable amount is known about the kinds of learning experiences that support transfer. Information that is anchored in just one specific context can reduce transfer. Abstract representations of information can help promote transfer as can teaching information in a range of different contexts.

Transfer is affected by the degree to which people learn with understanding rather than merely memorise sets of facts or follow a fixed set of procedures. So, to help pupils to develop transfer, we should:

1. Allow a sufficient amount of time for initial learning to take place.
2. Plan for distributed – or spaced – learning and engage in deliberate practice.

3. Make sure pupils are motivated to learn by planning work with sufficient challenge.
4. Teach information in multiple, contrasting contexts and/or in abstract form.
5. Teach metacognition so that pupils become expert at monitoring and regulating their learning.

CHAPTER TWENTY-THREE: SUMMARY OF STEP 1

Before we move on to Step 2 of our 3-step process of teaching for long-term learning, let's take stock...

The process of learning, we have said, is the interaction between our sensory memory and our long-term memory. Our sensory memory is made up of: what we see - this is called our iconic memory; what we hear - this is called our echoic memory; and what we touch - our haptic memory. Our long-term memory is where new information is stored and from which it can be recalled when needed, but we cannot directly access the information stored in our long-term memory - instead, this interaction between our sensory memory and our long-term memory occurs in the working memory.

In order to ensure our pupils learn, therefore, we need to stimulate their sensory memory, gain the attention of - and help them cheat - their working memory, and improve the strength with which information is stored in, and the ease and efficiency with which it can later be retrieved from, their long-term memory. In order to do this, we need to follow these three steps:

First, we need to stimulate pupils' senses in order to gain the active attention of their working memories.

Second, we need to make pupils think hard but efficiently about the curriculum content to be learned.

And third, we need to plan opportunities for pupils to engage in deliberate practice in order to ensure prior knowledge remains accessible.

In order to stimulate sensory memory, we need to:

1. Attend to the classroom culture.

Create an ethos - delivered through words and actions - in which pupils feel welcomed, valued, enthusiastic about learning, engaged in their learning, eager to experiment, and rewarded for their hard work. We do this by: greeting pupils at the door and using their names; encouraging everyone to contribute and explicitly teaching speaking and listening skills; modelling enthusiasm by being excited about teaching, ignoring anyone who advises 'don't smile till Christmas' - even if this means we have to put on an act some days; plan lessons on the premise of what pupils will think about rather than do - perhaps by framing lessons around a big question or hypothesis; model a growth mindset ethos in which mistakes are positively welcomed and everyone gets better at everything with hard work and practice.

2. Promote risk-taking and mistake-making.

Create a classroom in which taking risks and making mistakes is the default position and in which drafting and redrafting, improving work in response to feedback, is the norm. Provide opportunities for pupils to respond to feedback in the lesson in order to signal its importance and enable the teacher to recognise and celebrate progress.

Feedback should answer three fundamental questions: Where are pupils going? (This is about their goals and is 'feed up'); how are pupils going to get there? (This is 'feedback'); and where to next? (This is 'feed forward'). Feedback should operate on four levels: 1. Task level - how well tasks are understood and performed; 2. Process level - the process needed to understand and perform tasks; 3. Self-regulation level - self-monitoring and regulating of actions; and 4. Self level - personal evaluations by the pupil.

3. Reward hard work and effort.

Reward pupils' hard work as opposed to attainment because to do so creates a level playing field on which every pupil has equal chance of being recognised for the progress they have made from their individual starting points. Praise pupils for their 'growth-oriented processes' - what they accomplish through practice and persistence, not what they achieve through innate, inherited 'talent'. Avoid giving praise for the sake of it or praising pupils for doing no more than what's expected or for completing work below their 'struggle zone' (which is too easy and can be accomplished through habit) for this will demotivate them in the longer term.

4. Foster a sense of intrinsic motivation whereby pupils feel rewarded by the inhcrent satisfaction of completing a task and doing well, not by external awards

Intrinsic motivation is founded on pupils' autonomy (the desire to take control of their own learning), mastery (the urge to get better and better), and purpose (a yearning to do what they do in the service of a wider goal). Intrinsic motivation is the want to learn but it is contingent on pupils also developing the need to learn: pupils need to know why they're learning what they're learning and how that learning fits in to the bigger picture - why it matters and how and when they'll use it. Talking of which...

5. Articulate specific learning outcomes and task instructions.

Decide on a key take-away message for each lesson, the 'lead', which might be a big question that begs an answer or a hypothesis that demands to be proven or disproven. Use this to frame your learning outcomes so that pupils know what they're learning and why. Then share the success criteria and model excellence. Success criteria must be shared before a task is begun so pupils know how they will be assessed and what they are striving to achieve. These criteria should also be specific and match the objectives. Ideally, pupils should be involved in agreeing the criteria, too.

Once the success criteria have been agreed and shared, model what a perfect final product looks like (by, say, sharing a top mark essay) and deconstruct it to show pupils each of its constituent parts so that they can emulate it. Next, model a final product that's somewhat less than the best so that pupils can learn which pitfalls to avoid. Sharing learning outcomes and success criteria, then modelling excellence, will direct pupils' attentions to what they need to think about.

6. Create an open loop whereby practice leads to formative feedback which leads to yet more practice.

Promote a culture in which drafting and redrafting in response to feedback is considered the norm. Ensure that feedback leads to improvements and to further practice, which in turn should lead to more feedback and so on. Practice should involve: spaced repetition - whereby information is returned to for recap or reteaching but with increasingly long gaps so that pupils get to the point of almost forgetting it and retrieving it is hard; retrieval practice - whereby daily recaps, weekly quizzes and topic tests are used not for the purposes of assessment but for reinforcement and to provide pupils with feedback information on what they know and do not know (yet) and therefore need to practice; interleaved practice - whereby pupils are tested on information from different topics so that they are forced to make new connections between study material and improve their ability to transfer learning; and cognitive disfluency (sometimes called cognitive dissonance) - whereby pupils' initial learning of information (or encoding) is slowed down and made more difficult than it needs to be in order to improve its subsequent storage and retrieval strength.

7. Develop pupils' study skills.

Establish routines whereby pupils regularly: self-quiz - testing themselves on study notes; elaborate - relate new information to what they already know, explaining it to somebody else; generate - attempt to answer questions before being taught the answers; reflect - review their learning and how effectively they learnt; and calibrate - remove the illusion of knowing something by answering every question even if they think it's too easy and they know the answer.

8. Make ideas stick by grounding them in a sensory reality.

Make ideas tangible - for example, using analogy and metaphor to draw connections between new information and prior learning or to place new ideas into a useful context.

Make ideas real - for example, make abstract concepts concrete, show rather than tell, and appeal to pupils' emotions in order to make them feel and, therefore, make them care.

9. Dual code information by combining verbal instructions with visual ones.

Combine verbal instructions (whether written down or spoken) with visuals such as graphics and charts so that pupils can utilise the verbal and visual processing powers contained in working memory, thus increasing their capacity to handle information.

Images - diagrams, graphs, infographics and so on, rather than just pictures used for illustrative purposes - get coded twice, first visually then verbally, and therefore leave double the amount of traces in long-term memory.

10. Improve pupils' ability to transfer their learning.

Help pupils to connect what they learn in one topic to what they learn in another, and indeed to other situations in life, and help them connect their learning from one context to another context. We can this by: ensuring pupils are afforded a sufficient amount of time to explore the underlying concepts and ideas in a topic; teaching less curriculum content but in greater depth; giving pupils information in a variety of contexts; and teaching metacognition so that pupils can become more aware of themselves as learners and develop the ability to actively monitor their learning strategies and assess their readiness for particular activities and assessments.

STEP TWO:

MAKE PUPILS THINK HARD BUT EFFICIENTLY TO ENCODE INFORMATION IN LONG-TERM MEMORY

CHAPTER TWENTY-FOUR:
THE STRUGGLE ZONE

In Step 1 of our three-step process of teaching of long-term learning, we examined ways of stimulating our pupils' senses in order to gain the attention of their working memories.

Now that we've got that attention, we need to make sure our pupils think hard but efficiently about the curriculum content we need them to learn...

In this section of the book covering Step 2, we will tackle those two components in turn: first, we will explore ways to ensure our pupils are made to think **hard**; second, we will examine ways to help pupils to think **efficiently**, thus cheating the limited capacity of their working memories whilst rising to the challenge of an increasingly complex curriculum.

Let's start with thinking hard...

If I were to ask you to calculate 57 x 3489 in your heads, no cheating, and in the space of a minute, I'm confident most of you would fail. And in the process of failing, you'd likely do one of two things...

Either: you'd decide the task was unachievable - especially with the time constraints attached - and therefore not even attempt it.

Or: you'd try and try to complete the task but fail to do so because to succeed would involve processing too much information all at once. Your working memory wouldn't be able to cope with the demands you'd placed upon it, and in just sixty seconds, and you'd reach the point of cognitive overload.

Whichever of these two paths you'd take, you wouldn't get the answer and would, therefore, have encoded nothing into long-term memory.

Put simply, you'd neither learn something new nor practice something that you already knew.

This complex thing called 'learning' would not occur.

The task would prove utterly pointless.

Now, if I were to ask you to calculate 2 x 10, once again in your heads and in the space of a minute, I'm confident all of you would succeed this time. And you wouldn't need a full minute to do so either! In fact, you'd proffer your answer instantaneously.

But, and here's the rub, you wouldn't have calculated anything; you'd have given your answer automatically. In other words, you wouldn't have engaged the attention of your working memory, at least not in any meaningful sense, because you've practised your times tables to the point of automaticity whereby you can reel them off through habit, without thinking about them, just as you tie your shoe laces or button your shirt without thinking about it. Most of the time, you drive your car without thinking about that, too; you've done it so many times that the task no longer needs to engage your active attention, which helps explain why you sometimes arrive at your destination with absolutely no memory of the journey.

And because you answered 2 x 10 without thinking about it, as was the case with the first sum, you didn't learn anything new or practice something that you already knew.

In other words, this task - though ostensibly a success - was also pointless. Learning did not occur.

In Thinking Fast and Slow, Daniel Kahneman summarises his own research - and that of other cognitive scientists - in mapping the roles of the two interacting systems of the human brain:

"System 1" thinks fast. That is to say it's instinctive and intuitive. It can react more quickly than conscious thought. But it is also prone to error. And we cannot turn it off. We cannot see a word in a language we speak and choose not to read it.

"System 2" thinks slow. That is to say it works rationally and methodically.   It can assess and analyse choices in a sophisticated and analytical way. But it is slower and because this thinking is hard work, our minds try to avoid it.

We are always trying to shut this system down to save energy. And if we over-load this system, it's in danger of interfering with our basic functions (such as our perception).

For example, driving while talking on our mobile phone - even using hands free - increases the likelihood of having an accident because a conversation requires us to think and so we see and perceive less.

Kahneman argues that System 2 can shape System 1 by providing constant exposure to experiences that encode behaviours until they become more instinctual. We see a situation over and over and learn to recognise and react to it; ultimately it shapes our instinctual responses.

This is much of what we do when we engage in work that is pitch perfect - targeted at our 'sweet spot'.

Understanding the two systems and how they interact is incredibly useful for teachers because it helps us to understand how we can shape students' thinking.

In particular, it shows that decision-making starts with perception, and so systematic exposure to situations where students learn to perceive and recognise viable solutions is critical. This is why it's necessary to build "knowledge" ...

If we want to develop our students' problem-solving abilities, we must first teach them background knowledge. Indeed, problem-solving is not a skill our students can develop without background knowledge. In Practice Perfect, Doug Lemov says: "You essentially recognise a situation visually faster than you can consciously think. Then you associate this cue with knowledge of viable choices stored in long-term memory."

Herbert Simon, meanwhile, says, "Intuition is nothing more than and nothing less than recognition."

As I argued in the previous section of this book, if we want our pupils to learn anything - by which I mean, encode information in their long-term memories - then we need to stimulate their senses in order to gain the active attention of their working memories, then we need to get them thinking hard. In other words, we need to give them work to do that's challenging but achievable because: If the work's too easy, pupils will complete it through habit; if the work's too hard, pupils will be unable to complete it. In both cases, learning will fail.

So, we need to pitch work in pupils' 'struggle zone', what they can do with time, effort and support. This is sometimes referred to as the 'zone of proximal development', a term invented by the Russian psychologist Lev Vygotsky and defined by him in 1978 as "the distance between the actual developmental level as determined by independent problem-solving and the level of potential development as determined through problem-solving under adult guidance, or in collaboration with more capable peers".

In fact, that sentence is a perfect example of why we need to set hard work...

If you're like me, you probably had to read Vygotsky's definition a couple of times before you could make proper sense of it. His sentence is long and complex, it is just hard enough for me to be challenged by it but not too hard for me to be put off by it. If it contained lots of words with which I was unfamiliar, I'd likely give up or shy away from it, deeming it beyond my current reach. If it was short and simple, I'd probably skim over it without really taking it in because I didn't have to think about it. But it is difficult and achievable; it is just beyond my current ability but without my reach.

As such, I had to read it a couple of times to make the necessary connections between words I already knew and a context or meaning that was new to me. But I made sense of it eventually and, consequently, I learnt what Vygotsky meant by the term 'zone of proximal development'.

The fact I worked hard at understanding Vygotsky's definition, and had to stop and think about it, means I'm not just able to overcome a challenge and succeed, thus engaging the active attention of my working memory and helping me to learn, but I'm also much more likely to remember it later. In other words, because the work was pitched in my struggle zone, beyond my current abilities but within my reach, I improved the storage and retrieval strength of the information I encoded in long-term memory.

Working on problems that are too easy or too difficult is not enjoyable because there is no sense of progress, and thus we become frustrated. Working on problems that are pitched in our struggle zone, however, is rewarding.

This is why giving pupils work to do that is too easy for them and which they can therefore accomplish without thinking - in the misguided belief that it will give them a sense of success and thus motivate them - doesn't work. Instead, we are motivated by thinking hard and overcoming difficulty; we are motivated by overcoming challenges.

So how can we ensure that our pupils are made to think hard?

Sometimes, we need to place artificial barriers in the way of their initial encoding of information so that the information is stored more effectively and can more easily be retrieved later. These artificial barriers, or road-blocks in our thinking, are what Robert Bjork called 'desirable difficulties'.

We will explore desirable difficulties in the next chapter...

CHAPTER TWENTY-FIVE:
DESIRABLE DIFFICULTIES

Robert Bjork, a cognitive psychologist at UCLA, coined the terms 'storage strength' (SS) and 'retrieval strength' (RS) in order to help improve our understanding of how we learn (which is to say, how we commit things to long-term memory).

Storage strength is the measure of how effectively we have encoded something. Studying something in greater detail increases the chance of us storing it in our long-term memory. The better it is learned, the higher the SS. If it has a high SS, it is more likely to be stored in our long-term memory (rather than remain in our working memory to be quickly forgotten) and more likely to be ready to be 'retrieved' later.

Retrieval strength, meanwhile, is the measure of how easily we can access a memory of something we've learned. In other words, RS is our ability to recall information later. RS decreases over time - which is why we forget things as we get older - and the lower the SS, the faster the RS will decrease.

Put simply, if we want to learn something well enough so that it will be accessible to us in the future (rather than quickly forgotten), then we need to learn it in greater depth, and we need to 'over-learn' it.

Bjork identified several conditions which over time increase SS and RS and which therefore lead to information being retained for longer. These conditions, Bjork cautioned, "slow down the apparent learning, but under most circumstances help long term retention, and help transfer of knowledge, from what you learnt to new situations".

Bjork called these conditions 'desirable difficulties' because they are ways of teaching which are intentionally challenging to pupils because difficulty and hard work are what assists their long-term learning.

Put simply, then, Bjork argued that teachers should spend longer teaching fewer things but in greater detail. In other words, our pupils should learn less content but in more depth.

I'll give you an example in a moment but first answer me this question before we go on: How many animals of each kind did Moses take onto the Ark?

The more quick-witted, eagle-eyed among you will have spotted my deliberate mistake and answered 'none'. But I bet some of you said 'two', didn't you? I've asked this question during several conference speeches and training events and some members of the audience always say 'two'.

If you said 'two' then you fell into the trap of skimming the question too quickly and offering the obvious answer. The fact is, the question asks you how animals Moses took onto the Ark when, in fact, Moses didn't build an ark; it was Noah.

That question was a perfect example of work that is too simple, too easy, too obvious. Because it has all the hallmarks of a straightforward question, some of you put two and two together (pun very much intended) and made five. You skimmed over the words and filled in the gaps then offered an answer out of habit. That answer happened to be wrong, but you were convinced of its accuracy.

There are several ways to help pupils avoid falling into this trap - each of which is an example of a desirable difficulty, a barrier that slows down the initial encoding of information so that it is stored more securely and can be more easily retrieved from long-term memory...

Firstly, we can use more complex language constructions. For example, instead of asking a question worded as a simple sentence ('How many animals of each kind did Moses take onto the Ark?'), we could ask it using a complex sentence ('In the biblical story, to save them from the flood, how many animals of each kind did Moses take onto the Ark?').

Secondly, we could put a deliberate block in the way - something incongruous that stops pupils in their tracks or a gap which pupils must fill in ('How many animals of each kind did _____ take onto the Ark?').

Thirdly, and this is rather counter-intuitive, we could use a hard-to-decipher font for written information on the board or on handouts. If the font causes us to stop, slow down and concentrate more, then we are forced to think harder and therefore more likely to encode information into long-term memory from where we can retrieve it later.

In Visible Learning (2012), John Hattie echoed Bjork's belief that teachers should slow down learning and set challenging work. He said that the best way for pupils to learn is not always pleasurable for them: "Learning is not always... easy; it requires over-learning at certain points, spiralling up and down the knowledge continuum, building a working relationship with others in grappling with challenging tasks".

Hattie went on to say that the most "accomplished teachers set tasks that [have] a greater degree of challenge".

The cognitive scientist Daniel Willingham argues that a lack of space in working memory is a functional bottleneck of human cognition. In Why Don't Students Like School?, he says: "Working memory is more or less fixed – you get what you get, and practice does not change it... there are, however, ways to cheat this limitation".

One way to cheat the limited size of your working memory, so says Willingham, is through factual knowledge. The second way is to make the processes that manipulate information in working memory more efficient.

One useful example of this is learning to read...

Once we have 'mastered' reading in the sense that we know the sound each letter makes and how letters combine to make words, we still keep practising our reading not just to get faster at reading but in order to get so good at recognising the letters and words and the sounds they make that word recognition becomes automatic... we see words and understand them and how they sound without having to think about it and this automaticity frees up precious space in our working memories which used to be used to retrieve sounds and meanings from our long-term memories but which we can now devote to thinking about the meanings of sentences and texts.

Eventually, we get so good at reading that we have enough working memory to be able to recognise allusions and make other connections between the text we are reading and all the background knowledge we already possess.

What's true of reading is true of all the skills our pupils use in all the subjects we teach.

In conclusion, we should not be afraid to set our pupils work to do which is hard, which challenges them and makes them think. We should avoid setting work which is too easy and which pupils have already mastered. And we should avoid setting work which is too hard and which pupils cannot possibly master at the moment. Instead, we should ensure we set work that is pitched within the 'zone of proximal development': work that is hard but accessible; work that is challenging but achievable.

We should not set work which is too easy because if pupils do not have to think about it, they will not think about it. They will rely on their memory instead and complete tasks out of habit without engaging any cognitive processes, which is to say that their brains will not have to release dopamine in order to forge new connections, and they will not therefore feel any sense of reward and will become apathetic and bored.

Perhaps more importantly, if pupils successfully complete tasks without having to think about them, new connections will not be made, information will not enter their long-term memories and they will not, therefore, be able to recall that information later.

In short, if the work is too easy pupils will not learn.

Nor should we set work for our pupils to do which is too hard because if pupils cannot access it, they will be unable to forge new connections in their brains, their brains will not release dopamine and they will become frustrated and demotivated.

In short, if the work is too hard pupils will not learn.

And how do we make sure that the work we set falls squarely within the 'zone of proximal development'? Simply by knowing our pupils because regular assessment of our pupils will inform us where each of them is now - what they can and cannot do and, therefore, where the gaps in their learning are - and this, in turn, will inform us where their zone of proximal development currently sits.

Assessment is a form of planning. If you can confidently answer the following questions about each of your pupils, then you can plan for progress:

- Where are they now?
- Where do they need to be?
- How can they get there?

Planning for progress is at the heart of effective teaching and pupils only make progress when they are challenged and engaged. They are only challenged and engaged when the work they are asked to do is not too hard and not too easy but just right. Great teachers, therefore, are like Goldilocks: they know when the conditions are just right for learning to take place. Great teachers serve a rich diet of porridge that's heated to the optimum temperature - neither too hot nor too cold - each and every day.

CHAPTER TWENTY-SIX:
THE DANGERS OF DIFFERENTIATION

In Chapters Twenty-Four and Twenty-Five, I argued the importance of pitching work in pupils' 'struggle zones' - work that is hard but achievable; beyond pupils' current capabilities but within their reach.

I said we can do this by regarding assessment as a form of planning.

But, when teaching a class of pupils with different starting points, where do we pitch learning?   In this chapter and in Chapter Twenty-Seven, I will argue that the perfect pitch is high, that we should provide high levels of challenge and teach to the top...

Broadly speaking, we might say there are two approaches to differentiation: teaching to the middle; and teaching to the top (I don't think any teacher actively sets out to teach to the bottom, dumbing down for all but the lowest-performing pupils in their class).

Every class, whether set or streamed, will have a distribution of prior attainment; pupils will have a range of starting points and, although some gaps between pupils' performances will narrow through the course of the academic year, there will always been differences.   Teaching to the middle means pitching the lesson to the centre of the bell curve - teaching what the 'average' pupil can do and what will fill the gaps in the average pupils' current performance.

Scaffolding will be required for those pupils to the left of the bell curve in order to bridge the gap between their current performance and the performance of the average pupil in that class, whereas additional stretch and challenge will be needed for those pupils to the right of the bell curve in order to propel them further forwards from their more advanced starting points.

Teaching to the top, meanwhile, is about pitching learning at what the most able - or highest performing - pupils will be able to do with time, effort and support.

I'll return to the notion of 'teaching to the top' in a moment but, before I go on, I have an admission to make: I don't like the terms 'less able' and 'more able'. Less able than what, exactly? Less able than the more able? That's a pretty banal and facile statement. Less able than they could be? Than we want them to be? Less able than the average pupil? If so, what's 'average'?

No one is 'average'; rather, we are all made up of myriad individual characteristics. If you take an average of each of us (height, weight, IQ, shoe size, etc), you won't find any individual who is average in all respects.

This is known as the 'jaggedness principle'.

In the 1940s, the US Air Force had to refit fighter planes with adjustable seats because the cockpits had been designed around the average range of ten body measurements taken from a population of 4,063 pilots. But because no individual met all those criteria, they ended up with a seat which didn't fit a single pilot.

Not to be deterred by the jaggedness principle, as recently as 2011 the Australian Bureau of Statistics used the national census to find the average Australian. They announced that she was a 37-year-old woman with a son and a daughter aged six and nine. She was 5'4" and weighed 11 stone. She lived in a three-bedroom house, had about $200,000 still to pay on her mortgage and her family originally came from the UK. However, when they checked this description against the census data they couldn't find a single person in the whole country who fit.

So 'average' doesn't exist and we'd be wise not to compare pupils to the average, deeming some to be 'less able' and others 'more'.

What's more, the term 'less able' implies a fixed state of affairs. The 'less able' are destined to remain less able ad infinitum. They will always reside to the left of our graph, there to languish in the shadow of the bell curve.

No, I don't like the term 'less able' at all.

I prefer 'lower performing' and even that niggles. But for all its faults, at least 'lower performing' has the advantage of being less permanent, less immobile. Someone who is lower performing can improve their performance and become a better performer or a higher performer.

But this still implies an arbitrary comparison. What are we using as our measuring stick? The most recent summative assessment data? But surely this only tested pupils on their mastery of the most recent topic? Key Stage 2 SATs results? But surely this only tested pupils in English and maths, and even then, on a narrow field of study within these two subjects? Teachers' predictions for end of year or end of course outcomes? The latest university admissions data shows the weakness in that, with only 16% of A Level predictions bearing fruit.

Whatever stick we use to beat less able pupils with, it will be - like all sticks, I suppose - narrow. Someone who is deemed less able by one measure might well be more able by another. We are in danger of arbitrarily writing off some pupils because they didn't perform as well on a test than other pupils. We are defining them by way of a snapshot taken through a pinhole lens.

Whatever term we want to use - and I will stick with 'lower performing' for the purposes of this article - we must first accept that pupils cannot be pigeonholed in this way. All pupils - like all human beings - are different, unique, individual.

We should not pool the 'less able' into a homogenous group and assume that what works with one of them will work with all and that what has been proven to work with 'less able' pupils in another school, in another district, in another country, (according to research evidence and meta-analyses) will work in our classroom.

As I said at the start of this chapter, I do not think teaching to the middle is very effective because differentiation in this guise (scaffolding for lower-performing pupils whilst stretching and challenging higher-performing ones - and therefore - by definition - expecting less of lower-performing pupils), carries with it an inherent danger...

It is, by any other name, 'dumbing down'.

Differentiation of this kind is delivered by means of placing limits on learning, lowering a glass ceiling on top of pupils' ambitions. Differentiation of this kind might take the form of using Bloom's taxonomy to target questions at different pupils. For example, the teacher might start a classroom discussion by asking a question from the bottom of the taxonomy - a knowledge-based question which requires only a recall of facts - to a lower-performing pupil before moving up the taxonomy with higher performing pupils.

But sticking to the bottom of Bloom's taxonomy does not allow lower-performing pupils to deepen their understanding; rather, it leads to surface learning. And, to complicate matters further, this approach is guilty of assuming that because the taxonomy grows in difficulty, the bottom end isn't as important and that higher-performing pupils don't need to waste their time down there. Instead, they should be floating around the pyramid's apex like Bisto kids following the gravy trail.

Yes, Bloom is a spectrum of task difficulty: it goes from easy - such as recalling knowledge - to harder - such as evaluating an argument. But it is a spectrum because it explores the full range of cognitive learning. Knowledge is just as important as evaluation. Without knowledge, pupils can't access the higher bits. In other words, without the bottom layers of the pyramid - the foundations - the whole structure crumbles and falls to the sandy desert plain.

In order to show their complete mastery of a topic, every pupil (no matter their current level of performance) should be able to answer a combination of recall-type questions (these are questions which can be answered in a short period regardless of prior learning) and developmental-type questions (these are questions which stretch pupils and develop the skills required for academic success).

Every pupil at every level of their academic development needs to answer questions on the full spectrum of Bloom's taxonomy; every pupil needs access to both mastery and developmental questions.

Let me cite a familiar example often used in teacher-training...

First read this extract from The Jabberwocky by Lewis Carroll:

> 'Twas brillig, and the slithy toves
> Did gyre and gimble in the wabe;
> All mimsy were the borogroves,

And the mome raths outgrabe.

Now answer me this:
1. What were the slithy toves doing in the wabe?

How about this:
2. How would you describe the state of the borogroves?

And:
3. What can you say about the mome raths?

I bet you had no difficulty answering these questions and you even, by default, used quotations from the text, didn't you? But did you need to understand the poem in order to answer these questions? Or were you simply regurgitating isolated facts?

Now try this question:
4. Were the borogroves justified in feeling mimsy?

And:
5. How effective was the mome raths' strategy?

You'll note that questions 1 to 3 were from the bottom of Bloom's taxonomy whereas 4 and 5 were from the top. This activity demonstrates the fact that questions and tasks which remain at the very base of Bloom's pyramid create the false impression of learning, or 'surface learning', without actually helping pupils to develop and deepen their understanding of a topic.

So, to summarise, we should ensure that every pupil moves up and down the taxonomy by asking questions and setting tasks which use the following stems:

Knowledge: state; recall
Comprehension: explain; interpret
Application: apply; use

Analysis: analyse; classify; compare; give reasons; explain the cause and effects

Synthesis: solve; create; design; invent; suggest improvements for; provide constructive feedback on

Evaluation: strengths / weaknesses; advantages / disadvantages; give the arguments for and against; compare and contrast.

In conclusion, we differentiate in the sense of 'dumbing down' at our peril. Placing artificial limits on what we expect our lower-performing pupils to do isn't the answer to the question of 'How do we teach less able pupils?'

...So, what is?

We will answer this question in Chapter Twenty-Seven...

Matt Bromley

CHAPTER TWENTY-SEVEN:
TEACHING TO THE TOP

In Chapter Twenty-Six, I said that teaching to the middle of the bell curve - pitching learning to the average pupil whilst scaffolding for the lower-performing and stretching and challenging the higher-performing - was a form of dumbing down. I said that a far more effective way to pitch learning and ensure every pupil achieves their potential was to teach to the top - pitch learning to the highest-performing pupil in the class, accepting that will take some pupils longer and that they will require more support but that every pupil will get there eventually.

Teaching to the top is a way of modelling high expectations for all our pupils, no matter their starting points and their most recent performance.

So, we should teach to the top, not the middle, and ensure our classrooms provide challenge for all...

Of course, some pupils fear challenge. We need to eliminate - or at least mitigate - pupils' feelings of fear and hesitation by creating a classroom environment which encourages the making of mistakes as a sign of learning, and which explicitly says (through our choice of language, our modelling and thinking aloud, and the routines we engage in) there is nothing to fear by trying your best and pushing yourself to do hard work.

After all, challenge is innate...

In their lives outside the school gates, pupils are always seeking hard things to do such as Pokémon Go! and FIFA. They are the YouTube generation who spend hours watching video tutorials, looking at graphic organisers on Pinterest or reading articles on Buzzfeed so they can learn by increments and improve their performance in, say, Minecraft, baking, football, make-up and nail art, hair design, and so on.

They love challenge when it is private because, in the safety of their bedrooms, there isn't the fear of humiliation or peer pressure.

To promote challenge in the classroom, therefore, we need to reduce the threat level, we need to ensure no one feels humiliated if they fall short of a challenge. Rather, they need to know they will learn from the experience and perform better next time. They will learn by increments.

Of course, to set the right level of challenge for our pupils - hard but achievable with time, effort and support - we need to identify (perhaps using low-stakes quizzes, hinge questions, exit tickets and other forms of 'live' assessment in class) pupils' zones of proximal development.

What else can we do to help lower-performing pupils learn and make progress...?

First, as I argued earlier, we can put blocks in the way of pupils' initial learning (or encoding) - what Robert Bjork calls 'desirable difficulties' - in order to bolster their subsequent storage and retrieval strength.

Second, we can 'chunk' information, ensuring we teach knowledge before skill. And we can link new learning with prior learning so that pupils can cheat their limited working memories.

Third, we can provide opportunities for our pupils to engage in deliberate practice, repeating learning at least three times but doing so in a different way each time, allowing pupils to do something new with the learning every time they encounter it in order to forge myriad connections and improve 'transfer'.

And if all this works with lower-performing pupils then it will work with all pupils.

That's the beauty of this 'teaching to the top' approach to supporting lower-performing pupils: if you have high expectations of all your pupils and if you model grade 9 work rather than grade 5 work, then although some pupils will fall short, simply because they have aimed high they are more likely to achieve a better grade than if you'd placed artificial limits in the way of their learning.

What's more, why show pupils anything other than the very best? Why model the mediocre?

As Matthew Arnold said in Culture and Anarchy, "Culture...is a study of perfection, [it] seeks to...make the best that has been thought and known in the world current everywhere; to make all men live in an atmosphere of sweetness and light".

So, let's bring our all our pupils, no matter their starting points and current performance, out into the light and watch them grow and blossom.

CHAPTER TWENTY-EIGHT:
TEACHER EXPLANATIONS

Once we've engaged the active attention of our pupils' working memories by setting work that is hard but achievable with time, effort and support, work that is just beyond their current abilities but within their reach, what's the best way of teaching the information we need them to encode in long-term memory?

The most effective, expedient way for pupils to acquire new information is for the teacher – that educated, experienced, expert at the front of the classroom – to tell them, then show them, what they need to know.

This is not to suggest that sometimes, for some purposes, other approaches are not also effective, but direct instruction (note the lower case, Direct Instruction, when capitalised, denotes a particular type of lesson whereby the teacher sticks strictly to a script) remains the most efficient and the least likely to lead to misconceptions amongst pupils and a misunderstanding by the teacher of what pupils can and cannot do.

Therefore, rather than designing convoluted ways of enabling a pupil to "discover" new knowledge for him or herself, perhaps as a result of engaging in a range of group activities, teachers should - when teaching something for the first time - take the shortest, simplest path: they should explicitly tell them then show them what they need to know.

In short, we should make effective use of teacher explanations (telling) and modelling (showing).

We will explore the art of good teacher explanations in this chapter and the art of good modelling in Chapter Twenty-Nine. But first let us examine the importance of clear learning outcomes and assessment criteria. We talked about learning outcomes in Chapter Seventeen but I'd like to – albeit briefly – return to the subject here because they are integral to teacher explanations...

Learning outcomes - and indeed shorter-term task instructions - must be specific. Learning outcomes and the criteria against which pupils will be assessed must be joined-up - in other words, what we expect of pupils and how we assess the extent to which they have achieved it must correspond.

The assessment criteria must also be shared with pupils before they embark on a task and, ideally, pupils should be involved in agreeing that success criteria. A class discussion about 'what a good one looks like' not only makes it clear how pupils will eventually be judged – therefore, improving their chances of success and mitigating any feelings of unfairness and arbitrariness – it also ensures pupils take ownership of the task and have a vested interest in completing it to the best of their abilities.

The assessment criteria should allow for a degree of creativity and flair, and not be too prescriptive, and feedback should be formative, focused on what pupils need to do to improve ("Your essay was well-structured and had many good features including the use of signposts and a balanced argument but, next time, consider including persuasive devices such as rhetorical questions..."); rather than summative and final ("You got 20 out of 40, that's a grade 3 which is below target").

In short, we need to share the "bigger picture" with pupils, to make explicit what they are learning, why they are learning it, what success looks like and how they'll be assessed and given feedback.

Once the learning outcomes have been articulated, pupils should be able to answer the following questions:

- What do I have to understand by the end of this lesson/unit/module?
- What am I expected to produce in order to demonstrate my understanding? What will that understanding look like in practice?
- What knowledge and skills should I currently possess, or will I need to acquire, in order to meet the assessment criteria and, therefore, demonstrate my understanding?
- What resources and assistance will be available to help me?
- How does the work I am doing today relate to what we did previously?
- How will the work I am doing today help me to meet the final assessment criteria?
- What aspects of today's and future work demands the most attention?
- What are the strengths and weaknesses in my current performance? What can I do to improve?
- How will my final work be assessed?

A word of advice: Sharing learning outcomes and assessment criteria does not mean that every lesson must start with a set of objectives scribed on the board which pupils have to copy down. In fact, it definitely does not mean this. Lessons are artificial blocks of study not a complete learning sequence. Not every lesson, therefore, needs to start with objectives and there is nothing to be gained by getting pupils to copy verbatim from the board. Rather, the direction of travel should be shared with pupils when you begin a new topic or module, then periodically repeated and reinforced.

How to write learning outcomes

Learning outcomes should be measurable statements that articulate what pupils should know and/or be able to do by the end of a lesson or sequence of lessons. The best learning outcomes are pupil-centred rather than teacher-centred, and are specific and measurable, thus providing a means of determining the content, organisation, and assessment of the lesson or topic.

Learning outcomes can help pupils to acquire foundational knowledge and can improve their short-term retention, as well as improve higher-order cognitive processing such as the application of knowledge and the transferability of knowledge, not just its initial acquisition.

The best learning outcomes can actually shape what pupils learn because when pupils are clear about what they're expected to know they can direct their attention towards those ideas or concepts.

Once you've written your learning outcomes, check their validity by asking yourself these three questions:

- Does this learning outcome identify what pupils will be able to do after the lesson?
- Does it focus on specific and concrete actions and will I be able to observe that pupils have achieved the outcome? Is it clear to me how a pupil's achievement of the outcome will be measured?
- Does the outcome align with the level of knowledge expected of pupils at this stage?

How to share learning outcomes

Sharing the learning outcomes at the start of a lesson or sequence of lessons is an important element of direct instruction because knowing the learning outcomes in advance helps pupils to practice metacognitive skills and to become more self-regulated.

Having clear learning outcomes helps pupils to narrow their focus to the most important knowledge and skills, and outcomes can help pupils to organise their notes, track their progress towards meeting the outcomes, and improve their self-study.

Sharing learning outcomes prior to studying a topic can also increase pupils' levels of engagement because learning outcomes give pupils a clearer sense of purpose and may even pique their curiosity about the topic they're about to study.

Sharing learning outcomes can also increase pupils' levels of motivation because when pupils understand what is expected of them, they are more likely to feel confident that they can meet those expectations.

Perhaps the most important aspect of sharing learning outcomes, though, is checking that pupils understand them. To be certain of this, it's important to engage pupils in class discussion. For example, you may ask pupils what - in their own words - they think the learning outcomes mean. You may ask how they will know that they've achieved the learning outcomes, and why they think it's important to do so. You may also ask pupils how the learning outcomes relate to what they've previously learnt and how they think achieving the learning outcomes will help them with their future learning.

Once we've articulated learning outcomes, we - the experts in the room - need to introduce our pupils - the novices - to new knowledge and/or skills. The best way to do this, as I said at the beginning of this chapter, is through the artful use of direct instruction...

Teacher explanations

Research shows that active and guided instruction is much more effective than unguided, facilitative instruction. For example, Kirschner, Sweller and Clark (2006) compared guided models of teaching – such as direct instruction – with discovery learning methods – such as problem-based learning, inquiry learning, experiential learning, and constructivist learning. They found that the latter methods didn't work as well as the former. It didn't matter, they argued, if pupils preferred less guided methods, they still learned less from them (see also Clark, 1989).

In Visible Learning, Professor John Hattie found that the average effect size for teaching strategies which involved the teacher as a "facilitator" was 0.17, whereas the average effect size for strategies where the teacher acted as an "activator" was 0.60. Direct instruction had an effect size of 0.59 compared to problem-based learning with an effect size of just 0.15.

So direct instruction – teacher explanations and modelling; telling and showing – is clearly more effective than discovery learning approaches. But what, exactly, does direct instruction look like in practice?

Direct instruction is sometimes regarded as a passive mode of teaching, the pouring of information from one container (the teacher's mind) into another (the pupil's mind). Indeed, some academics believe that direct instruction is an undesirable form of teaching. McKeen et al (1972), for example, describe it as "authoritarian". Borko & Wildman (1986) say it is "regimented". And Edwards (1981) says it is akin to "fact accumulation at the expense of thinking skill development".

Even advocates of the form cannot quite agree on what it looks like in practice. Indeed, the term "direct instruction" has been used for more than a century to refer to any academic instruction that is led by the teacher.

For example, it featured in Joseph Meyer Rice's 1893 book, The Public School System of the United States, in which Rice complained "in many of the grades the children received direct instruction for no more than two or two-and-a-half of the five hours spent in school, the pupils being engaged in busy-work more than half the time".

Whichever definition of direct instruction you settle upon, it is likely to be built of the following cornerstones...

Firstly, the teacher will reduce the difficulty of a task during initial practice. Direct instruction is about the teacher presenting new material to pupils in small "chunks".

Secondly, the teacher will provide scaffolds and support. Direct instruction is about the teacher modelling a new procedure by, among other strategies, thinking aloud, guiding pupils' initial practice and providing pupils with cues.

Thirdly, the teacher will provide supportive feedback. Direct instruction is also about the teacher providing systematic corrections and feedback, providing pupils with "fix-up" strategies, and providing expert models of the completed task.

And finally, the teacher will provide opportunities for extensive independent practice. Direct instruction is about affording pupils plenty of opportunities to practice new knowledge and skills.

No matter your definition, research evidence suggests direct instruction really works and is certainly more effective than discovery learning.

But direct instruction – like all teaching strategies – only works if it is done well. So, what makes direct instruction (teacher explanations) work in practice?

I will now look at five ways of making teacher explanations work: the use of metaphors and analogies; dual coding; pitch; reciprocity; and models...

Metaphors and analogies

First, good teacher explanations need to contextualise information so that abstract ideas or hitherto alien concepts, are made concrete, tangible, and real, and so that they are related to pupils' own lives and experiences.

Dual coding

Second, teacher explanations should make use of dual coding. In other words, teachers' verbal instructions, as well as any text-based explanations displayed on the board or in handouts, should be paired with and complemented by visuals such as diagrams, charts, graphics and moving images.

Pitch

Third, teacher explanations should be pitched in what Lev Vygotsky calls the "zone of proximal development". In other words, they should be differentiated so that they are challenging and yet accessible to all pupils.

Reciprocity

Fourth, teacher explanations should be reciprocated, with pupils explaining concepts back to the teacher as well as to each other. This works on the basis that only once you teach something have you truly learned it. Learning by teaching works because, by teaching, pupils gain feedback and make better sense of a topic. Learning by teaching also works because it is a form of learning by doing, of practising, and thus addresses the want and the need to learn.

Models

Finally, teacher explanations should make effective and plentiful use of models – exemplars of both good and bad work, as well as exemplars from a range of different contexts

– which show pupils what a final product should look like and what makes such products work.

In the next chapter, we will explore the use of models in more detail...

CHAPTER TWENTY-NINE:
TEACHER MODELLING

In the previous chapter we said that the cornerstones of direct instruction were:

1. The teacher will reduce the difficulty of a task during initial practice. Direct instruction is about the teacher presenting new material to pupils in small "chunks".
2. The teacher will provide scaffolds and support. Direct instruction is about the teacher modelling a new procedure by, among other strategies, thinking aloud, guiding pupils' initial practice and providing pupils with cues.
3. The teacher will provide supportive feedback. Direct instruction is also about the teacher providing systematic corrections and feedback, providing pupils with "fix-up" strategies, and providing expert models of the completed task.
4. The teacher will provide opportunities for extensive independent practice. Direct instruction is about affording pupils plenty of opportunities to practise new knowledge and skills.

No matter your definition, research evidence suggests direct instruction really works and is certainly more effective than discovery learning. But direct instruction – like all teaching strategies – only works if it is done well. So, what makes direct instruction (teacher explanations) work in practice?

In Chapter Twenty-Eight, we looked at four ways of making teacher explanations work:

1. The use of metaphors and analogies;
2. Dual coding;
3. Pitch; and
4. Reciprocity.

Now let us turn our attention to a fifth and final strategy which helps make a success of direct instruction: teacher modelling...

Teacher explanations should make effective and plentiful use of models – exemplars of both good and bad work, as well as exemplars from a range of different contexts – which show pupils what a final product should look like and what makes such products work. Let's explore the use of models in more detail...

Good models demonstrate what works as well as what doesn't. It is important to show pupils what excellence looks like by sharing models of the very best work, giving them something to aspire to and an understanding of how to produce high quality work of their own. But it is equally important to show pupils models of ineffective work, work that isn't quite the best (or perhaps is so very far from being the best) so that pupils can learn what not to do and how to avoid making the same mistakes themselves.

All the models that are shared should be dissected in front of pupils, with the teacher demonstrating the dissection process, before pupils get their hands dirty dissecting another model for themselves and each other. For example, if a model of a persuasive speech is shown on the board, the teacher should analyse it using text marking, pointing out and then annotating how it works, what makes it effective, breaking it apart to identify and discuss each of its component parts. Then the teacher should reconstruct the speech, explaining how the component parts hang together to create an effective argument, how the whole becomes something much greater than the sum of its parts.

Once pupils know how to dissect models, they should be afforded the opportunity to do so without the teacher's guidance, perhaps by teaching other pupils. In order to prepare pupils for this, it is important that the teacher offers encouragement, gives specific instructions, uses thought or sentence stems to provide pupils with the right language, and – as I say above – directly demonstrates the process first.

Teacher explanations and modelling are not only proven strategies in the classroom, they're also strategies that will be very familiar to pupils as staples of popular television talent shows such as the *The Great British Bake Off* and *Masterchef*.

In both these shows, the judges – who are professional bakers and chefs – are shown making a dish first: they show us how it's done. Thus, they provide us with a model, an exemplar on which the television audience can base their later judgments. By so doing, they also prove that they are still the experts, that they can do what they require their pupils to do, thus establishing their credibility.

In much the same way, it is powerful for teachers to complete any task they ask their pupils to do and to do so publicly. This shows pupils that the teacher is an expert and doesn't expect pupils to do anything he or she isn't also willing to do. It also provides the class with an exemplar, a model on which to base judgments of their own work. For example, if a teacher asks their class to write an essay, they should sit at their desk and write the essay, too. Not only does this provide an exemplar to display on the board at the end which the teacher and then pupils can dissect (providing an initial model for sharing, thus removing pupils' fear of being the first to be critiqued and encouraging them to share their work next), it also forces pupils to work independently because the teacher cannot help them while he or she is also writing the essay.

In conclusion, direct instruction – the use of teacher explanations (telling) and models (showing) – are highly effective strategies to use in the classroom. What's more, they are the most expedient means of teaching pupils what they need to know.

What teacher explanations and modelling have in common is that they are largely verbal exercises - they rely on good oral communication. Teacher talk and pupil talk are crucial means by which pupils will deepen their knowledge and develop their understanding.

In Chapter Thirty we will explore the importance of speaking and listening in the classroom and then, in Chapter Thirty-One, we will examine the role of questioning.

CHAPTER THIRTY:
ORACY

In this section of the book - the second of our three steps of teaching for long-term learning - we are exploring ways of utilising pupils' working memories.

Once we have created a positive learning environment which stimulates sensory memory, we need to make pupils think hard but efficiently in order to gain the attention of - but cheat - working memory. Only once we have accomplished this, can we plan for deliberate practice in order to improve storage in, and retrieval from, long-term memory.

So far in this section we have said that we must pitch work in pupils' 'struggle zones'. In other words, we must give pupils work to do that is challenging but achievable with time, effort and support, and work that is just beyond pupils' current capabilities but within their reach, because if the work is too easy, pupils will complete it out of habit, that is to say with near automaticity - without thinking about it and therefore without learning, and if the work is too difficult, pupils will do one of two things: either they will not even attempt it (judging it to be a fruitless task) or else they will attempt it but quickly overload their working memory and fail to complete the task.

We have also said that we must plan for desirable difficulties. In other words, we must position roadblocks along pupils' learning journeys to slow down their initial encoding of new information in order to improve the subsequent storage

269

strength of that information, and the ease and efficiency with which that information can later be retrieved from long-term memory.

We must also provide high levels of challenge for every pupil but reduce the threat level. One way to do this is to teach the knowledge and skills the top-performing pupil in the class will be able to master with the benefit of time, effort and support. In other words, we must model high expectations of all pupils, no matter their starting points and backgrounds.

So far, we have also said that we must make effective use of teacher explanations because the most effective way of making pupils think hard - and the best way of ensuring pupils focus their attention on the right things - is for the expert teacher to provide direct instruction of new knowledge and skills. And once we have told pupils something, we must make effective use of teacher modelling. In other words, once the teacher has introduced new curriculum content, they need to model excellence, they need to tell then show pupils what's expected.

Next, we must promote classroom talk by providing plentiful opportunities for pupils to engage in discussions and debate. Speaking and listening – or oracy - helps to make pupils think hard and deepen their understanding of key concepts.

Speaking and thinking are intricately linked because the process of speaking helps pupils to learn by articulating their thoughts and developing the concepts they use in order to better understand the world. Speaking and listening also level the playing field because most pupils are better able to articulate their thinking verbally than in writing, particularly in the early stages of their education. In short, classroom discussion is the best means of engaging all pupils and the best way of developing their knowledge and understanding.

The teaching of oracy skills should come first, followed by reading then writing, because - in order to develop pupils' language capability and support their reading and writing - there first need to be purposeful speaking and listening activities which provide a foundation for thinking and communication. For speaking and listening to be effective in making pupils think hard, there needs to be an agreed set of rules for classroom talk, speaking and listening skills must be explicitly taught, and the teacher needs to model good speaking and listening strategies at all times.

In this chapter we will explore the importance of speaking and listening further and then, in Chapter Thirty-One, we will home in on the use of classroom questioning.

Classroom discussion

The Russian psychologist, Lev Vygotsky - yes, he of the 'zone of proximal development' fame - once said that speaking and thinking were intricately linked because the process of speaking helps us to learn by articulating our thoughts and developing the concepts we use to understand the world.

Vygotsky argued that, "Up to a certain point in time, [thought and speech] follow different lines, independently of each other [but] at a certain point these lines meet, whereupon thought becomes verbal and speech rational".

Stricht's Law tells us that "Reading ability in children cannot exceed their listening ability" and Myhill and Fisher say that "Spoken language forms a constraint, a ceiling not only on the ability to comprehend but also on the ability to write, beyond which literacy cannot progress".

In short, classroom discussion is the best means we have of engaging all our pupils - irrespective of their current abilities - and the best way to develop their knowledge and understanding of any given topic.

In 2017, the Education Endowment Foundation produced a guidance report called 'Improving Literacy in Key Stage 2' which recommended the teaching of literacy be carried out in a sequence beginning with speaking and listening, followed by reading then writing.

The report argued that, in order to develop pupils' language capability and support their reading and writing, there needed to be "purposeful speaking and listening activities [which provided] a foundation for thinking and communication". They suggested the following:

- Re-reading books aloud and discussing them;
- Activities that extend pupils' expressive and receptive vocabulary;
- Collaborative learning activities where pupils can share their thought processes;
- Structured questioning to develop reading comprehension;
- Teachers modelling inference-making by thinking aloud; and
- Pupils articulating their ideas verbally before they start writing.

The EEF recommended these activities be followed by strategies to support pupils in developing fluent reading capabilities, helping them to read quickly, accurately and with appropriate stress and intonation. They suggested the following activities:

- Guided oral reading instruction whereby teachers model fluent reading of a text, then pupils read the same text aloud with appropriate feedback; and
- Repeated reading whereby pupils re-read a short and meaningful passage a set number of times or until they reach a suitable level of fluency.

Next, the EEF says, we should teach reading comprehension strategies through modelling and supported practice. Comprehension, they say, can be improved by teaching specific strategies that pupils can apply both to monitor and overcome barriers to comprehension, including: prediction; questioning; clarifying; summarising; inference; and activating prior knowledge.

Having completed the reading phase, we should teach writing composition strategies through modelling and supported practice. Purpose and audience are, the EEF argues, central to effective writing. Pupils need to have a reason to write and someone to write for. Writing can be thought of as a process made up of seven components: planning; drafting; sharing; evaluating; revising; editing; and publishing.

"Effective writers use a number of strategies to support each component of the writing process," according to the report. For example, "pupils' planning could be improved by teaching the strategies of goal setting and activating prior knowledge."

The final stage of the process is to develop pupils' transcription and sentence construction skills through extensive practice.

"A fluent writing style," the report says, "supports composition because pupils' cognitive resources are freed from focusing on handwriting, spelling, and sentence construction and can be redirected towards writing composition."

Spelling should be taught explicitly, and diagnostic assessments should be used to focus pupils' attention on the spelling they find difficult.

The central premise behind the report, then, is that speaking and listening are at the heart of language, not only as foundations for reading and writing, but also as essential skills for thinking and communication. Speaking and listening can be used to model and develop expressive and receptive language.

For example, speaking can be used to help pupils articulate their ideas before writing - thus ensuring they're not preoccupied and hindered by their handwriting and spelling.

And listening can also be used to help pupils develop inference skills without the need to process a written text.

What's more, reading to pupils and discussing what you're reading exposes them to an increasingly wide range of texts which will, in turn, develop their language capability.

Classroom discussions are critical to extending pupils' receptive and expressive vocabularies. As the report says, "While pupils may have the decoding skills required to say a word out loud, they will only be able to understand what it means if it is already in their vocabulary.

Of course, talk alone is not enough – classroom talk must be focussed on what needs to be developed. An unfocussed piece of writing will lead to unfocussed results, and so it is with speaking. There are several learning activities that help facilitate and support talk so that it is purposeful, structured, and appropriate which we'll come to in a moment...

Firstly, let's discuss the importance of exploratory talk in our classrooms. Exploratory talk is - as the name might suggest - talk which helps pupils to explore ideas in order to come to a better understanding of something. It is important that pupils are made to feel comfortable with one another and with their teacher so that they can begin to share incomplete ideas, revise their own thinking, and challenge each other's thinking.

Dylan William says that teachers in the UK are likely to ask more questions than teachers in the highest-performing countries and that we tend to think less about the questions we ask. In other words, we engage in Q&As whereby we ask a question - often closed - a pupil answers it, we respond then ask another question, ad infinitum. It's the same with how we group our pupils. The result being that we tend to fall into the familiar routine of asking our pupils to 'talk to your neighbour about...'.

In the next chapter we will home in on the part questioning can play in promoting classroom talk...

CHAPTER THIRTY-ONE:
CLOSED QUESTIONS

Once we've explained and modelled new information for our pupils, we need them to engage with that information in order to deepen their understanding of it and improve their chances of transferring the information between contexts. As such, we need to provide plentiful opportunities for pupils to engage in speaking and listening activities and one of the best ways to do this is to ask questions...

In many ways, the art of asking good questions is what teaching's all about. Indeed, Socrates argued that "questioning is the only defensible form of teaching".

It could be argued that there are only two valid reasons for asking a question in class: either to provide information to the teacher about what to do next, or to cause pupils to think.

If so, then the latter involves *dialogic* questioning, which is to say questions that encourage discussion, questions that are open, philosophical, and challenging. And dialogic questions – such as Socratic questions – don't just cause thinking, they promote critical thinking. Open questions which cause pupils to think in this way are widely regarded in academia as effective teaching strategies.

However, what is perhaps less widely regarded, or at any rate less fashionable to admit to these days, is that closed questions can continue to play a vital role in an effective classroom. Indeed, if there are two reasons for asking questions (to provide information to the teacher and to cause thinking) and open questions accomplish the latter, then closed questions can help us to achieve the former. In other words, closed questions are great assessment tools to use in the classroom. They can provide valuable assessment information to the teacher about their pupils' learning and progress, about who has "got it" and who has not, and about what needs reteaching, recapping or developing further.

What's more, closed questions used as a form of assessment reduce the marking load on teachers and make assessment "live" and responsive. Further, closed questions used as a form of assessment turn assessment into a means of learning, they are assessment *as* learning rather than assessment *for* learning. And one of the most effective forms of closed questions is the "hinge question". Hinge questions are multiple-choice questions so, before we go any further, let's explain and defend the humble multiple-choice question which, although once a staple of schooling, has become somewhat unfashionable in recent years.

So, are multiple-choice questions:

A. Useful diagnostic tools.
B. A complete waste of time.

Closed questions for assessment

With open questions, the rubric defines the rigour. With multiple-choice questions, however, the options define the rigour. This is particularly true of hinge questions which can be used just as effectively with the most able pupils as with the less able.

The trick to making multiple-choice questions effective is to create several wrong options which are nevertheless plausible and closely related to the right answer. The best "wrong" options also uncover common misconceptions or false assumptions. As such, the best way to create the wrong options in a way which makes them plausible is to mine a class's work – or look back to a previous year when the topic was last taught – for pupils' common misconceptions, misunderstandings and mistakes.

If nothing else, trawling through pupils' work to discover what they tend to get wrong and what tends to stump them, helps inform the lesson planning process, allowing the teacher to dedicate more time to those elements with which pupils most often struggle.

This act of mining pupils' work for misconceptions and then applying the findings in a way that helps anticipate pupils' difficulties and questions, is the difference between content knowledge and pedagogical content knowledge, between knowing your subject and knowing how to teach your subject in a way which makes sense to pupils.

Analysing misconceptions also helps an expert teacher to view a topic through the lens of the novice pupil, to narrow the knowledge gap between them, and to improve the lesson planning process.

A hinge is a point in a lesson when a teacher needs to check whether pupils have grasped a key concept and are ready to move on to study another. Usually, pupils' ability to understand the next concept being taught is contingent on their mastery of the concept that has just been taught. It is important, therefore, that the teacher assesses pupils' levels of mastery before moving on, and this is exactly what a hinge question can do.

A hinge question is a diagnostic tool which a teacher employs when their pupils reach the "hinge" point. Pupils' responses provide the teacher with valuable evidence about what their pupils know, don't know and need to do next. A class's response to a hinge question should inform the teacher whether to completely reteach the topic, recap the main points, or move on to the next topic.

Of course, not every pupil in a class is likely to answer a hinge question in the same way, so the teacher needs to decide on the level of mastery they will accept. We'll explore this situation in a moment but we're getting ahead of ourselves...

A hinge question, then, is a multiple-choice question which provides an immediate check of pupils' understanding. Crucially, a hinge question provides a check of understanding for every pupil in a class. A hinge question informs the teacher if pupils have understood what they have taught and, if not, what pupils have misunderstood.

As I say above, a hinge question should be asked at the end of an activity as the teacher moves from teaching one key concept to another, when the teaching of the second concept is reliant on understanding the first. Every pupil must respond within a set timeframe, ideally one to two minutes. A hinge question is a quick assessment – a line in the sand – and, therefore, responses should be instinctive and almost immediate. All pupils must participate in the process. As such, it is best to avoid a "hands up" approach and instead employ a tactic that ensures every pupil shows the teacher their answer at the same time. This enables the teacher to assess every pupil and prevents pupils from being unduly influenced by their peers.

Simultaneous, all-class responses can be achieved by using mini whiteboards on which pupils write their answers then hold them up when instructed. Alternatively, voting buttons could be used, perhaps on iPads, with the responses – anonymised, of course; perhaps reported as a percentage response against each option – displayed on the interactive whiteboard. Or, perhaps more simply, pupils could hold up lettered, numbered or coloured cards to indicate their answer. A set of four cards could be kept on desks or given to pupils to retain in their books or planners in order to reduce the logistical strain and permit hinge questions to become a quick, simple, everyday feature of lessons.

The teacher must be able to interpret pupils' responses quickly, ideally within a minute, so that the flow of the lesson isn't stunted. Before pupils show their responses, the teacher – as I say above – needs to set a pass rate for what they consider to be an acceptable level of "mastery". For example, the teacher might decide that they will move on to the next topic if more than 80 per cent of pupils answer the hinge question correctly.

The teacher will then need to consider what to do to support the 20 per cent who got the question wrong. The teacher could set a task for the 80 per cent to do while working with the 20 per cent, scaffolding their learning, recapping on key points, and so on. Or perhaps the teacher could enlist some of the 80 per cent as peer-teachers to explain the topic to the 20 per cent. This notion of pupils acting as teachers is proven to be extremely effective.

If the teacher has just concluded a topic on word classes (nouns, verbs, adjectives, adverbs and so on) and wishes to assess whether pupils can identify a verb, they might ask the following: The cat purred loudly at me. Where is the verb in this sentence? Is it word A, B, C or D?

If the teacher has just taught rhetorical devices (persuasive writing techniques), he/she might ask the following: which of these is alliteration?

A. The golden disc of the sun burned.
B. The sizzling summer sun smiled sweetly.
C. I felt the red-hot sun on my back.
D. The trees swayed gently in the wind.

And, finally, if I wanted to ascertain whether you had understood the main thrust of this chapter, I might ask the following: which of these sentences best summarises the main point of the chapter?

A. It is about the importance of asking closed questions.
B. It is about the use of hinge questions to assess learning.
C. It is about questioning as a means of deepening understanding.
D. It is about teacher explanations and modelling.

In each case, it is feasible and even advisable to explore the reasons why some pupils have answered incorrectly. For example, if a pupil had responded to the question about alliteration with "A" then the teacher might ask the pupil why they responded thus. This can lead to a discussion – and a reaffirmation – about what alliteration is. But it might also lead to an interesting debate about the use of metaphor in option "A" whereby the sun is compared to a golden disc, and of the differences between a metaphor and alliteration.

Once these discussions have concluded, the teacher might also ask the class if they could have written a better set of options. Perhaps the teacher could ask the class if they can generate a better hinge question to have asked at this point in the lesson. All these discussions have the potential to generate rich and meaningful conversations about what has been learned, and how that learning can be demonstrated and assessed.

If time is of the essence, the teacher could give the hinge a quick oil by asking a binary question (which has a yes or no answer), such as "Do you agree with this statement...?" pupils could respond with a thumbs up or thumbs down. Though limited in its application and rather "rough and ready", this approach can provide a quick assessment of pupils' learning and progress and provide valuable information to the teacher about whether or not they can move on.

In the next chapter we will look at open questions to promote debate and to deepen understanding.

Matt Bromley

CHAPTER THIRTY-TWO:
OPEN QUESTIONS

As I explained in the previous chapter, fundamentally, there are only two reasons for asking a question in class: either to provide information to the teacher (or indeed the pupil) about what to do next, or to cause pupils to think.

The former, I said, involves using closed questions (such as multiple-choice questions at 'hinge' points in lessons) as a means of assessment.

Closed questions can provide valuable information to the teacher about their pupils' learning and progress, about who has "got it" and who has not, and about what needs reteaching, recapping or developing further. What's more, closed questions used as a form of assessment in this way can help reduce the marking load and make marking "live" and responsive. Closed questions used as a form of assessment also have the advantage of turning assessment into a means of learning, they are assessment *as* learning rather than assessment *for* learning.

The latter – questions which cause pupils to think – involves the use of open questions (such as dialogic or Socratic questions) and these are the subject of this chapter...

Dialogic questions are questions that encourage discussion, questions that are open, philosophical, and challenging. Dialogic questions – such as Socratic questions – don't just cause thinking, they promote critical thinking.

Critical thinking provides pupils with the tools they need to be able to monitor, assess and reconstitute their thoughts and actions. Critical thinking also provides pupils with a powerful inner voice for reasoning.

If it can be said that the act of thinking has three possible functions – to express a subjective preference, to establish an objective fact, or to formulate the best solution to a problem from various competing points of view – then critical thinking enables pupils to determine which of these three functions a question requires, and then to come to a conclusion. John Dewey described critical thinking as a process "in which the thinker turns a subject over in the mind, giving it serious and consecutive consideration".

Open questions which cause pupils to think are well known to be effective teaching strategies – as Socrates said, "questioning is the only defensible form of teaching". Indeed, the very term "education" comes from the Latin "ex duco" which means "to lead out" because Socrates and his contemporaries taught by asking questions in order "to lead out" answers from their pupils.

It is also well known that thinking is driven, not by answers, but by questions. And we might go as far as to argue that every intellectual field is born of questions to which answers are either required or else desired. Professor Robert Coe says that "learning happens when people have to think hard", and big, open, philosophical questions – when skilfully managed – can certainly accomplish that aim.

Dialogic teaching strategies, then, make use of the power of talk in order to stimulate and extend pupils' thinking, as well as to advance their learning and understanding. Dialogic teaching enables the teacher to diagnose and assess pupils' understandings and misunderstandings through speaking and listening, and questioning.

Dialogic teaching is collective because teachers and pupils address learning tasks together, whether as a group or as a whole class; it is reciprocal because teachers and pupils listen to each other, share ideas and consider alternative points of view; it is supportive because pupils articulate their ideas without the fear of failure and help each other to reach a common understanding; it is cumulative because teachers and pupils build on their own and each other's ideas and connect them into coherent lines of thinking and enquiry; and it is purposeful because teachers plan and steer classroom talk with specific educational goals in view.

As I say above, one popular dialogic technique is the use of Socratic questions which challenge, deepen and polish pupils' understandings. Socratic questioning can be used to:

- Control a discussion.
- Explore more complex ideas.
- Uncover assumptions.
- Analyse concepts and ideas.
- Distinguish between what pupils know and do not know.

Broadly speaking, Socratic questioning performs two functions in the classroom:

1. To deeply probe pupil thinking, to help pupils begin to distinguish what they know or understand from what they do not know or understand.

2. To foster pupils' abilities to ask Socratic questions and to help pupils acquire the powerful tools of Socratic dialogue so that they can use these tools in everyday life (in questioning themselves and others).

The six Socratic questions

There are six types of Socratic question which should be used in order. They are as follows:

1 Conceptual clarification questions

The first type of Socratic question is used in order to get pupils to clarify their thinking. These questions might be:

"Why do you say that?"
"What exactly does this mean?"
"Could you explain that further?"
"What do we already know about that?"
"Can you give me an example?"
"Are you saying ... or ...?"
"Can you rephrase that, please?"

2 Probing assumptions questions

The second type of Socratic question is used in order to challenge pupils about their pre-existing assumptions, and to make them think about their hitherto unquestioned beliefs. This might include the following questions:

"Is that always the case?"
"Why do you think that assumption holds here?"
"Please explain why/how ...?"
"How can you verify/disprove that assumption?"
"What would happen if ...?"
"Do you agree or disagree with ...?"

3 Probing rationale, reasons and evidence questions

The third type of Socratic question is used in order to uncover – and interrogate – the evidence or reasoning upon which pupils base their argument. In practice, a teacher might ask:

"Why do you say that?"

"Is there reason to doubt the evidence?"
"How do you know this?"
"Show me ... ?"
"Can you give me an example of that?"
"Are those reasons good enough?"
"How might it be refuted?"

4 Questioning viewpoints/perspectives questions

The fourth type of Socratic question is used in order to explore alternative points of view and, importantly, to show pupils that there are other, equally valid viewpoints. This might include asking the following questions:

"What is the counter-argument?"
"Can anyone see this another way?"
"What is the difference between ... and ...?"
"Why is it better than ...?"
"What are the strengths and weaknesses of ...?"
"How are ... and ... similar?"
"How could you look another way at this?"

5 Probing implications and consequences questions

The fifth type of Socratic question is used in order to explore the implications and consequences of an argument, and to consider whether the argument makes sense and if its consequences are desirable. In practice, this might include the following questions:

"But if ... happened, what else would then result?"
"How does ... affect .... ?"
"What are the implications of ...?"
"How does ... fit with what we learned before?"
"Why is ... important?"
"What is the best ...? Why?"

6 Questioning the question questions (if you see what I mean)

The sixth and final type of Socratic question is used in order to question the initial question. This involves pupils in understanding why the teacher asked the question he/she did and perhaps proposing alternative questions. For example, the teacher might ask:

"Why do you think that I asked that question?"
"Why was that question important?"
"Am I making sense? Why not?"
"What else might I ask?"
"What does that mean?"

Ideally, all six questions should be asked of the same pupil as a follow-up to the initial "big question". In other words, the teacher asks a question to which the pupil offers their initial response. Then the teacher drills down and interrogates the pupil's response by asking the six Socratic questions in order. While one pupil is being interrogated, the rest of the class should observe and, at the end, offer comments or be questioned themselves.

However, this isn't always feasible or desirable and so the six Socratic questions can instead be asked of six or more different pupils or be used to frame every pupil's written response. In fact, the six Socratic questions can act as extremely useful writing prompts to ensure pupils' essays are balanced, detailed and considered.

Socratic seminars

Socratic questions can also be used to help pupils respond to a text. This technique is often referred to as a Socratic seminar. The purpose of a Socratic seminar is to achieve a deeper understanding about the ideas and values contained in a text.

In the seminar, pupils systematically question and examine the issues and principles related to a particular text, and then articulate different points of view. The class discussion helps pupils to construct meaning through a process of disciplined analysis, interpretation, listening, and active participation.

In a Socratic seminar, pupils carry the burden of responsibility for the quality of the discussion. Good discussions occur when pupils have studied the text closely in advance, and then – during the seminar – listen actively, share their ideas and questions in response to the ideas and questions of others, and search for evidence in the text to support their ideas. A seminar discussion is not about right answers; it is not a debate. Instead, pupils should be encouraged to think aloud and to exchange ideas openly while examining each other's ideas in a rigorous, thoughtful, manner.

There are three basic elements to a Socratic seminar: Text; classroom environment; and questions. Let's explore each in turn...

1. Text

The text (which may be a book, an article, a short video or audio clip, or an object or artefact) should contain important and powerful ideas and values relevant to the topic being taught. The text should be pitched at the appropriate level for pupils in the class in terms of its language and the complexity of its argument, and it should relate directly to the core concepts of the content being studied.

It is beneficial if there is a certain degree of ambiguity in the text and, therefore, the potential for different interpretations because this makes for richer discussions. It helps if all pupils have read the text in advance.

2. Classroom environment

Ideally, the classroom should be arranged so that pupils can look at each other directly, as this promotes discussion and enables pupils to display and respond to active listening cues such as body language.

An agreed set of discussion "norms" or classroom rules should be displayed. More on this in a moment.

3. Questions

It is best for the teacher to prepare several questions in advance, in addition to the questions which pupils may bring to class having read the text.

The questions should be open-ended and reflect a genuine curiosity. There should be no right answer.

At the end, it is useful to debrief pupils and encourage them to reflect on how successful they feel the seminar has been.

Here are some sample questions which could serve as the key question or which could help pupils to interpret the text:

- What is the main idea/underlying value in the text?
- What is the author's purpose or perspective?
- What does (a particular phrase) mean?
- What might be a good title for the text?
- What is the most important word/sentence/paragraph?

Here are some sample questions which could help move the discussion along:

- Who has a different perspective?
- Who has not yet had a chance to speak?
- Where do you find evidence for that in the text?
- Can you clarify what you mean by that?
- How does that relate to what (someone else) said?

- Is there something in the text that is unclear to you?
- Has anyone changed their mind?

Here are some sample questions which could help bring the discussion to a logical conclusion:

- How do the ideas in the text relate to our lives?
- What do they mean for us personally?
- Why is this material important?
- Is it right that...?
- Do you agree with the author?

And here are some sample questions for the final debriefing:

- Do you feel like you understand the text at a deeper level?
- How was the process for us?
- Did we adhere to our norms?
- Did you achieve your goals to participate?
- What was one thing you noticed about the seminar?

A thinking classroom

Finally, in order to develop dialogic questioning, teachers need to establish clear rules and boundaries, and model good thinking, learning, and speaking and listening strategies. It is also important to establish a positive learning environment which fosters pupils' confidence and encourages all pupils to participate fully, promoting both tolerance and respect for each other's views.

A set of classroom rules might look something like this:

- Respect each other's ideas, views and opinions: One voice at a time; say what you think; say why you think it.
- Listen and reflect on what others say.
- Build on what others say.
- Support and include each other.
- Confidentially share partial ideas.
- Ask when you don't understand.

- Try to reach an agreement.
- Seek clarity from each other.
- Speak calmly – be noise aware.

And a "thinking classroom" might be built on the following foundations:

- Follow the classroom rules.
- Listen to others, add or build on their ideas.
- Never put others down or intimidate them.
- During thinking time, actively consider all ideas and ask new questions.
- Test ideas and subject them to scrutiny or challenge.
- Respect the views and ideas of others.
- Weigh the value of different viewpoints and evidence.

In the Uncommon Schools network in the US, teachers use a mnemonic to quickly remind pupils what's expected of them and how to behave during classroom discussions and debate. For example, STAR stands for: Sit up. Tracker the speaker. Ask and answer questions. Respect those around you. Whereas SLANT stands for: Sit up. Listen. Ask and answer questions. Nod your head. Track the speaker.

It might also be helpful to provide pupils with some of the language they require in order engage in polite and professional discourse. Diplomacy, after all, is a taught skill.

Here, by way of conclusion, are some examples of thought or sentence stems which could be shared and explained, discussed and agreed, then perhaps displayed on the wall as a constant reminder of how to debate:

Example statements to develop independence:

- I acknowledge your views but have a slightly different point, which is...
- I am starting to think that...
- My studies suggest that...

- That's a good idea but I think we could...

Example statements to show respect for others:

- Like others, I think that...
- That's a good point, I agree with it and I think that...
- I want to build on that point by...

Example statements to develop a high confidence environment:

- My initial thoughts are...
- I am starting to think that...
- I'm not sure if others would agree but...
- Just a thought, but it could be that...

Example statements to encourage collaboration:

- In our discussions we were thinking that...
- Between us we thought that...
- Overall, we concluded that...
- Building on what was said earlier, we...

CHAPTER THIRTY-THREE:
COGNITIVE LOAD

Cognitive load is the amount of mental effort it takes to do a task. As I explained earlier, there are three sources of cognitive load for every task:

1. Intrinsic load - the amount of mental activity involved in performing the task. For instance, in working out a maths problem you must do several mathematical procedures. This effort is intrinsic to the task itself.

2. Germane load - the amount of mental effort involved in deep learning and trying to understand the task or material. For instance, if I read an unfamiliar text, much of my effort would be focused on trying to make sense out of it.

3. Extraneous load - the amount of mental effort required to process and understand the immediate environment, especially the instructional context. Disorganised instruction, for example, contributes extraneous load to a task.

Every kind of learning involves a combination of these three sources of mental effort. Our capacity - and indeed our pupils' capacity - to process information is, as we have already seen, limited. People can manipulate only a few pieces of information at any one time.

Pupils are often asked to take in large amounts of new information that exceed their processing capacity, resulting in cognitive overload which, in turn, causes learning to fail. However, we can improve our pupils' capacity for learning by managing and reducing the cognitive load required in our lessons.

1. Build on pupils' prior knowledge

It is easier for pupils to make sense of new information when it is clearly related to what they already know (prior knowledge). Large amounts of unfamiliar material automatically increase cognitive load.

2. Segment material

By segmenting the subject matter, you help pupils process shorter or smaller chunks of material. You can do this by using pauses to note breaking points between topics [which also gives pupils a chance to catch up], by making explicit the transitions from one topic to another, and by making explicit references to how ideas and topics are related to one another.

3. Increase coherence and eliminate irrelevant material

Well-organised information is better understood and remembered. Pupils may not be able to impose coherence on disorganised information.

Irrelevant material also poses problems for pupils because they don't always know that it is irrelevant or tangential and so devote mental effort to trying to connect it to the topic at hand.

You should try to reduce extraneous material or move it into a designated part of the lesson where pupils understand that it is not critical.

4. Develop automated routines and knowledge

It is not possible to increase your working memory capacity, but it is possible to reduce the cognitive load of some tasks by automating them. In other words, there are always some procedures and concepts that will be used repeatedly in a class. Pupils will benefit by 'over-learning' these until they become automated. An automated routine is a procedure that you can perform with almost no mental effort, e.g., your times tables.

5. Scaffold complex tasks, processes and procedures

Scaffolding involves providing support that simplifies complex tasks. Stabilisers (or training wheels) scaffold the complex task of learning to ride a bicycle. They provide support, so the novice can learn to pedal, steer and brake without also concentrating on maintaining their balance. Once these aspects of cycling become familiar, there is more space in working memory to concentrate on balance and the training wheels can come off.

Using a worked example involves scaffolding in which the entire solution is available, so the pupil can explore different aspects of the problem without holding all the parts in working memory.

Here are some other tips for reducing pupils' cognitive load...

If there is a particularly difficult topic or assignment, try doing a cognitive task analysis in order to identify the background knowledge, intellectual skills, procedures and decisions that pupils will need in order to successfully grasp the topic or complete the assignment. You may discover hidden complexities that overload pupils. The analysis may also help you identify ways to scaffold the topic, break it up into its component parts, and find appropriate sequences for pupils to learn the topic.

We are the experts in the room and our pupils arc the novices. The gap between us is significant. Sometimes it is hard for experts to remember what it was like not to know their subject. Much of what experts know becomes tacit understanding that is invisible to pupils. To appreciate the complexity of the subject and the assignments we set, we should step into the novice's shoes and feel what it's like not to have extensive background knowledge or experience with our disciplinary thinking, conventions and expertise. Viewing our chosen field from a novice's perspective can help us to identify and better understand why some concepts, assumptions, and procedures prove particularly challenging for our pupils.

Lesson organisation

We could paint the big picture of learning for pupils, connecting each lesson with its predecessor and successor. We could also be explicit about how the lesson will be structured, providing an outline which we return to at key transitions throughout the lesson. We could also use a chronology that makes logical sense and, when using supporting materials such as presentation slides, we could ensure we only conveyed one message per slide, which was summarised in the title. We could try to make sure the slides made sense on their own as much as possible. We could also explicitly link new material to prior learning and make clear delineations and transitions between topics. We could organise topics into chunks with breaks in direct instruction for problem-solving activities and group work which are designed to apply or solidify the information that's just been presented.

Slides and visuals

Slides should be visually clean and concise with simple fonts and uncluttered backgrounds. It may help to use a high contrast between fonts and backgrounds. We could use bullet points with short phrases rather than complete sentences and avoid large blocks of text. We could also try to avoid figures and pictures that are purely for visual appearances - everything should be directly relevant to ideas we are trying to convey. We could include titles and labels for all the figures and diagrams we use and highlight any important takeaway messages. We could emphasise any important points by using bold or italicised text, a large font, and/or colours. We could avoid distracting animations that are irrelevant. And we could use a blank slide when we are talking to the class so that our pupils' attention is not split between verbal input and unrelated visual input.

Classroom atmosphere and pace

We could ensure we display slides long enough for pupils to absorb and/or record the information. In so doing, we should remember that it takes much longer to process information when seeing it for the first time. We could solicit ongoing feedback from pupils on our pacing. If we expect pupils to take notes whilst we're talking or showing slides, we could provide a skeleton framework for note taking such as a graphic organiser. We could try reducing potential distractions in the classroom by ensuring the temperature, noise, and light are suitable, too.

In Chapter Sixty-Two we will return to cognitive load and explore the importance of classroom consistency in order to lighten the load on our pupils' working memories and in Chapter Sixty-Three we will explore some practical ways of doing so by 'teaching by algorithm'.

But, for now, this brings us to the end of the second leg of the journey. So far, we have examined how to create a positive learning environment in order to stimulate sensory memory, and how to make pupils think hard but efficiently in order to gain the attention of - but cheat - working memory.

In the third and final part of our 3-step process of teaching for long-term learning, we will explore ways of planning for deliberate practice in order to improve storage in, and retrieval from, long-term memory. But before we embark on the third leg of this journey, let us summarise Step 2...

CHAPTER THIRTY-FOUR:
SUMMARY OF STEP 2

Before we move on to the final step of our 3-stage process of teaching for long-term learning, let's once again take stock...

The process of learning is the interaction between our sensory memory and our long-term memory. Our sensory memory is made up of: what we see - this is called our iconic memory; what we hear - this is called our echoic memory; and what we touch - our haptic memory. Our long-term memory is where new information is stored and from which it can be recalled when needed, but we cannot directly access the information stored in our long-term memory - instead, this interaction between our sensory memory and our long-term memory occurs in the working memory.

In order to ensure our pupils learn, therefore, we need to stimulate their sensory memory, gain the attention of - and help them cheat - their working memory, and improve the strength with which information is stored in, and the ease and efficiency with which it can later be retrieved from, their long-term memory. In order to do this, we need to follow these three steps:

First, we need to stimulate pupils' senses in order to gain the active attention of their working memories.

Second, we need to make pupils think hard but efficiently about the curriculum content to be learned.

And third, we need to plan opportunities for pupils to engage in deliberate practice in order to ensure prior knowledge remains accessible.

In order to make pupils think hard but efficiently so that we gain the attention of their working memories, we need to:

1. Pitch work in pupils' 'struggle zones'

Work that is pitched in the 'struggle zone' is work that is challenging but achievable with time, effort and support; work that is just beyond pupils' current capabilities but within their reach. If the work is too easy, pupils will complete it out of habit, that is to say with near automaticity - without thinking about it and therefore without learning. If the work is too difficult, pupils will do one of two things: either they will not even attempt it (judging it to be a fruitless task); or else they will attempt it but quickly overload their working memory and fail to complete the task. Either way, learning - or the deliberate practice of prior learning - will not occur and pupils will become demotivated.

Knowing where pupils' struggle zones are located involves lots of data in the widest sense of the word - knowing what pupils can do and cannot yet do (perhaps through frequent, formative assessments such as quizzes and the use of hinge questions), knowing how pupils like to learn and what motivates them, and knowing what barriers to learning - including misconceptions - pupils are likely to face.

2. Plan for desirable difficulties

Position roadblocks along pupils' learning journeys to slow down their initial encoding of new information in order to improve the subsequent storage strength of that information, and the ease and efficiency with which that information can later be retrieved from long-term memory.

Spaced and interleaved practice are forms of desirable difficulty, but so too is using more complex language and a hard-to-decipher font in written materials. Whatever roadblock is used, it is important to remember that learning should not be easy or indeed pleasurable - rather, it should involve over-learning, spiralling up and down the knowledge continuum, grappling with challenging tasks.

3. Provide high levels of challenge for every pupil but reduce the threat level

Have high expectations of every pupil in the class - ensuring there is no hiding place and no dumbing down of materials or outcomes. But encourage pupils to accept the challenge by creating a culture in which the threat level is reduced or removed. This means fostering an ethos - through your words and actions and through the way you manage pupils' interactions - in which no pupil feels humiliated if they fall short of a difficult task and every pupil knows that they will learn from the experience of making mistakes and will perform better next time.

4. Teach the knowledge and skills the top-performing pupil in the class will be able to master with the benefit of time, effort and support

In other words, don't pitch class work to the middle of the bell curve, teaching the 'average' pupil then scaffolding the lower performing pupils and stretching the higher-performing. Instead, teach the knowledge and skills that the top-performing pupil in the class will be able to master with time, effort and support. Teaching to the top also means modelling high expectations of all pupils, no matter their starting points and backgrounds.

Teaching to the top could take the form of mastery learning whereby every pupil in the class is taught the same content and is expected to achieve the same outcomes, albeit acknowledging that some pupils will take longer than others to achieve those outcomes and will need more support along the way. In other words, mastery learning is not about dumbing down, placing a glass ceiling on what some pupils can achieve. Mastery learning - first proposed by Benjamin Bloom in 1968 - insists that every pupil achieves a certain level of mastery (say, 80% in a test) before moving on to the next thing. If a pupil does not achieve 80%, they are given extra support and more time before being tested again.

Mastery learning is about focusing on the amount of time and support different pupils get in order to achieve the same learning goals, rather than focusing on differences in ability and lowering the intended outcomes for some. In a mastery learning classroom, all pupils achieve the same level of learning eventually and any failure is attributed to failures of instruction and insufficient time, not to pupils' abilities.

5. Make effective use of teacher explanations

The most effective way of making pupils think hard - and the best way of ensuring pupils focus their attention on the right things - is for the expert teacher to provide direct instruction of new knowledge and skills.

Direct instruction works best when: the teacher presents new information in small chunks; the teacher thinks aloud to make what they do implicitly explicit, to make the invisible visible; the teacher makes use of metaphors and analogies to contextualise new information, making abstract and alien concepts more concrete, tangible and relatable; the teacher makes use of dual coding - combining verbal instructions with visuals such as charts and graphics; and, once explanations have been given, the teacher affords pupils plenty of opportunity to practice and then provides systematic corrections and feedback guiding pupils' practice and providing cues when required.

6. Make effective use of teacher modelling

Once the teacher has introduced new curriculum content, they need to model excellence. In other words, they need to tell then show pupils what's expected. Good models demonstrate what works as well as what doesn't; good models provide pupils with a picture of the final product, an example of excellence, something to aim for and achieve, but they also provide examples of work that is not quite so good in order that pupils know what mistakes to avoid. Models should be deconstructed by the teacher in order to analyse their components - the individual pieces of the jigsaw that go to make up the whole picture. Then the models should be reconstructed to see how the product works as a whole.

7. Promote classroom talk

We need to provide plentiful opportunities for pupils to engage in classroom talk - including whole-class questioning - in order to make them think hard and deepen their understanding of key concepts. Speaking and thinking are intricately linked because the process of speaking helps pupils to learn by articulating their thoughts and developing the concepts they use in order to better understand the world. Speaking and listening also level the playing field because most pupils are better able to articulate their thinking verbally than in writing, particularly in the early stages of their education. In short, classroom discussion is the best means of engaging all pupils and the best way of developing their knowledge and understanding.

The teaching of oracy skills should come first, followed by reading then writing, because - in order to develop pupils' language capability and support their reading and writing - there first needs to be purposeful speaking and listening activities which provide a foundation for thinking and communication. For speaking and listening to be effective in making pupils think hard, there needs to be an agreed set of rules for classroom talk, speaking and listening skills must be explicitly taught, and the teacher needs to model good speaking and listening strategies at all times.

8. Use closed questioning as a form of assessment

There are two reasons for asking a question in class: either to provide information to the teacher about what to do next, or to cause pupils to think.

Using closed questions - such as multiple choice or hinge questions - as a form of assessment provides valuable information to the teacher about pupils' learning and progress, about who has 'got it' and who has not, and about what needs reteaching, recapping or developing further. What's more, closed questions used as a form of assessment reduce the marking load on teachers and make assessment 'live' and responsive. Further, closed questions used as a form of assessment turn assessment into a means of learning, they are assessment as learning rather than assessment for learning.

9. Use open questions to deepen pupils' understanding

Using open questions to deepen pupils' understanding involves engaging in a form of dialogic teaching, which is to say asking big, philosophical questions which challenge pupils' thinking and encourage discussion. Dialogic questions – such as Socratic questions – don't just cause thinking, they promote critical thinking, too.

Teaching through the use of dialogic questions is: collective because teachers and pupils address learning tasks together, whether as a group or as a whole class; reciprocal because teachers and pupils listen to each other, share ideas and consider alternative points of view; supportive because pupils articulate their ideas without the fear of failure and help each other to reach a common understanding; cumulative because teachers and pupils build on their own and each other's ideas and connect them into coherent lines of thinking and enquiry; and purposeful because teachers plan and steer classroom talk with specific educational goals in view.

Socratic questioning can be used to: Control a discussion; explore more complex ideas; uncover assumptions; analyse concepts and ideas; and distinguish between what pupils know and do not know.

10. Organise learning materials to support cognitive load

For example, we could make sure each slide of a PowerPoint presentation conveys just one message which is summarised in the title. We could ensure slides and other visuals are clean and concise with simple backgrounds, the avoidance of large blocks of text and pictures or animations which are there purely for presentational purposes. We could highlight important 'take-away' information, emphasising key points via coloured, bold or large fonts. And we could make sure we display information for long enough for pupils to absorb it and reduce potential distractions around the information.

STEP THREE:

EMBED DELIBERATE PRACTICE TO IMPROVE PUPILS' STORAGE IN AND RETRIEVAL FROM LONG-TERM MEMORY

CHAPTER THIRTY-FIVE:
DELIBERATE PRACTICE

This section of the book is all about practicing what has gone before. In other words, once we have successfully stimulated our pupils' sensory memories in order to gain the attention of their working memories, and once we have helped pupils to think hard but efficiently about curriculum content in order to encode new information into their long-term memories, all the hard work has been done.

However, do not be fooled into thinking this also means 'job done'...

Encoding new information into long-term memory may be synonymous with 'learning' but it is most certainly not the end of the learning *process* because, without the provision of deliberate practice, all this new information pupils have encoded could be lost or at least hidden beyond reach. And if pupils can't get ready access to what they've just learnt, can we truly claim to have taught them and can they truly claim to have learnt, at least in any meaningful, useful sense?

Remember what I said earlier about my childhood telephone number: I successfully encoded it in long-term memory but cannot access it without help. It's in there somewhere but I can't find it and so, if tested on it, I would fail. The same is true of the curriculum content we teach our pupils - they may well encode it but if we do not help them to retrieve it whenever it's needed - such as in a test - then all our - and their - hard work will have been for naught.

This is why we should teach less so that our pupils can learn more. In other words, we should try to cover less curriculum content but do so in a deeper way - ensuring we build into our lesson planning routines plenty of opportunities to repeat and reinforce prior learning, and indeed to connect prior learning to myriad new contexts. Learning is iterative; we cannot carve a straight path through the curriculum; we must meander and retrace our footsteps over and again like the New Year's Eve reveller in search of the house keys he lost in the snow on the way to a party. (Yes, dear reader, that reveller was me).

It might help to think of the curriculum as being a 'T' shape where the '–' is the breadth and the '|' is the depth. We need to strike a balance between the two so that we cover sufficient curriculum content to prepare our pupils for the next stage – including for formal assessments – and yet cover that content in sufficient depth so as to make the content meaningful, useful and useable. Depth, in part, requires there to be connections between what we are learning today and what we learnt yesterday, between related topics and within and across subject disciplines where relevant.

Put another way, we want to spin a spider's web in pupils' long-term memories that binds all their prior learning together in ever more complex and ever-expanding patterns. Engaging in retrieval practice activities will enable us to do this because we will pull from long-term memory what pupils learnt previously and connect it to what they are learning now.

What is deliberate practice?

Deliberate practice is about repeating prior learning but doing so in certain targeted ways so that each time we return to something we've already taught; we require our pupils to engage with the material in a way that makes it challenging to them. This is why we should space out practice sessions, leaving increasingly long gaps before returning to material. By waiting until pupils get to the point of almost forgetting something, we make the process of recall hard and, as such, pupils must think. Spaced practice, therefore, is about emulating the conditions in which material was learnt initially - ensuring pupils think hard but efficiently about work that is beyond their current capabilities but within their reach.

Interleaved practice, meanwhile, is about mixing up study topics so that pupils can revise prior learning but in new ways so that they make new connections and thus strengthen the storage of information in long-term memory. Interleaving also enables pupils to see the connections that exist between different study topics and to place prior learning within the context of new learning.

As you know by now, in order to ensure our pupils learn we need to stimulate their sensory memory, gain the attention of - and help them cheat - their working memory, and improve the strength with which information is stored in, and the ease and efficiency with which it can later be retrieved from, their long-term memory. In order to do this, we need to create a positive learning environment, make pupils think hard but efficiently, and plan for deliberate practice.

So, why is deliberate practice so integral to the learning process and what form should this practice take...?

To answer these questions, we need to understand how our brains work...

Our brains are like the back of an electrician's van: a tangle of coloured wires – about 100 billion to be imprecise. These wires are called neurones and they are connected to each other by synapses. Whenever we do something – think, move, read this book – our brain sends a signal down these neurones to our muscles.

In other words, every skill we possess – swinging a golf club, writing great fiction, playing the piano – is created by chains of nerve fibres carrying small electrical impulses like the signals travelling through a circuit.

Each time we practise something, a different highly specific circuit is illuminated in our heads like fairy lights strung round a Christmas tree. It is these circuits, not our muscles, that control our thoughts and movements. Indeed, the circuit is the movement because it dictates the content of each thought and the timing and strength of each muscle contraction.

More importantly, each time we practise something – be it a mental or physical skill – our nerve fibres are coated in a layer of insulation called myelin which acts in much the same way as the rubber insulation that coats a copper wire or the yellow foam in your loft: it makes the electrical impulses stronger and faster by preventing the signals from leaking.

Each time we practise a skill, a new layer of myelin is added to the neurone like the lagging on a boiler. The thicker the myelin gets, the better it insulates our nerve fibres and, therefore, the faster our movements and thoughts become.

But that's not all. As well as getting faster, our thoughts and movements also become more accurate as we add more and more layers of myelin. Why? Because myelin regulates the velocity with which those electrical impulses travel through our nerve fibres, speeding up or slowing down the signals so that they hit our synapses at exactly the right moment. And timing is all important because neurones are binary: either they fire or they don't. Whether or not they fire is dependent on whether the incoming impulse is big enough to exceed their so-called "threshold of activation".

Imagine, for example, a skill circuit where two neurones must combine – doubling their impulses – to make a third high-threshold neurone fire, for example, to serve an ace in a game of tennis. To combine their forces effectively, the two incoming impulses must arrive at almost exactly the same time (and by "almost", I mean within about four milliseconds of each other). If the first two signals arrive more than four milliseconds apart, the third neurone won't fire, and the tennis ball will be called out.

Left to their own devices, because our brain has so many connections, our genes are unable to code our neurones to time things as accurately as this. That's why we coat our nerve fibres with layers of insulation called myelin to help us achieve such precision.

If you are feeling somewhat dubious that myelin can hold the key to developing every imaginable human skill – from playing sports to playing Schubert – then remember this: everything on Earth is made from the same stuff – atoms. We may not closely resemble a fish or a tree, but we are all made from the same material and share the same cellular mechanism to convert food into energy.

Myelin is also universal: everyone can grow it, most swiftly during childhood but also throughout life. And it is indiscriminate: its growth enables the development of all manner of skills, both mental and physical.

In short, although skills vary in every which way – learning to play tennis is as different from learning to sing as learning to sing is from learning to write poetry – they all, without exception, rely on us growing more layers of myelin around our neurones which, in turn, relies on us practising over and over and over again.

Every skill is improved and perfected by performing it repeatedly because this helps us improve by honing our neural circuitry. And yet not all forms of practice are equal. We create myelin most effectively when we engage in deliberate practice, which is sometimes called deep practice.

In Chapter Thirty-Six, we will explore what deliberate - or deep - practice looks like in, well, practice...

CHAPTER THIRTY-SIX:
DEEP PRACTICE

To recap: Once we've taught something for the first time and that information has been encoded into pupils' long-term memories, we need to plan opportunities for pupils to repeat that learning over and over. The more pupils repeat their prior learning, the stronger the storage of that information becomes and the more efficient they become at retrieving that information from long-term memory and returning it to their working memory in order to use it.

Every piece of knowledge and every skill is improved and perfected by performing it repeatedly because repetition hones neural circuitry. And yet not all forms of practice are equal... we best improve storage and retrieval strength when we engage in deliberate practice, which is to say that every time we repeat prior learning we must make sure that practice is targeted and mistake-focused - in other words, that it responds to feedback and seeks to close the gaps in pupils' knowledge.

Slowing learning down and ensuring pupils struggle helps to pitch learning in the 'sweet spot' between what pupils can do and what pupils are trying to do.

In short, pupils need to: practice, attend to mistakes, and practice some more because, although re-studying information when it is fresh in your mind feels good because it feels familiar, it is misleading. The reason it feels familiar might simply be down to its recency, not a reflection of how well it has been learnt. The best time to re-study something is after you have forgotten it, when it is no longer familiar.

Deliberate or deep practice, then, is about struggling in certain targeted ways – placing artificial barriers in the way of our success in order to make it harder to learn something. In other words, you slow your learning down and force yourself to make mistakes.

This is what Robert Bjork calls 'desirable difficulties'. By slowing down and making mistakes – by creating desirable difficulties – we ensure that we are operating at the edges of our ability. So, the best form of practice – and therefore the best way to create more myelin – is to set yourself a target just beyond your current ability but within your reach.

This is where Vygotsky and his 'zone of proximal development' comes in handy…

My loose interpretation of Vygotsky is this: we should perform tasks that are challenging but attainable. If the task is beyond our present ability, then we will give up easily and learn nothing; if the task is too easy we will perform it out of habit without trying and will again learn nothing.

But if the task is hard yet just within our grasp, then we will learn. And because we struggle but overcome the challenge, our brains are rewarded with a dose of the naturally occurring chemical dopamine which makes us feel good and – though there is some debate about this – might just motivate us to keep on learning.

In The Talent Code, Daniel Coyle provides a useful example of deep practice. He presents two lists of word pairs as follows:

List 1:
ocean/breeze
leaf/tree
sweet/sour
movie/actress
gasoline/engine
school/college
turkey/stuffing
fruit/vegetable
computer/chip
chair/couch

List 2:
bread/b_tter
music/l_rics
sh_e/sock
phone/bo_k
chi_s/salsa
pen_il/paper
river/b_at
be_r/wine
television/rad_o
l_nch/dinner

If we are given the first list to memorise in, say, a minute, on average we are likely to remember seven of the pairs.

But if we are given the second list, we are likely to remember more than seven pairs because we have placed an artificial barrier in the way of our learning.

Because we must fill in the missing letters, although this may take but a microsecond, we have to stop and stumble until we work it out. That microsecond, Coyle argues, makes all the difference – in that moment, we don't practise any harder, but we do practise deeper. We slow down and locate what Robert Bjork calls "the sweet spot".

This spot is the "optimal gap between what [we] know and what [we're] trying to do" and "when [we] find that sweet spot, learning takes off".

Let's return to the subject of the previous chapter: myelin, our magic insulation...

The idea behind 'desirable difficulties' is that targeted, mistake-focused practice is the most effective means of developing skills.

And it is quite so effective because the best way to build a fast and accurate neural circuit is – to quote Coyle – "to fire it, attend to mistakes, then fire it again, over and over". Why? Because "struggle is not an option, it's a biological requirement".

The second key ingredient to skills development – after deep practice – is passion. You see, to be passionate about developing a skill is crucial because without passion you don't have the determination, or the persistence needed in order to dedicate the vast amounts of time and energy that are required of you to practice deeply. If you are not passionate, you don't work hard enough and therefore you don't create myelin.

In summary, and to quote Daniel Coyle again, practice does not make perfect, instead "practice makes myelin, and myelin makes perfect". And, as we have seen, myelin operates by a few fundamental principles...

First, myelin is not built to respond to fond wishes or vague ideas; it is built to respond to actions – the electrical impulses travelling down nerve fibres. It responds to urgent repetition.

Second, myelin is universal in that it works on all skills. Regardless of its use, it grows according to the same rules.

Third, myelin wraps but it doesn't unwrap. Once a skill circuit is insulated, it can't be uninsulated except through age or disease.

Finally, although we retain the ability to create myelin all our lives, age has an effect. As children, myelin arrives in a series of waves, some of them determined by genes, some dependent on activity.

These waves last into our 30s, creating critical periods during which time the brain is extraordinarily receptive to learning new skills. We continue to experience a net gain of myelin until the age of 50 but at that point the balance tips toward a net loss.

The next time you venture into the loft, take a moment to admire the effects of insulation. When put to use in your house, it traps heat in and saves you money on your energy bill. When put to use in your brain, it traps electrical impulses and makes you perform every human skill faster and more accurately. And the insulation in your brain, unlike that in your loft, is free – you can make as much of it as you want so long as you're willing to practice and practice.

We can't move on without mentioning Anders Ericsson...

Anders Ericsson is the foremost expert on deliberate practice. In his book, Peak, he offers the following advice:

1. Deliberate practice needs to push pupils to the edge of their comfort zone and often just beyond it. However, deliberate practice is - Ericsson argues - hard to sustain.

2. The goal of a practice session must be very specific and concrete, and improvement is fastest when pupils focus on one small, defined aspect of the skill at a time. "We're working on..." is insufficient if you want to improve. "We're improving the accuracy of our passing when advancing up the field" is therefore better. And even this more specific goal would get

subdivided during a PE lesson on football. First, we'd work on the accuracy of passes, and then perhaps focus on ensuring that they were driven fast but on the pitch to expedite the speed of attack.

Deliberate practice, Ericsson says, requires locked-in, full mental engagement. Crucially, deliberate practice also requires feedback, and a culture of response to the feedback.

And finally, Ericsson argues that success starts with "mental representations". In other words, the first step towards improving is perception and one of the things practice should do is present pupils with constant iterations of important scenarios so they learn to read them quickly, intuitively, instinctively.

CHAPTER THIRTY-SEVEN:
SPACED PRACTICE

There are two forms of deliberate practice that are proven to be particularly effective: spaced practice and interleaved practice. We will consider spaced practice in this chapter and interleaved practice in Chapter Thirty-Eight.

Spaced practice is also called distributed practice and it is a straightforward and easy-to-use technique...

Consider the following examples:

A Year 7 pupil studies for a spelling test. Using a worksheet to guide her practice, she might take one of two approaches. She could practice spelling the words by writing each one several times directly below the word printed on the sheet. After practicing one word repeatedly, she would move on to the next one and practice writing that word several times below it. This kind of practice is called massed practice, because the pupil practices each word multiple times together, before moving to the next one.

An alternative strategy for the pupil would be to practice writing each word only once, and after transcribing the final word, going back and writing each one again, and so forth, until the practice is complete. This kind of practice is called distributed practice, because practice with any one word is distributed across time (and the time between practicing any one word is filled with another activity—in this case, writing other words).

In this example, the pupil either masses or distributes her practices during a single session.

Now, imagine a Year 11 pupil trying to learn some basic concepts for an upcoming exam. He might read over his notes diligently, in a single session the night before the exam, until he thinks he is ready for the test - a study tactic called cramming, which practically all pupils use.

Or, as an alternative, he might study his notes and texts during a shorter session several evenings before the exam and then study them again the evening before. In this case, the pupil distributes his studying across two sessions.

Pupils will retain knowledge and skills for a longer period when they distribute their practice than when they mass it, even if they use the same amount of time massing and distributing their practice.

Unfortunately, however, many pupils believe that massed practice is better than distributed practice...

One reason for this misconception is that pupils become familiar and facile with the target material quickly during a massed practice session, but learning appears to proceed more slowly with distributed practice.

For instance, the Year 7 pupil quickly writes the correct word after practicing it several times in succession, but when the same practice is distributed, she may still struggle after several attempts. Likewise, the Year 11 pupil may quickly become familiar with his notes after reading them twice during a single session, but when distributing his practice across two study sessions, he may realise how much he has forgotten and use extra time getting back up to speed.

In both cases, learning itself feels tougher when it is distributed instead of massed, but the competency and learning that pupils may feel (and teachers may see) during massed practice is often ephemeral. By contrast, distributed practice may take more effort, but it is essential for obtaining knowledge in a manner that will be maintained (or easily relearned) over longer, educationally relevant periods of time.

Most pupils, whether they realise it or not, use distributed practice to master many different activities, but not when they are studying...

For instance, when preparing for a music recital, most pupil violinists will practice a piece nightly until they have mastered it; they will not just do all the practice the night before the recital, because everyone knows that this kind of practice will likely not be successful.

Similarly, when playing computer games, pupils see their abilities and skills improve dramatically over time in large part because they keep coming back to play the game in a distributed fashion.

In these and many other cases, pupils realise that more practice or play during a current session will not help much, and they may even see their performance weaken near the end of a session, so, of course, they take a break and return to the activity later. However, for whatever reason, pupils don't typically use distributed practice as they work toward mastering course content.

To distribute practice over time, pupils should set aside blocks of time throughout each week to study the content for each class. Each study block will be briefer than an all-night cram session, and it should involve studying (and using practice tests) for material that was recently introduced in class and for material they studied in previous sessions.

To use distributed practice successfully, teachers should focus on helping pupils map out how many study sessions they will need before an exam, when those sessions should take place (such as which evenings of the week), and what they should practice during each session. For any given class, two short study blocks per week may be enough to begin studying new material and to restudy previously covered material.

Ideally, pupils will use practice tests to study the previously covered material. If they do, they will quickly retrieve the previously learned material after just a handful of sessions, which will leave more time for studying new material.

Of course, pupils may need help setting up their study schedules (especially when they are younger), and they may need some encouragement to use the strategy. But by using distributed practice (especially if it is combined with practice testing), many pupils will begin to master material they never thought they could learn.

Teachers can also use distributed practice in the classroom. The idea is to return to the most important material and concepts repeatedly across several school days. For instance, if weekly quizzes are already being administered, a teacher could easily include content that repeats across quizzes, so pupils will relearn some concepts in a distributed manner.

Repeating key points across lectures not only highlights the importance of the content but also gives pupils distributed practice. Administering a cumulative exam that forces pupils to review the most important information is another way to encourage them to study content in a distributed fashion.

Now let's turn our attention to interleaved practice...

CHAPTER THIRTY-EIGHT:
INTERLEAVED PRACTICE

With interleaved practice, we focus on each aspect of a topic for a shorter period but return to it more often in-between studying other aspects of the same or related topic. This is the opposite of cramming, or blocked practice, and has been proven to be more effective in terms of long-term information-retention. As well as improving the storage and retrieval strength of information from each aspect of a topic, interleaving helps pupils to forge new connections between these aspects and therefore improve their ability to transfer their learning from one context to another. So, how does it work...?

Interleaved practice involves not only distributing practice across a study session but also mixing up the order of materials across different areas of related study. Distributed practice is better than massed practice, but the former typically refers to distributing the practice of the same problem across time. Thus, for spelling, a pupil would benefit from writing each word on a worksheet once, and then cycling through the words until each has been spelled correctly several times.

Interleaved practice is like distributed practice in that it involves spacing one's practice across time, but it specifically refers to practicing different types of problems across time.

Consider how a standard science or maths textbook encourages massed practice: In a text, pupils may learn about adding and subtracting real numbers, and then spend a block of practice adding real numbers, followed by a block of practice subtracting. The next chapter would introduce multiplying and dividing real numbers, and then practice would focus first on multiplying real numbers, and then on dividing them, and so forth.

Thus, pupils are massing their practice of similar problems. They practice several instances of one type of problem (e.g., addition) before practicing the next type (e.g., subtraction). In this example, interleaving would involve solving one problem from each type (adding, subtracting, multiplying, and dividing) before solving a new problem from each type.

One aspect of massed practice that pupils may find appealing is that their performance will quickly improve as they work with a particular problem. Unfortunately, such fluent performance can be misleading; pupils believe that they have learned a problem well when in fact their learning is fleeting.

Why does interleaving work so well? In contrast to massed practice, interleaving problems requires distributing practice, which by itself benefits pupil achievement. Moreover, massed practice robs pupils of the opportunity to practice identifying problems, whereas interleaved practice forces pupils to practice doing so.

When pupils use massed practice, after they correctly solve a problem or two of a certain type, they can almost robotically apply the same steps to the next problem. That is, they do not have to figure out what kind of problem they are solving; they just must apply the same rules to the next problem.

For interleaving, when a new problem is presented, pupils need to figure out which kind of problem it is first, and what steps they need to take to solve it. This is often a difficult aspect of solving problems.

Teachers often demonstrate how to do a few problems (whether writing compound sentences or adding fractions), and then ask pupils to complete a set of similar problems on their own. Pupils learn more, however, when they are given incremental guidance on problem solving.

Another type of interleaving is giving pupils problems to do which have worked-out solutions alternated with problems that the pupils must solve for themselves. Solved problems help pupils focus on the underlying principles that apply to each situation, instead of promoting the mechanical solution of problems. Here's how it works...

First, you interleave worked examples with problem-solving exercises. For example, you get pupils to alternate between reading already worked solutions and trying to solve problems on their own.

Second, as pupils begin to develop greater expertise, you reduce the number of worked examples you provide and increase the number of problems that pupils must solve independently.

Third, you offer explanations alongside solved problems to help pupils comprehend the underlying principles, thus taking them beyond the mechanics of problem solving.

CHAPTER THIRTY-NINE: MULTIPLE CONTEXTS

So far in this section of the book covering step 3 of our process of teaching for long-term learning – the step that deals with deliberate practice – we have discussed the importance of repetition as a means of developing layers of myelin around the neurones to improve our knowledge and skills. We have also talked about two forms of deliberate practice: spaced practice and interleaved practice. But that's not all. As well as spacing out practice sessions and mixing up study topics, we should re-teach information in a range of contexts and provide opportunities for our pupils to demonstrate their learning in different ways. Allow me to explain...

Each time we return to recap, re-teach or test pupils on their prior learning, we should do something different with the information, make new connections, and require pupils to present their learning using different methods and media.

Permit me to engage you in a short exercise to illustrate the effects of this teaching and learning strategy on the long-term memory...

Please close your eyes and think of a famous person. Bring an image of their face into your mind's eye.

Now think about a mode of transport. Again, picture this vehicle.

Now think about a famous location, perhaps a monument or building. Picture it.

Now put your famous person into your mode of transport.

Now put your famous person, still in your vehicle of choice, next to your famous location.

Hold that image.

Ok, here's what just happened...

Simply by dragging an image of a famous person out of your long-term memory and into your working memory where you could think about it, you improved the storage and retrieval strength of that image in your long-term memory. In other words, the next time you're asked to think about that particular person, you'll be able to do so more easily and efficiently. The same applies to the transport and location.

But, because you not only retrieved those three separate images but also connected them in new ways, you have further improved the storage and retrieval strength of all three. Put simply, when the images are encoded again – in other words, returned to long-term memory – they will be dusted off and stored within easier reach. But you'll also store two new images alongside the original three. Now you'll have an image of the famous person, an image of the mode of transport, and an image of the famous monument or building, plus you'll have a new image of the famous person in the vehicle, and yet another new image of the famous person in the vehicle next to the building.

By making new connections - and creating new images - you have increased the storage space each image takes up and have therefore made it easier to retrieve the images next time. And don't forget that long-term memory, unlike working memory, is limitless - you have plenty of room in there to keep forging new connections all your life without running out of space.

In the classroom, this means that every time you return to prior learning, you should get pupils to do different things with it, not just repeat it verbatim. For example, pupils could test themselves, test each other, devise quizzes, give presentations to the class, teach each other, write an essay, draw a diagram, create a knowledge organiser, and so on. Talking of which...

Before we move on and look at some study skills our pupils can use outside the classroom and independently of us, here are some more tips for planning opportunities for deliberate practice in your classroom...

A four-stage cognitive process

When planning for deliberate practice we need to be aware that deep learning is a complex cognitive process that, broadly speaking, occurs in four stages:

1. Attention,
2. Encoding,
3. Storage, and
4. Retrieval.

Let's look at each...

1. Attention

There are two main types of attention: goal-oriented and stimulus-oriented.

Goal-oriented attention is gained through motivation, curiosity, and other self-driven forces – in other words, we actively attend to something – and is retained through intent.

Stimulus-oriented attention is gained through the sensory stimuli that surround us – in other words, our response to sights and sounds – and is retained subconsciously, thus overriding our goal-oriented attention.

These goal-oriented and stimulus-oriented attention-grabbers operate at the same time and our ability to regulate them, i.e. to stay focused on our goal-directed attention and limit the influence of our stimulus-driven attention, is one of the keys to learning.

As such, it is important when engaging in deliberate practice that we tell our pupils why. Pupils often respond to the prospect of a practice session - or revision class - with the question, 'Why are we doing this again? We've already done this.' Therefore, in order to motivate our pupils to practice prior learning and pay attention to what we need them to think about, we need to share the cognitive science. So, tell them about this book. Tell them what you've learnt about how the brain works and about the importance of deliberate practice. Explaining the rationale behind your methods will help motivate pupils to practice and thus engage their goal-oriented attention.

In order to engage pupils' stimulus-oriented attention we need to return to Step 1 of our learning process and consider what we said about creating a positive learning environment that engages the iconic, echoic and haptic memories, and thus stimulates pupils' senses and gets them to focus on what we need them to think about and learn. When planning for deliberate practice, it is just as important as when first teaching something that we begin by asking, 'What do we need pupils to think about in this session?' and work backwards from there.

2. Encoding

When we are exposed to new information, we process it then attempt to connect it to existing information (in other words, we try to assimilate new knowledge with prior knowledge in an attempt to provide a context within which to make sense of it).

The richer – sensorily and emotionally – the new information is, and the deeper the existing information is engrained, the more strongly new information will be encoded in our long-term memories. We can infer from this that effective learning is the result of two things:

1. Multi-sensory and emotional experiences: The richer our sensory-emotional experience of new information, the more deeply we will encode it. For instance, if we are made to feel something, we are more likely to encode new information. We can take from this, therefore, the importance of letting pupils see and feel something for themselves, rather than just telling them. We can also take away the importance of making ideas concrete because this, in turn, makes them more credible.

2. Contextualised information (prior knowledge): When we have strong, vivid prior knowledge about a subject, we have easier access and greater insight into any new knowledge related to that subject that we acquire. In other words, when we have previous experience of something, we can encode new information about it more effectively and more richly. Let me explain...

According to Harvey and Goudvis (2000), schema theory is the notion that our previous experiences, knowledge, and emotions affect what and how we acquire new information. In the case of reading comprehension, for example, schema is the kind of background knowledge and experience we bring to a new text. Experienced readers draw on prior knowledge and experience to help them understand what they are reading, and then they use that knowledge to help them make new connections. Less experienced readers, however, often read through a text without stopping to consider whether the text makes any sense to them based on their own background knowledge, and do not consider whether their knowledge can be used to help them understand confusing or challenging ideas and words.

It follows, therefore, that teaching pupils how to connect new information to their prior knowledge will help them to better comprehend what they are studying. And this is an important part of deliberate practice sessions - when we return to previously taught curriculum content in order to recap or reteach it, we need to connect it to new contexts.

Keene and Zimmerman (1997) say that we should teach pupils to make three types of connections: how to connect new information to their own experiences, to other information they've studied, and to the wider world.

3. Storage

Memories fade away if they are neglected but can get stronger with repeated use. Making new associations with prior learning strengthens our memories because the number of connections we make influences the number of times memories are revisited, which in turn influences the length of time we retain a memory. When we connect different pieces of information with each other, we retain them for longer, because we retrieve them more often.

It follows that the more often we connect what we are teaching today to what we taught previously, the better the information will be learnt. Equally, the more we connect what we're teaching today to contextual information the better our pupils will learn.

4. Retrieval

We forget about half of the information that enters our working memories every hour, and two-thirds of the information we process disappears every day. But there are things we can do as teachers in our deliberate practice sessions to help our pupils retrieve important information more easily. One of those things, as I have already explained, is to plan learning in such a way as to allow purposeful practice, which is to say, the opposite of cramming. Rather than focusing on one topic for a long period of time and never returning to it again, purposeful practice focuses on each topic for a shorter period, but returns to it several times, with increasingly lengthy gaps and in-between studying other topics.

In practice, this means we should plan opportunities for our pupils not only to revise information they have previously learnt, but to reorganise that information by writing about it or talking about it.

Our pupils will forge new connections if they retrieve information from their long-term memories and re-encode it with new information.

CHAPTER FORTY:
QUIZZING

As I explained earlier, the use of practice tests or short, perhaps multiple-choice, quizzes can improve pupils' learning in both direct and indirect ways. Unlike simply re-reading study notes, when pupils are tested (or test themselves) and correctly retrieve an answer from their long-term memories, that memory is further improved. But practice tests also help when pupils fail to retrieve a correct answer. Such a failure signals that the answer needs to be revisited, re-studied perhaps. This helps pupils make decisions about what to dedicate most of their time practicing.

Practice tests should be regarded as a learning tool rather than an assessment tool and therefore be low-stakes (or indeed no stakes) in order to reduce anxiety. Practice tests should also be given frequently, perhaps weekly or even - on a small scale - at the start or end of every lesson. Questions should test pupils on a mixture of topics, modelling interleaving, and questions should be returned to at increasingly prolonged intervals, modelling spacing.

Of course, the problem with practice tests is the word 'test' - that term, like 'exam' and indeed 'quiz' are four-letter words that provoke anxiety in many pupils, if not some teachers. Such anxiety may not be misplaced, given the high stakes of exams. However, by viewing tests as the end-all assessments administered only after learning is complete, teachers and pupils are missing out on the benefits of one of the most effective strategies for improving pupil learning.

In 1909, a doctoral pupil at the University of Illinois demonstrated that practice tests improve pupil performance, and more than 100 years of research has revealed that taking practice tests (versus merely rereading the material to be learned) can substantially boost pupil learning.

As I say above, the use of practice tests can improve pupil learning in both direct and indirect ways. Consider two pupils who have just read a chapter in a textbook: Both pupils review the most important information in the chapter, but one pupil reads the information again, whereas the other pupil hides the answers and attempts to recall the information from memory. Compared with the first pupil, the second pupil, by testing himself, is boosting his long-term memory.

Thus, unlike simply reading a text, when pupils correctly retrieve an answer from memory, the correct retrieval can have a direct effect on memory.

Practice tests can also have an indirect effect on pupil learning. When a pupil fails to retrieve a correct answer during a practice test, that failure signals that the answer needs to be restudied; in this way, practice tests can help pupils make better decisions about what needs further practice and what does not. In fact, most pupils who use practice tests report that they do so to figure out what they know and do not know.

So how might pupils use practice tests to best harness the power of retrieval practice?

First, pupil learning can benefit from almost any kind of practice test, whether it involves completing a short essay where pupils need to retrieve content from memory or answering questions in a multiple-choice format. Research suggests, however, that pupils will benefit most from tests that require recall from memory, and not from tests that merely ask them to recognise the correct answer. They may need to work a bit harder to recall key materials (especially lengthy ones) from memory, but the pay-off will be great in the long run. Another benefit of encouraging pupils to recall key information from memory is that it does not require creating a bank of test questions to serve as practice tests.

Second, pupils should be encouraged to take notes in a manner that will foster practice tests. For instance, as they read a chapter in their textbook, they should be encouraged to make flashcards, with the key term on one side and the correct answer on the other. When taking notes in class, teachers should encourage pupils to leave room on each page (or on the back pages of notes) for practice tests. In both cases, as the material becomes more complex (and lengthy), teachers should encourage pupils to write down their answers when they are testing themselves. For instance, when they are studying concepts on flashcards, they should first write down the answer (or definition) of the concept they are studying, and then they should compare their written answer with the correct one. For notes, they can hide key ideas or concepts with their hand and then attempt to write them out in the remaining space; by using this strategy, they can compare their answer with the correct one and easily keep track of their progress.

Third, and perhaps most importantly, pupils should continue testing themselves, with feedback, until they correctly recall each concept at least once from memory. For flashcards, if they correctly recall an answer, they can pull the card from the stack; if they do not recall it correctly, they should place it at the back of the stack. For notes, they should try to recall all the important ideas and concepts from memory, and then go back through their notes once again and attempt to correctly recall anything they did not get right during their first pass. If pupils persist until they recall each idea or concept correctly, they will enhance their chances of remembering the concepts during the actual exam. They should also be encouraged to "get it right" on more than one occasion, such as by returning to the deck of cards on another day and relearning the materials.

Using practice tests may not come naturally to pupils, so teachers can play an important role in informing them about the power of practice tests and how they apply to the content being taught in class. Not only can pupils benefit from using practice tests when studying alone, but teachers can give practice tests in the classroom. The idea is for teachers to choose the most important ideas and then take a couple of minutes at the beginning or end of each class to test pupils. After all pupils answer a question, teachers can provide the correct answer and give feedback. The more closely the practice questions match the information that will be tested in the actual exam, the better pupils will do. Thus, this in-class 'testing time' should be devoted to the most critical information that will appear on the actual exam. Even using the same questions during practice and during the test is a reasonable strategy. It not only ensures that pupils will learn what their teachers have decided is most important but will also affirm to pupils that they should take practice quizzes seriously.

CHAPTER FORTY-ONE:
STUDY SKILLS

An assumption that teachers sometimes make - particularly when planning revision sessions - is that pupils have - somehow, somewhere - acquired an armoury of study skills and, perhaps by a process of osmosis, have become adept at working independently. Study skills, however, are not innate; rather, they must be taught, the implicit must be made explicit, and the invisible made visible.

Teaching study skills is about breaking down broad tasks into their constituent parts, modelling each process, then providing opportunities for pupils to practice and refine them. For example, if an assignment requires pupils to research information for an essay, we must explicitly teach them how to use multiple sources, how to skim and scan for key facts, and how to distinguish between fact and opinion and detect bias. We must then teach them how to use evidence to support an argument, including how to embed quotations, and how to write a bibliography citing their sources.

Before pupils write their essays, we must teach them how to craft a logical argument, using text markers such as 'Firstly', 'Secondly' and 'Thirdly'; 'However", 'Therefore', and 'In conclusion'.

If we expect pupils to work independently, perhaps drafting and re-drafting work based on feedback, and to do so outside of lessons and without our support, we must teach them how

345

to manage and organise their time, how to avoid cramming by distributing and spacing practice, and interleaving study topics, and how to self-assess then re-draft, referring back to the success criteria.

Likewise, if we expect pupils to engage in classroom debates, we must teach them active listening skills and turn-taking, as well as how to agree or disagree with someone else's contributions without it becoming personal.

If we expect pupils to adopt a growth mindset, willingly accepting and acting on feedback, taking risks and regarding mistakes as an integral part of the learning process, then we must teach and model resilience.

Growth mindset behaviours are likely to be developed in primary school but resilience and reflection become increasingly important as pupils travel through the education system because, as Draper (1998), and Smith and Pourchot (1998) found, whilst both children and young adults learn through experience and test all new learning against their prior experiences, the life experiences and contexts that older pupils bring with them to the classroom - and therefore how they respond to setbacks and assimilate new information within the context of prior knowledge - are different to the experiences and contexts that tend to accompany younger pupils.

In short, older pupils - particularly those in post-16 education - carry with them more prior knowledge and experiences and this colours how they learn new information and what they do with this new information.

Explicitly teaching and modelling study skills, therefore, is one means of helping pupils to engage in deliberate practice outside the classroom, but we shouldn't just teach skills at the start of a pupil's first year in school or at the beginning of a new course. Instead, we must teach skills on a sliding scale as pupils progress from one year to the next, from one key stage to the next, and from one phase of education to the next. For example, although we might start by teaching pupils how to write a simple bibliography, as they progress towards level 3 programmes at post-16, we need to move on to Harvard referencing.

A useful starting point when planning the teaching of skills is to map the skills pupils need and when they need them. This needs to be done for every subject and for every key stage and level of qualification, noting the difference between a skill required in, say, Year 7 and a similar skill - albeit more developed and complex - at GCSE and A Level. Likewise, we should map the skills development required of FE learners as they progress from a Level 2 qualification to a Level 3 and 4 and so on, moving perhaps into HE.

Skills maps should be shared across subject disciplines to ensure that common skills used in more than subject are taught in the same way, rather than confusingly and contradictorily, and to ensure explicit links are made between the skills used in different subject to aide pupils' transferability of those skills.

Next, we should carry out an audit of pupils' existing skills and identify any gaps. This will, in turn, inform us of where to start and on which skills we should spend most of our time.

Once we have a skills map, we need to decide how and by whom these skills will be taught. For example, will it be the teacher's responsibility to explicitly teach and model skills before pupils are required to use them, or will a form tutor be responsible for delivering study skills tutorials in standalone sessions?

Once a skill has been taught for the first time, we need to decide if it needs to be re-taught again when it is needed next (and, if so, whether we need to completely re-teach it or just recap and practice).

Note-making

One of the most impactful self-study strategies we can teach our pupils is that of note-making.

The act of note-making (rather than note-taking) is an art form. Note-making is about forming a point of view, reasoning, analysing and weighing statements and arguments, to develop a sense of curiosity and wonder.

The secret of good note-making lies in the way in which making notes - and the finished notes themselves - can shape a pupil's thinking. Learning to take attentive, analytical notes (selecting and analysing information before committing one's thoughts and ideas to paper) helps pupils to develop their own arguments and participate in debates. Debates, after all, are really all about note-making; dissecting your opponent's idea, reducing it to a single sentence.

In this sense, verbatim transcription (note-taking) is never the objective: rather, pupils should use the act of making notes to synthesise what they've learnt and to leave more traces in long-term memory. In short, pupils' notes should be the result of analysis, evaluation and synthesis; they should provide a thoughtful summarisation of the key points rather than be verbatim transcriptions of what the teacher has said.

Note-making can help pupils develop critical thinking skills and help them prepare for practice tests. Perhaps pupils' notes could consist of flashcards or blank spaces on which to test themselves later. Whilst pupils are making notes, they should periodically pause to ask themselves questions such as: What are the key ideas here? What terms are new to me and what do they mean? How do the ideas here relate to what I already know?

I favour the Cornell model of note-making because it promotes active processing and subsequent retrieval practice. It's easy to teach and simple to incorporate into any lesson.

Self-explanation

Imagine a pupil reading an introductory passage on photosynthesis: "It is a process in which a plant converts carbon dioxide and water into sugar, which is its food. The process gives off oxygen." If the pupil were using elaborative interrogation - or self-explanation - while reading and making revision notes, she would not just write out the key point, but she would also try to explain why this fact is true...

In this case, she might think that it must be true because everything that lives needs some kind of food, and sugar is something that she eats as food. She may not come up with exactly the right explanation but trying to elaborate on why a fact may be true, even when the explanations are not entirely on the mark, can still benefit understanding and retention.

If the pupil were using self-explanation, then she would try to explain how this new information is related to information that she already knows...

In this case, perhaps she might consider how the conversion is like how her own body changes food into energy.

Pupils can also self-explain when they solve problems of any sort and decide how to proceed; they merely explain to themselves why they made a particular decision.

While practicing problems, the success rate of solving them is no different for pupils who self-explain their decisions compared with those who do not. However, in solving new problems that involve transferring what one has learned during practice, those who initially used self-explanation perform better than those who did not use this technique. In fact, in one experiment where pupils learned to solve logical-reasoning problems, final test performance was three times better (about 90 percent versus less than 30 percent) for pupils who self-explained during practice than for those who did not.

One reason these two strategies can promote learning and comprehension and boost problem-solving performance is that they encourage pupils to actively process the content they are focusing on and integrate it with their prior knowledge.

Even young pupils should have little trouble using elaborative interrogation, because it simply involves encouraging them to ask the question "why?" when they are studying. The difference between this type of "why" and the "why" asked in early childhood (when this is a common question to parents) is that pupils must take the time to develop answers.

It should not be too difficult, or require much time, to teach most pupils how to take advantage of self-explanation. Nevertheless, younger pupils or those who need more support may benefit from some coaching.

For instance, as noted above, paraphrases and self-explanations are not the same and lead to different learning outcomes. In much the same way, using a word to define that word is not definition but repetition. As such, teachers should help younger pupils distinguish between an explanation of an idea and its paraphrase. Even so, a gentle reminder to use elaborative interrogation or self-explanation may be all most pupils need to keep them using these strategies as they learn new course content and prepare for examinations.

Dual coding

Another important consideration for pupils who engage in note-making and self-explanation is dual coding. I explained earlier that we receive information through two primary pathways — auditory (for the spoken word) and visual (for the written word and graphic or pictorial representation).

Learning increases when we convey study material both verbally and through graphics that convey key concepts and ideas. Graphics include illustrations, diagrams, and flow charts, as well as animation or video. Simple images in drawings or photos are not sufficient, unless they are carefully chosen to convey entire concepts.

What works for the teacher also works for the pupil and so pupils should make use of dual coding when writing study guides or even just scribbling revision notes to aid their self-explanation.

Linking concrete and abstract concepts

When engaging in note-making and self-explanation, pupils should also try to link concrete and abstract concepts. In other words, they should try to find tangible examples that illuminate overarching ideas and also explain how the examples and big ideas connect.

Presenting concrete examples helps pupils understand new ideas, while connecting those examples to abstract ideas allows pupils to apply concepts in new situations. For example, when self-studying (or revising) the general principle that all organisms are adapted to their environments, it will help pupils to think about an animal with which they are familiar (such as a squirrel) and consider how these everyday creatures must cope with the weather, rather than focus solely on the more exotic animals cited in textbooks (such as polar bears).

Matt Bromley

CHAPTER FORTY-TWO:
REVISION

Revision has become synonymous with dull, repetitious labour, revisiting by rote what pupils have already studied, sitting past paper after past paper in silent rows, receiving nothing in return but a miserly missive in blood-red ink. 'Revision' implies going over old ground without seeking to learn from it and make improvements, and without seeking to introduce new concepts and spark fresh ideas.

'Practice', however, implies doing something new, incrementally improving your performance through a process of trial and error (or perhaps, as one teacher put it to me recently, "trial and *improvement*"), and doing so by receiving feedback, learning from your mistakes, and making tweaks in order to achieve marginal gains.

In short, deliberate practice sessions should avoid learning by rote, reading and rereading the original study materials. They should, instead, make use of self-quizzing.

Self-quizzing - like practice tests in class - is about retrieving knowledge and skills from memory and is far more effective than simply re-reading one's study notes.

Along the way, pupils should also be encouraged to elaborate - which is to say, they should find additional layers of meaning in new materials, relate new material to what they already know, explain new material to other pupils, and explain how new material relates to the wider world and to their own experiences. Pupils should also be encouraged to reflect on what they've learnt and then adjust their judgment to reflect the reality - in other words, they should actively answer every question and re-cap on every idea even if they think they know the answers. Sometimes, pupils can assume they know something when, in reality, they don't, or they did but have forgotten it. By answering every question - writing down the answers or saying them out loud - pupils will remove this dangerous illusion of knowing.

As I explained in the previous chapter, in order for practice testing to be most effective, pupils should be encouraged to leave spaces in their study notes where they can test themselves later. When they test themselves, they should be encouraged to write their answers down, not simply say them aloud or in their heads.

The act of writing the answers boosts long-term retrieval and also uncovers false assumptions about what they know and don't know. Sometimes we can fool ourselves into thinking we know the answer when we don't. Writing the answer out in full quickly unmasks this misconception.

Also, we should encourage pupils to produce flashcards whereby they write a question or key term on one side and the correct answer on the other. They should then test themselves on all the questions and if they don't answer a question right the first time, they should continue testing themselves until they get it right. They might manage this by removing flashcards once they've given the right answer but replacing cards in the pack if they get the answer wrong.

If pupils persist until they answer each question correctly or positively recall each idea or concept, they will enhance their chances of remembering the concepts during the final exam. But they shouldn't stop there...

Pupils should also be encouraged to "get it right" on more than one occasion. For example, they could return to the full deck of flashcards on another day (once they have already mastered them all) and re-test themselves.

As well as using practice tests as a means of self-study, pupils can benefit from using practice tests in class. For example, teachers could choose the most important ideas from recent lessons and dedicate a couple of minutes at the beginning or end of each class to test pupils on them.

Once all the pupils have answered a question, the teacher should share the correct answer and give feedback. The more closely the practice questions test pupils on the information that will be tested in the exam, the better pupils will perform in the end.

I talked about the importance of spacing and interleaving in Chapters Thirty-Seven and Thirty-Eight, but these strategies are not the exclusive property of the teacher; rather, pupils should also employ these approaches when engaging in self-quizzing and other forms of self-study...

Imagine we're trying to learn some key facts relating to Shakespeare's Macbeth for an upcoming exam. We might diligently read all our study notes in a single session the night before the exam, until we think we are ready for the test. This strategy is commonly called cramming. Alternatively, we might study our notes during the course of several shorter sessions on two or three separate nights leading up to the exam, repeating the same "revision" exercise a number of times on different days.

If we opted for the second tactic – studying for a shorter period each night but doing so over several nights rather than cramming all our exam preparation into one long session – we would be able to retain the knowledge for a longer period even though, taken together, we dedicated the same amount of time.

Unfortunately, despite this fact, most pupils still prefer to cram for reasons I explained earlier. In short, learning feels slower and harder when it is distributed rather than massed. However, the sense of success pupils feel (and their teachers appear to see) during massed practice is often short-lived and their learning is often superficial.

So, although distributed practice takes more effort, it is essential for learning information in a way that will be retained (or more easily relearned) and retrievable over a longer period.

In short, massed practice leads to ephemeral and facile learning whereas distributed practice bolsters a pupil's storage and retrieval strength, ensuring their learning is both deep and longer lived.

So how can we help pupils to distribute their practice?

First, we should help pupils to map-out how many study sessions they will need before an exam, when those sessions should take place (which evenings of the week and between what times), and what they should practise during each session. Two short study blocks per week should be sufficient to begin studying new material as well as to restudy previously learned material. Pupils should be able to retrieve previous material more easily after just a few study sessions which leaves more time for studying new material.

Second, we should use distributed practice in the classroom by repeatedly going back over the most important knowledge and concepts. For example, we could use weekly quizzes that repeat content several times so that pupils relearn some concepts in a distributed manner. Repeating key points in several quizzes not only highlights the importance of that content but also affords pupils the opportunity to engage in distributed practice.

Third, we should set a cumulative exam that forces pupils to review the most important information they have studied this year.

CHAPTER FORTY-THREE:
SELF-STUDY

So far in this final stage of our 3-step process for teaching for long-term learning, I have advocated the use of spaced and interleaved practice and extolled the virtues of desirable difficulties. I have also talked about the importance of repeating learning several times and in different contexts, and of pupils demonstrating their learning in myriad ways. I have explored the self-study skills that are proven to help pupils make better progress outside of the classroom including self-quizzing, note-making and self-explanation. And I have discussed ways for pupils to space and interleave their independent revision.

Before we conclude our journey, I'd like to share a pertinent memory ...

Several years ago, while working as a Deputy Headteacher, I interviewed 50 pupils in Years 11 and 13 who had achieved high grades in their GCSE and A level exams. What I discovered was, depending on your point of view, either a set of amazing coincidences or the secret to exam success...

For example, every pupil I interviewed had an attendance of more than 93 per cent; 90 per cent of them had a perfect attendance record.

Every pupil I interviewed told me that they used their planners regularly and considered themselves to be well-organised. As a result, all the pupils I interviewed completed their homework on time and without fail.

Every pupil I interviewed told me they always asked for help from their teachers when they got stuck. They didn't regard doing so as a sign of weakness, rather a sign of strength. Admitting they didn't know something and asking questions meant they learnt something new and increased their intelligence.

Most of the pupils I interviewed were involved in clubs, sports, or hobbies at lunchtime, after school and/or at weekends. Though not all were sporting, they did all have get-up-and-go attitudes. They didn't spend every evening and weekend watching television. They were sociable and, in order to unwind, they read books. Lots of books. In fact, the school library confirmed that my cohort of high-achievers were among the biggest borrowers in school.

All the pupils in the survey believed that doing well in school would increase their chances of getting higher paid and more interesting jobs later in life. Many of them had a clear idea about the kind of job they wanted to do and knew what was needed in order to get it. They had researched the entry requirements and had then mapped out the necessary school, college, and/or university paths. They had connected what they were doing in school with achieving their future ambitions. School work and good exam results had a purpose, they were means to an important end.

In short, every pupil who achieved high grades regularly attended school, was well-organised, completed work on time, and had an end goal in mind. The cause was diligent study and determination; the effect was high achievement.

As such, these young people can teach all our pupils a valuable lesson: that the recipe for success is to:

- Have good attendance and punctuality.
- Be organised and complete all work on time.
- Be willing to ask for help when you're stuck.
- Have something to aim for and be ambitious.
- Map out your career path and be determined to succeed.

But telling our pupils to study hard isn't enough; they need to know how to study...

One means of becoming better organised pupil is to acquire effective study skills like the ones I shared in the previous chapters. There are, however, according to Paul C Brown et al in Make It Stick, a few more study skills worthy of our pupils' attention. They are:

Elaboration

Elaboration is the process of finding additional layers of meaning in new material. It involves relating new material to what pupils already know, explaining it to somebody else, or explaining how it relates to the wider world. An effective form of elaboration is to use a metaphor or image for the new material.

Generation

Generation is when pupils attempt to answer a question or solve a problem before being shown the answer or the solution. The act of filling in a missing word (the cloze test) results in better learning and a stronger memory of the text than simply reading the text. Before reading new class material, ask pupils to explain the key ideas they expect to find and how they expect these ideas will relate to their prior knowledge.

Reflection

Reflection involves taking a moment to review what has been learned. Pupils ask questions such as:

- What went well? What could have gone better?
- What other knowledge or experience does it remind me of?
- What might I need to learn in order to achieve better mastery?
- What strategies could I use next time to getter better results?

Calibration

Calibration is achieved when pupils adjust their judgment to reflect reality – in other words, they become certain that their sense of what they know and can do is accurate. Often when we revise information, we look at a question and convince ourselves that we know the answer, then move on to the next question without making an effort to actually answer the previous one.

If we do not write down an answer, we may create the illusion of knowing when in fact we'd find it difficult giving a response. We need to teach our pupils to remove the illusion of knowing and actually answer all the questions even if they think they know the answer and that it is too easy.

And, finally, here are some other useful self-study strategies we would do well to teach our pupils:

- Anticipate test questions during lessons.
- Read study guides, find terms they can't recall or don't know and learn them.
- Copy key terms and their definitions into a notebook.
- Reorganise class material into a study guide.
- Copy out key concepts and regularly test themselves on them.
- Space out revision and practice activities.

CHAPTER FORTY-FOUR:
A 4-STEP TEACHING SEQUENCE

Before we conclude our 3-step process of teaching for long-term learning, I'd like to explore a useful teaching sequence for introducing pupils to new information.

As I explained earlier, research by Kirschner, Sweller and Clark (2006) compared guided models of teaching, such as direct instruction, with discovery learning methods, such as problem-based learning, inquiry learning, experiential learning, and constructivist learning, and found that the latter methods didn't work as well as the former. It didn't matter, they argued, if pupils preferred less guided methods, they still learned less from them (see also Clark, 1989).

In his book, Visible Learning, Professor John Hattie found that the average effect size for teaching strategies which involved the teacher as a "facilitator" was 0.17, whereas the average effect size for strategies where the teacher acted as an "activator" was 0.60.

Direct instruction had an effect size of 0.59 compared to problem-based learning with an effect size of just 0.15.

Therefore, direct instruction – it seems – is more effective than discovery learning approaches. But what, exactly, does good direct instruction look like in practice?

Personally, I think direct instruction works best when it follows this four-step sequence:

1. Telling
2. Showing
3. Doing
4. Practising

Telling – or teacher explanation – works best when the teacher presents new material to pupils in small "chunks" and provides scaffolds and targeted support.

Showing – or teacher modelling – works best when the teacher models a new procedure by, among other strategies, thinking aloud, guiding pupils' initial practice and providing pupils with cues.

Doing – or co-construction – works best when the teacher provides pupils with "fix-up" strategies – corrections and "live" feedback.

Practising – or independent work – works best when the teacher provides planned opportunities in class for extensive independent practice.

Of course, the learning process does not end here. Rather, pupils need to garner feedback on their independent practice and then act on that feedback in order to improve by increments. We'll return to the importance of this "feedback loop" later. But first, let's take a look at each of the four steps in our teaching sequence.

Telling

The most effective, expedient way for pupils to acquire new information is for the teacher – that educated, experienced expert at the front of class – to tell them what they need to know.

This is not to suggest that sometimes, for some purposes, other approaches are not also effective, but teacher explanations remain the most efficient method of teaching – not to mention the least likely to lead to misconceptions among pupils and a misunderstanding by the teacher of what pupils can and cannot do. So, what are good explanations made of?

First, good explanations involve metaphors and analogies because this enables the teacher to contextualise new information so that abstract ideas or hitherto alien concepts are made concrete, tangible, and real, and so that they are related to pupils' own lives and experiences.

Second, good explanations make effective use of dual coding. In other words, teachers' verbal instructions, as well as any text-based explanations displayed on the board or in handouts are paired with and complemented by visuals such as diagrams, charts, graphics and moving images.

And finally, good explanations are reciprocated, with pupils explaining concepts back to the teacher as well as to each other. This works on the basis that only once you teach something have you truly learned it. Learning by teaching works because, by teaching, pupils gain feedback and make better sense of a topic. Learning by teaching also works because it is a form of learning by doing, of practising, and thus provides a source of both intrinsic and extrinsic motivation.

Showing

Once teachers have explained something, they should make effective and plentiful use of models – exemplars of both good and bad work, as well as exemplars from a range of different contexts – which show pupils what a final product should look like and what makes such products work.

Good models demonstrate what works as well as what doesn't. It is important to show pupils what excellence looks like by sharing models of the very best work, giving them something to aspire to, and an understanding of how to produce high-quality work of their own.

But it is equally important to show pupils models of ineffective work, work that isn't quite the best (or perhaps is so very far from being the best) so that pupils can learn what not to do and how to avoid making the same mistakes themselves.

All the models that are shared should be dissected in front of pupils, with the teacher demonstrating the dissection process.

For example, if a model of a persuasive speech is shown on the board, the teacher should analyse it using text marking, pointing out and then annotating how it works, what makes it effective, breaking it apart to identify and discuss each of its component parts. Then the teacher should reconstruct the speech, explaining how the component parts hang together to create an effective argument, how the whole becomes something much greater than the sum of its parts.

Once pupils know how to dissect models, they should be afforded the opportunity to do so without the teacher's guidance, perhaps by teaching other pupils. In order to prepare pupils for this, it is important that the teacher offers encouragement, gives specific instructions, uses thought or sentence stems to provide pupils with the right language, and – as I say above – directly demonstrates the process first.

Doing

Once the teacher has modelled something at the front of class, it is important to do so again but, this time, with pupils' help. Co-construction (or joint construction) works well because the teacher engages pupils' thought processes and helps them by questioning their decisions and by prompting further decision-making.

The teacher's role is not to construct another model herself but to ask targeted questions of pupils to encourage them to complete the model together, as well as to provide corrections and feedback along the way, and drip-feed key vocabulary into the mix.

For instance, and to return to the example above, if a teacher has explained to a class how to write a persuasive speech and then modelled doing so on the whiteboard while thinking aloud, she might then ask the class to produce a persuasive speech of their own.

The teacher may begin by asking the class to determine an audience and purpose for the speech, then prompt pupils to debate and decide upon the tone of the writing.

The teacher might ask a pupil to come up and write the first sentence and then ask other pupils to comment on it. She might drip-feed technical vocabulary into the conversation where appropriate (reminding pupils, for example, that placing two contrasting ideas side-by-side is called "juxtaposition") and she might encourage pupils to repeat it and use the correct term in future. She might ask pupils to model their thought processes, thinking aloud as they write, explaining the reasons for their choices.

The teacher, therefore, will mostly be engaged in asking open questions, such as: "Why did you choose that word? "Is there another word which might fit better or have more impact? Why is this word better than this one? Should we use a short sentence here? Why/why not? What is the effect of this, do you think?"

Practising

Once the class has constructed a model together, they need to do so independently.

Independent practice not only provides a crucial third opportunity for pupils to practise – after teacher modelling and co-construction – it also enables pupils to demonstrate their own understanding and for the teacher to assess the extent to which they have "got it".

Until a pupil completes a task by themselves, we – and perhaps they – cannot be certain that they can do it or that information has been encoded in long-term memory.

If pupils succeed, the teacher can move on. If not, the teacher can use the feedback information to guide further teaching of the subject, perhaps re-teaching key elements of it or engaging those pupils who have succeeded in teaching those who have not.

The feedback loop

The four-part teaching sequence is not the end of the learning process, because once pupils have practised new learning we need to provide planned opportunities for them to be assessed (by themselves, by each other, or by us) and receive feedback on what they have mastered and what they still need to practise. Then, crucially, we need to provide planned opportunities in class for them to act upon that feedback.

Failure is the best teacher. Pupils learn through practice, by making mistakes, and by experimenting. They also learn best when engaged in a process of trial and error and when they repeat actions several times, making incremental improvements each time.

If we do not provide lesson time for pupils to respond to feedback and improve their work, we send a negative message about the importance of redrafting work and learning from our mistakes. What's more, if pupils do not respond to feedback in class, the teacher cannot see progress being made and cannot, therefore, recognise and celebrate it.

We explored feedback in Chapters Seven, Eighteen and Nineteen, but here is a brief reminder of some best practice advice...

Feedback needs to motivate pupils to make progress. In this regard, short verbal feedback is often more motivational than long written comments on pupils' work. Indeed, some pupils find written comments demotivating because they ruin the presentation of their work, are confusing or overwhelming. Feedback should also prompt further thinking and drafting, perhaps by posing questions on which the pupil has to ruminate and act, as opposed to ready-made suggestions and solutions.

I think it is useful to remember that the term "feedback" originated from the field of engineering where it formed part of a loop: feedback in engineering terms was about the discrepancy between the current state and the desired state of something, but this alone was deemed useless unless there was also a mechanism within the feedback loop to bring the current state closer to the desired state. In other words, feedback was about correction and progress.

As such, simply telling pupils that their current performance falls short of where they need to be isn't feedback in the original engineering sense of the term. Rather, to be effective, feedback must also embody a mode of progression for pupils.

The best feedback causes thinking. In practice, this means that the teacher should be clear and constructive about pupils' weaknesses, offering suggestions on how they might be addressed, identify pupils' strengths and offer advice on how to develop them, and then – crucially – provide planned opportunities in class for pupils to improve upon their work.

And that is the four-part teaching sequence I recommend you follow, no matter what you're teaching and to whom. Tell pupils what you need them to know, show them what it looks like and how it works, produce a model of excellence together, plan opportunities for pupils to practise their learning independently, then make sure practice leads to quality feedback that pupils act upon in class so that progress becomes visible for all and the importance of learning from mistakes is writ large.

The bigger picture

The best lessons are small pieces of a much larger jigsaw; they do not operate in isolation. Learning, after all, is a lengthy, complex process.

As such, when using our 4-step teaching sequence, we also need to connect each lesson with its predecessors and with its successors. We need to explain how today's lesson will consolidate and extend what was studied last lesson, and how it will be further extended and then assessed later.

One way of connecting lessons in this way is to consider pupils' starting points: what prior knowledge do they bring to this lesson? What misconceptions and unanswered questions do they have? And what are their interests and talents (in as far as these may influence the way they learn and the way we teach)?

Once the answers to these questions have been ascertained, we need to use the information as rich diagnostic data in order to determine – or at least influence – the way in which we plan our lessons.
Here is a step-by-step guide to the lesson planning process…

Part 1: The KWL chart

One common diagnostic technique and a means of acquiring data on pupils' starting points is asking pupils at the beginning of a lesson or new topic to identify what they already know (or think they know) about what they are about to study. Their responses can then be listed in a table or on a graphic organiser. The contents of the first column provide us with a sense of pupils' prior knowledge, while also unmasking any misconceptions that may exist and therefore may need to be addressed.

Next, we should ask pupils to identify "what I want to learn" about the topic and ask them to raise any questions they may have at this early stage. These responses can be recorded in the second column to serve as indicators of areas of interest.

As the unit unfolds, the knowledge and skills that pupils begin to acquire should be recorded in the third column of the table, providing a record for pupils of "what I have learned".

An alternative to this is to begin a lesson or topic with an initial assessment, perhaps a low-stakes multiple-choice quiz. The results of these pre-tests can yield invaluable evidence about pupils' prior knowledge and misconceptions and, when repeated at various stages of the teaching sequence, can provide evidence of pupils' growing knowledge and understanding.

Regardless of the approach taken, information from diagnostic assessments can guide us in our planning so that lessons are more responsive to pupils' needs and their existing knowledge base.

An important practical implication, of course, is that we must remember to plan opportunities for assessments and allow sufficient 'wriggle room' to make adjustments based on the feedback garnered by the assessments.

In-built flexibility like this is not just advisable, it is a key aspect of effective lesson-planning because it enables learning to be personalised to match the needs and pace of pupils' learning. It also ensures that gaps in pupils' learning are identified and filled, which in turn will avoid an off-the-peg, one-size-fits-all approach to lesson-planning and enable good progress to be made by all.

Part 2: The big idea

Once we've connected the learning, we need to consider how pupils will be engaged in exploring the big ideas and questions around which we have framed our lessons and topics. We also need to consider what approaches, including direct instruction, will best support and equip our pupils for their final assessment. And we need to consider what homework tasks and additional interventions may be needed in order to enable pupils to develop and deepen their understanding of important ideas.

It's easy to assume that what we need to do in order to fill gaps in pupils' knowledge is to teach more knowledge, cover more curriculum content. But deep understanding requires an iterative mix of experiences, reflections on those experiences, and targeted instruction in light of those experiences. Good lesson design, therefore, involves the provision of sufficient real or simulated experiences in order to enable pupils' understanding to develop.

It is our job to equip and enable pupils to eventually perform with understanding and increasing autonomy. That is very different from preparing them for a test. In order to do this, we should ask ourselves, 'What kinds of knowledge, skill and routines are prerequisites for a successful pupil outcome?' and 'What kinds of tasks and activities will help pupils develop and deepen their understanding of key ideas?'

We often complain that pupils cannot transfer what they have been taught into new problems and tasks. Yet, we rarely plan opportunities to help pupils learn how to transfer knowledge to different situations. In other words, the problem is typically regarded as a pupil deficit rather than a teaching need.

Part 3: Dig deep and repeat

Trying to cover too many topics too quickly can hinder pupils' learning and their ability to transfer their learning, because pupils end up learning isolated sets of facts that are not organised and connected, or they're introduced to ideas they cannot possibly grasp because they lack the background knowledge necessary to make those ideas meaningful.

Accordingly, we need to provide pupils with opportunities to engage with sufficient, specific information that's relevant to the topic they're learning. Also, we need to providing enough time for pupils to be able to process information. In other words, learning cannot be rushed; the complex cognitive activity involved in integrating information takes time.

Therefore, when planning lessons, we should aim to cover less curriculum content but to cover that content in greater depth. We should provide opportunities for pupils to explore subject matter from a range of perspectives and to provide sufficient experience and context.

Finally, we should provide opportunities for pupils to repeat learning several times so that it penetrates their long-term memories. Tests are a good way of "interrupting forgetting" because they reveal what's actually been learnt as well as what gaps exist.

Part 4: Make learning stick

In order to ensure that, once pupils have thought about and encoded the knowledge and skills that we needed them to acquire, that knowledge and those skills 'stick', we need to make ideas tangible because pupils find it hard to care about or understand abstract concepts. If we ground an abstract concept in sensory reality and thus engage our pupils' emotions, our pupils are made to care about something, they are made to feel something, and this is an important part of the learning process.

What's more, when we are exposed to new information, we process it and then attempt to connect it to existing information (in other words, we try to assimilate new knowledge with prior knowledge). As I have already explained, the richer – sensorily and emotionally – new information is, and the deeper the existing information is ingrained, the stronger we will encode that new information in our long-term memories.

Ensuring our lessons provide variety and novelty, therefore, helps to appeal to pupils' senses and engage their emotions – if nothing else, simply by piquing their interest in something out of the ordinary, we are making them think – and therefore the information we teach them is more likely to be retained over the long-term.

A concluding caveat

As with all teaching advice, you should be influence by it but informed by your own experiences and by the context within which you work. Be attuned to your classroom environment, learn to read the dynamics of the room so that you can be flexible and fluid in your approach. Don't stick slavishly to a lesson plan; adapt and adjust to the here-and-now circumstances of the classroom for learning often takes place when and where you least expect it.

CHAPTER FORTY-FIVE:
SUMMARY OF STEP 3

We've reached the end of our 3-step process of teaching for long-term learning so, before we move on, let's take stock...

The process of learning, we have said, is the interaction between our sensory memory and our long-term memory. Our sensory memory is made up of: what we see - this is called our iconic memory; what we hear - this is called our echoic memory; and what we touch - our haptic memory. Our long-term memory is where new information is stored and from which it can be recalled when needed, but we cannot directly access the information stored in our long-term memory - instead, this interaction between our sensory memory and our long-term memory occurs in the working memory.

In order to ensure our pupils learn, therefore, we need to stimulate their sensory memory, gain the attention of - and help them cheat - their working memory, and improve the strength with which information is stored in, and the ease and efficiency with which it can later be retrieved from, their long-term memory. In order to do this, we need to follow these three steps:

First, we need to stimulate pupils' senses in order to gain the active attention of their working memories.

Second, we need to make pupils think hard but efficiently about the curriculum content to be learned.

And third, we need to plan opportunities for pupils to engage in deliberate practice in order to ensure prior knowledge remains accessible.

In order to improve the storage and retrieval strength of the information pupils have encoded into long-term memory, we need to:

1. Repeat learning at least three times.

Once we've taught something for the first time and that information has been encoded into pupils' long-term memories, we need to plan opportunities for pupils to repeat that learning over and over. The more pupils repeat their prior learning, the stronger the storage of that information becomes and the more efficient they become at retrieving that information from long-term memory and returning it to their working memory in order to use it. Every piece of knowledge and every skill is improved and perfected by performing it repeatedly because repetition hones neural circuitry. And yet not all forms of practice are equal... we best improve storage and retrieval strength when we engage in deliberate practice. Talking of which...

2. Make pupils struggle in targeted ways.

We need to plan for deliberate practice by making pupils struggle in certain targeted ways, slowing their initial learning down so that pupils stop and stumble, and crucially must think harder, to make sense of something. Moreover, we need to ensure that practice is targeted and mistake-focused - in other words, that it responds to feedback and seeks to close the gaps in pupils' knowledge. Slowing learning down and ensuring pupils struggle helps to pitch learning in the 'sweet spot' between what pupils can do and what pupils are trying to do.

3. Space practice sessions out.

Leave increasingly long gaps before returning to a topic so that pupils get to the point of almost forgetting what they'd previously learnt and must - once again - think hard about that information to retrieve it from their long-term memories.

4. Interleave practice topics.

Focus on each topic for a shorter period but return to it more often in-between studying other topics. This is the opposite of cramming, or blocked practice, and has been proven to be more effective in terms of long-term information-retention. As well as improving the storage and retrieval strength of information from each topic, interleaving helps pupils to forge new connections between topics and therefore improve their ability to transfer their learning from one context to another.

5. Repeat learning in multiple contexts.

Each time we return to recap, reteach or test pupils on their prior learning, we should do something different with the information, make new connections, and require pupils to demonstrate their learning in different ways.

In the classroom, this means that every time you return to prior learning, you should get pupils to do different things with it, not just repeat it verbatim. For example, pupils could test themselves, test each other, devise quizzes, give presentations to the class, teach each other, write an essay, draw a diagram, create a graphic organiser, and so on. Talking of which...

6. Set practice tests to boost learning.

The use of practice tests or short, perhaps multiple-choice, quizzes can improve pupils' learning in both direct and indirect ways. Unlike simply re-reading study notes, when pupils are tested (or test themselves) and correctly retrieve an answer from their long-term memories, that memory is further improved. But practice tests also help when pupils fail to retrieve a correct answer. Such a failure signals that the answer needs to be revisited, re-studied perhaps. This helps pupils make decisions about what to dedicate most of their time practising.

7. Explicitly teach pupils how to take good study notes.

Pupils' notes should be the result of analysis, evaluation and synthesis; they should provide a thoughtful summarisation of the key points rather than be verbatim transcriptions of what the teacher has said. Note-taking can help pupils develop critical thinking skills and help them prepare for practice tests. Perhaps pupils' notes could consist of flashcards or blank spaces on which to test themselves later. Whilst pupils are taking notes, they should periodically pause to ask themselves questions such as: What are the key ideas here? What terms are new to me and what do they mean? How do the ideas here relate to what I already know?

8. Encourage pupils to test themselves on prior learning.

Self-quizzing - like practice tests in class - is about retrieving knowledge and skills from memory and is far more effective than simply re-reading one's study notes.

Along the way, pupils should also be encouraged to elaborate - which is to say, they should find additional layers of meaning in new materials, relate new material to what they already know, explain new material to other pupils, and explain how new material relates to the wider world and to their own experiences. Pupils should also be encouraged to reflect on what they've learnt and then adjust their judgment to reflect the reality - in other words, they should actively answer every question and re-cap on every idea even if they think they know the answers. Sometimes, pupils can assume they know something when, in reality, they don't or they did but have forgotten it. By answering every question - writing down the answers or saying them out loud - pupils will remove this dangerous illusion of knowing.

9. Plan for daily free recall.

Develop a routine whereby pupils spend ten minutes at the end of every lesson filling a blank piece of paper with everything they can remember from that lesson. Start the next lesson with a recap quiz. Set a weekly homework whereby pupils create summary sheets for the previous week's learning. These could be annotated notes, perhaps with diagrams. The purpose of this task is to stimulate retrieval and reflection and to capture the previous week's learning before it is lost.

10. Use graphic organisers to capture key learning and frame revision.

Graphic organisers - also called knowledge organisers - can help to focus pupils' attentions on the key concepts and vocabulary they need to learn. The content of these organisers could be used to frame the daily recaps and weekly quizzes, as well as the end-of-topic tests. Indeed, it is good practice to only test pupils on the contents of the graphic organiser for that topic. Graphic organisers are also useful planning tools for the teacher - they help the teacher focus on the curriculum content that's most important for pupils to learn and therefore help to remove erroneous or irrelevant details. Graphic organisers can also be used to help make learning objectives and success criteria more specific and focused.

Matt Bromley

PART FOUR:

EQUAL ACCESS TO LONG-TERM LEARNING

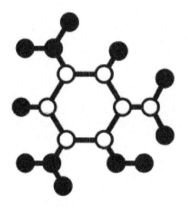

CHAPTER FORTY-SIX:
DELIVERING A DIFFERENTIATED
CURRICULUM

Before I delve into differentiation, I want to bridge the gap, so to speak, between the advice I've shared thus far on curriculum implementation and the advice that follows on differentiation. After all, at its heart, differentiation is about delivering the curriculum in a way that makes sense to all pupils irrespective of background, starting point and need, and in a manner that enables every pupil to access curriculum content and achieve.

Instruction to deliver

Although teacher autonomy is important - teaching is a profession after all - pupils undoubtedly benefit from a degree of consistency in approaches to pedagogy. Pupils like routine, after all.

In her book Student-Centred Leadership, Vivianne Robinson argues that, although "feet of varying shapes should not be shoved into the same ill-fitting shoe", in the sense of professional practice – teaching and teacher-learning – one size *does* fit all. In other words, although it is assumed that any loss of teacher autonomy is undesirable because it somehow reduces the professionalism of teachers, this isn't necessarily the case...

Although there can be no question that increased coherence (requiring teachers to teach in a consistent manner) means reducing individual autonomy, this does not necessarily imply a decrease in professionalism. After all, doctors are regarded as professionals precisely *because* they have mastered complex sets of shared diagnostic and treatment practices. They exercise their judgment about how those procedures are to be applied in any individual case and are held accountable for those judgments.

Teachers, too, need sufficient autonomy within which to exercise professional judgment about how to use the framework they're given and to contribute to evaluative discussions about its adequacy. But that autonomy should also be constrained by the need to ensure effective teaching practice – that is, practice under which all pupils achieve to a high level.

We may encourage collective autonomy (teachers working together to improve their practice), but curtail individual autonomy (teachers working in a purely idiosyncratic way) because standard professional practice provides the scaffolding that's required for the exercise of truly professional rather than idiosyncratic judgment. In other words, although we should not eradicate *individuality*, we should eliminate *individualism* (habitual or enforced patterns of working alone). Eliminating individualism should not be about making everyone the same and plunging them into groupthink; it should be about achieving collective responsibility.

In his book, Good to Great, Jim Collins expounds the importance of having a set of consistent systems and structures which dictate what staff can and cannot do and which governs how they should and should not operate. He uses the analogy of an airline pilot. A pilot, he says, operates within a very strict system and does not have the freedom to go outside of that system. Yet at the same time, the crucial decisions – whether to take off, whether to land, whether to abort, whether to land elsewhere – rest with the pilot. Collins says that great organisations have a culture of discipline which involves a duality. On the one hand, it requires people to adhere to a consistent system; yet, on the other hand, it gives people freedom and responsibility within the framework of that system.

In other words, schools can excel at delivering a great curriculum if they do so in a consistent manner. They must have strong values and high expectations. Their achievements will not happen by chance but through highly reflective, carefully planned strategies. There needs to be a high degree of internal consistency.

So, what 'routines' enable teachers to deliver the curriculum in the most effective manner and, furthermore, what teaching strategies best ensure a differentiated approach to curriculum delivery that meets the needs of every pupil? First and foremost, I would return you to the 4-step teaching sequence I shared in Chapter Forty-Four...

All mental activity – and *all* activity is mental activity, of course - is a delicate balance between intrinsic load (the space in working memory dedicated to performing a task), germane load (the space in working memory dedicated to trying to understand the task), and extraneous load (the space in working memory dedicated to understanding and responding to the instructional context).

Making the instructional context familiar helps to automate these processes which, in turn, frees up space in working memory to focus more on performing the task. This explains why, when we first learn to drive a car, we must focus on the various actions required to, say, change gear and we cannot do this well whilst also holding a conversation. As we grow used to changing gear, however, we free up the space used to understand the instructional context, and this enables us to multi-task.

We will return to these ideas in greater detail in Chapters Sixty-Two and Sixty-Three but, for now, suffice to say, when teaching the curriculum in a differentiated way, we can free up much needed space in pupils' working memories by following a familiar pedagogical routine – by using a consistent teaching sequence - in every lesson and in every subject across the curriculum.

What's more, pupils with learning difficulties and disabilities, and other vulnerable learners, benefit even more from a consistent routine so following a familiar teaching sequence is the first step towards effective differentiation.

My 4-step teaching sequence, you will recall, is as follows:

1. Telling
2. Showing
3. Doing
4. Practising

I'll provide a brief summary below in case you're dipping in and out of this book at random, but feel free to skip to Chapter Forty-Seven if you have only recently read about my 4-step teaching sequence...

Telling is the most effective, expedient way for pupils to acquire new information. And the best teacher explanations – or direct instruction - are often formed of three features:

Firstly, good teacher explanations involve metaphors and analogies because this enables the teacher to contextualise new information so that abstract ideas or hitherto alien concepts are made concrete, tangible, and real, and so that they are related to pupils' own lives and experiences.

Secondly, good explanations make effective use of dual coding. In other words, teachers' verbal instructions, as well as any text-based explanations displayed on the board or in handouts, are paired with and complemented by visuals such as diagrams, charts, graphics and moving images.

Finally, good explanations are reciprocated, with pupils explaining concepts back to the teacher as well as to each other. This works on the basis that only once you teach something do you truly learn it. Learning by teaching works because, by teaching, pupils gain feedback and make better sense of a topic. Learning by teaching also works because it is a form of learning by doing, of practising, and thus provides a source of both intrinsic and extrinsic motivation.

Showing is the effective and plentiful use of models – exemplars of both good and bad work, as well as exemplars from a range of different contexts – which show pupils what a final product should look like and what makes such products work. It is important to show pupils what excellence looks like by sharing models of the very best work, giving them something to aspire to and an understanding of how to produce high quality work of their own. But it is equally important to show pupils models of ineffective work, work that isn't quite the best (or perhaps is so very far from being the best) so that pupils can learn what not to do and how to avoid making the same mistakes themselves. Whilst modelling, the teacher should think aloud in order to make visible the invisible decision-making process and to make explicit what experts do implicitly.

Doing works well because by engaging in co-construction the teacher engages pupils' thought processes and helps them by questioning their decisions and by prompting further decision-making. The teacher's role is not to construct another model herself but to ask targeted questions of pupils to encourage them to complete the model together, as well as to provide corrections and feedback along the way, and drip-feed key vocabulary into the mix. During co-construction, the teacher will mostly be engaged in asking open questions such as, 'Why did you choose that word?' 'Is there another word which might fit better or have more impact?' 'Why is this word better than this one?' 'Should we use a short sentence here?' 'Why?/Why not?' and 'What is the effect of this, do you think?'

Practising is the opportunity for pupils to complete work independently. Independent practice enables pupils to demonstrate their own understanding and for the teacher to assess the extent to which they have 'got it'. Until a pupil completes a task by themselves, we - and perhaps they - cannot be certain they can do so or that information has been encoded in long-term memory. If pupils succeed, the teacher can move on. If not, the teacher can use the feedback information to guide further teaching of the subject, perhaps re-teaching key elements of it or engaging those pupils who have succeeded in teaching those who have not.

In the next chapter I will explain that effective differentiation is about ensuring every pupil, no matter their background and starting point, is headed towards the same destination, albeit their route and pace may differ. In other words, we should not 'dumb down' and expect less of some pupils, but should have high expectations of every pupil...

Matt Bromley

CHAPTER FORTY-SEVEN:
SAME DESTINATION, DIFFERENT ROUTE

In Chapter Forty-Six, I explained that differentiation was – fundamentally – about enabling every pupil, no matter their background and starting point, to access the curriculum and achieve. I said that we can do this best by building routines into our teaching and learning practices. In particular, I advocated a 4-step teaching sequence. I'd now like to offer some health-warnings about using some traditional forms of differentiation...

When we talk about differentiation, we often have in mind ways of scaffolding learning for our 'less able' pupils. But pupils – like learning – are complex and no pupil is uniformly 'less able' than another. Rather, some pupils have acquired more knowledge and skills in one area than another pupil or have practised a task more often. Of course, some pupils have additional and different needs – such as those young people with learning difficulties or disabilities – and they require a different approach. But to say they are 'less able' is, I think, an unhelpful misnomer.

To suggest a pupil is 'less able' implies there is an average pupil against which we are comparing all others. But there is no such thing as 'average'; rather, we are all made up of myriad individual characteristics. If you take an average of each of us (height, weight, IQ, shoe size, etc), you won't find any individual who is average in all respects. This is known as the Jaggedness Principle...

The Jaggedness Principle

Readers of the first book in this series on School and College Curriculum Design which covered 'intent', will be familiar with what follows but for the benefit of new readers and to refresh the memories of those who read Book One some time ago, here is a summary...

In the 1940s, the US Air Force had to refit fighter planes with adjustable seats because the cockpits had been designed around the average range of 10 body measurements taken from a population of 4,063 pilots. But because no individual met all those criteria, they ended up with a seat which didn't fit a single pilot.

'Average' doesn't exist and we'd be wise not to compare pupils to the average, deeming some to be 'less able' and others 'more able'.

What's more, the term "less able" infers an immovable position – if you are 'less able' you are destined to remain so ad infinitum, living life languishing in the left-hand shadow of the bell-curve.

I'm not suggesting that every pupil performs the same – or has the same capacity to do so. We are not all born equal. But defining someone as less able as a result of a test – whether that be Key Stage 2 SATs, Year 7 CATs or GCSE outcomes - means we are in danger of arbitrarily writing off some pupils by means of a snapshot taken through a pinhole lens.

When approaching differentiation, therefore, we would be wise to remember that all pupils – like all human beings – are different, unique, individual. Differentiation, therefore, should not be about treating 'less able' pupils – or indeed those with SEND or eligible for Pupil Premium funding – as a homogenous group. Rather, we should treat each pupil on an individual basis. Nor should we assume that what works with one pupil will work with all and that what was proven to work with 'less able' pupils in another school, in another district, in another country, (according to research evidence and meta-analyses) will work in our classroom.

Teach to the top

All this rather begs the question: 'What does work?'

Differentiation in the guise of teaching to the middle and scaffolding for lower-performing pupils while stretching and challenging higher-performing ones (and therefore expecting less of lower-performing pupils), carries with it an inherent danger: it is, by any another name, 'dumbing down'.

Differentiation of this kind is delivered by means of placing limits on learning, lowering a glass ceiling on top of pupils' ambitions. Differentiation of this kind might take the form of differentiated questions using Bloom's Taxonomy. For example, the teacher might start a classroom discussion by asking a question from the bottom of the taxonomy – a knowledge-based question which requires a recall of facts – to a lower-performing pupil before moving up the taxonomy with higher-performing pupils.

But sticking to the bottom of Bloom's Taxonomy does not allow lower-performing pupils to deepen their understanding; rather, it leads to surface learning. What's more, this approach is guilty of assuming that because the taxonomy grows in difficulty, the bottom end isn't as important and that higher-performing pupils don't need to waste their time down there. It's true that Bloom is a spectrum of task difficulty: it goes from easy – such as recalling knowledge – to harder – such as evaluating an argument. But it is a spectrum because it explores the full range of cognitive learning. Knowledge is just as important as evaluation. Without knowledge, pupils can't access the higher bits. In other words, without the bottom layers of the pyramid – the foundations – the whole structure crumbles.

To demonstrate their complete mastery of a topic, every pupil (no matter their current level of performance) should be able to answer a combination of recall-type questions (these are questions which can be answered in a short period regardless of prior learning) and developmental-type questions (these are questions which stretch pupils and develop the skills required for academic success). Every pupil at every level of their academic development needs to answer questions on the full spectrum of Bloom's Taxonomy; every pupil needs access to both mastery and developmental questions.

Rather than expecting different outcomes of different pupils, we should have high expectations that all our pupils will reach the same destination, albeit some will take a different route and need more time to do so.

This notion that all pupils achieve the same outcome forms the basis of 'mastery learning'...

Mastery learning

Mastery learning is founded on the belief that all pupils are capable of learning anything if that learning is presented in the right way. Mastery learning works on the basis that understanding is the result of intention and effort, and that difficulty is enjoyable.

In practical terms, mastery learning, which was first introduced into the UK system in maths and modelled on practices popular in China and Singapore but which is now gaining traction in other subjects, is about pupils demonstrating they have mastered something before being able to move on to the next thing. The teacher decides the level of mastery required – 80 or 90 per cent, say – and pupils are given opportunities to learn through a variety of instructional methods before taking a test. If pupils do not attain the right level of mastery in the test, they are given additional instructional activities to complete before retaking the test (which is usually in a different form or uses different questions).

One benefit of the mastery approach is that it avoids the negative effects of differentiation which can translate as lower expectations of what the so-called 'less able' pupils are able to achieve. With differentiation, activities can also be oversimplified. Mastery, however, allows teachers to genuinely challenge pupils. Here's how it works...

In a traditional classroom, as I have already explained, the teacher tends to teach to the middle and when the middle is ready, the teacher moves on to the next topic. This sends a signal to the class that everyone learns in the same way and requires the same activities. This approach also tells pupils that once the majority of the class has learnt something, all pupils move on. Many pupils learn nothing but are compelled to move on whether they are ready to do so or not. Those pupils who are ready to move on faster than the middle, meanwhile, have to wait for the majority to catch up.

But with mastery learning, the teacher sends a very different signal to their pupils: that everyone will learn and succeed, that the teacher is not going to move on until everyone is ready to do so. With mastery, the teacher also makes it explicit that every pupil will get a minimum of, say, 80 per cent in tests and that the teacher and/or teaching assistant will keep working with them until they do so.

The teacher can tell the faster pupils that they can move on whenever they are ready, that they will not be held back. The teacher makes it clear that people learn different things in different ways and at different paces.

Although, at its heart, mastery learning is about handing over responsibility for learning to pupils, it is not the same as independent learning or self-teaching. In fact, teachers who employ a mastery approach tend to interact more not less with individual pupils compared to more traditional instructional methods. By using a variety of resource materials (such as texts at different reading levels) and addressing various learning styles (by presenting information visually, verbally, and in writing), teachers can address differences in preferred learning styles and achievement levels.

By allowing pupils some options about how they work (for example, independently or in groups) or how they communicate their learning (visually, verbally, or in writing), teachers can personalise the learning still further.

Mastery learning, as I explained in Book One of this series, meshes perfectly with the 'progression model' of curriculum planning and sequencing I advocated as a means of identifying the way-points of our curriculum.

In short, differentiation should be about ensuring every pupil is headed toward the same destination. We should not 'dumb down' or expect less of lower-performing pupils; rather, we should articulate the same high expectations of all – expectations regularly reinforced through our language and our actions – but accept that some pupils, some of the time, will need different levels of support, different kinds of support, and to be afforded different timescales to reach that destination.

Learning how to fall

When approaching differentiation, we'd be wise to remember that all pupils – like all human beings – are different, unique, individual. Differentiation, therefore, should not be about treating 'less able' pupils – or indeed those with SEND or eligible for Pupil Premium funding – as a homogenous group. Rather, we should treat each pupil on an individual basis. Instead of expecting different outcomes of different pupils, we should have high expectations that all our pupils will reach the same destination, albeit some will take a different route and need more time to do so.

Of course, some pupils fear challenge. We need to eliminate – or at least mitigate – their feelings of fear and hesitation by creating a classroom environment which encourages the making of mistakes as an integral part of the learning process, and a pedagogical culture which explicitly says (through our choice of language, our modelling and thinking aloud, and the routines in which we engage) that there is nothing to fear by trying your best and pushing yourself to do hard work. After all, challenge is innate. Pupils love challenge when it is private because, in the safety of their own homes or when with trusted friends, there isn't the fear of humiliation or peer pressure.

To promote challenge in the classroom, therefore, we need to reduce the threat level, we need to ensure no-one feels humiliated if they fall short of a challenge. Rather, they need to know that they will learn from the experience and perform better next time. They will learn by increments.

Reducing the threat level

When I talk about reducing the threat level, I mean we need to create a positive learning environment in which pupils' senses are stimulated so that they pay attention to the right things and are made to think hard but efficiently about curriculum content. I refer, too, to an environment in which pupils are challenged by hard work but know that they are safe to take risks and make mistakes. What I do not mean to imply is that our classroom should be regarded as an easy, fun place to be. As I explained in Chapter Ten, there's nothing wrong with pupils enjoying themselves whilst they learn, and we certainly wouldn't want school to be a dull and boring place. However, fun is never the goal. Rather, we need pupils to think and work hard.

As I explained earlier, a positive learning environment is, to my mind, one in which all pupils:

- Feel welcomed,
- Feel valued,
- Are enthusiastic about learning,
- Are engaged in their learning,
- Are eager to experiment, and
- Feel rewarded for their hard work.

Behind all of these characteristics and any more we care to mention, I said, there is a simple, albeit oxymoronic, aim: to ensure pupils are comfortable with discomfort. In other words, we want our pupils to know that the work they'll be asked to do in our classrooms will be tough, that they will be challenged with hard work and made to think. We want our pupils to know that there will be no hiding place in our classrooms; they must ask and answer questions and attempt everything we ask of them.

However, in so doing, we want them to feel safe and protected, we want them to be eager for challenge, and to willingly attempt hard work because they know that we've strung a safety net beneath them: yes, they might falter but we will catch them if they fall. We also want our pupils to know that taking risks and making mistakes is not just accepted in our classrooms but is positively and proactively welcomed as an essential part of the learning process. Indeed, the only people who don't make mistakes either never get any better at anything or have reached the point of automaticity - they have fully mastered something and so can now do it through habit. Our pupils are not at the point of automaticity and so must make mistakes if they are to get better in our subject. If they don't make mistakes, they cannot receive feedback; if they don't receive feedback, they will not know how to improve; if they don't know how to improve, then they are unlikely to do so.

Of course, in order to set the right level of challenge for our pupils – hard but achievable with time, effort and support – we need to locate, perhaps through the use of exit tickets or hinge questions, pupils' 'struggle zones' – the point just beyond their current capability but within their reach, something they cannot yet do but will be able to with time, effort and support.

Talking of which... in the next chapter, I will explain how to use exit tickets and hinge questions in order to enable differentiated instruction.

CHAPTER FORTY-EIGHT:
FIND THE SWEET SPOT

In the previous chapter, I explained that, rather than differentiate by task, we should teach to the top and ensure our classroom provides challenge for all. I conceded that, naturally, some pupils fear challenge and so we need to eliminate – or at least mitigate – their feelings of fear and hesitation by creating a classroom environment which encourages the making of mistakes as an integral part of the learning process, and a pedagogical culture which explicitly communicates (through our choice of language, our modelling and thinking aloud, and through the routines in which we engage) that there is nothing to fear by trying your best and pushing yourself to do hard work.

Finding the right level of challenge for our pupils – work that is hard but achievable with time, effort and support – is not easy. So how can we locate pupils' 'struggle zones'? How can we ascertain where to pitch learning in our classrooms?

Two methods spring readily to mind: exit tickets and hinge questions.

I gave an overview of these strategies, along with the KWL chart, in Book One of this series on School and College Curriculum Design as part of a discussion about identifying curriculum starting points so readers of that book who, unlike me, are blessed with perfect recall, may wish to skip to the section below on high expectations. For the rest of you, we'll now take a quick look at each of these strategies in turn...

Exit tickets

One way to determine the current location of pupils' 'struggle zones' is to issue exit tickets at the end of the lesson. Exit tickets are slips of paper on which are written questions to which pupils provide responses. Exit tickets act as quick, informal assessments of learning that enable teachers to rapidly evaluate their pupils' understanding of the lesson content. They also help pupils to reflect on what they have understood and not understood, and they enable pupils to express what or how they are thinking about new information and, by so doing, they encourage pupils to think more critically.

According to Fisher and Frey (2004), there are three categories of exit slips:

1. Prompts that document learning:
E.g. Write one thing you learned today; Discuss how today's lesson could be used in the real world; etc.

2. Prompts that emphasise the process of learning:
E.g. I didn't understand...; Write one question you have about today's lesson; etc.

3. Prompts to evaluate the effectiveness of instruction:
E.g. Did you enjoy working in small groups today?; Did you find peer-assessment helpful?; etc.

Other useful exit ticket prompts might include:

- I would like to learn more about...
- Next lesson, I'd like you to explain more about...
- The thing I found easiest today was...
- The thing I found hardest today was...

I would go further than Fisher and Frey and suggest that the most effective exit tickets pose questions specific to the curriculum content of the lesson and require pupils to explicitly demonstrate their grasp of that content. For example, if I'd taught pupils how to use an apostrophe correctly, rather than ask them to vaguely comment on something they thought they'd learnt, my exit ticket might require pupils to add an apostrophe to three sentences whereby one would be an apostrophe for possession, one for omission and at least one would require a decision to be made about whether to use -s' or -s's. I could see at a glance if pupils had understood how to use apostrophes by assessing the three sentences.

Doug Lemov, in his book, Teach Like a Champion, says that exit tickets allow teachers to "know how effective [their] lesson was, as measured by how well [pupils] learned it, not how well [they] thought [they] taught it."

A good exit ticket, therefore, must be closely aligned to the lesson's objectives. A good exit ticket must also:

* Assess pupils' understanding in all aspects of the lesson
* Differentiate accurately between levels of understanding
* Be quick to answer and assess

Limiting the amount of space available for pupils to respond ensures the task is kept focused and, by the same token, writing a single question which incorporates the whole lesson helps to make assessing exit tickets more manageable.

Talking of which... when assessing the exit tickets pupils have handed in on their way out of the room, we are likely to find that:

* All pupils got the right answer – in which case we can move on to the next topic, or...
* All pupils got the wrong answer – in which case we can re-teach the topic next lesson before moving on, or most likely....
* Some pupils got the right answer but some got it wrong – in which case we can briefly recap on the topic next lesson (perhaps as a starter activity), get a pupil who 'got it' to peer-teach the topic or share their work as an exemplar to deconstruct (or group pupils to do this in pairs), and/or sit down with the pupils who didn't get it when there's a suitable opportunity next lesson and re-teach them whilst the others move on to the next topic.

A caveat: learning is not always observable in a lesson. We can assess pupils' performances - the immediate regurgitation of what they've just seen or heard - but learning only becomes evident at a later time. What's more, performance is often a poor proxy for learning – those pupils who appear to struggle initially often learn better long-term. Exit tickets, because they review pupils' understanding at the end of the lesson not days or weeks later, are in danger of assessing performance rather than learning so some caution should be applied and the questions should be revisited again at a later stage, but they remain a helpful means of reviewing the success of the lesson and can provide a useful focus for the next lesson's starter activity.

To mitigate the limitations of exit tickets, it is worthwhile repeating the task in a later lesson and comparing responses – do pupils still claim to understand what they said they'd learnt last time? Do we need to recap or re-teach a topic in light of their long-term retrieval ability?

Hinge questions

Another useful strategy – though one that's harder to get right – is the use of hinge questions...

Hinge questions are multiple choice questions so, before we go any further, let's explain and defend the humble multiple-choice question which, although once a staple of schooling, has become unfashionable in recent years...

With open questions, the rubric defines the rigour. With multiple choice questions, however, the options define the rigour. This is particularly true of hinge questions which can be used just as effectively with the most able pupils as with the less able. The trick to making multiple choice questions effective is to create several wrong options which are nevertheless plausible and closely related to the right answer.

The best 'wrong' options also uncover common misconceptions or false assumptions. As such, the best way to create the wrong options in a way which makes them plausible is to mine a class's work - or look back to a previous year when the topic was last taught - for pupils' common misconceptions, misunderstandings and mistakes. If nothing else, trawling through pupils' work to discover what they tend to get wrong and what tends to stump them, helps inform the lesson planning process, allowing the teacher to dedicate more time to those elements with which pupils most often struggle.

This act of mining pupils' work for misconceptions and then applying the findings in a way that helps anticipate pupils' difficulties and questions, is the difference between content knowledge and pedagogical content knowledge, between knowing your subject and knowing how to teach your subject in a way which makes sense to pupils. Analysing misconceptions also helps an expert teacher to view a topic through the lens of the novice pupil, to narrow the knowledge gap between them and improve the lesson planning process.

A 'hinge' is a point in a lesson when a teacher needs to check whether or not pupils have grasped a key concept and are ready to move on to study another. Usually, pupils' mastery of the concept that has just been taught is contingent on them being able to understand the next concept. It's important, therefore, that the teacher assesses pupils' levels of mastery before moving on... and this is exactly what a hinge question can do...

A hinge question is a diagnostic tool which a teacher employs when their pupils reach the 'hinge' point. Pupils' responses provide the teacher with valuable evidence about what their pupils know, don't know and need to do next. A class's response to a hinge question should inform the teacher whether to completely re-teach the topic, recap the main points, or move on to the next topic.

A hinge question, then, is a multiple-choice question which provides an immediate check of pupils' understanding. Crucially, a hinge question provides a check of understanding for every pupil in a class. A hinge question informs the teacher if pupils have understood what they've taught and, if not, what they have misunderstood. As I say above, a hinge question should be asked at the end of an activity as the teacher moves from teaching one key concept to another, when the teaching of the second concept is reliant on understanding the first.

Every pupil must respond within a set timeframe, ideally one to two minutes. A hinge question is a quick assessment - a line in the sand - and, therefore, responses should be instinctive and almost immediate. All pupils must participate in the process. As such, it's best to avoid a 'hands up' approach and instead employ a tactic that ensures every pupil shows the teacher their answer at the same time. This enables the teacher to assess every pupil and prevents pupils from being unduly influenced by their peers.

Simultaneous, all-class responses can be achieved by using mini whiteboards on which pupils write their answers then hold them up when instructed. Alternatively, voting buttons could be used, perhaps on iPads, with the responses - anonymised, of course; perhaps reported as a percentage response against each option - displayed on the interactive whiteboard. Or, perhaps more simply, pupils could hold up lettered, numbered, or coloured cards to indicate their answer. A set of four cards could be kept on desks or given to pupils to retain in their books or planners in order to reduce the logistical strain and permit hinge questions to become a quick, simple, everyday feature of lessons.

The teacher must be able to interpret pupils' responses quickly, ideally within a minute, so that the flow of the lesson isn't stunted. Before pupils show their responses, the teacher - as I say above - needs to set a pass rate for what they consider to be an acceptable level of 'mastery'. For example, the teacher might decide that they'll move on to the next topic if more than eighty per cent of pupils answer the hinge question correctly. They'll then need to consider what they'll do to support the twenty per cent who got the question wrong.

The teacher could set a task for the eighty per cent to do whist working with the twenty per cent, scaffolding their learning, recapping on key points, and so on. Or perhaps the teacher could enlist some of the eighty per cent as peer-teachers to explain the topic to the twenty per cent.

Now let's take a look the importance of high expectations and examine what they might look like in the classroom.

High expectations

So far in Part Four of this book on ensuring equal access to long-term learning, I've explained that differentiation is – fundamentally – about enabling every pupil, no matter their background and starting point, to access an ambitious curriculum and achieve. The best way of doing this is by building routines into our teaching and learning practices. In particular, I've advocated a 4-step teaching sequence.

Also in this section of the book, I've explained that to suggest a pupil is 'less able' implies there is an average pupil against which we are comparing all others. But there is no such thing as 'average'. What's more, the term 'less able' infers an immovable position – if you are 'less able' you are destined to remain so *ad infinitum*, living life languishing in the left-hand shadow of the bell-curve.

When approaching differentiation, therefore, we'd be wise to remember that all pupils – like all human beings – are different, unique, individual. Differentiation, therefore, should not be about treating 'less able' pupils as a homogenous group. Rather, we should treat each pupil on an individual basis. We should not 'dumb down' or expect less of lower-performing pupils; we should articulate the same high expectations, regularly reinforced through our language and our actions – but accept that some pupils, some of the time, will need different levels of support, different kinds of support, and be afforded different timescales to reach that destination.

We should, therefore, teach to the top and ensure our classroom provides challenge for all. Of course, some pupils fear challenge and so we need to eliminate – or at least mitigate – their feelings of fear and hesitation by creating a classroom environment which encourages the making of mistakes as an integral part of the learning process, and a pedagogical culture which explicitly communicates (through our choice of language, our modelling and thinking aloud, and through the routines in which we engage) that there is nothing to fear by trying your best and pushing yourself to do hard work.

To promote challenge in the classroom, therefore, we need to reduce the threat level, we need to ensure no one feels humiliated if they fall short of a challenge. Rather, they need to know that they will learn from the experience and perform better next time.

The Pygmalion Effect

Once we've created a positive learning environment in which pupils willingly accept challenge, we need to model high expectations of all.

Robert Rosenthal and Lenore Jacobson conducted research in the 1960s which showed that, when teachers expected an enhanced performance from their pupils, their pupils' performance was indeed enhanced. Their study supported the hypothesis – known as the Pygmalion Effect – that reality can be positively or negatively influenced by other people's expectations. In other words, the higher the expectations you have of somebody, the better they perform.

This research led Rosenthal to predict that teachers subconsciously behave in ways that facilitate and encourage their pupils' success. In other words, teachers perpetrate the Pygmalion Effect: when they have high expectations of their pupils, their pupils perform well.

It follows, therefore, that having high expectations of pupils is not only a nice thing to do, it actually leads to improved performance. But saying and doing are two very different things. After all, what do high expectations actually look like in practice? Well, as with most teaching strategies, having high expectations is simply about establishing a set of clear rules and routines. Doug Lemov shares a few such routines in his book, Teach Like a Champion...

Lemov says that teachers who have high expectations operate, amongst other things, a "No opt out" policy. In other words, a teaching sequence that begins with a pupil unable to answer a question should end with the same pupil answering that question as often as possible.

Lemov also says that teachers who have high expectations always insist that "Right is right". In other words, they set and defend a high standard of correctness in their classroom. For example:

- They use simple positive language to express their appreciation of what a pupil has done and to express their expectation that he or she will now complete the task. For example: "You're almost there. Can you find the last piece?";
- They insist that pupils answer the question they have been asked not a different question entirely. These teachers are clear that the right answer to any question other than the one they have asked is, by definition, wrong.

- As well as insisting on the right answer, teachers with high expectations insist that pupils answer the right question at the right time. They protect the integrity of their lesson by not jumping ahead to engage an exciting right answer at the wrong time.
- These teachers insist their pupils use precise, technical vocabulary.

Lemov says that teachers who have high expectations "Stretch it". In other words, a sequence of learning does not end with a right answer; these teachers reward right answers with follow-up questions that extend knowledge and test for reliability. For example, they ask how or why, ask for another way to answer, ask for a better word, ask for evidence, ask pupils to integrate a related skill, and/or ask pupils to apply the same skill in a new setting.

Lemov says that, for the teachers who have high expectations of their pupils, "Format matters". In other words, it is not just what their pupils say that matters but how they say it. To succeed, pupils must take their knowledge and express it in the language of opportunity.

As well as having high expectations of our pupils, we should insist that our pupils have high expectations of themselves, because only by believing in yourself and in your own ability to get better will you actually do so. But what does *this* look like in practice?

First, pupils should have a growth mindset and believe that they can get better at anything if they work hard. This means having a thirst for knowledge, this means accepting that work needs to be drafted and redrafted, and this means following the maxim that if it isn't excellent, it isn't finished (never settling for work that is less than their best). This also means setting aspirational goals for themselves and expecting to achieve them.

Second, pupils should embrace challenge and enjoy hard work because they know it will help them to learn. This means actively engaging in lessons and readily accepting any new challenges that are presented. It also means exerting a lot of effort and engaging in deliberate practice. It means pushing themselves in lessons, practising something over and over again, and regarding additional study opportunities such as homework as an important way of consolidating and deepening their learning rather than as an onerous chore.

Third, pupils should seek out and welcome feedback. They should value other people's opinions and advice and use it to help them improve their work. Feedback should be given and received with kindness in a manner that is helpful and not unduly critical, and yet it should be constructive and specific about what needs to be improved.

Fourth, pupils should be resilient. By being resilient – not giving up easily when things get hard – they will overcome obstacles. Moreover, they will be happy to make mistakes because they know they will learn from them. In practice, this means that pupils ask good questions in order to further their learning, this means pupils always try and solve problems for themselves before asking others for help.

Finally, pupils should be inspired by other's success. They should seek out examples of great work, discovering what makes it great then using this knowledge to inform their own work. They should take collective responsibility for the work of the class and have a vested interest in everyone's success.

This means that pupils support each other and encourage each other to succeed. This means that pupils work well in groups and are confident expressing their views and sharing their ideas. This means that pupils are good at giving each other feedback that is – as I say above – kind, specific and helpful.

Lesson design

What else can we do to help the so-called 'lower-performing pupils' to learn and make progress?

First, we can put blocks in the way of pupils' initial learning (or encoding) – what, as we discovered in Chapter Thirty-Six, Robert Bjork calls "desirable difficulties" – in order to bolster their subsequent storage and retrieval strength.

Second, we can "chunk" information, ensuring we teach knowledge before skill. And we can link new learning with prior learning so that pupils can cheat their limited working memories.

Third, as we discussed in Chapter Thirty-Five, we can provide opportunities for our pupils to engage in deliberate practice, repeating learning at least three times but doing so in a different way each time, allowing pupils to do something new with the learning every time they encounter it in order to forge myriad connections and improve "transfer".

And if all this works with lower-performing pupils then it will work with all pupils.

That's the beauty of a 'teaching to the top' approach: if you have high expectations of all your pupils and if you model, say, grade 9 work rather than grade 5 work, then although some pupils will fall short, because they have all aimed high they are more likely to achieve a better grade than if you'd placed artificial limits in the way of their learning. The key is in deconstructing models of excellence 'live' in front of pupils so that they can see how excellence is forged in the red-hot furnace of experience, so that they can see the steps they need to take to travel from novice towards expertise, and so the invisible is made visible and the implicit is made explicit.

What's more, why would we show pupils anything other than the very best? Why model the mediocre? As Matthew Arnold said in Culture and Anarchy, "Culture ... is a study of perfection, [it] seeks to [...] make the best that has been thought and known in the world current everywhere; to make all men live in an atmosphere of sweetness and light".

So, let's bring all our pupils, no matter their starting points and current performance, out into the light and watch them grow.

In Chapter Forty-Nine, I'll review eight of the most common forms of differentiation in use in our classrooms today and analyse their respective advantages and disadvantages. Then I'll examine the role that teaching assistants (TAs) or additional learning support (ALS) can play in ensuring that learning is differentiated.

CHAPTER FORTY-NINE:
DIFFERENT FORMS OF DIFFERENTIATION

Differentiation wears many guises. I'd like to review eight of the most common forms of differentiation in use in our classrooms today and analyse, as I see them, their relative advantages and disadvantages. I do so not to imply that I know what works best for you and your pupils, but simply to provide you with the space and opportunity to step back and consider each of these approaches afresh. I would not profess to know what works for you and I would never presume to teach grandma how to suck eggs. All I ask is that you keep an open mind to what might and might not be the most effective strategies...

Differentiation by task

What is it? The teacher gives different pupils different tasks, the level of difficulty of which is determined by the pupil's 'ability'.

What are the advantages? It allows the task to be set to test the mastery of skills of different groups of pupils dependent on their needs.

What are the disadvantages? It can be time-consuming, and it can lead to difficulties comparing pupils' achievements because we can't assess the same things. It also places a limit on what some pupils can achieve.

Differentiation by resource

What is it? The teacher gives different pupils different resources to support their learning, such as scaffolded worksheets or texts at differing word levels.

What are the advantages? It allows pupils of different abilities to access the curriculum but in a manner appropriate to them.

What are the disadvantages? It can be very time-consuming and promote learned helplessness.

Differentiation by assessment

What is it? The teacher gives different pupils different assessment tasks based on what they need them to demonstrate.

What are the advantages? It allows an assessment task to be set to test the mastery of skills of different groups of pupils dependent on their needs. It can be quick to prepare because it can simply consist of different questions

What are the disadvantages? It can be time-consuming and can lead to difficulties in comparing pupil achievements because different assessments may not be testing the same thing. What's more, it runs counter to current examination practice in most subjects whereby papers are no longer tiered, and every pupil is assessed in the same manner.

Differentiation by pace

What is it? The teacher allows pupils differing timescales to read the end goal, accepting that every pupil learns at a different pace.

What are the advantages? It allows pupils to work at their own pace whilst striving towards the same destination.

What are the disadvantages? It may mean that some pupils do not reach their destination and therefore do not cover all the curriculum content. It may mean the teacher loses the integrity of their carefully planned and sequenced curriculum and that whole-class instruction becomes difficult.

Differentiation by support

What is it? The teacher offers different levels of support to different pupils.

What are the advantages? Pupils receive personalized support from the teacher, teaching assistant or other pupils.

What are the disadvantages? It is difficult for the teacher to manage whole class progress and know exactly what has been taught and learnt so they can assess pupil progress and move through the curriculum.

Differentiation by extension

What is it? The teacher provides additional tasks to pupils who finish soonest, enabling them to move on to more difficult content whilst the rest of the class catches up.

What are the advantages? It allows the teacher to set a task that tests pupils' mastery of skills. It can be quick to prepare if it takes the form of questions of differing difficulty.

What are the disadvantages? It can be time-consuming if it takes the form of different detailed activities. It can lead to difficulties in comparing achievement because different tasks may not be testing the same thing.

Differentiation by dialogue

What is it? The teacher uses one-to-one or small group discussions – such as verbal feedback – to provide assessment information and support which enables pupils to make progress.

What are the advantages? It is an integral part of the lesson, builds rapport, enables the teacher to gain crucial assessment information and personalise the learning, and can be applied to all.

What are the disadvantages? It is sometimes difficult to carve out sufficient time in a lesson to talk to pupils on an individual basis without slowing the flow of the curriculum. Some pupils may receive a lot of feedback information whilst others – whom the teacher deems to be making sufficient progress – are largely ignored.

Differentiation by grouping

What is it? The teacher places pupils into different groups depending on their current progress and their strengths and weaknesses, in order to carry out different tasks, use different resources, undertake different assessments, work at a different pace, access a different level of support, work on extension tasks, and so on.

What are the advantages? Differentiated grouping allows different groups to be tracked differently, it encourages collaborative learning and allows pupils to support each other. Sometimes, pupils are placed in groups of similar 'ability'; other times, 'less able' pupils are placed with their 'more able' peers who offer support, perhaps in the form of peer-teaching.

What are the disadvantages? It can lead to stigmatisation if some groups are deemed 'less able'. Like all group work, it can lead to off-task learning or to some pupils doing all the work whilst others 'coast' if it is not tightly controlled and if the teacher doesn't explicitly teach group work skills or behaviours first.

Adapting the learning environment for pupils with additional needs

In Chapter Ten, I said that creating a positive physical environment in which to learn is crucial to ensuring that *every* pupil makes progress. But environmental factors such as these become even more critical to pupils' success when those pupils have additional and different needs including SEND. As such, as an appendix to this chapter on differentiation approaches, I'd like to explore some best practice advice on creating an effective learning environment for pupils with SEND – what we might class as our ninth strategy: *differentiation by environment*.

According to a 2014 report by the charity Mencap, 65% of parents of children with SEND believed their child had received a poorer quality of education than their peers without SEND, in large part because their child had sometimes been removed from the classroom and taught separately, but also because the physical, social, emotional and learning environment in their main classroom had not just adjusted to meet their needs.

In 2013, the University of London's Institute of Education reported that pupils with SEND were routinely segregated from their teachers and classmates, spending more than a quarter of their time in school away from qualified teachers and the classroom.

What's more, when pupils with SEND *are* taken out of their normal classrooms, they tend to be housed in smaller rooms that are not as comfortable or conducive to learning. It is not atypical, for example, for these pupils to be taught (either in small groups or on the basis of one-to-one tuition) in rooms which have ill-matched and broken tables and chairs, and which were designed for other purposes such as the dining hall, library, computer room, and staff offices. These rooms by their nature are often adjacent to busy or noisy spaces, such as staff rooms, playgrounds or corridors, and have become dumping grounds for unused stationery or broken equipment. Sometimes, these rooms are also poorly ventilated or heated, and have little natural light.

Both the Teacher Standards (2012) and the SEND Code of Practice (2014) require teachers to ensure all the pupils in their classes can access learning, and this - it is made explicitly clear - means adapting their learning environment, for example by providing visual timetables, writing frames and mind-maps, or by providing physical resources such as sloped writing boards.

Pupils with SEND also tend to respond best when the classroom is tidy and organised, when the teacher sits with the pupil at the front of the class and provides handouts which summarise and clarify the key points from the lesson rather than expecting pupils to copy copiously from the board.

The best learning environments have a range of resources such as personalised dictionaries, writing frames, lists of sentence starters, lists of linking words, mini-whiteboards and coloured pens, pastel coloured paper and notebooks, aide memoire to support individual learning activities, and tailored handouts to support specific tasks.

Pupils who are susceptible to visual stress are best supported by coloured overlays, cream paper for handouts and exercise books, pastel or cream backgrounds on computer screens and PowerPoint presentations, a font size no smaller than 12 point for paper and 28 point for PowerPoint, texts in a sans serif font such as Arial, Verdana, Tahoma, and Comic Sans, left-justified text, and the use of bold to emphasise text but the avoidance of italics, underlining and capitals.

Classroom displays work best for pupils with SEND when they are informative, interactive and relevant, are uncluttered so that key information can quickly and easily be found and can be seen from every position in the classroom. Displays also work best when there is a good use of colour, when they contain key words that are explicitly taught to and understood by all pupils and then frequently referenced in lessons, and when they celebrate pupils' work and make them feel valued.

The learning environments that work best for pupils with SEND are also:

1. Suitably adapted to the needs of pupils with SEND
2. Quiet and distraction-free
3. Fitted with good lighting, heating and ventilation
4. Visually attractive and inspiring
5. Stocked with requisite resources and equipment, all within easy reach of pupils and adults including, for example, a white board, flip chart, and writing resources, but which is also clutter-free.
6. Equipped with the appropriate furniture and space, including chairs and a table at the right height.

But, as we saw in Chapter Eleven, there's far more to creating a positive learning environment adapted to the needs of pupils with SEND than these physical attributes. A classroom is more than just the bricks and mortar of the built environment, after all. A positive learning environment is also about how the teacher teaches and about the culture or ethos they create?

Accordingly, let's briefly explore the pedagogical and emotional features of a SEND classroom in more detail...

The SEND Code of Practice says that 'Special educational provision is underpinned by high quality teaching and is compromised by anything less.' Providing an inclusive learning environment whereby pupils' needs are met without drawing attention to their difficulties, therefore, is crucial because this will maximise their learning potential but limit any feelings they may have of embarrassment and frustration.

Here are some practical tips for:

- Supporting pupils with memory difficulties
- Teaching spelling
- Teaching reading
- Teaching writing
- Teaching through intervention

Supporting SEND pupils with memory difficulties

When supporting pupils with memory difficulties, the teacher could:

- Revisit previous learning at the beginning of the lesson, allowing pupils to recall and make associations with new learning.
- Give an overview of the lesson so the pupils can see the outcome and make sense of the content.
- Revisit learning at regular intervals throughout the lesson.
- 'Chunk' new information and regularly check understanding.
- Use a step-by-step approach to completing any task with regular checkpoints for monitoring progress and giving feedback.
- When giving instructions, limit the number, repeat them and provide notes and a checklist.

- Use simple, concise sentences when giving direct instruction
- Consider the pace of delivery – speak more slowly if necessary.
- Use songs, rhyme and rap to aid memorisation.
- Allow 'wait time' for pupils to process information before articulating an answer.
- Allow pupils to work collaboratively.
- Ensure that the tasks are relevant to the learning and eliminate those that will interfere with that learning, such as copying from the board or writing the date and title.
- When pupils are on task, avoid interrupting their learning.
- At the end of the lesson, summarise the learning and say what the next lesson will be about. Paint the big picture for pupils, showing how each lesson fits in and builds upon the last.

Supporting SEND pupils with spelling

When teaching spelling, the teacher could:

- Provide subject-specific key words in handouts.
- Encourage pupils to take risks with their spelling, suggesting that they underline these words.
- Encourage a metacognitive approach by asking pupils to analyse their spelling mistakes and identify the learning required.

Supporting SEND pupils with reading

When teaching reading, the teacher could:

- Only ask a pupil to read aloud if you know they want to.
- Ensure that books are at the right level of difficulty for pupils.
- Use audiobooks when appropriate.
- Teach reading skills, such as skimming, scanning and close reading.
- Encourage pupils to condense and make sense of what they read, for example by making mind maps and drawing diagrams and flow charts.
- Explicitly teach key vocabulary pupils will encounter in the text before they start reading.

- Encourage the pupils to take question the writer's techniques and intentions and consider their own views and experiences in relation to the text.
- Instil in pupils a desire to read by providing reading materials that are of interest to them.

Supporting SEND pupils with writing

When teaching writing, the teacher could:

- Check pupils' understanding of the task before they begin writing.
- Use ICT to improve written outcomes, for example voice recognition software or mind mapping software.
- Provide examples and model good practice.
- Break down a writing task into manageable chunks.
- Teach, model and encourage pupils to plan.
- Give specific feedback at each stage so pupils know what to repeat or improve.
- Provide a mix of written and verbal feedback.
- Improve proofreading by building in proofreading time in lessons, using a 'buddying' system, teaching and modelling strategies, providing proofreading checklists, encouraging pupils to read work aloud, and leaving 'thinking time' between writing and proofreading.

Supporting SEND pupils through intervention

When teaching through additional interventions, the teacher could:

- Ensure the lessons are structured, cumulative and multi-sensory.
- Ensure the pupil governs the pace of delivery
- Ensure the specific needs of the pupil are met
- Ensure the knowledge and skills taught in the intervention session are transferred back to the classroom
- Ensure progress is reviewed at regular intervals and is tracked
- Ensure the pupil enjoys the learning and feels motivated, confident and self-empowered.

In the next chapter, by way of illustration, I'll home in on ways to support pupils with a particular – and commonplace – learning difficulty...

CHAPTER FIFTY:
HOW TO SUPPORT CHILDREN WITH SLCN

In this chapter we are going to explore ways of supporting pupils with a particular form of SEND called SLCN. We'll do this in order to exemplify a wider point. In other words, the advice contained within this chapter and the ones that follow can be adapted and applied to support pupils with many other forms of SEND and indeed some disadvantaged pupils.

Before we begin, though, I'd like you to answer, with honesty, a simple question: What does SLCN stand for?

If you don't know, don't worry - you're not alone. I polled several secondary school teachers before I began writing this book and was unsurprised to find a majority hadn't heard of the acronym.

And yet SLCN is a major cause of SEND in school pupils and college learners and prevents many pupils from accessing the curriculum and fulfilling their potential.

So, before we go on, let's define SLCN...

What is SLCN?

SLCN stands for speech, language and communication needs.

All children and young people need good speech, language and communication skills in order to access the school

419

curriculum, make good progress and achieve good outcomes from school and from life. After all, speech, language and communication underpin basic literacy.

But, as well as being integral to literacy and therefore academic success, speech, language and communication skills are also closely linked to pupil behaviour and to their social, emotional and mental health and wellbeing. After all, if pupils cannot communicate effectively, they cannot interact with their peers or express their feelings. Let's call this *emotional literacy*.

Speech, language and communication may sound tautologous but there are important differences between the three elements of SLCN. Let's deconstruct the acronym...

S stands for speech: Pupils need to be able to speak fluently - which is to say with a clear voice, using appropriate pitch, volume and intonation, and without too much hesitation - in order to express themselves and demonstrate their understanding in every school subject. Being able to speak enables pupils to clearly convey their learning.

L stands for language: Pupils need to command a range of appropriate vocabulary in order to facilitate and further their learning across the curriculum. For example, they need to understand instructions from teachers and others. Pupils also need to be able to use verbal reasoning in order to acquire, process, analyse and understand the new information they encounter every day at school.

C stands for communication: Pupils need to know how to adapt their communication style in order to suit the purpose and audience. They need to be able to use and follow the non-verbal rules of communication such as active listening and taking conversational turns, and they need to be able to use language to explain, describe, persuade and so on.

Why is SLCN important to schools and FE colleges?

Language development is something generally associated with early years education. However, language and communication skills continue to develop throughout pupils' teenage years. Pupils continue learning new vocabulary and complex language structures to enhance their learning and interaction with others. It is therefore important for secondary teachers and FE college teachers, not just their primary school colleagues whom we tend to think are more crucial to pupils' language acquisition and development, to be able to encourage and extend this development. Put simply, language and communication between teachers and pupils enables learning.

Furthermore, pupils need the ability to use language for negotiation, compromise, resolving conflict, developing relationships and for managing and regulating their emotions. All pupils need the skills required to be proficient communicators; for attainment, behaviour, emotional and social development and their readiness for the workplace.

However, there are many pupils who struggle to develop these skills. For some pupils this may mean specialist support is needed and/or access to alternative and augmentative means of communication such as signs, symbols and communication aids. For others, however, tailored support from within school can make a considerable difference. Without this support, pupils with SLCN will struggle to understand instructions, access the curriculum, manage their behaviour and reach targets that could otherwise be well within their grasp.

It is therefore vital that secondary school teachers and FE college teachers, not just primary school teachers, understand how to support and guide pupils, students and learners with SLCN.

The policy context

It's over a decade since the term SLCN entered the popular lexicon...

In 2008, John Bercow, the former Speaker of the House of Commons who was then a backbench Conservative Party MP, chaired an independent cross-party commission into the way in which children and young people with speech, language and communication needs were supported. The commission's report, entitled the 'Bercow review of services for children and young people (0-19) with speech, language and communication needs', identified five key themes:

1. *Communication is crucial to children's life chances* and yet awareness of its importance among the public and decision makers is not sufficient.

2. *Strategic system-wide approaches to supporting SLCN are rare*; very often SLCN does not feature in national or local policies.

3. *Services are inaccessible and inequitable*. Too often support for children's SLCN is planned and funded based on the available resources, rather than what is needed, leading to an unacceptable level of variation across the country.

4. *Support that makes a difference is based on the evidence of what works*. However, service design and cuts frequently do not take account of the evidence we have.

5. *Too many children with SLCN are being missed* and are not getting the vital support they need.

To address these five key themes, the commission set out forty recommendations. Chief amongst them were the following:

Firstly, the commission said that communication was critical. Everyone must understand speech, language and communication better. To achieve this aim, clear messages and information should be developed for parents and carers.

Support for speech, language and communication should be recognised as essential to improving social mobility, health inequality and employment.

Secondly, the commission argued for a strategy for system change. What was needed, it said, was a clear unified message from the top in order to enable change. A new cross-government strategy for children should be developed, with speech, language and communication at its core. Proposals to transform provision for children and young people's mental health should be strengthened to recognise the importance of SLCN in mental health.

Thirdly, there should be an accessible and equitable service. Children and young people with SLCN should get the support they need, wherever they live. Local areas should be provided with data on estimated SLCN in their population. A programme of training on joint commissioning for SLCN should be funded.

Fourthly, support needed to make a difference. As such, decisions about SLCN support should be made based on what we know will make the greatest impact. Government should support the development of evidence-based integrated pathways for children and young people with SLCN. An evaluation programme for innovative models of school-based support should be funded. Ofsted training should ensure inspectors focus on progress in speech, language and communication. Health providers should be supported to collect data on the quality and outcomes of their intervention.

Finally, there needed to be better early identification and intervention. It is essential, the commission said, that the signs of SLCN are spotted early and acted on. Understanding of speech, language and communication should be embedded in initial qualifications and continuing professional development for all relevant practitioners. Commissioners should ensure that there is a system in place to follow up with children who are not brought to appointments.

In its response, published in December 2008 and called 'Better Communication: An action plan to improve services for children and young people with speech, language and communication needs', the government accepted many of the review's recommendations. The government's subsequent action plan contained a range of initiatives to improve services for children and young people with SLCN and to raise awareness of the importance of speech, language and communication across the whole children's workforce.

But it wasn't enough.

Ten years on...

In March 2018, marking ten years since the Bercow Review was published, the Royal College of Speech and Language Therapists (RCPLT) published a progress report. In the foreword, John Bercow said that "The 10th anniversary of the original report provides an ideal opportunity to look again at provision for children and young people with communication difficulties, and ensure their needs are placed at the heart of local and national policy, where they belong."

In the years following the report's publication, a number of its recommendations were implemented, including changes within the commissioning and provider landscape. However, the RCSLT argues that, as a nation, we are still to grasp the significance of SLCN and as a result, hundreds of thousands of children and their families continue to suffer needlessly.

More than 1.4 million children and young people in the UK have speech, language and communication needs). Language disorders alone are one of the most common disorders in childhood, affecting nearly 10% of children and young people everywhere throughout their lives. What's more, in areas of social disadvantage this number can rise to 50% of all children and young people, including those with delayed language as well as children with identified SLCN.

Poor understanding of and insufficient resourcing for SLCN mean too many children and young people receive inadequate, ineffective and inequitable support, impacting on their educational outcomes, their employability and their mental health.

The RCSLT say that, "without a shift in approach, children and young people will continue to leave school without basic language and literacy skills... we will continue having disproportionate numbers of young people with SLCN who are not in education, employment or training, who need mental health support or who are in contact within the youth justice system... [and] children and young people with lifelong communication needs will not get the support and adjustments they require."

In the remainder of this chapter, I will explore what more schools and colleges can do to help support pupils, students and learners with SLCN.

The first action I recommend schools and colleges take is to ensure they are correctly identifying pupils with SLCN. And, as I said at the beginning of this chapter, it's an action that holds water for all pupils with SEND because the first step towards supporting these pupils is to identify the learning difficulties that may hinder them in accessing our ambitious curriculum.

Identification of need

DfE census data from January 2018 shows that the percentage of pupils with special educational needs increased from 14.4% in 2017 to 14.6% and that the percentage of pupils with a statement or education health and care plan (EHCP) increased from 2.8% in 2017 to 2.9%. A further 1,022,535 pupils were on SEN support in January 2018, this equates to 11.7% of the total pupil population, an increase from 11.6% in 2017.

The 2018 data shows that SLCN remains one of the most significant causes of SEN with 22.8% of pupils with SEN support and 14.6% of pupils with a statement or EHCP being identified as having SLCN as their primary need.

So why, if SLCN is so prevalent, with most statistics suggesting an average 7% of young people have some form of SLCN, that's an average of two pupils in every class, are many secondary school teachers seemingly unaware of it?

One reason, I think, is the fact that pupils' needs are often being wrongly identified and coded when they move from primary school to secondary school and, as a consequence, from secondary school to FE college. This has legal implications because, according to the SEND Code of Practice (2014), schools have a statutory duty to publish information on their website about how they implement their policy for SEN (known as the SEN Information Report) and this must include information on 'policies for identifying children and young people with SEN and assessing their needs'. If SLCN is not being correctly identified, those policies are clearly ineffective, and pupils may suffer the consequences.

The charity The Communication Trust believes that an average of 40% of children with SLCN are not being identified as such and, they say, the most difficult to spot are older pupils, particularly those who have difficulties with vocabulary (45% not identified), those who struggle with formulating sentences (52% not identified) and children with difficulties understanding (48% not identified). That's not to say that primary school pupils are always identified correctly and supported – they're not – but it is to argue that a far greater proportion of pupils go unidentified or wrongly coded when they transfer to secondary school. Take, for example, that last statistic: 48% of pupils with difficulties understanding are not identified in secondary schools. In primary, it's only 29% which is still clearly a concern but nevertheless highlights the discrepancy.

Ofsted have reported on this problem of identification. They say that inspection evidence suggests some children and young people have been "allocated support for their behaviour when, in fact, they had specific communication needs."

The Communications Trust says that, because "SLCN is often under-identified, [...] it's important to think about how many pupils you might typically expect to have SLCN in your school. This way you can see if your current data suggests there could be pupils who have not been identified or who have been misidentified."

Identification is key across all phases of education, from early years through primary, secondary and beyond. SLCN can be complex and difficult to identify, so an ongoing focus on identification is absolutely imperative. If an average 7% of young people have SLCN, and your school has a close-to-average SEN population of 14-15% overall, you can expect your school population to mirror this. In other words, you can expect two in every class of thirty pupils to have some form of SLCN.

In May 2010 the government published a report called 'The transitions between categories of special educational needs of pupils with Speech, Language and Communication Needs (SLCN) and Autism Spectrum Disorder (ASD) as they progress through the education system,' in which it argued that pupils who initially had SLCN and who changed their category of primary need when they transferred from primary school to secondary school, were most likely to be identified as having moderate learning difficulties (MLD) or specific learning difficulties (SLD).

The report went on to argue that "the decline in the proportion of pupils identified as having SLCN as the pupils progress through secondary school needs close monitoring to ensure that [...] pupils are being properly identified in terms of their special needs in the first instance [and that] pupils who do have SLCN receive adequate support as they progress through secondary school."

The report also found that, although the main problem was that many pupils were not identified as SLCN, some who were identified as such were in fact pupils for whom English was an additional language.

The report concluded that further investigation was needed in order to determine whether there was systematic misidentification of children's needs and specifically if those with EAL often have their needs mistakenly identified as SLCN.

So how can schools, colleges and teachers identify pupils with SLCN..?

Identifying pupils with SLCN

There are several common risk factors to look out for. For example, boys are more likely (at a ratio of 2.5:1) to have SLCN than girls. Summer-born pupils are 1.65 times more likely to have SLCN than those born in the autumn. And pupils eligible for free school meals are 2.3 times more likely to have SLCN than those not eligible.

SLCN may manifest itself in pupils' limited social interactions, poor literacy skills, poor behaviour, low self-esteem and poor levels of achievement.

Here are some more tips for identifying pupils with SLCN:

A pupil who is experiencing <u>difficulties with receptive language</u> may do some of the following:

- They may have a limited vocabulary knowledge compared with other children of their age.
- They may not volunteer answers in class.
- They may parrot what you've said but without understanding it.

- When you ask them a question, they may appear to be answering a different question.
- They may have difficulty following instructions. They may appear forgetful or may take time to decipher/process more complex and/or longer sentences.
- They may show disruptive behaviour or become quiet and withdrawn. This may be because they are unable to understand what is being asked of them, are frustrated, or are frightened of failing.
- They may appear to stop concentrating when you are talking to them in a group. They may not be able to understand what you are saying, and so switch off.
- After an instruction to the group, they may look around the room at what the other pupils are doing before they start the activity. They may not have understood the instruction and are using their peers' actions as clues to help them carry out the activity.
- In activities that involve a lot of talking, like class discussions, they may be quiet and not join in, or they may join in but give inappropriate answers.

A pupil who is experiencing <u>difficulties with expressive language</u> may do some of the following:

- They may use the wrong words for things or use a word that sounds similar
- They may use very general words where a more specific word would be better.
- Their language may sound immature compared with other children of their age.
- They may omit the endings of words.
- They may miss out the small parts of a sentence like determiners such as 'the' and 'a'.
- They may wrongly order the words in a sentence, and/or miss important information in a sentence.
- They may seem to be struggling to express themselves, for example they may know a word but appear not be able to access it, resulting in lots of fillers or gesticulation.

A pupil who is experiencing difficulties with social communication/pragmatic language, may do some of the following:

- They may find it difficult to take turns in conversation.
- They may find it difficult to follow social conventions and may have difficulties initiating and maintaining conversations.
- They may find it difficult to understand non-literal language such as metaphors and sarcasm, which they take literally.
- They may have poor eye contact - not appearing to look at you or at peers when talking with them.
- They may show some disruptive or difficult behaviour due to difficulties understanding how to use language flexibly for a range of purposes.
- They may not use much expression in their face or tone of voice.
- They may talk about the same topic of conversation over and over and/or change topic frequently.

A pupil who is experiencing difficulties with speech sounds may do some of the following:

- They may be unintelligible to unfamiliar listeners.
- They may omit parts of words and/or have difficulties making some specific sounds in speech.
- During phonics work, they may not be able to produce - or discern the difference between - some of the sounds.

One form of SLCN is stammering although this does not always manifest itself as you might expect. A pupil with a stammer may do some of the following:

- They may prolong sounds (e.g. Sssssssorry)
- They may 'block', meaning that, when they are attempting a word, they make no sound at all or make a strangled sound.
- They may repeat sounds or parts of a word (e.g S s si sir, or p p please)

Understandably, some pupils become tense because of their stammer. They may have some tension in their face – particularly in the muscles around the eyes, lips or neck, and/or make extra movements when they speak, as though they are trying to force words out. They may blink or tap their hands or feet. Some pupils also try to mask their stammer. They may, for example, avoid speaking in certain situations or to certain people. They may also change the word they were going to use mid-sentence.

What can teachers do to help?

A small number of pupils with the most severe SLCN will require specialist support such as speech and language therapy. Some will require some targeted interventions outside of the classroom. Most will require some tailored support in the classroom. And all will benefit from quality first teaching and from a learning environment that supports their development.

Before I proffer my own advice on how to support pupils with SLCN, let us hear what the pupils themselves say...

According to the charity, I CAN, pupils with SLCN say that to help them access the curriculum and make better progress they want:

- Opportunities to ask questions and seek clarifications
- Teachers to use drawings and diagrams such as mind-maps to support verbal instructions
- Teachers to explain what they need to include in their answers to questions
- The use of bullet points instead of writing on the whiteboard and in handouts
- To learn the vocabulary that they need to know *before* a lesson
- Lessons where the teacher talks briefly and then they work in groups
- Thinking time after a question is asked
- Opportunities to work with a partner

In Chapters Fifty-One and Fifty-Two, I will share some proven strategies for supporting pupils with additional and different needs such as SLCN. I will do so under the following headings:

- Quality first teaching
- In-class differentiation and additional interventions

I'll stress again that the advice I offer in relation to pupils with SLCN can, in most cases, be applied to other pupils who may be at some disadvantage in terms of accessing our ambitious curriculum and of achieving long-term learning.

CHAPTER FIFTY-ONE:
QUALITY FIRST TEACHING

The best way to improve outcomes for pupils with additional and different needs including those with SLCN, is through quality first teaching because, if we improve the quality of timetabled teaching in the classroom, all pupils - including those with SEND - will make better progress.

A study by Hanushek and Rivkin (2006) found that teacher effectiveness had more impact on outcomes than anything else - pupils in the classroom of the most effective teacher out of a group of fifty teachers took just six months to make the same amount of progress that pupils taught by the least effective teacher out of fifty took two years to achieve – in other words, between the most and least effective teacher out of fifty, there was eighteen months' wasted time.

What's more, Hamre and Pianta's research (2005) showed that, in the classrooms of the most effective teachers, socio-economic differences were null and void - in other words, pupils from the most disadvantaged backgrounds made the same progress as the least disadvantaged.

Since the National Strategies were launched in the late-1990s, it has been common practice to talk of three waves of intervention for pupils with SEND. The 3-wave model is often expressed as a pyramid similar to Bloom's taxonomy whereby Wave 1 sits at the bottom and thus provides the foundations on which all other forms of SEND support are built.

433

According to the National Strategies, Wave 1 is "quality inclusive teaching which takes into account the learning needs of all the pupils in the classroom". As such, if we do not first provide pupils with quality classroom teaching, then no amount of additional intervention and support will help them to catch up.

A 2008 government paper defined the key characteristics of quality first teaching as follows:

- highly focused lesson design with sharp objectives
- high demands of pupil involvement and engagement with their learning
- high levels of interaction for all pupils
- appropriate use of teacher questioning, modelling and explaining
- an emphasis on learning through dialogue, with regular opportunities for pupils to talk both individually and in groups
- an expectation that pupils will accept responsibility for their own learning and work independently
- regular use of encouragement and authentic praise to engage and motivate pupils.

National Strategy guidance also said that quality first teaching includes a balance between the following approaches:

- directing and telling
- demonstrating
- explaining and illustrating
- questioning and discussing
- exploring and investigating
- consolidating and embedding
- reflecting on and talking through a process
- reflecting and evaluating
- summarising and reminding
- guided learning

In Chapter Forty-Four, I argued that quality first teaching occurs when we introduce pupils to new curriculum content in four distinct stages:

1. Telling
2. Showing
3. Doing
4. Practising

I won't repeat that advice again here but I would like to add some further tips to consider when using direct instruction ('telling') with pupils with additional and different needs such as SLCN...

Because pupils with SLCN:
- Find it difficult to listen to and understand lots of spoken language,
- Need more time to process spoken language,
- Can find it hard to separate out sounds, words, phrases,
- ...and yet can have visual strengths...

They will benefit from direct instruction in which their teachers:
- Cut down the amount of language used,
- Repeat important information several times,
- Build in time for processing answers to questions,
- Slow down and repeat instructions,
- Think aloud,
- Use visuals,
- Display key words on the board,
- Use sentence stems, mnemonics and other 'schema'.

Increasingly independent

Ultimately, whatever form it takes, 'quality first teaching' should ensure that all pupils, including those with SEND:

- Are engaged - in the sense of being active participants in the process of learning not passive recipients of information
- Are highly motivated to learn and enthusiastic about learning

- Are challenged by hard work and know that making mistakes is an essential part of learning
- Receive effective feedback about where they are now, where they need to go next and how they will get there
- As a result of feedback, make progress over time and become increasingly independent and resilient learners.

One way to enable pupils to become increasingly independent and resilient is to employ the popular '3B4ME' method which encourages pupils to persevere when they get stuck and overcome challenges by themselves. It works like this:

When a pupil experiences difficulty, before they ask for help, they must first use:

1. Brain (think for themselves)
2. Buddy (ask a peer)
3. Book or board (use classroom resources including wall displays and textbooks).

It's good to [teach] talk

It is also helpful to teach pupils with SEND (including those with SLCN) how to engage in classroom discussions, and for the teacher to consider the way in which they and other adults speak to pupils...

Pupil talk

In order to help pupils with SEND including SLCN to engage in classroom discussions and question-and-answer sessions, teachers need to teach pupils how to talk and work in groups. They need to provide plenty of opportunities for pupils to talk in class, to a partner, to a small group, to adults, and to the whole class. Teachers should also scaffold the questions they ask in order to build pupil confidence. They should give pupils time to process questions and instructions, building in 'thinking time'. And they should make pupils aware of the range of resources available to support them.

Teacher talk

It is important that teachers and other adults working with pupils with SEND including SLCN carefully consider the way in which they talk. For example, they should be cognisant of the length and complexity of the language they use with pupils and consider the range and level of questions pupils understand. They should encourage pupils to engage in discussions with peers. They should model and scaffold if needed and teach pupils how to recognise when they need help and how to ask for it. They should frequently check for understanding, perhaps involving other adults in the class where relevant.

The importance of literacy

The Educational Endowment Foundation report entitled 'Preparing for Literacy: Improving Communication, Language and Literacy in the Early Years' (2018), argues that approaches that emphasise spoken language and verbal interaction can support the development of communication and language [and], in turn, communication and language [can] provide the foundations for learning and thinking and underpin the development of later literacy skills." Their advice, though aimed at early years' teaching, could prove helpful for key stage 3 teachers of pupils with SEND including SLCN...

"Focusing on language and communication," the EEF say, "is especially important for young children and will support the development of a range of early literacy skills as well as their wider knowledge and understanding. In addition, developing communication and language is linked to other important outcomes including children's self-regulation, socio-emotional development, and reasoning."

A wide range of activities can be used to develop communication and language including:

- Shared reading,
- Storytelling, and
- Explicitly extending children's vocabulary.

These activities should be embedded within a curriculum of rich and varied experiences. Developing vocabulary is important for later literacy development, but it should not – the EEF warn - be seen as a silver bullet; "it should form part of a broad approach to improving communication, language, and literacy."

In terms of shared reading, the EEF recommend using the PEER framework and this might be a useful tool to help pupils with SLCN to read aloud. It is a simple sequence that can be used to support shared, or 'dialogic', reading. When reading together, adults can pause and:

- Prompt the pupil to say something about the book;
- Evaluate their response;
- Expand their response by rephrasing or adding information to it; and
- Repeat the prompt to help them learn from the expansion.

There are five main types of prompts that can be used as part of the PEER sequence. The prompts can be remembered using the acronym CROWD:

- Completion—leave a blank at the end of a sentence for pupils to complete (this works particularly well with books with rhymes or repetitive phrases);
- Recall—ask pupils about something they have already read (these prompts support pupils to understand the story plot);
- Open-ended—often with a focus on pictures in books (this works well with illustrations and encourages pupils to express their ideas);
- Wh—prompts that begin with 'who', 'what', 'where', 'why', and 'when' ('what' questions can be used to develop vocabulary); and

- Distancing—connects the book to pupils' own life experiences and provides an opportunity for high quality discussion.

More strategies

Here are some more 'quality first teaching' strategies that work particularly well for pupils with SLCN – and indeed for all pupils:

- KWL charts
- Dual coding, including the use of mind-maps
- Thinking time
- Explicit vocabulary instruction

KWL charts

One common diagnostic technique – and one I mentioned earlier in this book – is asking pupils at the beginning of a lesson or new topic to identify what they already know (or think they know) about what they are about to study. Their responses can then be listed in a table or on a graphic organiser. The contents of the first column provide us with a sense of pupils' prior knowledge, while also unmasking any misconceptions that may exist and therefore may need to be addressed.

Next, we should ask pupils to identify "what I want to learn" about the topic and ask them to raise any questions they may have at this early stage. These responses can be recorded in the second column to serve as indicators of areas of interest.

As the unit unfolds, the knowledge and skills that pupils begin to acquire should be recorded in the third column of the table, providing a record for pupils of "what I have learned".

An alternative to this is to begin a lesson or topic with an initial assessment, perhaps a low-stakes multiple-choice quiz. The results of these pre-tests can yield invaluable evidence about pupils' prior knowledge and misconceptions and, when repeated at various stages of the teaching sequence, can provide evidence of pupils' growing knowledge and understanding.

Regardless of the approach taken, information from diagnostic assessments can guide us in our planning so that lessons are more responsive to pupils' needs and their existing knowledge-base - surely the very definition of differentiation.

An important practical implication, of course, is that we must remember to plan opportunities for assessments and allow sufficient 'wriggle room' to make adjustments based on the feedback garnered by the assessments.

In-built flexibility like this is not just advisable, it is a key aspect of effective lesson-planning and differentiation because it enables learning to be personalised to match the needs and pace of pupils' learning - which is essential if we are to support pupils with SLCN. It also ensures that gaps in pupils' learning are identified and filled, which in turn will avoid an off-the-peg, one-size-fits-all approach to lesson-planning and enable good progress to be made by all pupils, irrespective of their additional and different needs.

Before we move on, let us explore some further strategies for quality first teaching that work particularly well for pupils with SLCN – and indeed for all pupils:

- Dual coding, including the use of mind-maps
- Thinking time
- Explicit vocabulary instruction

Dual coding

Dual coding, as we discovered in Chapter Twenty-One, is the combination of words and images. We have two specific yet connected cognitive subsystems: one specialises in representing and processing non-verbal objects or events; the other specialises in language. In other words, we process verbal and visual information separately and so can double the capacity of our working memory if we utilise both verbal and visual processing at the same time.

What's more, dual coding allows us to boost the information traces in our long-term memory (as two connected traces are stronger than one single trace) and it enables us to recall - or recognise - the information in two different ways.

By combining an image with a complementary word (written or preferably spoken), we're utilising both a verbal/semantic process (deciphering spoken/written words) and an iconic process (deciphering images).

Dual coding works particularly well for pupils with SLCN because, as we have already seen, these pupils tend to have strong visual processing capabilities and benefit from the use of diagrams such as mind-maps and from short bullet-points rather than lots of dense text.

However, as with all teaching strategies, dual coding only works when it's done well. Reading a text aloud in parallel with the same written text onscreen (such as reading text verbatim from a PowerPoint slide) – even if this is short bullet points - is a bad combination because pupils are required to conduct one and the same verbal/semantic decoding process in two different ways - rather than splitting and therefore doubling working memory capacity, it requires pupils to process twice the information using one process, thus halving working memory capacity! As a result, working memory becomes overloaded in what's known as 'the redundancy effect'.

The best way to make use of dual coding is to, for example, explain a visual (a diagram, graph, mind-map, etc) verbally, not through text on the visual. If there is writing on the visual, it's best not to explain it. Furthermore, we should present visuals and text at the same time so that pupils don't have to remember one part while processing the other.

Thinking time

In Chapter Thirty-Two, I talked about the role open questions – and classroom discussion – can play in helping pupils to learn. One important feature of effective classroom questioning is 'thinking time', sometimes referred to as 'wait time'...

In 1974, Mary Budd Rowe conducted research into the way in which teachers asked pupils questions in the classroom. Her findings on 'thinking time' – the amount of time, once a question has been asked, that a teacher allows to elapse before asking someone else or providing an answer themselves – were quite astonishing.

Rowe found that, on average, teachers left less than one second before answering their own question or before asking someone else to answer it.

Rowe also found that thinking time of less than one second prevented most pupils taking part in classroom discussions because such a short interval did not allow enough time for pupils to think through the question and then formulate an answer. This is particularly pronounced for pupils with SEND including SLCN who often struggle to process information, formulate their thoughts and articulate an answer clearly and concisely.

Rowe's research concluded that teachers, acknowledging their wait time was insufficient, compromised by asking more simple, closed questions where straightforward recall – as opposed to higher-order thinking – was enough for pupils to be able to provide an answer. As a further consequence of this, classroom talk was superficial.

The teachers involved in Rowe's research were encouraged to increase the amount of time they gave pupils to answer their questions. Teachers achieved this by allowing a period of time to elapse before pupils were allowed to put their hands up and answer. This extra time was used for one of the following purposes:

Thinking time – allowing pupils time to process the question and think through their answers before anyone was allowed to volunteer a response aloud;

Paired discussion time – allowing pupils to think about the question with a partner for a certain amount of time before giving an answer;

Writing time – allowing pupils to draft their thoughts on paper first before giving their responses.

Most of the above involves pupils working together to discuss their thoughts before sharing them with the whole class. In this way, effective questioning involves pupils taking group responsibility – if pupils have time to discuss the answer in pairs or groups before anyone responds verbally, pupils are more ready to offer answers and to attempt more difficult thinking, because they know that others will help them.

Having 'talking partners' as a regular feature of lessons is more democratic, too, because it allows every pupil in the room to think, to articulate and therefore to extend their learning. This has two advantages: firstly, pupils with SEND including SLCN, and those who are reluctant to volunteer answers, get to find their voice; secondly, the garrulous, over-confident pupils get to learn to listen to others. In short, it creates a spirit or ethos of cooperation which is at the heart of formative assessment.

Once the teachers in Rowe's study had had the opportunity to get used to increasing their wait time, Rowe went back to look at the effect it had had. She found:

- pupils' answers were longer
- pupils' failure to respond had decreased

- responses were more confident
- pupils challenged and/or improved other pupils' answers
- more alternative explanations were being offered

Teachers involved in the King's Medway Oxfordshire Formative Assessment (or KMOFA for short) project which began in 1999 and was undertaken by Professors Paul Black and Dylan Wiliam as part of their initial research into the effects of formative assessment, found that "increasing waiting time after asking questions proved difficult to start with...the pause after asking the question was sometimes painful [and] unnatural... [but] given more thinking time, students seemed to realise that a more thoughtful answer was required [and that they now] give an answer and an explanation without additional prompting."

For obvious reasons, pupils with SEND including SLCN particularly benefit from being afforded more thinking time to process what has been asked and to articulate a response. To ensure thinking time is especially effective for pupils with SLCN, the teacher and/or teaching assistant can warn pupils they're going to ask a question, explicitly teach clarification questions, model asking questions, use strategies such as 'snow-balling', flag up questions at the beginning of the lesson, provide a list of key questions in advance , and ask pupils to draw and/or write down an answer before they put their hand up.

Explicit vocabulary instruction

Department for Education research suggests that, by the age of seven, the gap in the vocabulary known by children in the top and bottom quartiles is something like 4,000 words (children in the top quartile know around 7,000 words). For this reason, when teaching pupils with SEND including SLCN, teachers need to be mindful of the importance of vocabulary and support its development so that pupils who, because of a specific need, did not develop this foundational knowledge before they started school and through primary school are now helped to access the curriculum.

One way to do this is to plan group work activities which provide an opportunity for pupils with SEND including SLCN to mingle with pupils with a more developed vocabulary, to hear language being used by pupils of their own age and in ways that they might not otherwise encounter.

Another solution is to model the clear and correct use of spoken language. In other words, we should give unambiguous instructions, use accurate descriptive and positional language, utilise precise terminology where appropriate, and give clear feedback.

Next, teachers can use simple, direct language and place verbs at the beginning of instructions. "Teacher talk" is not necessarily better than the language pupils access in other environments but it is different. As a result, pupils' language proficiency might be different from that required to access the curriculum, or even to understand simple classroom instructions. Confusion and disobedience can result from the fact that pupils are unfamiliar with the language structures and "lexical density" of the more formal teacherly language of the classroom. This does not mean that teachers should use the same language as their pupils, but that they might sometimes need to use simpler language and emphasise important words.

Furthermore, teachers can teach active listening skills. Most pupils can hear but are not naturally active listeners. Active listening requires selective and sustained attention, working memory, cognitive processing, and information storage and recall mechanisms. Teachers can help pupils develop these skills by giving them tasks such as listening for specific or key information, listening to answer specific questions, and listening to follow instructions.

Teachers can also teach note-taking skills whereby pupils have to write down the key points ascertained from a piece of spoken language. What's more, they can develop communication skills such as turn-taking and the use of eye contact.

And teachers can build on pupils' language by elaborating on their answers to questions, adding new information, extending the conversation through further questioning, or reinforcing the language through repetition.

To help pupils build their vocabularies, teachers can also:

- Use fewer "what?" questions and use more "why?" and "how?" questions.
- Give pupils time to rehearse answers to questions, perhaps by discussing their answers in pairs before sharing them more widely.
- After each question has been asked, give pupils thinking time before they are expected to share their answers.
- Enforce a "no-hands-up" policy as often as possible.
- Model the kind of language they expect pupils to use in group discussions and answers.
- Build pupils' vocabularies by explicitly teaching the key words in their subject and by repeating key words as often as possible; give key words as homework and test pupils on their spelling and meaning so that they become the expected discourse of all pupils.

In addition to the above, teachers of pupils with SLCN should make sure that the development of spoken language permeates the school day. After all, spoken language is used all day, every day so we should take advantage and build spoken language activities into daily routines, such as during tutor time (e.g. ask a question of each pupil that must be answered in a sentence), when handing out materials, when pupils enter and leave the classroom, and when giving instructions.

Teachers can also make sure that pupils have a regular opportunity to speak. The teacher tends to dominate classroom discussion – and it is right that teachers talk a lot because they are the experts in the room in possession of the knowledge and experience that pupils need. But it is also important that pupils get a chance to interact with the teacher and with each other and to do so beyond responding to closed questions.

What's more, teachers can plan opportunities for one-to-one discussion. Spoken language develops best through paired conversation and when one of the people in the pair has a better developed vocabulary. Therefore, it is worth investigating ways of pairing up pupils with people with more sophisticated language skills, perhaps an older pupil or a parent or volunteer. This could be a case of volunteers reading a book with a pupil or simply engaging in conversation. One-to-one conversation also enables young people with SLCN to develop conversational skills such as turn-taking, intonation and eye contact.

CHAPTER FIFTY-TWO:
IN-CLASS DIFFERENTIATION AND
ADDITIONAL INTERVENTIONS

In Chapter Fifty-One, I said that it's common practice to talk about three waves of intervention for disadvantaged pupils and those with SEND.

The 3-wave model is often expressed as a pyramid whereby Wave 1 sits at the bottom and thus provides the foundations on which all other forms of SEND support are built. I explored Wave 1 (quality first teaching) in the previous chapter.

We'll explore proven strategies for in-class differentiation (wave 2) and additional interventions (wave 3) shortly but, before we do, and to conclude my discussion of quality first teaching strategies from the previous chapter, I would like to add some further thoughts on the explicit teaching of vocabulary...

The Educational Endowment Foundation report, 'Preparing for Literacy: Improving Communication, Language and Literacy in the Early Years' (2018), claims that there is relatively limited evidence about how best to improve vocabulary, but the existing evidence suggests that the following should be considered:

- Providing pupils with a rich language environment (implicit approaches) as well as directly extending pupils' vocabulary (explicit approaches);

- Carefully selecting high-frequency words for explicit teaching;
- Developing the number of words pupils know (breadth) and their understanding of relationships between words and the contexts in which words can be used (depth); and
- Providing multiple opportunities to hear and use new vocabulary.

In terms of selecting high-frequency words for explicit instruction, it may be wise to begin by teaching the 'Tier 2' words identified by Isobel Beck. Tier 2 words are those words which appear commonly in written texts but not in spoken language. They are not subject-specific terminology nor necessarily complex words but are words that are vital to pupils' ability to access the school curriculum and to them being able to demonstrate their understanding.

Once these words have been identified, they need to be taught on a number of occasions and in different contexts. Beck offers this possible teaching sequence:

- Read a sentence in which the word appears
- Show pupils the word and get them to say it out loud
- Discuss possible meanings of the word
- Identify any parts of the word that may be familiar (e.g. Greek or Latinate roots, common prefixes and suffixes)
- Re-read the sentence with the word in it to detect any contextual clues
- Explicitly explain the meaning of the word through definition and the use of synonyms
- Provide several other examples of the word being used in context
- Ask pupils to use the word in sentences of their own.

The EEF also say that prioritising high-quality interactions with children will help to develop their communication and language. A distinction is sometimes drawn between talking with children and simply talking to children; talking to children tends to be more passive, while talking with children is based on their immediate experiences and activities and is likely to be more effective: "When done well, high quality interactions often look effortless, but they are not easy to do well and professional development is likely to be beneficial."

Multiple frameworks exist to help structure high quality interactions. Guided interaction occurs when a teacher and pupil collaborate on a task and the teacher's strategies are highly tuned to the pupil's capabilities and motivations. The teacher is responsive to the pupil's intentions, focuses on spontaneous learning, and provides opportunities for the pupil's feedback. Discussion is a key feature of this approach and the use of a variety of questions helps to develop and extend pupil's thinking.

Sustained shared thinking involves two or more people working together to solve a problem, clarify an issue, evaluate activities, or extend a narrative. Key features include all parties contributing to the interaction—one aimed at extending and developing pupils' thinking.

According to the EEF, techniques that teachers might use include:

- ***tuning in***: listening carefully to what is being said and observing what the pupil is doing;
- ***showing genuine interest***: giving whole attention, eye contact, and smiling and nodding;
- ***asking pupils to elaborate***: 'I really want to know more about this';
- ***re-capping***: 'so you think that...';
- ***giving their own experience***: 'I like to listen to music when cooking at home';
- ***clarifying ideas***: 'so you think we should wear coats in case it rains?';
- ***using encouragement to extend thinking***: 'you have thought really hard about your tower, but what can you do next?';
- ***suggesting***: 'you might want to try doing it like this';
- ***reminding***: 'don't forget that you said we should wear coats in case it rains'; and

- ***asking open questions***: 'how did you?', 'Why does this...?', 'What happens next?'

In-class differentiation and additional interventions

Even with the provision of 'quality first teaching' as outlined in the previous chapter and above, some pupils will require more - and more tailored - support in the guise of Wave 2 in-class differentiations and Wave 3 additional interventions which take place outside the classroom and off the taught timetable.

Such intervention strategies may take the form of one-to-one support from a teaching assistant (TA) or additional learning support (ALS), small group targeted teaching by a SEND or High Needs specialist, or support from external agencies such as speech and language therapists.

Before we explore some proven strategies for making Wave 2 and 3 interventions work, let us first be clear that the ultimate aim of such additional support, in most cases, is for it to become redundant over time. In other words, we want pupils with SEND to become increasingly independent and for the scaffolds to fall away. Indeed, this is the stated aim of Education Health and Care Plans (EHCPs) and High Needs funding: over time, discrete SEN funding should be reduced as its impact is felt and pupils require less and less support.

With this aim in mind, it is important to ensure that all strategic interventions aimed at pupils with SEND are monitored whilst they are happening. Often, schools review an intervention once it's ended - perhaps at the end of the term or year - to see whether or not pupils made expected progress and if the strategy was successful. This review data is also often used to evidence the impact of said strategies and, where applicable, to prove that SEND monies have been used effectively and have provided value for the public purse.

But an end-of-strategy review is not enough; rather, interventions for pupils with SEND must be monitored whilst they are still taking place in order to ascertain whether or not they are working, or working as well as they should be. If the monitoring data suggests a strategy is not having the desired effect, or not working for some pupils, then it must be stopped or changed before more time and money is wasted.

Another point worth making before we continue concerns the role of teaching assistants because it is often TAs not teachers who lead Wave 2 and 3 interventions for pupils with SEND.

As we discovered in Chapter Six, when the Educational Endowment Foundation (EEF) published the first iteration of its Teaching and Learning Toolkit, it claimed that TAs were 'not worth it'. However, if you look behind the headlines, you'll find an altogether more nuanced story... As with everything, the use of TAs only works if it's done well. In other words, it's not what you do but how you do it that matters.

Since it published its toolkit, the EEF has commissioned evaluations of six TA-led interventions, involving more than 2,000 children in around 150 schools. In each case, the TAs were trained to deliver structured sessions to small groups or individual pupils and all six trials showed TAs had a positive impact on learning.

So, the big question is this: what is the best way to utilise TAs? Here, as a reminder from Chapter Six, are some tips inspired by the EEF research:

- TAs should not be used as an informal teaching resource for pupils with SEND.
- TAs should be used to add value to what teachers do, rather than replace teachers – pupils with SEND need as much, if not more, exposure to the teacher as all other pupils.
- TAs should be used to help pupils with SEND to develop independent learning skills and manage their own learning. To achieve this, TAs need to be trained to avoid prioritising task

completion and instead concentrate on helping pupils with SEND to develop personal ownership of tasks.

- TAs should be fully prepared for their role in the classroom and need access to sufficient training and time to meet the teacher outside of class.

Furthermore, when supporting pupils with SEND in one-on-one or small group settings, TAs should use structured interventions.

The most effective intervention strategies are:

- Brief (20– 50mins),
- Regular (3–5 times per week),
- Sustained (running for 8–20 weeks),
- Carefully timetabled,
- Staffed by well-trained TAs (5–30 hours' training per intervention),
- Well-planned with structured resources and clear objectives,
- Assessed to identify appropriate pupils, guide areas for focus and track pupil progress, and
- Linked to classroom teaching.

Intervention strategies that work

Above I share some logistical features of effective intervention strategies, but the question remains, exactly what kind of support should be given to pupils with SEND during differentiated teaching and intervention sessions? Below, by way of illustration, are some suggestions specific to pupils with speech, language and communication needs (SLCN) – a particular form of SEND which we discussed in Chapter Fifty...

In terms of in-class differentiation, pupils with SLCN are often helped by:

- The use of modified language
- The use of visual prompts
- The pre-teaching of subject specific vocabulary, as appropriate

- Access to a social skills group

In terms of additional interventions, pupils with SLCN are often helped by:

- Small group or one-to-one support for language to address specifically identified pupil targets
- Access to explicit social skills teaching
- Access to additional ICT teaching such as touch typing, dictaphone, tablet and so on
- A referral to and advice from the speech and language therapy service and the Learning Language Service (LLS)
- Ongoing advice from specialist teachers
- Advice from an educational psychologist

A graduated approach to SEN support

The provision of SEN support including that for pupils with SLCN - as articulated in the SEND Code of Practice - often takes the form of a 4-part cycle of assess, plan, do, review. The cycle recommended by the SEND Code of Practice posits a 'graduated approach' whereby actions are reviewed and refined as our understanding of a pupil's needs - and indeed the support they require - increases.

The first part of the cycle is *assess*. At this stage, information is gathered from on-going, day-to-day assessments and this helps to form judgments about the progress an individual pupil with SEND is making, as well as to highlight any barriers that pupils may face. Where concerns about a pupil's progress persist, further discussions with the pupil, their parents and the SENCo may be necessary. It may also be necessary to conduct further specialist tests, or to request advice from a specialist such as, in the case of pupils with SLCN, a speech and language therapist.

The second part of the cycle is *plan*. At this stage, everyone needs to agree what additional and different support will be put in place as a result of the data gathered at the 'assess' stage. The planning stage should involve the pupil, their parents, and relevant school staff who know the pupil well.

The first step of the planning process is to agree some targets for the pupil in order to focus attention on what needs to improve first, and to give the pupil a clear idea of what they need to do to accelerate the pace of their progress.

To help the pupil achieve their targets, additional tailored support needs to be put in place, and this may include deploying specific teaching strategies, approaches or resources both in class and out of class such as those outlined above and in the previous article in this series.

Once targets are set and additional support agreed, clear and realistic timescales need to be set for monitoring and reviewing the plan. As I say above, it is crucial that additional interventions are subject to ongoing monitoring rather than just reviewed at their end-point.

The third part of the cycle is ***do***. At this stage, as the SEND Code of Practice makes clear, it is the responsibility of every staff member who comes into contact with the pupil with SEND - including, of course, their teachers - to implement the plan on a day-to-day basis. It is not the sole domain of the SENCo. In practice, this might involve:

- Delivering quality first teaching to the pupil in every lesson.
- Enacting any specific adjustments, strategies or approaches to classroom teaching as identified in the ISP.
- Liaising with teaching assistants who are providing in-class support to pupils with SEND.
- Implementing any targeted additional, out-of-class interventions as identified in the plan.
- Engaging in ongoing monitoring of pupil progress and responding to the data by making any necessary adjustments to planning and teaching.
- Communicating regularly with the pupil, their parents, the SENCo and any other staff and external agents who are involved.

The final stage of the cycle is **_review_**. At this stage, the school needs to formally evaluate how successfully the interventions and support they have offered have met the pupil's needs. At the review meeting, it is helpful to consider the following questions:

- What progress has the pupil made with regards addressing their speech, language and communication needs? Have they achieved their agreed targets and what is the evidence for this?
- What impact has the support/intervention had on the pupil being able to access the curriculum, make progress and communicate their learning? What are the pupil's, parents' and professionals' views on the effectiveness and impact of additional support/intervention?
- What changes need to be made to the pupil's targets and the specialist provision next term/year?

The SEND Code of Practice makes clear that the 4-step cycle of assess, plan, do, review is a process and is therefore continual. Even if a review shows a pupil has made good progress and no longer requires additional support in order to mitigate their speech, language and communication needs, they should still be monitored in order to ensure that their progress is sustained through inclusive quality first teaching.

Matt Bromley

CHAPTER FIFTY-THREE:
MOTIVATION MATTERS

In the chapters that follow, we will continue to explore ways of ensuring all our pupils, irrespective of their starting points, backgrounds and additional and different needs, are afforded equal access to our ambitious curriculum and to effective teaching for long-term learning. But, in so doing, we will turn our attention away from pupils with SEND and towards disadvantaged pupils such as those in receipt of the Pupil Premium Grant.

In Chapter Fifty-Four, we will explore the importance of identifying the academic barriers disadvantaged pupils face and emphasise that this should be done on a case-by-case basis because each pupil is different and will likely face different challenges and therefore require different solutions.

In Chapter Fifty-Five, we will discuss ways of planning solutions to help pupils overcome their barriers to learning and examine the central tenets of effective intervention strategies. In so doing, we will focus on one particularly impactful way of helping disadvantaged pupils – building cultural capital including in the form of explicitly teaching vocabulary.

And in Chapter Fifty-Six, we will examine how best to set the success criteria for such interventions and support so that we can be certain (or at least *more* certain) of their value.

But, before we do all this, I'd like to discuss the importance of developing pupils' intrinsic motivation...

When I started exercising about four years ago, following a bout of ill health, I could muster but fifteen minutes' half-hearted jogging on a treadmill whilst watching trash TV before collapsing, coughing and spluttering, to the floor. Until, that is, I had an idea. What I did next not only helped me conquer my natural phobia of physical activity, it also taught me a lesson about motivation, a secret I believe can help unlock the potential of our most reluctant, difficult-to-reach pupils and enable them to access our ambitious curriculum.

The only time I'd really enjoyed exercise was when, as a younger man, I went hiking or cycling in the Yorkshire Dales because the exercise had been a by-product of experiencing the beauty of the landscape. And so my first stab at a solution to my problem of motivation was to try to simulate the great outdoors indoors, to stimulate me visually and kinaesthetically (that is to say, I wanted to watch something that gave me the sensation of movement, of being outdoors, rather than stare at a static image of a beautiful landscape).

Watching TV shows whilst jogging hadn't inspired me to keep going or to run faster; I'd just wanted to stop, get off the treadmill and watch TV from the comfort of a sofa. There was, I think, too much of a discontent between what I was doing and what I was watching, it broke my concentration; it may have stimulated me but it also distracted me from the task and so I quickly grew bored of exercise. I needed to watch something that related to the physical activity I was engaged in so my body and mind were united in common cause.

Accordingly, I began watching videos of virtual runs because - as well as moving through some beautiful landscapes - the person who was running in front of me on the screen provided a focus - they were a pacesetter and I wished to keep up. I set my running pace by theirs and kept running because they kept running. What's more, because I now had a fixed destination to reach, I was determined not to give up until I had crossed that finish line.

The first thing I learnt about motivation, therefore, was the importance of having ***a destination to aim for*** and a ***model to follow***, an exemplar, someone to look up to, to aspire to, and on whom to base my technique. I realised it was important that this coach was regarded as an expert in their field, too, and that they set high expectations for me to follow.

But the running videos were only part of the solution; I also found motivation in music...

Now that I was watching a silent video of someone running, I could listen to music rather than the TV soundtrack. I quickly realised that music – particularly loud, fast music – made me run faster. Indeed, the louder and faster the music, the faster I ran. And music made me feel happier too which, in turn, made exercise feel less of a chore and more like an enjoyable way to relax and unwind.

The second thing I learnt about motivation, therefore, was the importance of ***personalisation*** – of being able to make choices and express preferences about the way you perform a task so that carrying out that task is made more enjoyable and you're more engaged in it.

I'm a rare breed: an English teacher who loves data. I was gifted a well-known brand of fitness watch for my birthday shortly after I took up running which monitors my heart rate and physical activity and uploads data to my smartphone then provides me with a range of graphs with which I can bore people at parties.

What this data did whilst I was in the early stages of my exercise routine a few years ago was provide me with rich information that allowed me to set short-, medium- and long-term goals, then monitor my ongoing progress and evaluate my outcomes.

My watch also regularly rewarded me for my achievements. I received notifications when I accomplished certain goals and was sent motivational messages about how close I was to achieving the next milestone. It was important that these milestones were within my reach - if it told me I could achieve my daily target by, say, going on a half-hour run just before bedtime, it would have demotivated me with a goal beyond my capabilities. If, however, it told me to climb the stairs a few times, it would've spurred me on.

The third thing I learnt about motivation, therefore, was the importance of having ***regular updates of progress*** towards my destination, which in turn provide a feeling of continuous movement in the right direction, as well as ***stretching but achievable step goals***.

In summary, then, I learnt that motivation requires:

1. A destination to aim for – knowing what the outcome looks like and not giving up until you reach it.

2. A model to follow – an exemplar on which to base your technique provided by someone who is regarded as an expert and who sets high expectations.

3. Regular checkpoints to show what progress has been made and what's still to do, coupled with regular celebrations of ongoing achievements and timely messages about upcoming milestones.

4. Personalisation – the ability to make choices about how to carry out tasks in order to increase enjoyment and engagement

If we want all our pupils to have equal access to our ambitious curriculum, we might want to think about adapting these four strategies to motivate them to rise to the challenge of hard work and to help them face setbacks with resilience and determination.

Two types of motivation

As we discovered in Chapters Fourteen and Fifteen, there are two types of motivation that matter most in the classroom: intrinsic and extrinsic.

1. Intrinsic motivation

Intrinsic motivation is the self-desire to seek out new things and new challenges, in order to gain new knowledge. Often, intrinsic motivation is driven by an inherent interest or enjoyment in the task itself, and exists within an individual rather than relying on external pressures or necessity.

Put simply, it's the desire to do something even though there is no reward except a sense of accomplishment at achieving that thing. Intrinsic motivation is a natural motivational tendency and is a critical element in cognitive, social, and physical development.

Pupils who are intrinsically motivated are more likely to engage in a task willingly as well as work to improve their skills, which - in turn - increase their capabilities. Pupils are likely to be intrinsically motivated if:

1. They attribute their educational results to factors under their own control, also known as *autonomy*.

2. They believe in their own ability to succeed in specific situations or to accomplish a task - also known as a sense of *self-efficacy*.

3. They are genuinely interested in accomplishing something to a high level of proficiency, knowledge and skill, not just in achieving good grades - also known as **mastery**.

2. *Extrinsic motivation*

If the 'want' to learn is concerned with intrinsic motivation, we might loosely argue that the 'need' to learn - the purpose - is linked to extrinsic motivation...

Extrinsic motivation refers to the performance of an activity in order to attain a desired outcome. Extrinsic motivation comes from influences outside an individual's control; a rationale, a necessity, a need. Common forms of extrinsic motivation are rewards (for example, money or prizes), or - conversely - the threat of punishment.

We can provide pupils with a rationale for learning by sharing the 'big picture' with them. In other words, we can continually explain how their learning fits in to the module, the course, the qualification, their careers and to success in work and life. For example, we can explain how today's lesson connects with yesterday's lesson and how the learning will be extended or consolidated next lesson, as well as how it will be assessed at a later stage. We can explain how this learning will become useful in later life, too. And we can connect the learning in one subject with the learning in other subjects, making explicit the transferability of knowledge and skills and the interconnectedness of skills in everyday life.

Either / or

This is not to suggest that pupils will possess either intrinsic or extrinsic motivation. Rather, it is desirable for pupils to possess or develop both. Pupils should both *want* and *need* to learn.

However, it is natural that some pupils will lack the *want* to learn and so instilling in them the *need* to learn becomes all the more important.

We all know - because we're mature and worldly adults - that learning is a reward in itself. We know that, although we might not use algebra in our everyday lives, it was something worth learning at school. We know, too, that understanding how rhythm and metre works in poetry is a good thing, even if it's not something we rely on every day. Knowing stuff makes us cultured, civilised people; it helps us to access and appreciate the world around us. Knowledge allows us to interpret, understand and synthesise new information more easily and quickly, and to create schemata in long-term memory that makes us more efficient thinkers.

But pupils cannot - and should not be expected to - understand this... yet.

So although painting the big picture of learning for our pupils (explaining how what we're teaching today consolidates and extends upon what pupils learnt yesterday, and how today's learning will be built upon and utilised in the future) is important because pupils need to regard the learning process as something long-term rather than an isolated chunk (the 'lesson') demarcated on a timetable and because it can help to develop pupils' intrinsic and extrinsic motivation, sometimes this simply isn't enough.

Telling pupils that paying attention in class today matters because what we intend to teach them will be useful in a few years' time when they sit an exam, go on to further or higher education, and get a job is, let's be honest, a bit of a hard sell.

After all, pupils have little regard for the future; to primary school pupils, secondary school seems like another planet; to key stage 3 pupils, GCSEs seem a long way off; and to FE learners, university or the world of work are but dreams, blurred specks on a distant horizon.

What pupils really need - if they are to be motivated to learn - is a more contemporary purpose and a more relevant rationale. In short, they need to know that paying attention in class is worth their time and energy now, in the short-term. The pay-off has to be immediate not years away. Moreover, pupils need the pay-off to be related to their individual aspirations.

So, what else can we do to motivate those pupils who cannot see a purpose in learning what we need to teach?

First, we can engender a culture of excellence in our classroom...

A culture of excellence

As we discovered earlier in our exploration of the learning environment, the first step towards motivating pupils to produce high-quality work is to set tasks which inspire and challenge them and which are predicated on the idea that every pupil will succeed, not just finish the task but produce work which represents personal excellence.

The most effective tasks offer pupils an opportunity to engage in genuine research not just that invented for the classroom. What's more, a pupil's finished product needs a real audience. This means there is a genuine reason to do the work well, not just because the teacher wants it that way. Not every piece of work can be of genuine importance, of course, but every piece of work can be displayed, presented, appreciated, and judged by people outside the classroom.

Classwork also works best when it is structured in such a way as to make it difficult for pupils to fall too far behind or fail. Tasks also work best when they are broken into a set of clear components so that pupils have to progress through checkpoints to ensure they are keeping up. Good tasks have in-built flexibility to allow for a range of abilities.

Classwork works best when it has in-built rubrics, checklists if you like, which make clear what is expected of each pupil at each stage of development. In other words, the rubric spells out exactly what components are required in the assignment, what the timeline for completion is, and on what qualities and dimensions the work will be judged.

However, it is not enough simply to make a list, a rubric, of what makes a good finished product, be that an essay or a science experiment. It is not enough to read a great piece of literature and analyse the writing, or to look at the work of a great scientist. If we want our pupils to write a strong essay, to design a strong experiment, we need to show them what a great essay or experiment looks like. We need to admire models, find inspiration in them, and analyse their strengths and weaknesses. In short, we need to work out what makes them strong.

Second, we can make learning meaningful...

Making learning meaningful

Pupils are motivated to learn when they regard classwork as personally meaningful and when learning fulfils an educational purpose...

Ensuring classwork is personally meaningful

Classwork can be made personally meaningful if we begin by triggering pupils' curiosity. In other words, at the start of the first lesson on a new topic we could use a 'hook' to engage our pupils' interest and initiate questioning. A hook can be anything: a video, a lively discussion, a guest speaker, a field trip, or a text.

Many pupils find schoolwork meaningless because they don't perceive a need to know what they're being taught. They are not motivated by their teacher's insistence that they should learn something because they'll need it later in life or for the next module on the course, or because it might be in the exam. With a compelling task, however, the reason for the learning becomes clear: pupils need to know this in order to meet the challenge they've just accepted.

Classwork can also be made personally meaningful to pupils if we pose a big question that captures the heart of a topic in clear, compelling language, and which gives pupils a sense of purpose and challenge. A big question should be provocative, open, and complex. The question can be abstract or concrete; or it can be focused on solving a problem. Without a big question, pupils may not understand why they are undertaking a task. They may know that the series of activities they are engaged in are in some way connected but may not be clear as to how or why.

Classwork can be made personally meaningful to pupils if they are given some choice about how to conduct the work and present their findings. Indeed, the more choice, the better. Where choice is limited, pupils can select what topic to study within a general big question or choose how to design, create, and present their findings.

Ensuring classwork fulfils an educational purpose

Classwork can fulfil an educational purpose if it provides opportunities to build metacognition and character skills such as collaboration, communication, and critical thinking – albeit in domain-specific ways – which will serve pupils well in the workplace as in life.

Classwork can fulfil an educational purpose if it makes learning meaningful by emphasising the need to create high-quality products and performances through the formal use of feedback and drafting. Pupils need to learn that most people's first attempts don't result in high quality. Instead, frequent revision is a feature of real-world work. In addition to providing direct feedback, we can coach pupils in using rubrics and other sets of assessment criteria in order for pupils to critique each other's work.

More tips for motivating pupils

Here are some other suggestions for motivating apathetic pupils:

1. Growth mindset: We could help unmotivated pupils to understand that setbacks and mistakes are a normal part of the learning process. As they begin to enjoy more success, their confidence will grow and they will be more willing to take risks.

2. Choice: We could provide unmotivated pupils with a choice of assignments. An unmotivated pupil is often more likely to work hard if they have a say in what they do in class and for homework.

3. Interest: We could try to incorporate pupils' interests into our lessons. For example, if a pupil has a paper round, we could design a maths question that requires them to calculate how much they would earn delivering papers under various conditions.

4. Real life: We could try to relate lessons to real life. Unmotivated pupils often want to know "Why do I have to know this?" We can help them to see how what they learn in school can be applied to life outside the classroom. For example, we could show how being able to count is essential when buying things.

5. Chunk it: We could break tasks down into manageable steps. Some pupils become demotivated because they find assignments too overwhelming. It may help, therefore, to present assignments in small chunks, thus allowing pupils to progress one step at a time. If we do this, it's important that pupils do not move on until they have completed each step and achieved their target. While adults tend to be good at seeing the big picture and breaking a task down into logical steps, this skill is rarely intuitive for pupils.

6. *Personal progress*: We could focus on pupils' individual progress rather than on their performance relative to the rest of the class. If we compare a pupil to classmates who consistently outperform them - even if their poor attainment is down to a lack of effort rather than ability - the pupil will become discouraged and may give up entirely. We can avoid this by focusing on the pupil's personal improvement. We could, for example, assess pupils through a portfolio assessment in which we evaluate work completed throughout the year and consider the progress the pupil has made from their starting point as the measure of their performance.

7. *Competition*: Although we should avoid comparing one pupil with another, there is no harm in comparing a pupil's earlier performance with their later performance - in other words, encouraging pupils to compete against themselves! We could, for example, assess initial performance to establish a baseline (say, in a pre-topic quiz), then keep track of how much a pupil improves (in speed, in accuracy, in detail) each time we re-test them on the same topic.

8. *Variety*: We could give pupils the knowledge they need - through direct instruction - but then allow time for them to work with that knowledge, to think about it and to apply it in practice, as well as give them a chance to contribute. There should be a variety of teaching and learning strategies, a balance between teacher-led and pupil-led approaches, and between individual, pair and group work.

9. *Model*: Enthusiasm is contagious. If we are not enthusiastic about teaching our subject and about teaching our pupils, then we can't expect our pupils to be enthusiastic about learning. Indeed, the Golem Effect has us believe that the lower our expectations of pupils, the worse they perform - and if pupils begin to exhibit behaviours in line with the labels we give them, then surely they will also mirror the attitudes we model. The Pygmalion Effect, meanwhile, has it that the higher our expectations of pupils, the better they perform. It follows, the more enthusiastic we are, the more enthusiastic our pupils will become.

10. *Safe space*: We could create a safe, supportive and sharing environment. This means modelling the growth mindset and making pupils comfortable with discomfort - eager and willing to take on challenges and accept that making mistakes is an integral part of the learning process - but it also means making the physical environment conducive to thinking and learning. Sitting in a moulded plastic chair all day listening to a teacher talk is uncomfortable and boring. As such, we should try to mix things up - give pupils a chance to get up and move around the room (or indeed out of it) and we, too, should vary our position in the room, moving in-between pupils, sometimes teaching from the back of the room.

11. *Realistic goals*: The Pygmalion Effect, as I have explained, dictates that we should have high expectations of every pupil. But we need to be careful to ensure that our expectations are also realistic. After all, to develop the drive to achieve, pupils need to believe that achievement is possible. A failure to attain unrealistic goals can disappoint and frustrate pupils. If the end goal seems unattainable, we could encourage pupils to focus on their continued improvement, on achieving step-goals, not just on their final grade in a test. We could also help pupils to evaluate their own progress by encouraging them to critique their work, to analyse their strengths, and tackle their weaknesses.

12. *Questions*: We could ask lots of questions in the classroom. Sometimes, the best way to teach something new is to tell pupils. But sometimes it will be more motivating to ask rather than tell. We could, for example, encourage pupils to suggest approaches to a problem or to guess the results of an experiment before they conduct it, asking 'What do you think will happen when we combine these two chemicals and why?'

13. *Concrete*: We could connect abstract learning to concrete examples. After all, the case-study method has proven very effective in medicine, law and business. Making the abstract concrete involves applying theories and concepts to a real-world scenario, using these formulations to analyse and make sense of situations involving real people and real stakes.

14. *Objectives*: We could clearly define the objectives. Pupils want and need to know what is expected of them in order to stay motivated to learn. At the beginning of the year, therefore, we should set out clear objectives, rules, and expectations of pupils so that there is no confusion and pupils have goals to work towards. We should re-state those objectives, rules and expectations at regular intervals, repeatedly reinforcing them.

15. *Model*: Ultimately, the best approach we can take is to be the model at all times: to remain, as difficult as it can be, the mature, adult in the room. That means we get to know and care about all our pupils; and that we're kind, and calm and patient. It also means we're respectful and supportive, and forever forgiving of our pupils' mistakes.

CHAPTER FIFTY-FOUR:
IDENTIFY THE BARRIERS

So far in Part Four of this book on ensuring equal access to an ambitious curriculum and to effective teaching for long-term learning, we have focused on ways to support pupils with SEND. But, of course, many other pupils struggle in school or college as well. For example, disadvantaged pupils, such as those eligible for the Pupil Premium Grant, are also – by definition – at a disadvantage when it comes to accessing our curriculum and achieving in school. Whether the source of their disadvantage is socio-economic, geographical, or as a consequence of their gender or ethnicity, they may require additional or different support in order to be afforded a fair chance of success.

In the next few chapters, by way of illustration, we will focus on strategies to support pupils eligible for the Pupil Premium but the advice I will share is equally applicable to other forms of disadvantaged pupil.

What is the Pupil Premium?

The Pupil Premium (which for the sake of brevity I will sometimes refer to as 'PP') was introduced by the Coalition Government in 2011 and is money given to schools to help support disadvantaged pupils. 'Disadvantage' here being defined by three categories:

Firstly, the Pupil Premium is awarded to pupils who are categorised as 'Ever 6 FSM'. In other words, it is given to pupils who are recorded in the January school census who are known to have been eligible for free school meals (FSM) in any of the previous six years, as well as those first known to be eligible that month.

Secondly, Pupil Premium funding is awarded to pupils who are adopted from care or who have left care. In other words, the funding is given to pupils who are recorded in the January school census and alternative provision census who were looked after by an English or Welsh local authority immediately before being adopted, or who left local authority care on a special guardianship order or child arrangements order (previously known as a residence order).

Finally, Pupil Premium funding is awarded to pupils who are categorised as 'Ever 5 service child' which means a pupil recorded in the January school census who was eligible for the service child premium in any of the previous four years as well as those recorded as a service child for the first time in the January school census.

Does the Pupil Premium work?

Since the Pupil Premium was introduced in 2011, its success has been variable...

The gap has closed fastest in schools with the highest concentration of disadvantaged pupils. In contrast, schools with the lowest proportions of disadvantaged pupils have seen the gap widen, particularly at key stages 2 and 4, suggesting that disadvantaged children are not prioritised when they are in the extreme minority.

What's more, the overall gap has widened. One in three children in the UK now grows up in poverty and the attainment gap between rich and poor is detectable at an early age. White working-class pupils (particularly boys) are among the lowest performers and the link between poverty and attainment is multi-racial.

The limited impact of PP can, I believe, be attributed to several factors...

Firstly, as I explained above, the PP is awarded to pupils who are eligible for free school meals (as well as those in care and care-leavers, and children from service families) but FSM eligibility is a poor proxy for educational and social disadvantage. Indeed, as many as 50-75% of FSM children are not in the lowest income households. What's more, it's often the time-poor and the poorly educated who are less engaged and motivated at school, rather than those facing economic deprivation.

That's not to suggest that a majority of pupils from poorer households do not have difficulties at school and are not deserving of additional funds to help close the gap between them and their better-off peers, but it is important to note that other pupils not currently in scope for the PP are also academically disadvantaged and are equally deserving of our attention.

Secondly, PP children are not a homogenous group. Indeed, the group mean often masks significant differences amongst all those eligible for the PP. It is wrong to group together those eligible for PP and assume they all face the same challenges and must therefore be served the same diet of interventions.

Thirdly, closing the gap is more difficult for some schools than others because the size of the 'gap' is necessarily dependent on the non-PP demographic in a school. Put simply, the more advantaged the non-PP cohort, the harder it is to close the gap. And yet we too often focus on measuring the disadvantage and do not consider the make-up of those pupils in a school who are not eligible for PP funding.

Finally, PP data is often meaningless because assessments change and the PP cohort itself changes over time - not least as a result of recent benefits reforms which have taken a large number of pupils out of eligibility despite no discernible differences in their circumstances. In other words, pupils who were previously eligible for the PP are no longer so but are just as disadvantaged socio-economically. Further, in-school sample sizes are usually too small to make inferences, and this also means that a school's 'closing the gap' data is largely meaningless.

All of which is not to suggest that we should abandon the PP or indeed all hope of closing the gap. If the government were to cease funding disadvantage and were to include the funds in school budgets then, I firmly believe, it would only be a matter of time before those funds were diminished or cut completely.

But we need to recognise the limitations of the current funding system and use common sense and pragmatism when analysing our data. Most importantly of all, we need to ensure that we focus on every child in a school not just those eligible for discrete funding, and work on a case-by-case basis to understand the barriers that some pupils face at school. Talking of which...

The three-point plan

In this chapter and the two that follow, I will be exploring my three-point plan for Pupil Premium success. That plan is as follows:

1. Identify the barriers
2. Plan the solutions
3. Agree the success criteria

In this chapter, we will take a close look at step one...

Identify the barriers

Before you can put in place Pupil Premium intervention strategies aimed at supporting disadvantaged pupils, you must first understand why a gap exists between the attainment of disadvantaged pupils and non-disadvantaged pupils.

In short, you need to ask yourself: What are the barriers to learning faced by my disadvantaged pupils?

This may sound obvious but it's a step often missed by schools and colleges who assume all pupils eligible for PP, or other sources of disadvantage funding, must be academically disadvantaged and similarly so. However, as I imply above, when identifying the barriers to learning in your school, it is important to remember that not all the pupils who are eligible for PP will face all, or even some, of the barriers to learning that I set out below, and there is no such thing as a typical disadvantaged pupil. Rather, each pupil must be treated on an individual basis and the support given must be tailored to meet their needs, not the needs of a homogenous group.

As such, schools and colleges should identify, on a case by case basis, what, if any, barriers to learning those pupils eligible for PP or other sources of funding face.

Let me emphasise this: not all pupils who come from socio-economically deprived homes will struggle at school and do less well than their affluent peers. A majority will, but it's not set in stone.

Likewise, not all pupils who come from affluent families will do well in school. It may be that some of these pupils have time-poor parents and spend their evenings plugged into a device rather than talking at the dinner table or reading books.

In short, avoid stereotypes and work hard to understand the truth for each of your pupils.

When seeking to identify barriers to learning, here are some possible answers to look out for...

- Pupils for whom English is an additional language having limited vocabulary;
- Poor attendance and punctuality;
- Mobility issues caused by a pupil moving between schools;
- Issues within a pupil's family unit;
- Medical issues, sometimes undiagnosed;
- A lack of sleep or poor nutrition;
- A lack of family engagement with learning;
- Education not being valued within local community;
- A lack of role models, especially male role models;
- A lack of self-confidence and self-esteem.

Plan the solutions

Once you have identified the barriers your disadvantaged pupils face towards learning, you need to plan the solutions.

In Chapter Fifty-Five I will explore step 2 of my three-point plan in more detail, but in this chapter, I'd like to focus on the most common cause of disadvantage amongst our pupils: language and literacy skills...

Language and literacy

Currently, about 1 in 3 young people grows up in poverty in the UK - in the last year or two, this proportion has risen from 1 in 4. What's worse, a report by the Resolution Foundation in February 2019 predicted that by 2023 37% of children would live in poverty - the highest proportion since the early 1990s.

The academic achievement gap between rich and poor is detectable from an early age - as early as 22 months in fact - and the gap continues to widen as children travel through the education system.

Children from the lowest income homes are half as likely to get five good GCSEs and go on to higher education as the national average. And white working-class pupils (particularly boys) are amongst our lowest performers.

What's more, the link between poverty and attainment is multi-racial - whatever their ethnic background, pupils eligible for free school meals underperform compared to those who are not.

In short, if you're a high ability pupil from a low-income home (and, therefore, a low social class), you're not going to do as well in school and in later life as a low ability pupil from a higher income home and higher social class.

Interestingly, the gap does not grow at a consistent rate. If you were to divide the gap that exists by the age of sixteen into fifths, two would already be present by the age of five, one would have developed during primary school and two during secondary school. Two-thirds of the primary school component develops during reception and key stage 1.

In other words, educational disadvantage starts early and these gaps are particularly pronounced in early language and literacy.

By the age of 3, more disadvantaged children are – on average – already almost 18 months behind their more affluent peers in their early language development. Around two fifths of disadvantaged five-year-olds are not meeting the expected literacy standard for their age.

The Pupil Premium should, therefore, be spent primarily on improving pupils' literacy and language skills.

Early intervention - language and literacy

Black and Wiliam (2018) argue that "Children from working class families, who are only familiar with the restricted code of their everyday language, may find it difficult to engage with the elaborated code that is required by the learning discourse of the classroom and which those from middle class families experience in their home lives."

Children born into families who read books, newspapers and magazines, visit museums, art galleries, zoos, and stately homes and gardens, take regular holidays, watch the nightly news and documentaries, and talk - around the dinner table, on weekend walks, in the car - about current affairs and about what they're reading or doing or watching - develop what's called *cultural capital.*

These children acquire, unknowingly perhaps, an awareness of the world around them, an understanding of how life works, and - crucially - a language with which to explain it all.   And this cultural capital provides a solid foundation on which they can build further knowledge, skills and understanding.

The unlucky ones - those children not born and brought up in such knowledge-rich environments, and who therefore do not develop this foundation of cultural capital - don't do as well in school because new knowledge and skills have nothing to 'stick' to or build upon.

These children may come from broken or transitory homes, be in care, have impoverished parents who work two or more jobs and so spend little time at home or are too exhausted when they get home from work to read to or converse with their children.

These parents may not themselves be well educated and so possess very little cultural capital of their own to pass on to their children. Maybe these parents came from disadvantaged backgrounds and so books and current affairs never featured in their lives and remain alien to them. Maybe they did not do well at school or did not enjoy their schooling and so do not know how to - or do not wish to - help prepare their child for the world of education.

Let's be clear - educational disadvantage is an accident of birth. It is not about ability, innate or otherwise.   But, unfortunately, a child's birth is often their destiny...

The Matthew Effect

The Matthew Effect is a term coined by Daniel Rigney in his book of the same name, using a title taken from a passage in the Bible (Matthew 13:12) that proclaims, 'The rich shall get richer and the poor shall get poorer".

In the context of academic disadvantage, the Matthew Effect posits that disadvantaged pupils shall get more disadvantaged because they do not possess the foundational knowledge that they need in order to access and understand the school curriculum.

It is not, as I said earlier, that these children are less able, but that they don't have the same amount of knowledge about the world as their more fortunate peers with which to make sense of new information and experiences.

Put simply, the more you know, the easier it is to know more and so the culturally rich will always stay ahead of the impoverished, and the gap between rich and poor will continue to grow as children travel through our education system.

The best use of Pupil Premium funding, therefore, is to help disadvantaged pupils to build their cultural capital.

Indeed, the new Education Inspection Framework also highlights the importance or cultural capital. It says that inspectors will judge the extent to which schools are equipping pupils with the knowledge and cultural capital they need to succeed in life. Ofsted say that their definition of this knowledge and cultural capital matches that found in the aims of the national curriculum: namely, that it is "the essential knowledge that pupils need to be educated citizens, introducing them to the best that has been thought and said and helping to engender an appreciation of human creativity and achievement".

Once you're clear that the best use of PP funding is to build cultural capital then all the hard work of action planning, implementing, monitoring and evaluating intervention strategies, and reporting the impact of your Pupil Premium activities becomes easier...

The next big question, then, is 'how?'

Cultural capital = word power

Cultural capital takes myriad forms and is highly complex. There is not one single solution, therefore, to the problem of improving pupils' cultural capital as a means of helping the more disadvantaged to access our ambitious curriculum. However, we have to start somewhere, and I would suggest you start with vocabulary. Why? Because, as I said earlier, a lack of early language and literacy skills is a major cause of disadvantage...

The size of a pupil's vocabulary in their early years of schooling (the number and variety of words that the young person knows) is a significant predictor of academic attainment in later schooling and of success in life.

Most children are experienced speakers of the language when they begin school but reading the language requires more complex, abstract vocabulary than that used in everyday conversation.

Young people who develop reading skills early in their lives by reading frequently add to their vocabularies exponentially over time.

In his book, The Matthew Effect, which I mentioned earlier, Daniel Rigney explains: "While good readers gain new skills very rapidly, and quickly move from learning to read to reading to learn, poor readers become increasingly frustrated with the act of reading, and try to avoid reading where possible.

"Pupils who begin with high verbal aptitudes find themselves in verbally enriched social environments and have a double advantage."

Furthermore, E D Hirsch, in his book, The Schools We Need, says that "The children who possess intellectual capital when they first arrive at school have the mental scaffolding and Velcro to catch hold of what is going on, and they can turn the new knowledge into still more Velcro to gain still more knowledge".

Department for Education data suggests that, by the age of seven, the gap in the vocabulary known by children in the top and bottom quartiles is something like 4,000 words (children in the top quartile know around 7,000 words).

For this reason, when planning to use the Pupil Premium or other forms of disadvantaged funding in order to build cultural capital, we need to understand the importance of vocabulary and support its development so that children who do not develop this foundational knowledge before they start school are helped to catch up.

So, what can we do to help the word poor become richer and, with it, to diminish the difference between the attainment of disadvantaged pupils and their non-disadvantaged peers?

Building word power

One answer is to plan group work activities which provide an opportunity for the word poor to mingle with the word rich, to hear language being used by pupils of their own age and in ways that they might not otherwise encounter. In other words, schools need to ensure that disadvantaged pupils have equal access to a knowledge-rich diet and provide cultural experiences in addition to, not in place of, the school curriculum.

This might involve spending Pupil Premium money on museum and gallery visits, or on mentors who talk with pupils about what's happening in the world, perhaps reading a daily newspaper with them before school or at lunchtime.

Another answer is to provide additional intervention classes for the disadvantaged (taking place outside the taught timetable to avoid withdrawing pupils from classes) in which we teach and model higher-order reading skills because, as the literate adults in the room, we teachers use these skills subconsciously all the time so we need to make the implicit explicit.

For example, we could use these intervention sessions to model:

- Moving quickly through and across texts
- Locating key pieces of information.
- Following the gist of articles
- Questioning a writer's facts or interpretation

- Linking one text with another
- Making judgments about whether one text is better than, more reliable than, or more interesting than another text

We can also use Pupil Premium funding to promote the love of reading for the sake of reading; encouraging pupils to see reading as something other than a functional activity.

It is the responsibility of every adult working in a school (not just teachers, and certainly not just English teachers) to show that reading because we like reading is one of the hallmarks of civilised adult life.

Community outreach

Finally, it's worth remembering that, although Pupil Premium funding is for the purposes of the school it is awarded to, it can also be used for the benefit of pupils registered at other maintained schools or academies and on community facilities such as services whose provision furthers any charitable purpose for the benefit of pupils at the school or their families, or people who live or work in the locality in which the school is situated.

We know that the attainment gap emerges early in a child's life and that, therefore, the child's family is crucial in helping to close that gap.

We know, too, that reading books from an early age is a vital weapon in the battle for social mobility.

As such, Pupil Premium funding can legitimately - and wisely - be used to support community projects such as reading mentor schemes, helping improve parents' literacy levels and encouraging parents and members of the community to engage with education.

The Pupil Premium grant can be used, for example, to fund a community outreach officer who helps educate disadvantaged or hard-to-reach parents in the locality about the work of the school, how best to support young people with their education, and as an advocate for the use of community facilities such as libraries, museums and galleries.

They could lead cultural visits after school, at weekends and in the holidays for those children who would not otherwise enjoy such experiences.

If the impact of such activity can be linked to an increase in literacy levels and cultural capital, then it is money well spent and will help to close the gap in a sustainable way.

Admittedly, this will involve some bravery on the part of secondary schools will not know with absolute certainty which pre-school or primary-age pupils are likely to attend their school aged 11 but they can make an educated guess and, even if some Pupil Premium money is spent on young people who do not go on to attend that school, it is still money well spent within the school community and schools have a duty to look beyond their gates and be a force for good in society.

CHAPTER FIFTY-FIVE:
PLAN THE SOLUTIONS

In Chapter Fifty-Four, I explained my three-point plan for helping disadvantaged pupils to access our ambitious curriculum. The three steps are:

1.   Identify the barriers
2.   Plan the solutions
3.   Agree the success criteria

I underlined the importance of *identifying the barriers* because not all pupils who are eligible for the Pupil Premium or other sources of disadvantaged funding are academically disadvantaged and even those who are will not face the same barriers to learning as each other. As such, it is crucial that schools treat each pupil as an individual and provide support on a case-by-case basis.

The second action in my three-point plan is to *plan the solutions*. Once we have identified the barriers each pupil faces, we must decide what action we can take to help them overcome those barriers and afford each pupil an equal chance of success at school.

There are, I believe, some common principles we need to consider when deciding which strategies to use...

Firstly, we should ensure our strategies promote an ethos of attainment for all pupils, rather than stereotyping disadvantaged pupils as a group with less potential to succeed.

Secondly, we should take an individualised approach to addressing barriers to learning and emotional support and do so at an early stage, rather than providing access to generic support as pupils near their end-of-key-stage assessments.

Thirdly, we should focus on outcomes for individual pupils rather than on providing generic strategies for whole cohorts.

Fourthly, we should deploy our best staff to support disadvantaged pupils; perhaps develop existing teachers' and TAs' skills rather than using additional staff who do not know the pupils well.

Fifthly, we should make decisions based on frequent assessment data, responding to changing evidence, rather than use a one-off decision point.

And finally, we should focus on high quality teaching first rather than on bolt-on strategies and activities outside school hours and outside the classroom.

In Chapter Fifty-Four, I articulated one such strategy: the building of cultural capital by closing the vocabulary gap. Although context is all and you must make decisions based on what you know about your own pupils, in addition to building cultural capital, I believe that disadvantaged funding can usefully be focused on:

1. Improving pupils' transitions between the key stages and phases of education
2. Developing pupils' cross curricular literacy skills
3. Developing pupils' cross curricular numeracy skills

Why use disadvantage funding to improve transition?

According to Galton (1999), almost forty per cent of pupils fail to make expected progress during the year immediately following a change of schools or settings. Although the affect of transition is particularly felt as pupils transfer from primary school to secondary school at age 11 - DfE data shows that average progress drops between Key Stage 2 and Key Stage 3 for reading, writing and maths – this is by no means the only transition that needs improving. Students' transfer from secondary school to FE College is similarly crucial and often mismanaged with college leaders and teachers wrongly assuming their adult learners are much more independent and mature than they are.

Whatever stage a pupil is at, when they transfer from one setting to another, the effects of transition are amplified by risk factors such as poverty and ethnicity. Those pupils eligible for PP and other forms of disadvantage funding are, therefore, amongst those most likely to suffer when they change schools. Although schools cannot mitigate all of the social and emotional affects of transition, they can do more to help pupils make the academic leap more smoothly and successfully.

There are five aspects of transition where disadvantage funding may be usefully employed...

- **Administration**: funding can be used to improve the general management of the transition process such as the formal liaison between a secondary school and its feeder primaries. In practice, this might take the form of the transfer of pupil records and achievement data, meetings with pupils and parents, and visits from headteachers, senior leaders and teachers.

- **Social and emotional**: funding can be used to help forge better links between pupils/parents and their new school prior to and immediately after transfer. It can also be used to smooth the pupil induction process into their new school and might take the form of induction days, open evenings, school orientation activities, team-building days, taster classes, the production and issuing of prospectuses and booklets, and so on.

- **Curriculum**: funding can be used to improve curriculum continuity between the various stages and phases of education by funding teachers to share plans that show what content is taught on either side of the transition. It could also fund cross-phase teaching, the teaching of bridging units – for example – at the end of Year 6 and start of Year 7, summer schools, joint CPD networks and INSET days, the sharing of good practice and shared planning, and teacher exchanges.

- **Pedagogy**: funding can be used establish a shared understanding of how pupils are taught - as well as how they learn - in order to achieve a greater continuity in classroom practice and teaching. This might be achieved by understanding differing teaching styles and skills, by engaging in shared CPD and teacher exchanges, and by primary and secondary teachers observing each other in practice.

- ***Management of learning***: funding can be used to ensure that pupils are active participants, rather than passive observers, in the transition process. This might be achieved by empowering pupils and their parents with information about achievement and empowering them with the confidence to articulate their learning needs in a new environment. This might take the form of giving information to parents/pupils, providing pupils with learning portfolios and samples of achievements, and raising pupils' awareness of their needs and talents by sharing and explaining data.

Why use disadvantage funding to improve literacy?

I've already talked about word power and teaching vocabulary but language and literacy is much more than that...

Disadvantage funding can be used to run interventions in which teachers or mentors model higher-order reading skills because, as the literate adults in the room, teachers use these skills unconsciously all the time so they need to make the implicit explicit. For example, intervention sessions could be used to model:

- Moving quickly through and across texts
- Locating key pieces of information.
- Following the gist of articles
- Questioning a writer's facts or interpretation
- Linking one text with another
- Making judgments about whether one text is better than, more reliable than, or more interesting than another text

As I said earlier, disadvantage funding could also be used to promote the love of reading for the sake of reading, too; encouraging our pupils to see reading as something other than a functional activity.

Why use disadvantage funding to improve numeracy?

Numeracy skills, like literacy skills, are gateway skills that enables pupils to access and succeed in the whole school curriculum. Numeracy skills are also vital for success in work and life and can help to mitigate the effects of socio-economic deprivation.

Numeracy can be divided into four categories:

1. Handling information;
2. Space, shape and measurements;
3. Operations and calculations; and
4. Numbers.

Handling information is about graphs and charts, comparing sets of data and types of data, processing data, and probability.

Space, shape and measurements is about both space, shape and measure, and solving problems with space, shape and measure.

Operations and calculations is about addition and subtraction, multiplication and division, number operations, and the effective use of calculators.

Numbers (and the use of the number system) is about using numbers, whole numbers, size and order, place value, patterns and sequences, and numbers 'in between' whole numbers.

In addition to those four categories, numeracy encompasses three sets of skills:

1. Reasoning;
2. Problem-solving; and
3. Decision-making.

Reasoning might involve identifying structures, being systematic, searching for patterns, developing logical thinking, and predicting and checking. Problem-solving might involve identifying the information needed to carry out a task, breaking down a problem or task into smaller parts, interpreting solutions in context, and making mental estimates to check the reasonableness of an answer. And decision-making might involve choosing appropriate strategies, identifying relevant information and choosing the right tools and equipment.

Disadvantage funding can be used to fund teacher professional development to raise awareness of how to teach numeracy across the curriculum...

For example, in English, numeracy can be developed by using non-fiction texts which include mathematical vocabulary, graphs, charts and tables.

In science, pupils will order numbers including decimals, calculate means, and percentages, use negative numbers when taking temperatures, substitute into formulae, rearrange equations, decide which graph to use to represent data, and plot, interpret and predict from graphs.

In ICT, pupils will collect and classify data, enter it into data handling software to produce graphs and tables, and interpret and explain the results. When they use computer models and simulations they will draw on their abilities to manipulate numbers and identify patterns and relationships.

In art and design and technology, pupils will use measurements and patterns, spatial ideas, the properties of shapes, and symmetry, and use multiplication and ratio to enlarge and reduce the size of objects.

In history, geography and RE, pupils will collect data and use measurements of different kinds. They will study maps and use coordinates and ideas of angles, direction, position, scale, and ratio. And they will use timelines similar to number lines.

Disadvantage funding can also be used for numeracy intervention strategies...

At the whole-school level, the PP and other forms of disadvantage funding may also be used to help create a positive environment that celebrates numeracy and provides pupils with role models by celebrating the numeracy successes of older pupils.

At subject level, PP funding may be used to help provide high quality exemplar materials and display examples of numeracy work within a subject context. Departments could highlight opportunities for the use of numeracy within their subject and ensure that the learning materials that are presented to pupils match both their capability in the subject and their numerical demands.

CHAPTER FIFTY-SIX:
AGREE THE SUCCESS CRITERIA

The third and final action on our three-point plan is to *agree the success criteria.*

Once you've identified the barriers to learning faced by your disadvantaged pupils and have planned the best solutions to help them overcome these barriers, you need to be clear about what success will look like. Ask yourself: what do I expect to see as an outcome? What is my aim here? For example, is it to:

- Raise attainment;
- Expedite progress;
- Improve attendance;
- Improve behaviour;
- Reduce exclusions;
- Improve parental engagement;
- Expand upon the number of opportunities afforded to disadvantaged pupils...?

Whatever your immediate goal is, ultimately you should be seeking to diminish the difference between the attainment of disadvantaged pupils in your school and non-disadvantaged pupils nationally, as well as narrowing your within-school gap. As such, if your initial aim is pastoral in nature, for example to improve behaviour and attendance, or reduce exclusions, then you must take it a step further and peg it to an academic outcome. Although pastoral outcomes are important, all our activity must ultimately lead to an academic success criterion - in other words, improving attainment.

The PP and other forms of disadvantaged funding exist to close the attainment gap, after all.

Monitoring *and* evaluating

In terms of ensuring you meet your success criteria, it's crucial that any intervention strategy is monitored as it's happening and not just evaluated once it's finished. The monitoring may involve more anecdotal data such as pupil and teacher feedback, but evidence must be gathered throughout the timespan of the intervention in order to ensure it is working – or working as well as it could – and so that timely decisions can be taken to stop or tweak an intervention if it is not having the desired effect on pupil progress. Waiting until the intervention has finished to evaluate its success is too late: if it did not work or did not work as well as it could have done, then time and money have been wasted.

When interventions work best

When setting the success criteria, it's important to consider the best individual approach. For example, evidence suggests that interventions work best when they are short term, intensive, focused, and tailored...

Short term

The best interventions help pupils to become increasingly independent over time. In other words, the scaffolds slowly fall away as the pupil. Interventions should, therefore, be planned to run for a finite amount of time, ideally less than a term. Of course, if the evidence shows the intervention is working but that further improvement is needed, then the intervention can be extended, but to slate an intervention for a year, say, is often misguided.

Intensive

Similarly, interventions should be intensive, perhaps with three or more sessions a week rather than just one. And those sessions should also be intensive in the sense of being short, say 20 to 50 minutes in length rather than an hour or more.

Focused

Interventions should be keenly focused on a pupil's areas of development rather than be generic. For example, rather than setting a goal of, say, 'improving a pupil's literacy skills', an intervention strategy should be focused on a specific aspect of literacy such as their knowledge of the plot of Stone Cold or their ability to use embedded quotations in an essay.

Tailored

Interventions need to be tailored to meet the needs of those pupils accessing them. They must be as personalised as any classroom learning and not be 'off the peg' programmes. Assessment data should be used to inform the intervention and to ensure it is being pitched appropriately to fill gaps in the pupil's knowledge.

So, what works?

Many schools turn to the EEF when deciding which intervention strategies will work best for those pupils eligible for PP and other types of disadvantage funding. If you refer to their toolkit, here's a quick reminder of the health warnings I issued in Chapter Five...

How does the EEF toolkit work?

The EEF teaching and learning toolkit is based on meta-analyses of other studies. A meta-analysis is a way of collating the outcomes of similar studies and converting the data into a common metric, then combining those in order to report an estimate which represents the impact or influence of interventions in that given area.

As I explained in Chapter Five, there are a number of advantages of meta-analyses when conducted as part of a systematic review. For example, they allow large amounts of information to be assimilated quickly. They also help reduce the delay between research 'discoveries' and the implementation of effective strategies. Meta-analyses enable the results of different studies to be compared, and in so doing highlight the reasons for any inconsistencies between similar studies.

However, meta-analyses are not without their problems. For example, it is a misconception that larger effect sizes are associated with greater educational significance, and it is a misconception that two or more different studies on the same interventions can have their effect sizes combined to give a meaningful estimate of the intervention's educational importance because studies that used different types of 'control group' cannot be accurately combined to create an effect size (not least because what constitutes 'business as usual' in each control group will be different to the others).

Likewise, unless the studies used the same range of pupils, the combined effect size is unlikely to be an accurate estimate of the 'true' effect size of a particular strategy. Also, the way in which researchers measure the effect can influence the effect size. What's more, increasing the number of test items can influence the effect size. If the number of questions used to measure the effectiveness of an intervention is increased, this may significantly increase the effect size.

This doesn't mean we shouldn't look to meta-analyses such as the EEF toolkit for advice on which interventions to use to support our disadvantaged pupils. But we should dig beneath the meta-analyses and analyse the original studies on which the effect sizes are based because the averages may hide huge variations depending on the nature of the intervention and the context in which it was used.

PART FIVE:

PUTTING IT ALL INTO PRACTICE

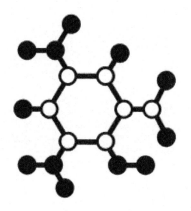

CHAPTER FIFTY-SEVEN:
CREATING THE CULTURE FOR
IMPLEMENTATION

In Book One of this series on School and College Curriculum Design, which was subtitled 'Intent' and explored all the planning that happens before teaching happens, I explained that, although the process of curriculum design is largely within the purview of middle leaders and teachers because subject specialists must design a curriculum that befits their discipline, senior leaders do still have a part to the play in the process. In particular, I argued that SLT have five key roles:

Firstly, I said, it is the responsibility of senior leaders to **agree the vision** for their whole school or college curriculum. This, as we have already explored, involves defining what is meant by the term 'curriculum' and making decisions about the national, basic, local and hidden curriculums.

Secondly, I said, senior leaders – particularly the curriculum and timetable leads – are key to determining how broad and balanced the whole school or college curriculum will be and why. They must make decisions about **which subject disciplines and vocations matter most** and **which subjects are afforded the most time** on the timetable. For example, senior leaders must be attuned to their community and learner needs and if their school population predominantly has English as an additional language (EAL), they may decide to timetable more English lessons.

Thirdly, I explained, senior leaders **articulate the purpose of education** in their school or college – and therefore guide middle leaders in determining the broad 'end-points' (schools) or 'body of knowledge' (FE) to be taught. For example, senior leaders must have an overview of what qualification types and levels are offered in their school or college, and must ensure that their offer meets local needs (including learner needs, employer needs, community needs, etc) and that each entry-point to their curriculum leads to a higher level of study and/or into meaningful employment rather than to a series of dead-ends. Only senior leaders have the necessary oversight of the whole school or college curriculum to be able to make these decisions.

Senior leaders can also help their middle leaders and subject specialists to determine the 'end-points' or 'body of knowledge' they plan to teach within their subjects by asking some broad questions about their curriculums.

Fourthly, and most pertinently to this chapter, I argued that senior leaders **create the culture** in which a curriculum can flourish.

Finally, and also crucial to this chapter and indeed the chapter that follows, I said that senior leaders should be the gatekeepers and defenders of staff skills and time. They have a duty to **provide appropriate training** to staff to ensure they are skilled at curriculum thinking, and they have a duty to **provide protected time** for staff to engage in the time-consuming task of designing, delivering and reviewing the curriculum in their subjects.

With a just focus on teacher workload, senior leaders must do all they can to prevent this renewed focus on curriculum design adding to teachers' workloads and must decide what to stop doing in order to carve out the time for teachers to focus their energy on 'the real substance of education'.

The fourth and fifth roles are critical to our current purposes because, if we are not careful, curriculum intent and implementation are in danger of becoming a fad to which a considerable amount of time is dedicated. I am not suggesting improving curriculum design and ensuring teaching leads to long-term learning are not important and deserving of more of our time – I think they are – but I am saying that, if we decide we need colleagues to dedicate more time to these important processes, then we must also decide what they can stop doing in order that their overall workload does not increase; rather, that they focus their time on doing the things that will have the biggest impact on pupils.

As well as protecting our colleagues' workloads, we need to ensure they are helped to develop the knowledge and skills required to engage in effective curriculum thinking, design and delivery. This includes designing programmes of CPD that perform a dual function: firstly, that they help teachers and middle leaders to develop their pedagogical content knowledge so that they know more about effective teaching strategies and approaches; and secondly, that they help teachers and middle leaders to develop their subject-specific knowledge so that they know more about their chosen disciplines.

But even this isn't enough. As well as protecting teacher workload and helping them to develop their knowledge and skills, we must also ensure that our school and college cultures, including - though not exclusively - our internal systems and structures, support the process of curriculum planning and teaching, rather than act in opposition. By 'systems and structures', I specifically mean three things: performance management and appraisal; quality assurance; and professional development.

In Book One in this series I tackled teacher workload and professional development, so I won't do so again here in any real detail. However, before we move on to other aspects of the culture, I would like to summarise the key points by way of providing some context to that which follows... if you have recently read Book One and don't require a reminder, you are welcome to skip forward to Chapter Fifty-Eight...

Creating the culture

In the best schools and colleges, I would argue, the staffroom remains a hub - it is busy with staff sharing and listening; offloading and laughing. Conversely, in the least successful schools and colleges, the staffroom is either non-existent or deserted; instead, staff work in departmental silos or, worse, alone in their classrooms.

In the best schools and colleges, I would argue, the canteen and corridors are calm, friendly places - respected and kept clean by everyone. People are polite, greeting you with a smile; and they are purposeful, focused on learning and teaching. In the least successful schools and colleges, meanwhile, there's a threatening atmosphere of chaos and confusion. There are no-go areas, behaviour isn't tackled because there is no leadership from the top: rather, behaviour is regarded as an individual teacher's responsibility, and if they can't manage it, they alone are to blame. In such circumstances, it won't be unusual to hear some staff unhelpfully say, "Well, he's always well-behaved with me."

In the best schools and colleges, leaders develop a 'no-blame' culture. They believe that, just because someone has made a mistake, this doesn't mean they should suddenly forget the important contribution which the same colleague makes every day. In fact, in such situations, they know that staff need to feel supported and trusted to learn from their mistake and to move on. When things are going well, meanwhile, the best leaders are generous with their praise and recognition.

Senior leaders in the best schools and colleges build trust and openness, and thus develop autonomy, mastery and purpose. They build for the future; they develop sustainable models of leadership by investing in their people and reducing attrition.

In terms of curriculum design, senior leaders in the best schools and colleges create a culture in which middle leaders and teachers are encouraged to honestly self-reflect and admit to mistakes. Middle leaders regularly review the effectiveness of their curriculum and make changes to it without fear. A curriculum must be a living, breathing thing – constantly under review and constantly evolving in response to the shifting landscape and to assessment data. If the initial draft of the curriculum doesn't work as well as anticipated, middle leaders must be given the breathing space of a no-blame culture to learn from their mistakes and to improve their curriculum.

Teacher professional development

Another of the five key aspects of senior curriculum leadership I outlined earlier was providing appropriate training to staff to ensure they are skilled at curriculum thinking. Teacher continuing professional development (CPD) is crucial if our curriculum is to be successful and it features prominently in Ofsted's new inspection framework...

Under Ofsted's 'quality of education' judgment, consideration is given to how school leaders align continuing professional development for teachers and staff with the curriculum, and the extent to which they develop teachers' knowledge over time.

Teacher professional development is also placed up-front and centre in 'leadership and management'; specifically, the twofold nature of CPD: developing subject knowledge *and* developing pedagogical content knowledge – the *what* and the *how* of teaching, if you like.

'Dual professionalism' is crucial to effective curriculum design and delivery because teachers need to deepen their understanding of their discipline *and* deepen their understanding of how to teach that discipline in a way that makes sense to pupils - seeing their expertise through the eyes of the novice pupil and pre-empting their likely misunderstandings, misconceptions and questions – if they are to have the knowledge and skills required of curriculum experts. Subject knowledge without pedagogical content knowledge is not enough; and vice versa.

Therefore, it is incumbent upon senior leaders to plan opportunities for their teachers to engage in professional development that aims to achieve these dual functions. Often, schools are good at providing staff with generic CPD such as a training course on feedback or metacognition – which absolutely have their value and should continue – but they are less effective at helping their staff to update and upskill their subject knowledge, including through an engagement with subject associations and by attending subject-specific training or reading academic research in their specialism.

Why CPD matters

With this in mind, let us start with this important - yet oft forgotten - truth about education: teachers - and what happens in their classrooms - are the main drivers of positive change in our schools. The only way to improve the quality of teaching, therefore, is to improve the quality of our teachers. And the only way to improve the quality of our teachers is to treat them fairly and with respect, and to train them well and continue to develop them throughout their careers.

Improving the quality of teachers requires systems of collaboration so that professional development becomes an everyday, collaborative exercise not an end of year 'sheep-dip' activity 'done to' teachers by school leaders.

Improving the quality of teachers requires professional development to be personalised, tailored to meet individual needs, so that it is made meaningful and encompasses all aspects of self-improvement activity - such as reading research, watching colleagues teach, working with a coach, and engaging in lesson study - not just attending a formal training course.

Improving the quality of teachers also requires professional development to recognise hard work in all its forms - even the quiet, 'just doing my job' kind - and to encourage rather than stifle team-work, and to favour collaboration over competition.

In short, improving the quality of teachers is about building a mature, adult culture in which teachers and senior leaders work together in the best interests of their pupils to improve the quality of teaching in their schools and colleges and to do so without fear or favour.

So how can schools and colleges ensure that they provide high quality professional development for their staff in order to support the process of curriculum development, and do so without drilling a big hole in their diminishing budgets?

The Standard for Teacher Professional Development (2016) - together with the ETF Professional Standards (FE colleges) and the DfE Teachers' Standards (schools) - may hold the key.

The five strands of the Standard are as follows:

1. Professional development should have a focus on improving and evaluating pupil outcomes.
2. Professional development should be underpinned by robust evidence and expertise.
3. Professional development should include collaboration and expert challenge.
4. Professional development programmes should be sustained over time.

5. Professional development must be prioritised by senior leadership.

So, what does this look like in practice and how can schools and colleges deliver it?

As the Standard suggests, the most effective professional development is collaborative and driven by teachers. Professional development, therefore, should involve responding to advice and feedback from colleagues, and reflecting systematically on the effectiveness of lessons and approaches to teaching. This might take the form of peer-observations and feedback, of peer-coaching, or of more formal lesson study activities. It might also take the form of peer-to-peer work scrutiny, both of pupils' marked work and assessment records, and of medium- and long-term planning documentation.

Having said this, and as Ofsted also recognises, professional development should not only be teacher-led or delivered in-house; rather, it requires the expertise of external providers. Otherwise, schools and colleges are in danger of becoming closed shops, working in silos and without suitable benchmarking from the wider profession and indeed from other related fields.

Whatever form it takes, the best professional development gives ownership to staff and creates the time and space needed for them to work together, sharing best practice and learning from each other's mistakes.

Another way to ensure that professional development is effective is to make it an unmissable event, tailored to meet the differing needs of departments and teachers. Every member of staff should recognise the importance of professional development as a mandatory part of their jobs – not as a voluntary extra. But they'll only do that when professional development is worth engaging with and it will only be worth engaging with when it is relevant, timely, keenly focused on real classroom practice, and genuinely and tangibly impactful.

In order to ensure relevance and focus, professional development should be influenced by research evidence but informed by context. In other words, it should take its lead from what the research evidence indicates works best, but be mindful of the unique circumstances of each school and college, subject, teacher and cohort of pupils.

As well as being unmissable, professional development should be regular, embedded and joined-up. Professional development should be seen as a collaborative enterprise involving all staff working together, rather than something which is 'done to' them by senior leaders.

Professional development also works best when it performs the twin functions of innovation and mastery. In other words, professional development should not solely be about learning new ways of working – professional development for *innovation* - although this is undoubtedly important. Rather, it should also be about helping teachers to get better at something they already do – professional development for *mastery*. Professional development for mastery is about recognising what already works well and what should therefore be embedded, consolidated, built upon, and shared.

I'd like to share two approaches to professional development which I think may help teachers to improve their curriculum knowledge and work more collaboratively on curriculum planning: lesson study and professional learning communities...

Lesson study

According to Vivianne Robinson (2009), "Taking part in collaborative enquiries into improving teaching and learning is the single most impactful action a school leader can take to improve educational outcomes for pupils."

Lesson Study is one way of achieving this and it can be used as an alternative to the high stakes lesson observation. Lesson Study is a planned programme of teacher enquiry which originated in Japan. It enables teachers to work collaboratively in order to explore and improve their own practice. However, it requires a strong commitment from staff and is time-consuming. As such, school leaders must be serious about setting time aside for teachers to meet, observe each other, and give feedback. This might involve getting cover for some lessons.

Lesson Study usually involves a group of between two and four teachers (most often it's three called a triad or four called a quad) working collaboratively to plan a lesson, predict pupil reactions to that lesson, observe the reality, interview pupils, and then reflect and repeat the process. The group works best when there is a range of teaching experience and when one member is a more senior member of staff.

When observing each other and interviewing pupils, the triad focuses on three "case study pupils" rather than the whole class. This allows a more detailed exploration of the effects of their teaching on pupils' learning.

Here's the process:

Firstly, perhaps with the help of a coach or subject leader, the triad/quad identifies a research question – using data collected from their assessments of pupils – such as 'What impact will peer-assessment have on the quality of the written work of Year 11 grade 3/4 borderline pupils in the response to non-fiction unit of GCSE English?'

The research question, like the one above, should be focused and specific; it should identify the learning outcome which the Lesson Study seeks to improve (e.g. the quality of written work); the pupils who will be involved in the study (Year 11 grade 3/4 borderline English pupils); the teaching and learning strategy which is to be tested (peer-assessment); and the unit or scheme of work (GCSE English 'response to non-fiction').

It's also important at the planning stage that the teachers in the triad identify the means by which they will evaluate the impact of their project. For example, the triad might want to create a test for pupils to complete before and after the project and agree a set of interview questions for pupils to answer.

Secondly, the lesson is planned collaboratively and is then taught and observed. The observation is focused on the case study pupils' learning and progress; it is not a general observation of the quality of teaching and learning. The process may be repeated, and the activities refined over time. Not all the lessons in the study need to be observed.

One alternative to 'live' peer-observation and a potential solution to the problem of cover – is to use video technology to record lessons for later viewing. Whatever method is used to observe lessons, it should be made clear that observations are not high stakes. Indeed, because the lessons have been co-planned, there should be less fear and more trust built into the process. Also, the foci of observation are the case study pupils rather than the teacher.

Thirdly, the case study pupils are interviewed in order to gain an insight into their responses to the activity. A discussion is held with the research group to analyse how pupils have responded to the teaching strategy, what progress they have made, what they found difficult and what can be learned about how to develop the teaching strategy further.

Finally, the outcomes are shared with a wider audience (perhaps the whole department or staff).

Here's the process again in summary form:

1. Three or four teachers plan a lesson together
2. The activity they plan addresses a specific learning outcome
3. Teachers predict how pupils will react to the activity
4. A case study of three pupils is selected, perhaps based on prior assessment
5. The lesson is taught and observed, particular attention is given to the case study pupils
6. An assessment is carried out and pupils are interviewed
7. The teachers reflect on their findings (in relation to their predictions) and plan their response

Lesson Study blends the features of professional learning that Cordingley (2004) identified as having the biggest impact on teaching and learning. Namely:

- the professional learning takes place over time (it is not a one-off event)
- the research takes place in classrooms with real pupils
- there is an element of collaborative enquiry between teachers trying to solve a problem

David Hargreaves (2011) calls this kind of approach 'joint professional development' (JPD as opposed to CPD).

In his paper on the subject of teaching schools (a concept which was introduced in 2011 based on the existing model of teaching hospitals), David Hargreaves argued that, "It will not be enough for teaching schools to continue [with the traditional model] of professional development. Their challenging task is to raise professional development to a new level through the exemplary use and dissemination of joint practice development [which] "captures a process that is truly collaborative, not one-way; the practice is being improved, not just moved from one person or place to another".

Joint practice development gives birth to innovation and grounds it in the routines of what teachers naturally do. Innovation is fused with and grows out of practice, and when the new practice is demonstrably superior, escape from the poorer practice is expedited.

If joint practice development replaced sharing good practice in the professional vocabulary of teachers, we would, I believe, see much more effective practice transfer in the spirit of innovation that is at the heart of a self-improving system.

"Mentoring and coaching between schools," Hargreaves says, "are at the heart of this effective practice transfer. A school that has not developed a strong mentoring and coaching culture is not likely to be successful either at moving professional knowledge and skills to partners or at rising to the level of joint practice development." He says effective use of coaching and mentoring is a means of nurturing talent and is of particular importance in leadership development "since leaders learn best with and from outstanding leaders."

Dudley (2013) says JPD helps teachers to:

- observe pupils' learning in much sharper detail than is usually possible
- observe the gaps between what they'd assumed was happening when pupils learned and what really happens
- discover how to plan learning which is better matched to the pupils' needs

- learn in a supportive community committed to helping pupils learn

Here are some useful rules for the triad or quad to observe:

- All members of the group should be treated as equals because they are all pupils irrespective of age, seniority, and experience.
- All members should be allowed to contribute, and their contributions should be treated positively, albeit challenged and analysed in a professional manner.
- The teacher who teaches the research lesson should be supported – observations should be focused on the case study pupils not on the teacher and their practice.
- Pupils' work and interview responses should inform the post-lesson discussion and pupil's responses to activities should be compared with the group's earlier predictions.
- All the findings should be shared with a wider audience and acted upon.

Professional learning communities

Another useful model of CPD which can help improve teachers' curriculum knowledge and engender more effective collaborative planning is the professional learning community…

As we discovered in Chapter Fourteen, Daniel Pink, in his book 'Drive' (2009), explores what motivates people at work. He argues that people tend to be motivated by autonomy – in other words, being accorded control over the way they work; mastery – being good at their jobs and getting better; and purpose – doing a job which is considered meaningful and worthy.

One way to promote autonomy, mastery, and purpose is through the establishment of professional learning communities in which teachers are provided with the time, space and – perhaps most importantly of all – the safety net they need in order to feel able and supported to take risks, to try out new teaching methods without fear or favour.

Joyce and Showers' report, 'Student achievement through staff development' (2002), explores the idea of professional learning communities further.

The authors argue that teaching has at least three times the effect on pupil achievement as any other factor and assert that teaching is best improved through experimentation. In other words, teachers need to be accorded the opportunity to try out new teaching strategies and then to candidly discuss with colleagues what worked and what did not.

Joyce and Showers suggest the following method:

Identify training needs: teachers ask themselves 'What do we feel are our most pressing needs? And 'What do our results tell us? Then a list of 10-20 ideas for improvement is drawn up, combined, compromised and prioritised into one common goal. This common goal is focused on a process designed to produce better outcomes which will directly affect pupils' experiences.

Training is devised: training is planned in the following sequence...

- Knowledge – new theories and rationale are explained
- Demonstration – new theories are modelled
- Practice – teachers try out the theories for themselves
- Peer coaching – teachers work together to solve the problems and answer the questions which arise during the 'practice' stage.

Training is delivered: the above training takes place over a period of time and is continually evaluated.

Joyce and Showers found that teachers must practice new methods 20-25 times if they are to learn how to use them as effectively as they do their usual methods.

There is a lot of research which underlines the importance of deliberate practice in achieving mastery and all insist that practice must be carried out over a long period of time. Most notably, there is the '10,000-hour rule' propounded by Malcolm Gladwell, Matthew Syed and others, which argues that in order to become an expert you must accrue 10,000 hours of practice.

Joyce and Showers also warn that the first few attempts at trying out a new teaching technique might fail but the teacher must remain positive and keep trying.

This process of experimentation works best – according to Joyce and Showers – when teachers:

- Practice the use of the new methods repeatedly over time
- Monitor the effect of the new methods on pupils
- Ask pupils their opinions on the new methods, garnering further suggestions
- Bring issues to peer coaching sessions for discussion
- Help and support others with their experimentation

It is important that leaders support experimentation by modelling what Joyce and Showers call an 'improvement and renewal' style of leadership. That is to say, they display an emphatic belief that it is always possible to get better, no matter how good you already are. And they display the belief that the factors which most affect pupil outcomes are in pupils' and teachers' control. They do not blame achievement on socio-economic factors nor suggest that ability is innate. They do not accept low standards.

What professional learning communities also do best is encourage risk-taking. Because they are about developing teaching expertise rather than judging colleagues' abilities, they encourage colleagues to try out new ways of teaching, some which will work and some which will not.

Risk-taking and innovation are key to the long-term development of teaching because they help us as professionals to keep on getting better over time. And as lead learners, teachers should model the process of learning for their pupils. We need to show our pupils that we are also learning all the time and that we are unafraid of trying new things even if that means we sometimes make mistakes. Actually, not "even if that means we make mistakes" but "exactly because it means we make mistakes". After all, to make mistakes is to learn; to learn is to increase our IQs. As Samuel Beckett wrote back in 1884, "Ever tried? Ever failed? Try again. Fail again. Fail better." Teachers need to model the "growth mindset" approach pioneered by Carol Dweck.

Professional learning communities also encourage teachers to do exactly what we want all of our pupils to do in order to achieve success: namely, to work outside their comfort zones, to try something difficult. And setting ourselves tough tasks is also to be encouraged because challenge leads to deeper learning and greater achievement. Challenge is, after all, a central feature of effective long-term learning. If you think back to a time when you've felt challenged either personally or professionally, you'll probably recall feeling discomfort. But, once you'd overcome the challenge and achieved, the sense of success with which you were rewarded felt far greater than if you'd achieved something easy without even breaking into a sweat.

Of course, engaging in professional development – as well as designing curricular – is a time-consuming task and senior leaders have a duty to protect their teachers' workloads. So, what can SLT do to balance the demands of the job with protecting staff health and wellbeing?

Teacher workload

If we are to encourage teachers and middle leaders to engage in the curriculum planning process, and to use research evidence to improve the chances that their teaching will enable pupils to transfer key knowledge into long-term memory, and if we recognise that to do so requires them to participate in more professional development, then we must carefully consider the impact of this on their work life balance and wellbeing.

This new focus on the intent, implementation and impact of the curriculum could, if left unchecked, lead to a significant increase in teacher workload. For example, in June 2019 I heard first-hand of middle leaders and teachers being mandated by their senior colleagues to re-write all their schemes of work for the next academic year in order to incorporate Ofsted's 3I's. This is not what Ofsted intended and certainly not what I wish to advocate with this series of books.

Although it's inevitable that a new, sharper focus on curriculum planning will create more work in the short-term, this increase must be balanced with reductions in the workload elsewhere. In simple terms, it is about protecting or reducing the overall workload of staff but refocusing their time and energies on what matters most and on what will have the biggest impact on pupils and students.

For example, I happen to think that time spent identifying the key concepts pupils must learn and the threshold concepts that lead towards those concepts is time well spent because this helps teachers to teach more effectively and helps pupils to learn more effectively. On the other hand, I happen to think that time spent on triple-marking, say, or on stamping books to record that verbal feedback has been given, is time wasted. So, if you currently require teachers to do all manner of things that do not lead to demonstrable academic gains for pupils – or not significant enough gains – then tell them to stop, carve out some time and use that more wisely.

What more can senior leaders do to help protect their staff from an unnecessary workload?

Firstly, consideration should be given to the nature of the work staff are expected to complete, and not solely the volume of it. Indeed, a recent UCL Institute of Education survey of around 1,200 current and former teachers found that it was the nature rather than the quantity of workload, linked to notions of "performativity and accountability", that was a crucial factor in determining staff satisfaction.

The UCL report found there was a contradiction between expectation and reality, the practices of being a teacher impeded some teachers' abilities to actually be teachers. Many of those surveyed by UCL thought they could cope with the amount of workload they were given, but a lack of support and a targets-driven accountability system was worse than they had thought and led to many teachers leaving the profession, and yet more teachers considering it.

The general response from government is that teaching will be improved by reducing workload, removing unnecessary tasks and increasing pay. This may help, say the UCL, but their survey also indicates that part of the problem lies within the culture of teaching, the constant scrutiny, the need to perform and hyper-critical management. Reducing workload will not address these cultural issues.

The UCL findings illustrate the link between workload fears and the reality of working within what the report authors (Dr Jane Perryman and Graham Calvert) call "the accountability performativity context".

This takes me back to my initial point: that the key to improving teacher workload is to focus teachers' time on what matters most and on what will have the biggest impact on pupil academic gains. If teachers know that what they're being asked to do is important and will help their pupils, they are likely to feel motivated to do it and not regard it as a burden. If they regard a task as purely fulfilling management purposes, however, they will begrudge doing it and regard it as a distraction from their core purpose which, in turn, will lead to feelings of being burdened and stressed.

In order to ensure that a teacher's workload is manageable and meaningful, I think senior leaders should consider the impact of their demands on staff's autonomy, mastery, and purpose...

In terms of **autonomy**, school and college leaders need to better understand what motivates staff, and accept that teachers need to feel valued, rewarded, and professionally developed.

In practice, rather than telling staff what to do or presenting them with a school improvement plan of actions, school leaders might invite staff to identify a problem that exists in their department or in the wider school. Then they might be afforded the time - and resources - to solve it in their own way, perhaps during twilight INSET or in staff meeting time.

It is important to end this process by implementing staff's innovations in order to make it clear that their contributions are valued. As I've already argued, autonomy should certainly be afforded in the way subject specialists design their disciplinary curriculums.

In terms of **mastery**, school and college leaders might wish to improve their system of performance management. In particular, they may wish to sharpen the focus on performance *improvement* and personal *development* rather than on compliance with a set of norms. They may also want to ensure that performance feedback derives from a wide range of sources, not just from observation and not just from the line manager.

School and college leaders might also introduce a means by which teachers can be recognised and rewarded for their contributions beyond exam results. This means being clear and transparent about what being a high value member of staff means, having clear and transparent processes for identifying such members of staff, and ensuring that staff know that their potential has been recognised. This might mean developing a no-blame culture of openness, offering high quality feedback that allows teachers to learn from their mistakes without fear or favour.

In terms of **purpose**, school and college leaders need to understand and articulate what their school has to offer teachers and what makes it unique. They should talk to existing staff and pupils about why it's a good place to be then communicate this clearly and frequently. They should also be clear about the school's direction of travel - about where it is headed and how it intends to get there – and this includes sharing their curriculum vision and explaining the purpose of education in their school.

Ways to reduce workload to make way for curriculum design

As well as considering teachers' autonomy, mastery and purpose, and focusing on the nature as well as the volume of work you give teachers and middle leaders to do, here are some other ways in which you might reduce workload in order to create the space for curriculum discussions and planning...

School calendar

It is, I think, helpful for senior leaders to ask themselves how the school calendar might add to a busy teacher's burden. Is there an avoidable congestion of parents' evenings and other late-night events such as open evenings, awards nights, drama productions, and so on? Are meetings and CPD events similarly congested, or do they all fall on the same night of the week which may cause difficulty for some staff?

Often, calendar congestion is the result of unintended consequences – senior leaders put together what they think is a sensible, logical plan for the year. I'm sure no one sets out to cause their colleagues difficulty! But, perhaps because they do not themselves teach a full timetable, they don't always consider the impact of their decisions on the full-time classroom teacher.

This can be solved – to some extent – by either consulting on the calendar before it is finalised, by forming a working party of staff from a wide variety of job-roles to co-produce the calendar, or by simply talking to teachers and other staff. Combing charts are sometimes helpful as a way of getting staff to set out their preferences before the school calendar and timetable are written. It's impossible to please everyone all the time, of course; but without consultation, it's likely many staff will be avoidably inconvenienced.

When I was a headteacher, I followed a simple maxim: before I took any decision, I asked myself: What will this feel like for a teacher with twenty-three lessons a week, teaching across all year groups and ability groups? Often the best teacher to have in mind is the one who teaches a minority subject to almost every child in the school.

This maxim proves particularly useful when writing the school timetable or scheduling reports and parents' evenings. What looks sensible on paper may be unworkable for the teacher who teaches several groups in the same year or every year group from 7 to 11.

Assessment schedule

What about the collection of data and the writing of reports? Is there a bottleneck at certain points of the year? More importantly, are the processes and systems used for data collection and reporting onerous and convoluted? Or do teachers lack the training to be able to use these systems quickly and fluently? Again, what are the implications of our scheduling decisions on the teacher who teaches right across the age and ability spectrum? Are we expecting a teacher to write hundreds of reports and meet hundreds of parents within a very short space of time?

School timetable

As well as looking again with fresh eyes at the annual calendar and assessment schedule, senior leaders may wish to consider the shape of the working week, for staff as a body and for individual teachers. For example, when timetabling, are we seeking to – wherever possible – provide a spread of PPA time and other non-teaching time or do some teachers teach several full days and then have an entire morning, afternoon or full day off-timetable?

When timetabling, have we considered the impact of the groups we have assigned to teachers? Are teachers being given too many different classes, perhaps because they teach split-classes or only one group in any year? Could we cut their planning load by giving them two or more classes from the same year group? Or could we do more to avoid split classes which in itself adds to a teacher's workload because they have to find time to liaise with their opposite number to discuss their planning and marking, and to compare notes on the progress being made by pupils. How are exam classes assigned? Do some teachers teach only exam classes and therefore have a much higher marking load not to mention the pressure applied through their accountability for outcomes?

How are we assigning teaching assistants (TAs) and additional learning support (ALS)? Could more be done to utilise TAs to support teachers? Do we take account of TAs' subject specialisms and interests to ensure they are supporting in subject disciplines about which they have knowledge?

For those teachers teaching a full day, have we also inadvertently scheduled their bus, break or lunch duty on the same day, meaning they have no downtime at all? How many duties do we expect staff to undertake and is this fair? Often it is middle leaders who suffer here because they are weighed down by duties and meetings as a perverse reward for being a member of the extended school leadership team but commonly, unlike the core-SLT, they continue to teach a heavy timetable.

Advantage of staff collaborative planning

In Chapters Sixty and Sixty-One, I will explore the importance of collaborative planning and explain how this can help improve the quality of our curriculum design, ensuring greater levels of consistency and continuity both in terms of *what* is taught and *how* it is taught.

I will also argue that collaborative planning can aide pupils' capacity to learn increasingly complex curriculum content by reducing the cognitive load weighing on their limited working memories.

But, for the purposes of this chapter, allow me to focus on the fact that, by engaging in collaborative planning, we can also reduce teacher workload.   After all, rather than every member of a department planning their own schemes of work and creating their own resources, the team do this collectively - and a scheme of work shared is a scheme of work halved, after all.

In order to put the above advice into practice, I'd suggest the following approach:

1. As a department, decide on the key concepts and ideas that need to be taught and for each identify a schema to help pupils process, retrieve and apply their knowledge - then work together to create that schema and ensure all the department use the same one and present it in the same way.   For example, for the use of rhetorical devices, all teachers agree to use the same version of AFOREST and does so using the same PowerPoint slide

2. As a department, identify the key concepts and ideas pupils are bringing to your subject from their previous school. Identify the language they have been taught - such as the technical vocabulary they've used - and their definitions. Ensure all teachers use the same language and definitions or, if it important to increase the complexity of this, explicitly signpost the change, linking the new language to what pupils already know and use.

3. Agree a set of classroom displays that will act as schema or aide memoir and place them in every room in the department and ideally in the same location. Refer to these displays as often as possible so that pupils automatically utilise them as and when required.

4. Establish consistent rules and routines for entering classrooms, for transitions between activities, for group work, for self- and peer-assessment, and for class debate and discussion.   Again, develop consistent schema to remind pupils of these rules - such as SLANT which is used by the Uncommon Schools network in America for class debates and stands for Sit up - Listen - Ask and answer questions - Nod - Track the speaker. Refer to three - using the same slide or display - whenever pupils engage in a relevant task until it becomes automated.

Naturally, teachers will want to tailor these collaborative plans to suit their style and their pupils' needs, but though the garnish may change, the 'meat' will stay the same. After all, all pupils should be working towards the same destinations and studying curriculum content in roughly the same order and at roughly the same pace.

In the next chapter, we will explore the importance of creating performance management and quality assurance processes that support, rather than obstruct, curriculum design and delivery.

CHAPTER FIFTY-EIGHT:
CREATING THE SYSTEMS FOR
IMPLEMENTATION

Once upon a time, not so long ago, teachers were judged by means of a single digit which graded an hour's performance, observed through the narrow lens of one lesson, with one class, and with the biased eyes of one observer. Tell your children that and they won't believe you. 'But that's ridiculous,' they'll protest, 'Surely no one thought that made any sense?' And the answer, of course, is the secret hidden in plain sight, the elephant in the room: it didn't.

If your school or college is still grading lesson observations and using this score as a proxy for quality assurance and performance management, then you have my deepest sympathies and urgent request that you enact change. I'm confident, though, that the tide has finally turned, and senior leaders are developing more robust, accurate and - above all - fair systems of performance management and quality assurance. I'm not quite so confident, however, that most schools and colleges have yet discovered a workable alternative.

When it comes to performance management, my philosophy is simple: it is no one's vocation to fail. In other words, no one wakes up in the morning determined to do the worst job they possibly can; no one opens their eyes, stretches and yawns, looks themselves up and down in the mirror and vows to fail as many pupils as they can before nightfall. But, despite the best of intentions, sometimes some people don't perform as well as we'd like.

When teachers under-perform, they need to be given time and support – including training – in order to improve. Many will. But those who don't need to leave the profession, ideally of their own volition and with our best wishes as they embark on a new career, but sometimes more forcibly. Retaining people who cannot perform the duties for which they are paid (from tax-payers' limited coffers) serves no one well, least of all our pupils.

Accountability – when managed fairly and accurately, honestly and transparently – is a good thing. It ensures the best people do the best jobs; it ensures the teaching profession – and our next generation – is kept safe. Arguing against ineffective systems of performance management (such as lesson observations) is not - therefore - akin to arguing against the need for accountability. Indeed, performance management matters and it is important school and college leaders get it right in order to help teachers improve, to reward hard work and challenge persistent underperformance.

A system of accountability based on lesson observations alone - or indeed any other single measure - is a broken one because lesson observations do not accurately or reliably measure the quality of teaching nor the effectiveness of teachers. What they do, however, is create a climate of fear; they straitjacket teachers. As a result of high-stakes lesson observations, teachers tend to do one of two things:

1. They over-plan, over-teach and proffer showcase lessons which bear no relation to their everyday practice.

2. They become stressed by the experience of being watched and so under-perform.

In short, high-stakes lesson observations - or any other single-source evaluation tool - do not allow observers to see the teacher as they would normally teach. But even if a teacher is brave enough to teach a 'normal' lesson and does not succumb to the natural stress of observation, the very presence of an observer in the room inevitably alters the classroom dynamics. This is called the Hawthorne Effect.

So, what's the answer?

First of all, let me be clear: I'm not suggesting we stop observing lessons altogether. In fact, I think walking into lessons to see what's happening is important. By observing the classroom environment, for example, we can see the rapport the teacher has established with pupils, we can see how well the teacher manages behaviour and utilises resources. Lesson observations also allow us to see the ways in which transitions are handled and tasks are organised. But observations alone do not enable us to accurately judge the quality of teaching. For that we need to triangulate what we see and hear in classrooms with other sources of information, not least our – much maligned but absolutely vital – professional judgment.

In other words, we should measure the quality of teaching in a holistic not isolated way.

The Measures of Effective Teaching (MET) project by the Bill and Melinda Gates Foundation was a three-year study which sought to determine how best to identify and promote great teaching. The project concluded that it was possible to identify - and therefore measure - great teaching by combining three types of measures, namely:

1. Classroom observations,
2. Pupil surveys, and
3. Pupil achievement gains (or outcomes).

The project report said that "Teaching is complex, and great practice takes time, passion, high-quality materials, and tailored feedback designed to help each teacher continuously grow and improve."

The project's report shows that a more balanced approach – one which incorporates multiple measures such as the pupil survey data and classroom observations – has two important advantages: teacher ratings are less likely to fluctuate from year to year, and the combination is more likely to identify teachers with better outcomes on pupil assessments.

The report also offered advice on how to improve the validity of lesson observations. It recommended averaging observations from more than one observer: "If we want students to learn more, teachers must become students of their own teaching. They need to see their own teaching in a new light. This is not about accountability. It's about providing the feedback every professional needs to strive towards excellence."

The project claimed we had to learn four lessons if we were to improve our systems of performance management:

Firstly, teachers generally appear to be managing their classrooms well, but are struggling with fundamental instructional skills.

Secondly, classroom observations can give teachers valuable feedback, but are of limited value for predicting future performance.

Thirdly, value-added analysis is more powerful than any other single measure in predicting a teacher's long-term contributions to pupil success.

And finally, evaluations that combine several strong performance measures will produce the most accurate results.

The solutions to these problems are as follows:

Firstly, we should base teacher evaluations on multiple measures of performance, including data on pupil academic progress.

Secondly, we should improve classroom observations by making them more frequent and robust.

Thirdly, we should use or modify an existing observation rubric instead of trying to reinvent the wheel.

Fourthly, we should give evaluators the training and ongoing support they need to be successful.

And finally, we should consider using pupil surveys as a component of teacher evaluation.

In terms of using multiple measures of effectiveness, the project found that using lesson observation alone had a positive correlation with outcomes of just 0.24. Using pupil surveys alone had a correlation of 0.37. Using value added data was the most accurate with a correlation of 0.69. But combining all three of these measures had a correlation of 0.72, proving yet again that using multiple measures of performance - measuring teacher effectiveness holistically - is the best solution.

So, if we accept that teaching is a highly complex job, what aspects of it should we measure? What elements of teaching matter most to us and lead to the most significant academic gains for pupils and, perhaps more pertinently, what elements of teaching can actually be observed and measured?

Measuring what matters most - and what can be measured

In attempting to answer this question, there are several useful starting points. Hopkins and Stern (1996), for example, conducted a synthesis of OECD findings from ten countries They concluded that excellent teachers in all these countries had the following traits in common:

- They made a passionate commitment to doing the best for their students.
- They had a love of children which was enacted in a warm, caring relationship.
- They had strong pedagogical content knowledge.
- They used a variety of models of teaching and learning.
- They had a collaborative working style and regularly worked with other teachers to plan, observe and discuss one another's work.
- They constantly questioned, reflected on, and modified their own practice in light of feedback.

The Education and Training Foundation's Professional Standards (2013) - which articulate what is expected of teachers in the further education sector - define the role of the effective teacher using three broad headings:

1. Professional values and attributes,
2. Professional knowledge and understanding,
3. Professional skills.

The Teachers' Standards - created by the government's Department for Education in 2011 - are intended to inform and support the performance management of teachers working in state schools in England. The standards are gathered under eight umbrella headings. According to the standards, great teachers:

1. Set high expectations which inspire, motivate and challenge pupils,
2. Promote good progress and outcomes by pupils,
3. Demonstrate good subject and curriculum knowledge,
4. Plan and teach well-structured lessons,
5. Adapt teaching to respond to the strengths and needs of all pupils,
6. Make accurate and productive use of assessment,

7. Manage behaviour effectively to ensure a good and safe learning environment, and
8. Fulfil wider professional responsibilities.

There are many such frameworks that seek to set out as succinctly as possible the roles and responsibilities, and the character traits and qualities, shared by the best teachers around the world. But one of my favoured sets of standards is The Danielson Framework (2013) which pithily yet comprehensively sets out what great teachers do. The standards are grouped under the following four headings:

1. Planning and preparation,
2. Classroom,
3. Instruction, and
4. Professional responsibilities.

Under '**planning and preparation**', Danielson says (and I have taken the liberty to abridge and paraphrase) that teachers should:

Demonstrate a good pedagogical knowledge

They do this by ensuring that their curriculum plans reflect important concepts in the discipline and accommodate prerequisite relationships among concepts and skills. They ensure they give clear and accurate classroom explanations, give accurate answers to students' questions and feedback to students that furthers learning. And they make interdisciplinary connections in plans and practice.

Maintain a good knowledge of students

They do this by gathering both formal and informal information about students which they use in planning instruction. They learn students' interests and needs and again use this to inform their planning. They participate in community cultural events.

Write learning outcomes that are of a challenging cognitive level

They do this by stating student learning not student activity, by ensuring outcomes are central to the discipline and related to those in other disciplines, and by ensuring outcomes can be assessed and differentiated for students of varied ability.

Maintain a knowledge of resources

They do this using material from a range of sources including a variety of texts, as well as internet resources and resources from the local community. They participate in professional education courses or professional groups.

Provide coherent instruction

They do this by ensuring their lessons support instructional outcomes and reflect important concepts, perhaps by creating instructional maps that indicate relationships to prior learning. They provide activities that represent high-level thinking and offer opportunities for student choice. They make use of varied resources and teach structured lessons.

Assess students

They do this ensuring their lesson plans correspond with assessments and instructional outcomes. They use assessment types that are suitable to the style of outcome and offer a variety of performance opportunities for students. They modify assessments for individual students as needed. They write clear expectations with descriptors for each level of performance. And they design formative assessments which inform minute-to-minute decision making by the teacher during instruction.

Under the '**classroom**' heading, Danielson says that teachers should:

Show respect and rapport for others

They do this by ensuring they engage in respectful talk, active listening, and turn-taking. They acknowledge students' backgrounds and their lives outside the classroom. Their body language is indicative of warmth and caring shown by teacher and students, and they are polite and encouraging at all times.

Create a culture of learning

They do this by believing in the value of what is being learned, by setting high expectations for all that are supported through both verbal and non-verbal behaviours, for both learning and participation. They have high expectations of students' work, too, and recognise effort and persistence on the part of students.

Develop effective classroom procedures

They do this by ensuring the smooth functioning of all routines, with little or no loss of instructional time. They ensure students play an important role in carrying out the routines and that they know what to do and where to move.

Manage student behaviour

They do this by setting out clear standards of conduct which are regularly referred to during a lesson. There is a notable absence of acrimony between teacher and students concerning behaviour. The teacher is constantly aware of student conduct and takes preventive action when needed. They reinforce positive behaviour.

Make good use of the physical space

They do this by creating a pleasant, inviting atmosphere, a safe environment that is accessible for all students. They make effective use of physical resources, including technology.

Under '**instruction**', Danielson says that teachers should:

Communicate effectively

They do this by having a clarity of lesson purpose, articulating clear directions and procedures specific to the lesson activities. They give clear explanations of concepts and strategies and use correct and imaginative use of language.

Make good use of questioning and classroom discussion

They do this by asking questions of high cognitive challenge. They use questions with multiple correct answers or multiple approaches, even when there is a single correct response, and make effective use of student responses and ideas. During discussions, the teacher steps out of the central, mediating role, and focuses on the reasoning exhibited by students, both in give-and-take with the teacher and with their classmates. There are high levels of student participation in discussion.

Engage students in learning

They do this by promoting enthusiasm, interest, thinking, and problem solving. Learning tasks require high-level student thinking and invite students to explain their thinking. Students are highly motivated to work on all tasks and persistent even when the tasks are challenging. Students are actively working rather than watching while their teacher works. There is a suitable pacing of the lesson: it is neither dragged out nor rushed, and there is time for closure and student reflection.

Use assessment wisely

They do this by paying close attention to evidence of student understanding, by posing specifically created questions to elicit evidence of student understanding, and by circulating to monitor student learning and to offer feedback. Students assess their own work against established criteria, too.

Be flexible and responsive

They do this by incorporating students' interests and daily events into a lesson, and by adjusting their instruction in response to evidence of student understanding (or indeed the lack of it).

And under '**professional responsibilities**', Danielson argues that teachers should:

Reflect on their teaching

They do this by adjusting their practice so that it draws on a repertoire of strategies. They maintain accurate records. They establish routines and systems that track student completion of assignments.

Communicate with families

They do this by sending appropriate information home regarding the curriculum and student progress. Communication is two-way and there are frequent opportunities for families to engage in the learning process.

Participate in the professional community

They do this by regularly working with colleagues to share and plan for student success. They take part in professional courses or communities that emphasise improving practice and engage in school initiatives.

Grow and develop their practice

They do this by regularly attending courses and workshops and engaging in regular academic reading. They take part in learning networks with colleagues, freely sharing insights.

Show professionalism

They do this by forging a reputation as being trustworthy. They frequently remind colleagues that students are the highest priority and challenge existing practice in order to put students first.

A balanced scorecard

Once you have agreed a set of expectations or standards against which your teachers can be measured for the purposes of performance management, it is important to build a workable system of recording, monitoring and tracking performance against those measures that lead to professional conversations and to the offer of support where performance is deemed to fall short.

One solution is the professional portfolio approach. This is not to be confused with a tick-box approach which mandates teachers to self-assess against a fixed set of criteria, often feeling the need to engineer evidence where none exists. Rather, it is about teachers taking genuine responsibility for their own development and taking their professional practice seriously. It is not essential that teachers gather evidence against every criteria. Instead, they take a pragmatic approach to identifying their own development needs and to monitoring and evaluating the impact of their efforts to improve their practice. The portfolio should be a living document, added to throughout the academic year so that it becomes a true record of developing practice as well as a means of reflecting on that practice, rather than being hurriedly compiled the day before an appraisal meeting. The contents of the portfolio then facilitate a professional discussion with a line manager.

Another possible solution is the 'balanced scorecard' approach – which works when criteria are quantifiable rather than qualitative – which is a means of aggregating a range of data. That data - soft and hard, narrative and numerical - can be drawn from in-year pupil progress, end-of-year pupil outcomes including value added scores, pupil voice surveys, a teacher's contribution to their own and others' professional development, evidence of professional conduct, a scrutiny of marked pupil work, evidence of medium- and long-term planning, and so on. The wider the net is cast, the more accurate, fair, and holistic the picture of performance will be.

Of course, such systems are premised on the understanding that no measure of teacher effective is perfect because teaching is a highly complex job. Such systems are also premised on the understanding that data is more than a spreadsheet; it is a conversation. In other words, the data recorded in a scorecard is just that - data. And data is the start of a discussion. Through discussion, data can be converted into meaningful information that will support improvements in teacher effectiveness and, moreover, improvements in outcomes for pupils.

Whilst accepting its limitations, one advantage of a scorecard – and indeed a portfolio – is that it can focus attentions where they're needed most, and it can help drive positive behaviours.

A scorecard places data centre-stage and puts it in the hands of teachers and school leaders, highlighting good performance to be shared and underperformance to be addressed.

Teachers and school leaders can see their pupils' progress 'live' and can therefore act on areas of concern in a much timelier fashion and before it is too late to affect change.

The scorecard can also shine a spotlight on those aspects of a teacher's performance that are of particular importance such as target-setting, assessment, and feedback.

When implemented well, School and college leaders can access - just one-click from login - a 'live' scorecard for their teams. The discussions that flow from the data are crucial because numbers only tell us so much. Professional judgments should always act as the breakwater between data and decision-making, particularly where appraisal outcomes are concerned.

It's also important that a scorecard permeates the whole school or college. Every member of staff working in that school or college should have a scorecard including the headteacher/principal in order to ensure consistency. No pupil should be allowed to fall through the net.

A balanced scorecard – or a portfolio – is only part of the solution, however. The best systems of quality assurance and performance management lead to formative feedback which helps teachers to improve their practice.

In other words, the best performance management processes do not merely draw lines in the sand but provide a roadmap to excellence and are intrinsically linked to professional development.

In fact, the best systems are not about performance *management* at all; rather, they are about performance *improvement...*

If performance improvement feedback is to be effective, it must be based on sound and, more importantly, fair information.

For example, when giving feedback on a lesson observation (which, as I've argued, should still form one piece of the quality assurance jigsaw), the observer should ensure their notes are short, simple observations of things seen, as opposed to subjective remarks about what they would have liked to have seen. Personal opinion, as difficult as it is, should be left at the door of any feedback discussion.

When giving performance feedback, it's also important to remember - common sense, I know, but it's often forgotten in the heat and urgency of the moment - to be polite, professional, and friendly throughout. Even if a teacher's performance is less than we desire, there is nothing to be gained by being confrontational or rude. As such, it's worth contemplating the language we use: our choice of words cannot be in direct conflict with any judgment or outcome. A useful word is 'interesting' because it doesn't imply good or bad - a lesson can be interesting because it is wonderful or because observing it is like rubber-necking a car crash.

Feedback sessions should begin by thanking the teacher for allowing us to observe their lesson, review the evidence of their marked work, or to engage in whatever quality assurance activity has led to the feedback, including taking a look at the data in their scorecard.

It's wise to remember that the observed lesson or the scrutinised paperwork was a mere snapshot and not wholly representative of the teacher's overall performance. Our feedback should make this point explicit - just as we would differentiate between a pupil and their actions when chastising them for misbehaving, we should also differentiate between the teacher as a person and a professional, and the snapshot of their performance we've seen.

As well as accepting the limitations of the snapshot, we should remember the Hawthorn Effect, too. By observing something we are changing its very nature.

In the best feedback sessions, the teacher talks a lot more than the leader who is giving the feedback. Not only is this good practice because it encourages the teacher to reflect on their own performance, it also helps the leader to avoid a difficult situation in which they have to impart bad news and invite argument.

Here are some useful questions with which to start a feedback session:

- What went well? What aspects of this performance are you most pleased with?
- If you were to teach this lesson again/mark this work again/etc, what would you do differently and why?
- Can you describe pupils' starting points and the level of progress they made in this sequence of lessons/with this project?
- Did all pupils make the progress you hoped they would? How do you know?

Having facilitated a discussion around these questions, we could ask the teacher to summarise their strengths and areas for development as they see them. If the teacher's opinion is less favourable than our own, we'll find ourselves in the enviable position of being able to impart positive, motivational news. If our opinions match, we can feel reassured we're in agreement. If the teacher's opinion is more favourable than our own, we need to find out why by taking an analytical approach, probing into some specifics, for example by asking about individual pupils and the progress they are making. By drilling down into the detail and analysing small parts of a teacher's performance, we should be able to unmask misunderstandings or misconceptions, and shine a light on those aspects of performance that require improvement.

Hopefully, taking an analytical approach - keeping the discussion professional and focused on the facts not on our own prejudices and preferences - will help the teacher to see that, on reflection, they've been too generous in their initial self-assessment and aspects of their performance can, with time and support, be even better. If not, then firmness may be needed. Being firm and being rude are not synonymous, and neither are being assertive and being aggressive.

Once the feedback has been concluded, we should move the meeting towards action. Whatever the outcome, there is always need of a follow-up. If the teacher's performance is excellent then the action might be to enlist the teacher to share their good practice, to help colleagues improve the quality of their teaching. Perhaps the teacher could lead a CPD session or video a part of their lesson and share it with colleagues in a staff meeting. If the performance has been less than desired then the action might be to engage the teacher in some professional development activities, perhaps observing a colleague and trying out some new approaches in their own classroom.

Whichever path is taken, it is important we end the feedback session with a clear plan of action, complete with reasonable timescales, and an agreed method for the teacher to report back on the progress they are making against this plan.

Quality assurance

In the third and final book in this series on School and College Curriculum Design, we will turn our attention to 'impact' and one aspect we will explore further is quality assurance. There, I will add to the above with a slightly different approach premised on agreeing a set of quality standards and carrying out supportive curriculum reviews in order to assess the effectiveness of each subject discipline's planning, and to identify their areas for improvement. I won't go into any detail here - after all, I want you to buy my next book! – but briefly...

Vision, mission and priorities

I'd suggest that the starting point of effective quality assurance is to consult upon, agree and communicate a vision for the quality of education in your school or college. This vision is unique because it reflects your local context.

The next stage is to write a short mission statement which articulates **how** that vision will be realised.

The third stage, once the vision and mission have been agreed, is to set the priorities for the next one to three years. These priorities should help focus the school or college on the actions it needs to take in order to achieve its vision and mission.

Quality standards

Next come the 'quality standards', the everyday behaviours and values you need your school or college to embody.

Here are some examples for the purposes of illustration:

1. The curriculum offer is relevant, up-to-date and meets the needs of learners, communities, and the regional economy
2. The curriculum is ambitious for all learners and addresses issues of social mobility
3. Curriculum leaders and teachers identify and provide equal access to the knowledge, skills and experiences learners need to thrive
4. The curriculum is planned and sequenced to ensure positive progression
5. Teaching and assessment ensure learners know and can do more, and remember what they have learned for the long term
6. Learners are supported to become increasingly independent and resilient
7. Learners are prepared for the next stage of their lives and progress to high quality destinations
8. There is a positive learning environment and there are clear expectations for behaviour, attendance and punctuality
9. Bullying, harassment and discrimination is not accepted, and issues are quickly and consistently dealt with
10. Learners are supported to develop research and study skills that help them academically
11. Learners are afforded opportunities for personal development beyond the academic curriculum
12. Learners are given planned opportunities to develop wider skills including through high quality work experience and enrichment opportunities
13. Learners receive effective information and advice about their next steps, including careers guidance

14. Leaders and managers engage with learners, parents, the community and employers to plan and support the curriculum

Self-assessment and review

Quality improvement is a cyclical – as opposed to a linear – process and, as such, does not have a natural start and end point. Each self-assessment informs future planning which informs the actions taken, and each action is reviewed to inform the next self-assessment and so on. However, for the purposes of explanation, I will begin with the subject self-evaluation...

The purpose of the subject self-evaluation is to critically reflect on past performance in order to improve future performance. Self-evaluation requires subject leaders to state their position at the end of each academic year, the actions they took in the previous year to get there, the positive impact of those actions on pupils, each with supporting evidence, and the areas for improvement that remain and that they therefore need to focus on in the year ahead.

The areas for improvement contained within the self-evaluation document should then be carried forward to the curriculum improvement plan and form the objectives for the year ahead...

The curriculum improvement plan should be a live document used to record the actions required in-year in order to improve the quality of education each subject discipline provides. Each action taken to improve the quality of provision should be added to the plan alongside emerging evidence of its impact on pupils.

To quality assure each subject's provision and to support their improvements, subject leaders should then receive around three curriculum reviews during the academic year, roughly one per term.

Each curriculum review should be a professional process used to support and challenge leaders. The process should begin and end with the improvement plan. The plan should be used to determine the nature of the review and to identify key areas of focus for the review. The outcome of the review process should, in turn, be an updated plan. The plan is the thing!

An effective review, I would argue, has three stages:

1. A professional conversation about subject purpose and intentions
2. A range of quality assurance activities (see below)
3. An action planning meeting to agree next steps

In Book Three in this series, I will explore each stage in detail. For now, suffice to say that, in line with what I say above about the nature of observation, there should be myriad forms of quality assurance activity that, when triangulated, paint a holistic picture of performance. I'd suggest these four cornerstones:

1. Lesson observations
2. Work scrutiny
3. Review of planning
4. Review of resources

CHAPTER FIFTY-NINE:
MANAGING CHANGE

The process of curriculum intent and implementation necessarily involves change because, if a school or college is to improve its curriculum design and ensure that all teachers translate that curriculum into practice in ways that lead to long-term learning it must, by definition, change.

As such, in addition to protecting teacher workload and providing a programme of effective professional development, managing change is an important consideration for senior leaders to make.

Many senior leaders enjoy working against a backdrop of continuous change because it makes their jobs interesting, challenging and varied. It gives them a chance to stamp their mark on their school or college, to show what they are capable of. And curriculum design is a case in point: many senior leaders have embraced the recently renewed focus on curriculum design because it has afforded them an opportunity to enact change and thus leave behind a legacy. But it's important to remember that not everyone shares this passion for change.

Indeed, I would suggest that leaders start this process with the knowledge that change can be uncomfortable, particularly for those who feel that change is being done to them not by them. Leaders should also bear in mind that many staff will resent change and will either refuse to engage with it or, worse, act to prevent it from happening.

So, what is the best way to manage change?

First, it is important to understand why other people might be resistant to it...

People are often resistant to change because:

- They are anxious of the impact it will have on their jobs
- They feel they have tried it before, and it didn't work
- They fear it will mean more work for them
- They do not understand the need for change, they like the status quo
- They fear failure
- They are scared by the pace of change and by being out of their comfort zone
- They fear change will prove too costly or a waste of time and money

People are also resistant to change because change implies that the status quo isn't good enough, that the way people work now is in some way inadequate. People also resent change because it signals the destruction of all they have worked hard to achieve. Change means abandoning what they know and what they like. All of these things may be true, of course: the status quo may not be good enough; the way people work now may indeed be inadequate. But it is unlikely your school curriculum and the way in which teachers teach are so thoroughly broken that they require a total transformation. It is more likely that there will be lots of things about your current practice that should be retained, preserved, protected. Even if wholesale change is needed, and this is rare, then the process of mending it should be done gradually and with the support of staff: this means careful management, a lot of tact and patience.

Once you understand people's resistance to change, you should consider engaging them in the process of change. As a starting point, I'd suggest it is important to:

Be open and honest about the need for change: involve your staff as early as possible, ideally involve them in the process of identifying the need for change in the first place.

Explain the rationale behind change: on what evidence have you based your decision to change? What do you hope this change will achieve and why is that important?

Outline the benefits of change for everyone: what is it in for staff, pupils, parents and governors? How will change make their working lives easier and more rewarding?

I would also suggest that senior leaders use the following behaviours when managing change:

1. Patience and self-control
Leaders need to stay calm and considered at all times, and they need to think and behave rationally.

2. Balance
Leaders need to balance the needs of pupils with the needs of staff.

3. Communication
Leaders need to keep others informed and involved at all times and ensure communication is genuinely two-way.

4. Problem-solving
Leaders needs to think through the options and find appropriate solutions.

5. Personal ownership
Leaders need to showing initiative and be conscientious; leaders need to take responsibility for their decisions and

actions and for the consequences of those decisions and actions.

Leaders of change also need enthusiasm, flexibility, energy and tenacity if they are to succeed in bringing about lasting, positive change which, in turn, leads to genuine and sustainable curriculum improvement.

I find a change management cycle useful when planning for change. The cycle I often use is as follows:

1. Mobilise
2. Discover
3. Deepen
4. Develop
5. Deliver

Let me explain what this change management cycle means in practice...

Mobilise

First, as I say above, it is important to understand why some colleagues may resist change. You need to tackle this head-on by explaining why change is necessary (where is the need, what is the rationale?) and by outlining the benefits of change for everyone involved. Then you need to involve your staff in the process of change: don't let them see change as something being done to them by the senior team, let them feel genuinely a part of the process and able to contribute to it and affect it. A good way to mobilise staff is to establish 'change teams' or working parties which will be the driving force behind change. Change teams should be representative of all staff and, in the case of curriculum change, of all subject disciplines. A sensible change team may be your middle leadership team of subject leaders and coordinators.

Discover

One of the first jobs for the change team is to identify and acknowledge the issues involved in change. It means developing a deeper understanding of what change will involve and how barriers will be overcome. This might involve members of the change team consulting with others and bringing ideas and issues back to the table. Discovering the issues may be as simple as conducting a SWOT analysis or may be more complex. Subject leaders might start by assessing the effectiveness of their existing curriculum plans and then estimate the scale of the task ahead, negotiating workable timescales and step goals for a review of the whole school curriculum.

Deepen

The change team then needs to develop a deeper knowledge and understanding of the size and scope of the changes that are required. They also need to know and understand the root causes of the issues that led to change being needed in the first place, as well as the issues that will inevitably arise whilst change is being enacted. This stage is about being forewarned and forearmed, about being prepared for the road ahead. It is also about setting the boundaries - knowing what will be included in the project and what will not - and setting appropriate timescales. A curriculum cannot be designed overnight and it might be the case that teachers are not yet suitably trained and skilled to be able to complete the task alone. This stage, therefore, is as much about understanding the barriers and limitations of curriculum change, such as identifying the training needs of staff, as it is about understanding what aspects of the curriculum actually need to change.

Develop

This stage is about suggesting solutions, coming up with specific improvements to the curriculum. It is about the change team taking action, trialling new ideas and finding out what is effective and what is not. It is important at this stage to prioritise those actions which will have the biggest or most immediate impact. Start with a splash not a ripple. You want other staff to see the impact of what you're doing, you want them to see that curriculum change is for the better, that you are getting results and making life easier. You want to win over your detractors and those most resistant to change, you want to convince them that what you're doing is right. For example, your change team may trial a new teaching method – baked into the curriculum – aimed at helping pupils to transfer key knowledge into long-term memory, let's say the use of daily low-stakes quizzes as a form of retrieval practice, and this may be videoed and played at a team meeting or on a training day in order to show all staff that such an approach works with your pupils and in your school. This may then encourage others to try it out, too.

Deliver

This stage is about making change happen. The change team now rolls out the curriculum changes they have developed and refined to the whole school curriculum in their subject. The plans formed in the 'develop' stage are now fully agreed and everyone begins to implement them, again starting with the high impact actions or 'quick wins'.

In summary, then, effective change requires:

Effective leadership

Effective leadership is democratic, it acts as a role model, it supports and encourages others. Why? Because effective leadership leads to people feeling involved and valued, provides broader, richer insights and ideas, and helps improve staff morale, as well as recruitment and retention; effective leadership also shares responsibility, leads to less stress, higher standards of teaching, effective collaboration and more honest relationships in which problems are aired and resolved faster.

An inclusive culture

An inclusive culture is one in which people know they can contribute and overcome barriers together, in which everyone is encouraged to play a part in driving the school's change agenda.

Broad collaboration

This means collaboration between schools, stakeholders and other organisations which helps embed a culture of openness to positive change.

Change teams

Change teams are working parties which are inclusive and representative of all areas of school, a team which acts as a communication channel between the senior team and the workforce and which makes staff feel involved in their school.

Avoiding common change management mistakes

Even if you follow all the above advice, and with the best will in the world and a prevailing wind, mistakes can and will be made, and your best laid schemes will not always go to plan. Some mistakes can be foreseen, however; and thus, they can be avoided or mitigated.

In an article for Harvard Business Review in 1995 called Leading Change, John Kotter explained why some attempts to change the way organisations work are unsuccessful.

The first mistake many organisations make when seeking to improve the way they work is to lack a sense of urgency. Effective change requires the aggressive cooperation of many individuals and yet, without motivation, these people will not help and the effort will go nowhere. Many organisations fail to establish a sense of urgency because they worry that their staff will become defensive and that morale will drop. They worry that events will spiral out of control and short-term results will be jeopardised.

A sense of urgency is created when a frank discussion is had about some potentially unpleasant or uncomfortable realities: namely, that the organisation's performance isn't as good as people think it is and/or that the tectonic plates on which the organisation is built, are shifting and sliding at a rapid pace and the organisation is losing its footing. The purpose of such discussions is to make it clear that the status quo is more dangerous than change.

You will know when the sense of urgency is at the right level when over 75% of school staff know that operating on a business-as-usual basis is inadvisable, unacceptable and unsustainable.

The second mistake many organisations make when seeking to improve is failing to create a powerful coalition of senior staff. A successful team might only consist of four or five people in the first phase but it needs to grow quickly before real progress can be made.

A guiding coalition develops a shared commitment to improving performance through change. Although not every senior member of staff will buy into the transformation effort to begin with, the coalition must be appropriately powerful in terms of job titles and status, reputations and relationships in order to affect change.

The third mistake is lacking a clear vision – the most successful guiding coalitions develop an image of the future that is easy to communicate and appeals to all its organisation's stakeholders. The vision clearly articulates the direction of travel the organisation will take in order to become successful. Often the first draft of the vision comes from an individual who drives change but it is later refined by many others.

Without a clear and positive vision for the future of the organisation, impetus can be lost and the purpose of change can become muddy and confused. A successful vision can be communicated in less than five minutes and can garner a reaction that shows that the audience both understand it and are interested in working towards it.

The fourth mistake is not communicating the vision effectively enough or frequently enough. Without a lot of effective communication, hearts and minds cannot be won. And the vision must be communicated repeatedly, it must be incorporated into everything the organisation says and does. Emails, newsletters, staff meetings, and appraisals are all focused on articulating and achieving the vision.

The vision is communicated in both words and actions, too: no one's behaviour must undermine the vision and senior staff must behave in a way that is wholly consistent with the vision.

The fifth mistake is failing to remove the barriers that stand in the way of achieving the vision. Although senior staff can empower others to take action simply by communicating the vision, this is not enough on its own. Instead, effective change requires the removal of any barriers to change.

Often, a member of staff understands and agrees with the vision but is prevented from helping to achieve it because there is a road block in their way. Sometimes this block is a process and sometimes it is a person. Sometimes people are fearful for their jobs, and/or appraisal systems make them act out of self-interest rather than in the best interests of the organisation.

The guiding coalition, therefore, need to understand what the barriers to their vision are and then actively work to remove them – this might mean changing policies and procedures and it might mean removing some rogue staff.

The sixth mistake is failing to plan for and create 'quick wins'. Most people need compelling evidence that change will be successful within a year or less before they will commit to it. Creating short-term 'wins', therefore, is important as a means of motivating staff and convincing them that change will work.

Creating quick wins is not the same as simply hoping for a win – a successful transformation effort involves leaders actively seeking out ways of improving performance. They establish short-term goals that act as checkpoints on the journey towards achieving the long-term vision, and they work hard to ensure that those goals are scored and, once they are scored, they reward their staff accordingly.

The seventh mistake is to declare victory too soon. It is good to set short-term goals along the way and to celebrate when you achieve them – but never forget that these are small battles in a much bigger war. It is important not to declare the war to be won too soon. Instead, use the credibility afforded by achieving short-term goals as a means of tackling the bigger issues. Start work on abolishing systems and structures that are inconsistent with the vision or that stand in the way of achieving that vision.

The final mistake is failing to reconcile the new vision with the organisation's established culture. Transformation is only successful and sustainable when it becomes the norm, the accepted culture, 'the way we do things around here'.

The vision has to become the expected and established way of working. There are two key factors to consider here:

Firstly, you need to signpost for staff how the new ways of working have explicitly led to improvements, make clear that the changes you've introduced have been successful in achieving a better performance. If you are not explicit about this, people are likely to make different connections or no connections at all. Communication is the key here: tell a story linking your vision and your changes to the successes you're subsequently enjoying, and tell that story relentlessly. Dedicate meetings and emails to explaining how success was achieved.

Secondly, you need to make sure that any new appointments, particularly new leaders and managers, are well matched to the vision and model the behaviours you need. A poor appointment at a senior level can undermine the vision and the transformation you have worked hard to achieve.

In conclusion, if we are to learn from these common mistakes, we should infer that an effective change management process - as well as following a cycle such as the one I set out above - follows these eight steps:

1. Establishing a sense of urgency
2. Forming a powerful guiding coalition
3. Creating a vision
4. Communicating the vision
5. Empowering others to act on the vision
6. Planning for and creating short-term wins
7. Consolidating improvements and producing still more change
8. Institutionalising new approaches

In Book Three in this series which will tackle the third and final 'I' of 'impact', I will expand on some of these ideas.

Matt Bromley

CHAPTER SIXTY:
CLASSROOM CONSISTENCY

In Chapter Fifty-Seven, I articulated the importance of collaborative planning and argued that, by working in teams to produce collective schemes of work and resources, teachers can reduce their individual workloads. But collaborative planning has two other crucial benefits: firstly, it ensures greater consistency and thus improves curriculum continuity; and secondly, it helps pupils to make more efficient use of their space-limited working memories. Let's explore these two benefits in more detail...

Life on Mars

I moved to a new house recently. Those who claim it's one of the most stressful things you can do in life are not wrong. The solicitor's bill alone was enough to send my blood pressure through the roof. But, contrary to popular opinion, the stress does not dissipate the moment the removals van pulls off the drive.

Coming to terms with life in a strange house is also challenging. Take, for example, cooking. In our old home, I would dance around the kitchen with balletic grace retrieving pots and pans, utensils, and ingredients from their various storage places. But now, in our new house, I struggle to find even the necessities to make the most basic of meals. (Beans on toast has become a regular fixture on the family menu).

Even if I could find what I needed, I'd still struggle because the cooker has a very tenuous relationship with both heat and time - gas mark 8 is the new gas mark 6 and what should take twenty minutes now takes in excess of two hours, or sometimes no more than two minutes - there's no rhyme nor reason to it; whenever I place a chicken in the oven I do so with a silent prayer, not knowing if it will emerge clucking or cremated.

We may as well have moved to Mars. They'd be better WIFI for starters.

But why should moving to a new house be so tough and what on Earth (or indeed Mars) has this got to do with teaching?

Here's the cognitive science

As I explained in Chapter Twelve, the working memory (sometimes called the short-term memory) is the place where we actively process information; it's where we think and do. In order to learn something new, we need first to wrestle with it in working memory then encode it into long-term memory from where we can retrieve it and use it later. But working memory is very small. Miller's Law posits that working memory is limited to seven plus or minus two unique concepts. In other words, we can only process - actively think about - between five and nine unique concepts at once. That rather begs the question: what is a unique concept? And the answer? Well, it depends...

I define a 'unique concept' as something which carries a single unit of meaning so it could be a letter, a word or a sentence depending on what meaning we attach to it. For example, the twenty letters H T N O M T S A L E S U O H D E V O M I contain no collective meaning for us and therefore take up twenty spaces in working memory which is beyond our capacity. If we tried to learn these letters in isolation, we would likely fail because we'd overpower working memory - what's called 'cognitive overload'.

However, if we combined those letters into words such as LAST, MOVED, MONTH, I and HOUSE then those twenty concepts could be chunked into five unique concepts - five units of meaning which we could easily hold in working memory.

But, if we then combined those five words into a single sentence - such as the first sentence of the paragraph that began this section on 'Life on Mars' (I MOVED HOUSE LAST MONTH) then we could chunk the information even further into just one unique concept and hold this plus much more besides in our working memory. We call this kind of 'chunking', schema - it's a way of forging connections, or mental maps, between the working memory and the long-term memory.

Anyway, I digress... although this point will prove helpful later so hold onto it if you can...

The war being waged in working memory

Working memory, then, is small and we can't make it any bigger.

Whenever we think about or do anything, we use working memory and it's not just the information we are thinking about that takes up space. In fact, there is a constant battle being fought in our working memories for its limited capacity. Every task - whether it's mental or physical - requires us to balance three forms of cognitive load: intrinsic load, germane load and extraneous load.

Intrinsic load is the amount of mental activity involved in *performing a task,* to actively think about what we're doing.

Germane load is the amount of mental effort involved in *trying to understand the task* - if the task is new or unfamiliar, we have to use some working memory capacity to try make sense of it and decide how to tackle it.

Extraneous load, meanwhile, is concerned with *understanding the immediate environment* within which we are trying to perform a task. Disorganised or unfamiliar contexts contribute extraneous load to a task. For example, if I am trying to read a challenging book, such as *Ulysses* by James Joyce, I will fare better if I am sitting in a quiet, comfortable room devoid of distractions than if I am on a noisy train being buffeted back and forth.

And that - along with the astronomical amounts solicitors charge for making a phone call - explains why moving to a new house is stressful: performing everyday tasks is made harder because the extraneous load is much greater when we perform those tasks in a strange new place. When I cooked in my old kitchen, with which I was familiar, I didn't have to think about where to find everything I needed, nor did I have to contend with a cooker that refused the obey the laws of physics. I became familiar with my environment over the course of time and through practice - through trial and error I learnt where everything was kept and how everything worked - and so automated all the decisions associated with navigating that environment.

Classroom consistency

And it is the same for our pupils. When they are learning in our classrooms, there is a war being waged in their working memories, too. If we present them with unfamiliar tasks which contain entirely new information and which is presented in a new way, then we are placing unsustainable demands on their working memories and learning is likely to fail.

We can't - and wouldn't want to - eliminate all the cognitive load because if everything was too familiar and undemanding - in other words, too easy - then pupils wouldn't have to think at all and therefore would not encode anything into long-term memory. No, work has got to be hard so that pupils are made to actively think about it. But we want the focus of their hard work in lessons to be on curriculum content, not on having to contend with a distracting instructional style or learning environment.

Let me give you an example... if I wanted pupils to learn some key facts about Shakespeare's life in order to aid their analysis of the authorial context of one of his sonnets, I could ask them to conduct some independent internet research. But there is a good chance, if they are not skilled and practiced internet researchers, that most if not all of their working memory capacity will be dedicated to the 'how?' not the 'what?' - in other words, they'd have to think so hard about how to conduct research (where to go, what to type in, how to sift through the search results and discern the trustworthy from the tosh, how to skim and scan for key facts, how to present their findings, and so on...) that they would not be able to actively attend to the facts about Shakespeare's life. And because they hadn't actively thought about those facts during their research, they are unlikely to encode them into long-term memory.

To help pupils to overcome these challenges and to mitigate these kinds of risks, we need to provide greater consistency in the way we teach our pupils... and that, in turn, means we need to plan together. Yes, this does mean less teacher autonomy in the sense of teachers working in isolation, but it also means more *collective autonomy* in the sense of teachers working together to ensure pupils learn more and achieve more.

Collective autonomy

What might this look like in practice? Let me give you an example...

When teaching persuasive writing in English, it helps if we provide pupils with schema to aide their retrieval of information from long-term memory. For example, in an exam we want our pupils to be able to remember which rhetorical devices and structural markers to use in order to write persuasively and so, to help, we might teach them a mnemonic like 'AFOREST' which in my version stands for 'Amazing opening - Facts - Opinions - Rhetorical questions - Statistics - Thought-providing ending'.

Remember earlier when I said that working memory is small, but we can cheat its limitations by chunking information into meaningful units such as words and sentences? Well, in the example above, pupils can do this by simply holding one word - AFOREST - in working memory which sparks a connection to more detailed information stowed in long-term memory. By chunking in this way, pupils can free up more working memory to think about the actual task in hand, i.e. the exam question and the topic on which they need to persuade.

However, if every teacher in an English department taught a different mnemonic or all used AFOREST but had different definitions for it (for example, one teacher has the A stand for 'Alliteration' rather than 'Amazing opening') or they all used the same word with the same definitions but presented it in an entirely different format (different font, different background image, etc) then although the mnemonic will go some way to helping them cheat their working memories, pupils would still have to dedicate more WM capacity than necessary to processing it and understanding it whenever they moved from one teacher to another.

The example I've provided above is small and simplistic for the purposes of easy illustration but often teachers working in blissful isolation create all sorts of roadblocks in the way of their pupils' cognition without thinking about it or meaning to. We teachers often use a different language (see 'connective' versus 'conjunction') or methods (see long division); we have different aide memoirs in our classrooms and/or in different locations of our rooms; and - perhaps most unhelpfully of all - we have differing sets of expectations and different systems for (or ways of applying) rewards and sanctions.

Every time teachers do things differently to one another; they require pupils to use some of their working memory to process the instructional context and learning environment. In short, the extraneous load gets bigger when teachers are left to their own devices. And that leaves less space for the intrinsic load and therefore means pupils perform less well.

For this reason, and spurred by my recent house move, I have come to recognise the importance of collective rather than individual autonomy, and now appreciate the need for greater consistency across a department and school. This means that teachers need to be afforded the time to get together as a subject team for curriculum planning and the creation of pooled resources.

CHAPTER SIXTY-ONE:
TEACHING BY ALGORITHM

In Chapter Sixty, I argued in favour of greater consistency in the way we plan and teach the curriculum in order to smooth pupils' transitions from class to class, teacher to teacher, and year to year, key stage to key stage and phase to phase of education.

Consistency is helpful not just to pupils but to staff too... so how might we help teachers to automate some of their regular routines in order to reduce their workloads and promote greater consistency? I think algorithms may hold the key...

In popular rhetoric, algorithms are something to be scared of, a form of artificial intelligence poised to take over the world. But are algorithms *really* to be feared? Or might they be helpful tools for automating regular, predictable processes so that we can speed up certain actions? And, if so, might we be able to make use of them in education to foster greater consistency, reduce teacher workload, and improve outcomes for pupils?

Although the word 'algorithm' sounds somewhat state-of-the-art, it is in fact very old. It was imported into English, via French and Latin, from the name of the 9th Century Arab mathematician al-Khwarizmi.

Originally 'algorithm' simply meant what we now call the 'Arabic' system of numbers (including zero). Later, it acquired a more specific mathematical sense denoting a procedure.

So, put simply, 'algorithm' is another name for a set of rules: 'If this, then that'. And, crucially, these rules are written by humans not machines.

If we thought of algorithms as mere flowcharts or checklists drafted by people, we'd be better able to see where responsibility really lies if, or when, they go wrong. Talking of which...

Recently, Facebook suggested I might like Nigel Farage's page. Either Facebook has a dark sense of humour or there's a gremlin in the algorithm.

Likewise, because I recently bought a car-boot protector from Amazon, I'm now being plagued by emails suggesting other car-boot protectors I might also wish to purchase. But surely the fact I've just bought a car-boot protector means I'm now highly unlikely to want another one? Again, the algorithm seems faulty.

These examples are mild but when algorithms control your satnav, say, the results can be more harmful...

In her book, Hello World, the mathematician Hannah Fry recounts the story of Robert Jones who, while driving home, noticed his fuel light was flashing. He only had a few miles to find a petrol station, but thankfully his satnav found a short cut, sending him on a narrow, winding path up the side of a valley. Jones followed the satnav's instructions but, as he drove, the road got steeper and narrower. After a couple of miles, it turned into a dirt track.

"Just a short while later," Fry tells us, "anyone who happened to be looking up from the valley below would have seen the nose of [Jones's] BMW appearing over the brink of the cliff above, saved from the 100ft drop only by the flimsy wooden fence at the edge he had just crashed into." Jones later told a local newspaper, "It kept insisting the path was a road. So I just trusted it. You don't expect to be taken nearly over a cliff."

So, algorithms are certainly not faultless, but this does not mean they are to be feared. In fact, algorithms are already proving very useful indeed...

Algorithms are everywhere and we use them every day without thinking about it. For example, if you've ever used Google Maps or an online search engine, then you've used an algorithm. Indeed, whenever you press a key on your keyboard, make a call, perform a calculation, open a phone app or press a button on your TV remote, an algorithm is triggered.

Algorithms are already used in our hospitals, our courtrooms and police stations, and our airports, feeding on our data and making decisions on our behalf. Algorithms can help diagnose breast cancer, catch serial killers, and avoid plane crashes.

Life would be much harder - and slower - without algorithms.

In short, knowing when to trust an algorithm and when to deviate from it and use human intuition is key to their success. When used wisely, they can help us be more productive.

Algorithms in education

So, with this in mind, how can algorithms be put to good use in education without losing our sense of humanity and professional autonomy and creativity?

To be clear, I'm not suggesting we allow robots into the classroom and outsource teaching to automatons. Rather, I'm suggesting that we can learn from the example of algorithms and create flowcharts and checklists (or what we might in education call 'rubrics') for all those regular routines we follow in school and college in order to help staff and pupils automate those processes and secure greater consistency. Talking of which...

In Chapter Sixty I explained why consistency is important in education. Whenever pupils are learning in our classrooms, I said, there is a war being waged in their working memories. If we present them with unfamiliar tasks which contain entirely new information and which is presented in a new way, then we are placing unsustainable demands on their working memories and learning is likely to fail.

We can't - and wouldn't want to - eliminate all the cognitive load, I explained, because if everything was too familiar and undemanding - in other words, too easy - then pupils wouldn't have to think at all and therefore would not encode anything into long-term memory.

Rather, work has got to be hard so that pupils are made to actively think about it. But we want the focus of their hard work to be on curriculum content not on having to contend with a distracting instructional style or learning environment.

Consistency is also key to ensuring we apply behaviour policies fairly and that every member of staff upholds high expectations - only by being consistent can schools create a culture of positive behaviour and win the war of attrition that is low-level disruption.

Algorithms for pupils

In order to help pupils focus on what matters most, we might draft rubrics that help them remember key routines or the ingredients of good work (e.g. 3B4me for independent study, STAR for self- and peer-assessment, FACT for giving peer feedback, PEE or PEEL for structuring analytical essays, AFOREST for persuasive writing, etc.). We might create algorithms to help pupils focus on how to behave in school and how to contribute to lessons (e.g. CARE for attitudes to learning, PARTNERS or GROUP for pupil interactions, SLANT for class discussions, etc.), and algorithms that help them with their learning (e.g. mnemonics for remembering spelling rules such as 'Big Elephants Can Always Upset Small Elephants', and how to proof-read their work).

The crucial point to make here, though, is not simply that mnemonics or checklists are helpful - teachers have been using these for years - but that all these rubrics must be the same across a subject discipline and, where possible, across an entire school or college, rather than created or tweaked by individual teachers, because if everyone does something slightly different, pupils will suffer.

A school or department might usefully create rubrics to help pupils with the following:

- entering and leaving a classroom
- behaviour expectations in and out of class
- equipment requirements and respecting property
- reporting concerns including bullying
- how to conduct research inc in the internet
- note-taking

- pair and group work
- making presentations in class
- critical thinking
- class debate and discussions
- self- and peer-assessment
- giving feedback
- proof-reading and redrafting work
- seeking help with work when stuck
- the presentation and submission of written work including homework
- acting on feedback to improve work
- independent study / revision skills and strategies

Here are some useful mnemonic-style rubrics you may wish to use with pupils...

How to SOAR:
Show integrity
Own your learning
Accept responsibility
Respect yourself and other

How to SUMmarise:
Shorter than the text
Use our own words
Main ideas only

Take CARE:
Courteous
Always prepared
Respect
Effort

When in assemblies in the school HALL:
Hands at your side
All eyes forward
Lips zipped
Low speed

Effective GROUP work:
Give thoughtful feedback
Respect others and their thoughts

On task at all times
Use quiet voices
Participate actively
Stay with your group

How to work with PARTNERS:
Participate actively
Ask questions
Respect your partner's ideas
Take turns to speak
Never give up
Explain your answers/ideas
Respect others' answers
Stay with your partner

The POWER of planning:
Prepare - list your ideas
Organise - structure your ideas into a response
Write the first draft
Edit the first draft, identify improvements
Re-write

THINK before speaking:
Is it:
True
Helpful
Inspiring
Necessary
Kind

Algorithms for new teachers

As I said at the beginning of this chapter, algorithms can also be used to help new teachers learn about a school's systems and structures, and policies and procedures. In the same way as they help cheat the limitations of pupils' working memories, checklists can help new teachers - who are not only new to their school, but new to the profession - to automate some regular routines so they can focus on the complex task of teaching.

For example, schools might create rubrics for lesson planning routines, resource-creation, behaviour systems (including how and when to apply rewards and sanctions), the setting, assessing and recording of homework, marking and feedback, and working with teaching assistants, to name just a few.

New teachers might also benefit from flowcharts to help them use the school's data systems including for recording attendance and lateness, as well as to navigate the school's procurement and reprographics procedures, and engage with performance management and professional development procedures, and so on.

Indeed, rubrics can form the basis of the new teacher's induction handbook.

Checklists are not only helpful for new teachers as part of their induction and probation; they can help all teachers to automate regular routines and ensure greater consistency between teachers and departments.

Checklists may be created to help ensure meetings are productive and focused, for example, and to improve the effectiveness of quality assurance processes. They may be used to improve parental and community engagement, and to ensure the school complies with health and safety legislation, as well as child protection procedures including on school trips.

In fact, the use of checklists is truly limitless!

How to write a rubric

Whatever you decide to write a rubric for, here are some questions to consider...

- Why do I need this rubric? Do I have clear and concise objectives for its use?
- What are the crucial steps people usually miss which I must include in my rubric?
- Is this rubric as simple as it can be but as comprehension as it needs to be?
- Can this rubric be read aloud easily and fluently whilst someone is performing the task?
- Have I used simple sentences and short words?
- Does the title accurately reflect the purpose of the rubric?
- Does it fit on one page?

- Is this rubric logically ordered and presented in a simple, uncluttered format?
- Do I include natural 'pauses' or checkpoints for long, complex processes and, if so, are there fewer than 10 actions between checkpoints?
- Is this rubric likely to be contradicted or confused by another checklist or process, or to become quickly outdated?
- Does the rubric include a creation date and the date it was last revised?
- Does it make clear who the rubric is aimed at?
- Have I trialled the rubric and modified it in response to any difficulties?

Above all, remember that good rubrics are precise - they don't try to spell out everything, they simply provide reminders of the most critical or important steps.

Schools and colleges - simplified

Checklists can also be helpful for the bigger things in education. For example, in previous chapters of this book and in previous books, I've shared my checklists for, amongst others, the 3-step learning process, the 4-part teaching sequence, the 5 features of a growth mindset classroom, the 8 cornerstones of excellent work, and the 4Cs for working with teaching assistants...

The 3-step learning algorithm

1. Stimulate pupils' senses to gain the attention of working memory
2. Make pupils think hard but efficiently about curriculum content
3. Plan for deliberate practice to retrieve prior learning from long-term memory

The 4-part teaching algorithm

1. Tell - make use of effective teacher explanations
2. Show - use teacher modelling whilst thinking aloud
3. Do - engage in co-construction with the class
4. Practice - ensure pupils practice independently

The 5 features of a growth mindset classroom algorithm

1. Use frequent, formative feedback
2. Provide high levels of challenge for every pupil
3. Explicitly welcome mistakes
4. Engage in deliberate practice
5. Reward effort not attainment

The 8 cornerstones of excellence algorithm

1. High quality work
2. Genuine research
3. A real audience
4. In-built differentiation
5. Collective responsibility
6. Class critique
7. Modelling success
8. Drafting and redrafting

The 4Cs of working effectively with teaching assistants

1. Consistency
2. Communication
3. Clarify
4. Connections

Returning, finally, to Hannah Fry's anecdote, she claims Robert Jones is not alone in trusting machines like his satnav: "All around us, algorithms provide a kind of convenient source of authority: an easy way to delegate responsibility, a short cut we take without thinking. Who is really going to click through to the second page of Google results every time and think critically about the information that has been served up? Or go to every airline to check if a comparison site is listing the cheapest deals? Or get out a ruler and a road map to confirm that their GPS is offering the shortest route?"

So maybe it's time to start trusting algorithms in education and allow the use of rubrics to foster greater consistency, reduce teacher workload and improve outcomes for pupils.

Matt Bromley

CHAPTER SIXTY-TWO:
IMPROVING TEACHER RECRUITMENT AND RETENTION

If we are to design an effective curriculum and translate it into practice in a way that leads to long-term learning, we need qualified, expert subject-specialist teachers. And yet this is easier said than done...

The teaching profession currently resembles a leaky sieve and the prevalence of unfulfilled teaching posts (23 per cent of secondary schools reported an unfilled vacancy in 2017, up 15.9 per cent on 2010), as well as a growth in the numbers of unqualified teachers in our classrooms (in November 2016 there were 500 fewer qualified teachers in service than in the previous year and 1400 more unqualified teachers), is proving to be both costly and damaging.

One in 10 teachers left the profession in 2016. Of these, an increasing proportion left for other sectors rather than retiring, suggesting working conditions rather than age were driving them out.

Although there are myriad reasons why teachers quit, topping the table in most surveys is workload...

According to a NAO survey, 67% of school leaders report that workload is a barrier to teacher retention. Meanwhile, a report by CooperGibson Research on behalf of the

Department for Education entitled 'Factors affecting teacher retention: qualitative investigation' published in March 2018, found that workload remained the most important factor influencing teachers' decisions to leave the profession and most solutions to addressing retention were linked in some way to workload.

So, the theory is simple: reduce teacher workload and solve the teacher retention crisis. But we have already explored ways to reduce teacher workload in Chapter Fifty-Seven so why bring it up again? Because, in truth, improving teacher recruitment and retention is not as simple as reducing teacher workload. Indeed, a report of the House of Commons Education Committee entitled 'Recruitment and retention of teachers' published in February 2017 concluded that workload concerns were not the only reason teachers appear to be leaving the profession. Rather, "overall job satisfaction comes out as the biggest driver [for intention to leave], and also things related to whether they feel supported and valued by management".

This sentiment is echoed in the NFER report, 'Engaging teachers: NFER Analysis of Teacher Retention', which says that "it is too simplistic to focus solely on workload as the reason ... teachers decide to leave".

As such, in this chapter, to complement my earlier advice on reducing teacher workload, I'd like to explore some of the other possible solutions to the problem of teacher recruitment and retention.

Firstly, I will examine the scale of the problem, and then analyse its nature.

Secondly, I will explore some potential solutions including improving pay and conditions, leadership practices, teacher training and professional development opportunities, and career progression and professional recognition.

In so doing, I will offer twelve solutions to the problem that are within the purview of school and college leaders.

But, before we begin, let's wrestle with some statistics that might help shed some light on the issues...

The scale of the recruitment and retention problem

Why do we have a teacher recruitment and retention crisis?

Firstly, **pupil numbers are growing**. This is due to a demographic bulge which is travelling through the education system, causing a large increase in pupil numbers at secondary level.

The secondary school population – not counting Year 12 and 13 students – is projected to rise from 2.72 million in 2017 to 3.03 million by 2021, a rise of 11.5 per cent over four years. By 2025 there is projected to be 3.3 million 11 to 15-year-olds in English schools, which is an increase of half a million compared to 2015. If we are to ensure these children are properly educated, we will need an extra 26,500 teachers in the classroom.

Secondly, **not enough new secondary school trainee teachers are coming into the profession**. Initial teacher training (ITT) figures for 2016/17 show a decrease in the overall number of recruits compared with 2015/16, with only 93 per cent of places being filled. The overall contribution to the secondary target was 89 per cent, meaning nearly 2,000 places went unfilled.

In truth, the situation is even worse than these figures suggest because, since 2015/16, ITT figures have included applicants for Teach First who were previously excluded from the statistics. This therefore boosted the overall figure for 2016/17 by more than 1,000 applicants. However, despite the inclusion of Teach First applicants in the ITT statistics, the overall Teacher Supply Model (TSM) target was still not met, just as it hadn't been met for the previous four years.

In 2016/17, the only subjects where the TSM recruitment target was met were biology, geography, history and PE. All other secondary subjects were under-recruited, and some by a significant margin. For instance, maths only recruited 84 per cent of the required number of trainees, physics 81 per cent, and computing just 68 per cent.

Thirdly, not only are we failing to recruit enough new teachers, we are also losing too many experienced ones. **Teachers are leaving the profession in record numbers.** One in 10 teachers left the profession in 2016. As I said above, an increasing proportion left the profession for other sectors rather than retiring.

The consequence of falling recruitment and retention rates is that the number of unfilled teaching post vacancies is at a record high in secondary, with 23 per cent of schools reporting an unfilled vacancy in 2017, up 15.9 per cent on 2010.

The leaving rate is highest among teachers who teach non-EBacc subjects, which might suggest that they have been incentivised to leave the profession because their subjects are no longer being taught as the school curriculum narrows, or that they have become more frustrated or disaffected at their subject taking lower priority. This may now change in response to the new Education Inspection Framework (EIF) with which Ofsted intends to tackle this narrowing of the curriculum, ensuring all pupils have access to a broad and balanced education and are properly prepared for the next stages of their education and lives. But any changes will take time to land.

The crisis in teacher recruitment and retention means that while schools are struggling to fill vacancies and retain experienced staff, **large numbers of pupils are being taught by unqualified teachers** – or at least teachers who do not have a relevant qualification in the subject they are being asked to teach.

In March 2016, for example, the then National Union of Teachers (NUT) found that only 63 per cent of physics and 75 per cent of chemistry teachers held a relevant post A level qualification in the subject they taught. For maths and English, these figures were 78 and 81 per cent respectively.

As such, high levels of attrition among qualified teachers is not only costly in financial terms; it also has an impact on the quality of education that schools can provide. In November 2016, for example, there were 500 fewer qualified teachers in service than in the previous year. Conversely, there were 1,400 more teachers in service without qualified teacher status than there had been the year before.

The nature of the recruitment and retention problem

As I explained above, the report by CooperGibson Research on behalf of the Department for Education (2018) states that workload is the most important factor influencing teachers' decisions to leave the profession and most suggested solutions to addressing retention were linked in some way to workload.

Although workload is key, teachers' decisions to leave the profession are generally driven by an accumulation of a range of different factors and over a sustained period of time. Few teachers quit based on a single issue. Having said this, CooperGibson did found that, for some teachers, there had been a specific 'trigger' point, for example around teaching performance resulting in involvement from the senior leadership team, feeling undervalued after an issue had been highlighted or a specific behavioural incident involving pupils and parents/carers.

When asked by researchers, teachers found it challenging to provide solutions to retention issues or suggestions for how issues they had faced could have been resolved. Nevertheless, they did provide some ideas for consideration. These related to:

Improving in-school support for teachers – greater levels of support and understanding from SLT was needed, for example in terms of the management of pupil behaviour, and the ability to have open and honest conversations. This would help support teachers' relationships with their SLT and reduce feelings of pressure in terms of scrutiny, accountability and workload. Considerations would be how the message to senior leaders and teachers can be strengthened to dispel the myths around inspection and the commitment to reduce workload. This would mean giving greater confidence and support to senior leaders to address workload and well-being.

Greater focus on progression opportunities - there was some evidence that the availability of wider progression opportunities may help support retention. This could be supported by communicating examples of how multi-academy trusts have developed alternative subject progression pathways, exploring transferability to other schools and supporting schools to consider job role swaps.

Reducing workload at a school level - for most teachers a significant reduction in their workload would have led them to reconsider their decision to leave. As well as supporting schools to implement recommendations of the Workload Review Groups, sharing and making accessible good practice examples of success in schools would be beneficial. Supporting teachers with confidence to plan and mark efficiently and effectively and supporting senior leaders to implement the necessary changes, would also be important contributions.

Improved working conditions – flexible working and part-time contracts were generally viewed positively. Some viewed these as a way to secure a better work-life balance. Increasing opportunities for flexible working may have a role in helping to retain teachers in the profession but offering such opportunities without addressing fundamental issues around teacher workload is unlikely to have a significant impact. Although pay was not the driver for many teachers, it was stated by most that the pay levels were not reflective of teachers' expertise, experience and dedication. Some suggestions included grants/funding for teacher training and better pay/incentives for staying in teaching.

Professional recognition and greater autonomy – although teachers were unclear on how this could be achieved for the profession as a whole, it was evident that teachers feeling more respected and valued would have gone some way to retaining them in the sector. Their suggestions related to how senior leaders trusted their work and gave them freedom and autonomy to mark and plan.

In addition, teachers felt strongly that **further subject specialist support for early career teachers** was needed, particularly around mentoring, providing networks and resources and using a database to track teachers and offer additional support if they decide to leave. Concerns were around not duplicating what was already available, having the time to use elements of the support package, confidentiality and independence of mentors, and the availability of mentors at a suitable time prior to making a decision to leave. Some also suggested the support package would be useful for those slightly later in their careers.

Teachers wanted their schools to commit to **implement the recommendations from the three Workload Review Group reports,** with evidence suggesting this assurance would be more likely to have an impact on retention/returning to the profession. There were concerns raised as to whether the recommendations would be implemented, and as such there could be a need to review progress across schools and support schools in communicating their workload reduction successes. Schools may also need support in overcoming some of the practical challenges of reducing workload.

With the above in mind, let us now consider in greater depth some possible solutions to this problem. In particular, we will explore the following:

- Pay and conditions
- Leadership practices
- Teacher training and professional development
- Career progression and professional recognition

Improving recruitment and retention by improving pay and conditions

As we have seen, workload is a major cause of teacher attrition. Reduce the volume of work teachers are expected to do – and thus improve their work life balances – and more teachers will stay in the profession. What's more, if we improve workload, the profession will become more attractive, more people will consider training to be a teacher and we will improve recruitment.

But, as I've already explained, workload is not the only factor that drives teachers out. Pay and conditions are also key to resolving the issue...

Solution 1: The nature of teachers' workloads

A recent UCL Institute of Education survey of around 1,200 current and former teachers found that it was **the nature rather than the quantity of workload** that was the crucial factor in driving teachers out of the classroom.

Underlying teachers' decisions to quit, the report concluded, was a perceived contradiction between expectations and reality – in other words, the practice of being a teacher impeded their ability to actually be a teacher.

Many of those surveyed by UCL imagined, before they started, that they could cope with the workload, but once in the classroom, a general lack of support from middle and senior leaders, together with the effects of a high stakes accountability system, were far worse than they had thought and it was this that led to many leaving, with many more actively considering quitting.

The general response from government is that teaching will be improved by reducing workload, removing unnecessary tasks and increasing pay. This may help, say the UCL, but their survey also indicates that part of the problem lies within the culture of teaching, the constant scrutiny, the need to perform, and hyper-critical management. Reducing workload alone will not therefore address these cultural issues.

The UCL findings illustrate the link between workload fears and the reality of working within what the report authors call "the accountability performativity context".

"Those who want to be teachers are committed to the profession and yet, somehow, that commitment is eroded in a very short space of time," say the report authors Dr Jane Perryman and Graham Calvert.

This notion of an 'accountability performativity context' is echoed in the 2018 NFER report, 'Early career continuing professional development: Exploratory research (Walker et al, 2018)' which argues that the translation of hopes and expectations to lived experiences of teaching leads to "practice shock", summarised by one participant as "When you go through your [initial teacher training] placements, you can't truly understand how much work there is to do, or how much responsibility comes with the job ... [which] hit me hard in the NQT year."

Unless such issues are addressed, the report says, there is a high risk of new teachers walking away from the profession before they might have anticipated doing so.

To help, the report said that early career teachers should have access to:

- *A supportive mentor* who is ideally a subject specialist and respected by the mentee as a practitioner in the classroom,
- *A balanced package of support* involving a standardised training programme alongside more personalised, teacher-led opportunities, and
- *A supportive school culture.*

Solution 2: Flexible working

According to the CooperGibson Research report (DfE 2018), **flexible working and part-time contracts** are also generally viewed positively by teachers and likely to improve recruitment and retention. Some viewed these as a way to secure a better work-life balance.

Although pay was not the driver for many teachers, it was stated by most who took part in the research that pay levels were not reflective of teachers' expertise, experience and dedication. Some suggestions included **grants/funding for teacher training** and **better pay/incentives for staying in teaching**.

A **'sympathetic timetable'** (e.g. focusing on fewer year groups as an early career teacher) was viewed positively by around one-third of secondary teachers. Considerations included how flexibility could be offered to early career teachers who want broader teaching experience, how pastoral responsibilities could be gently phased in and how these could be managed practically in school.

Solution 3: Pay

A Learning Policy Institute paper from the US entitled 'Teacher turnover: Why it matters and what we can do about it', authored by Carver-Thomas and Darling-Hammond and published in 2017, argues that previous research indicates that teachers are more likely to continue teaching and stay at their schools when their **wages increase and are comparable with job opportunities in other industries**.

In addition to wage comparability, data from the US National Center for Education Statistics 5-year longitudinal study show that teachers whose first-year salary was less than $40,000 (c£30,000 at the time of writing) had an attrition rate 10 percentage points higher than teachers who earned more in their first year.

Fair pay is clearly a factor in recruiting and retaining high quality teachers but the fact there is little data from the UK linking pay with recruitment and retention suggests it's by no means the most important aspect of teachers' working conditions affecting turnover.

Solution 4: School facilities

In a paper entitled 'The effects of school facility quality on teacher retention in urban school districts' by Jack Buckley of the Lynch School of Education, Boston College, Mark Schneider of the Department of Political Science, Stony Brook University, and Yi Shang of the Lynch School of Education, Boston College, published in February 2004, the authors posit that **the quality of school facilities** is a significant – albeit often overlooked – cause of teachers quitting the profession.

They investigated the importance of facility quality using data from a survey of K-12 (compulsory education) teachers in Washington, D.C and found in their sample that facility quality was an important predictor of the decision of teachers to leave their position. Here, the availability of resources such as textbooks and stationery, the quality of light and heat, and the general attractiveness of the teaching and learning environment were key drivers.

Improving recruitment and retention by improving leadership practices

Solution 5: Leadership support

In a paper entitled 'Is the Grass Greener Beyond Teaching?' published in December 2017 as part of the NFER's Teacher Retention and Turnover Research Research project, the author Jack Worth argues that there is a strong relationship between teacher job satisfaction and the leadership quality in their school, and that leadership is also associated with the extent to which teachers regard their workload as manageable.

The NFER concludes that **nurturing, supporting, and valuing teachers is vital to keep their job satisfaction and engagement high** and improve their retention in the profession. Senior leaders, they argue, should regularly monitor the job satisfaction and engagement of their staff.

According to the CooperGibson report I cite above (DfE 2018), greater levels of support and understanding from SLT is needed, for example, in terms of **the management of pupil behaviour**, and **the ability to have open and honest conversations**. This will help support teachers' relationships with their SLT and reduce feelings of pressure in terms of scrutiny, accountability and workload.

Solution 6: Encouragement and clarity of expectations

Meanwhile, the Learning Policy Institute paper by Carver-Thomas and Darling-Hammond (2017), says that school leadership, collegial relationships, and school culture are of particular importance to teacher retention.

With controls for student and teacher characteristics, their analysis found that the workplace condition most predictive of teacher turnover in the US was a perceived lack of administrative support, a construct that measures how teachers rate an administrator's ability to **encourage and acknowledge staff, communicate a clear vision,** and generally run a school well. When teachers strongly disagree that their administration is supportive, they are more than twice as likely to move schools or leave teaching than when they strongly agree that their administration is supportive.

While only a small body of research links headteachers/principals directly to student achievement (Branch, Hanushek & Rivkin, 2009; Hallinger & Heck, 1996), a much larger research base documents headteacher/principals' effects on school operations, through **motivating teachers and students, identifying and articulating vision and goals, developing high performance expectations, fostering communication, allocating resources, and developing organisational structures to support instruction and learning** (Knapp, Copland, Plecki & Portin, 2006; Lee, Bryk and Smith, 1993; Leithwood, Louis, Anderson & Wahlstrom, 2004).

Improving retention by improving <u>teacher training and professional development</u>

Solution 7: Initial teacher training

The Learning Policy Institute paper I cite above by Carver-Thomas and Darling-Hammond (2017), found that teachers' ITT route also influenced their subsequent retention rates.

Those who entered the profession through what the paper called "an alternative certification programme" - what we might equate to non-HEI routes into teaching such as School Direct or SCITT - are, Carver-Thomas and Darling-Hammond say, 25% more likely to leave their schools than are full-time teachers who entered teaching through a regular certification programme, holding all else constant. About 15% of all the teachers Carver-Thomas and Darling-Hammond surveyed (and about 1 in 4 first-year teachers) had entered teaching through an alternative pathway, which typically requires that a teacher work toward the requirements of a full credential while teaching and receiving little formal training beforehand. Alternative pathway teachers left their schools at rates about 28% greater than regular certification teachers when in high-minority schools.

These findings, argue Carver-Thomas and Darling-Hammond, are not surprising. Studies of the relationship between teacher training and teacher retention suggest teachers with the least preparation are 2 to 3 times more likely to leave the profession than those with the most comprehensive preparation - including student teaching and courses in teaching methods.

Quite often, Carver-Thomas and Darling-Hammond suggest, teachers choose alternative certification pathways because, without financial aid, they cannot afford to be without an income for the time it takes to undergo teacher training. Furthermore, candidates are less likely to be willing to go into debt for training if the financial rewards of the occupation are lower. It must therefore be made equally – or at least fairly - financially viable to train to be a teacher via every route and every route must offer parity of quality and fully prepare trainees for the classroom. Talking of which...

Buckley, Schneider and Shang (2014) say that **teachers who graduate from traditional university-based programmes have lower attrition rates** than teachers with other, non- traditional forms of preparation (Harris, Camp, and Adkison 2003). A large percentage of new teachers also report that the teacher preparation programmes they went through did not provide enough help for them to cope with their first-year experience, which intensifies the need for proper mentoring, professional development, and administrative support in their working environment (Tapper 1995).

Solution 8: Investment in CPD

Peter Sellen from EPI told the House of Commons Education Committee (2017) that "60% of teachers agreed that one of the key barriers to accessing professional development was their work schedule".

The pressure on teachers' time can mean professional development is squeezed out of timetables and not prioritised. ITT typically lasts for just one year and must cover a wide range of skills in this period. Continuing professional development (CPD) should follow on from this and act as **ongoing training throughout teachers' careers to improve their practice, develop new skills and maintain subject knowledge**. However, the House of Commons Education Committee argues that currently the teaching profession in England lacks clear, structured provision for CPD and a number of barriers act to reduce the amount of CPD done by teachers.

As well as struggling to find time for CPD, the current nature of the accountability system – the Committee argues - means senior leaders can be reluctant to release staff from the classroom. The Mathematical Association described the situation to the Committee thus: "Secondary and FE level schools are regularly unwilling and unable to release staff to attend professional development. Losing class time with high stakes exam classes is not permitted and funding is not available to support attendance to training events. We have experience of even free high-quality training events being cancelled due to lack of delegates, not because teachers did not want to attend but because they were not allowed to by their schools."

As well as CPD being available, therefore, **teachers must be given time to attend training**.

Analysis by the EPI of the Teaching and Learning International Survey (TALIS) 2013 showed that the number of days of CPD that English teachers carried out was fewer than most other OECD countries. **On average, English teachers spent four days doing CPD in one year, whereas teachers in Singapore spent 12 days and South Korea 15 days.** This is perhaps unsurprising, the Committee says, when you consider that teachers in Singapore are entitled to 100 hours of CPD per year, whereas England has no such entitlement. Singapore is not alone with this kind of commitment; somewhat closer to home, Scottish teachers are entitled to 35 hours of CPD per year.

Solution 9: CPD quality and relevance

In addition to the availability of CPD and the opportunity being afforded to teachers to attend training courses, the quality of CPD is also crucial to improving teacher retention. This, too, was raised at Committee hearings as an essential factor to teacher professionalism. UCL Institute for Education told the Committee that "evidence suggests **the best CPD is long-term, interspersed with episodes of practice, individually tailored and informed and challenged by external expertise**".

Schools deliver a lot of their CPD in-house, which can be very effective, but, the Committee says, **external expertise is often beneficial** too.

Professor Sir John Holman, President of the Royal Society of Chemistry, told the Committee "by and large, schools put a greater emphasis on generic things". Some 'generic' CPD, for example, behaviour management is very important, but Dr Bevan said: "Nearly all - and I am going to be a little mischievous in my description but I think it is fair - CPD currently being provided is driven by regulatory or statutory frameworks, so that is curriculum change, Ofsted, Prevent training. **Subject-specific CPD is necessary to develop specific skills related to the teaching of a subject,**

maintenance or acquisition of subject knowledge, and to improve practice".

One of the main reasons that teachers intend to leave the profession, the Committee found, is a lack of job satisfaction, and not feeling supported in their profession. Charles Tracy from the Institute of Physics said: "If they provide a culture of professional development and professional support for their staff, the staff will stay in the school and it works for them as well as the national system where they will stay in education.

The Committee also heard that teachers who are less supported and professionally confident are more likely to find their workload unmanageable, a key factor of teachers leaving the profession. A professional learning culture and support for teachers may also help improve the status of the profession, something which was a recurring theme of the Committee's inquiry.

Solution 10: Tailored support for new teachers

According to CooperGibson Research's report, 'Factors affecting teacher retention: qualitative investigation' (2018), teachers felt strongly that – in addition to the above - **further subject specialist support for early career teachers** was needed, particularly around mentoring, providing networks and resources and using a database to track teachers and offer additional support if they decide to leave. Concerns were around not duplicating what was already available, having the time to use elements of the support package, confidentiality and independence of mentors, and the availability of mentors at a suitable time prior to making a decision to leave. Some also suggested the support package would be useful for those slightly later in their careers.

Improving retention by improving <u>career progression and professional recognition</u>

Solution 11: Career progression opportunities

In a report entitled 'Leading Together: Why supporting school leadership matters' published in 2018, Teach First argued that nurturing existing talent in schools could help address the leadership shortage *and* help retain teachers in the profession.

The report claims that nine out of ten (88%) teachers say that if their school were to **offer excellent leadership development opportunities** this would have some impact on their likelihood of remaining at their school, with a third of teachers (34%) saying it would have a great impact. Importantly, this rises to 41% of those teachers considering leaving the profession within the next year.

The Teach First report goes on to say that offering meaningful development opportunities to those not yet in senior leadership – either middle leaders or classroom teachers with the potential to step-up – provides an opportunity to improve retention and keep talented people in schools.

Leadership development provides teachers with an additional incentive to stay in education, rather than seeking progression opportunities elsewhere. Providing teachers with **a positive and supportive culture of learning and development** could, therefore, support with morale and retention.

The CooperGibson Research report (DfE 2018), says there is evidence that **the availability of wider progression opportunities** may also help support retention. This could be supported by communicating examples of how multi-academy trusts (MATs) have developed **alternative subject progression pathways**, exploring **transferability to other schools** and supporting schools to consider **job role swaps**.

Solution 12: Professional recognition

In a discussion paper entitled 'Why Teach?' published by Pearson and LKMCo in October 2015, the authors argue that teachers who stay in the profession do so largely because they consider themselves to be good at it and because they enjoy making a difference to pupils' lives. Retention, therefore, depends on **ensuring teachers feel they can have an impact**: letting them 'get on with it' is therefore key in maintaining a motivated and committed workforce.

The Pearson/LKMCo paper draws heavily on research carried out by NFER in 2000 which outlined four reasons teachers remain in the profession:

1. Recognition of their work;
2. Pupil development and learning;
3. Manager approval;
4. Family and friends.

Similarly, Priyadharshini and Robinson-Pant (2003) find that job satisfaction depends on providing greater **intellectual challenge, autonomy and the opportunity to spend sufficient time with students**.

Birkeland and Johnson (2003), meanwhile, argue that teachers tend to stay in post when they can pursue **professional growth and development**, something particularly important to new or early-career teachers. A deeply rooted culture of professionalism can therefore ensure that even socio-economically disadvantaged schools retain teachers through "supportive administrators and colleagues, clear expectations for students and safe, orderly environments".

In a NFER paper entitled 'Engaging Teachers' by Sarah Lynch, Jack Worth, Susan Bamford, and Karen Wespieser published in September 2016, the authors claim that the more engaged teachers are, the less likely they are to consider leaving. Their research, based on responses to their Teacher Voice surveys in November 2015 and March 2016, suggests that a majority

(90 per cent) of teachers who report being 'engaged' are not considering leaving, compared with only a quarter of 'disengaged' teachers. But not all teachers in the survey fitted this pattern. Ten per cent of engaged teachers are considering leaving, and five per cent had also identified an alternative destination, so seem more certain about their decision.

The NFER suggests that effort be targeted at keeping the engaged teachers feeling valued and satisfied in their roles. Re-engaging ambivalent teachers could also help teacher retention. A third of ambivalent teachers in the survey are considering leaving, and as a third of teachers overall made up this group, that is approximately ten per cent of teachers who could potentially be retained if re-engaged. A quarter of disengaged teachers in the survey have no intention of leaving. It is perhaps not surprising that three-quarters of the disengaged teachers are considering leaving. Given the research evidence of the relationship between engagement factors and teacher quality, it may not be a negative consequence for the teaching profession if disengaged teachers leave. However, there could be opportunities within the sector to re-engage this group.

Conclusion

To conclude this chapter, I believe that schools and colleges can start to address the teacher recruitment and retention crisis if, in addition to dealing with the issue of workload, they also:

1. Address the nature of teachers' workloads
2. Provide more opportunities for flexible working
3. Improve pay and rewards
4. Improve the quality of school facilities
5. Improve the support leaders give to staff
6. Provide more encouragement to teachers and make expectations clearer
7. Improve the quality of initial teacher training
8. Improve the availability of continuing professional development

9. Improve the quality and relevance of CPD
10. Tailor the support offered to new teachers
11. Provide opportunities for career progression including into leadership positions
12. Improve the professional recognition and social standing of teachers

Matt Bromley

PART SIX:

END MATTER

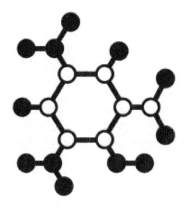

Matt Bromley

CONCLUSION

We've reached the end of our curriculum implementation journey. But, before you pop this book on a shelf, and sit in a dark room to eagerly await the third and final volume in this series on School and College Curriculum Design, let's take stock of what we've learned...

What is 'implementation'?

In the schools' inspection handbook, Ofsted defines implementation as the way in which "the curriculum is taught at subject and classroom level".

Accordingly, during an inspection, Ofsted will want to see how teachers enable pupils to understand key concepts, presenting information clearly and promoting appropriate discussion, how teachers check pupils' understanding effectively, identifying and correcting misunderstandings, and how teachers ensure that **pupils embed key concepts in their long-term memory** and apply them fluently.

Further, Ofsted will want to see if the subject curriculum that classes follow is designed and delivered in a way that allows pupils to transfer key knowledge to long-term memory and if it is sequenced so that **new knowledge and skills build on what has been taught before** and towards defined end points.

In the further education and skills inspection handbook, Ofsted argues that teachers need sufficient subject knowledge, pedagogical knowledge and pedagogical content knowledge to be able teach learners effectively.

Effective teaching and training should, Ofsted argues, ensure that learners in further education and skills settings **know more and remember what they have learned** within the context of the approach that teachers have selected to serve the aims of their curriculum. Consequently, learners will be able to apply vocational and technical skills fluently and independently.

In short, Ofsted's definition of effective curriculum implementation is high quality teaching which leads to long-term learning.

Evidence-informed teaching

One of the best ways to ensure we implement the curriculum effectively – that is to say, in a way that leads to long-term learning – is to follow the evidence...

These days, there's a surfeit of research evidence about what works and what doesn't. From the darkness there is light.

Evidence tells us, for example, that **feedback** is a highly effective teaching strategy. It tops the EEF chart as the most impactful tool at a teacher's disposal and so it would follow that schools should invest time and money in improving the effectiveness of feedback...

However, caution should be exercised because the term 'feedback' is a slippery one and can mean many different things.

The EEF say that feedback is "information given to the learner or teacher about the learner's performance relative to learning goals or outcomes. It should aim towards (and be capable of producing) improvement in students' learning. Feedback redirects or refocuses either the teacher's or the learner's actions to achieve a goal, by aligning effort and activity with an outcome."

Feedback, say the EEF, can be about "the output of the activity, the process of the activity, the student's management of their learning or self-regulation, or them as individuals (which tends to be the least effective)."

According to the EEF, studies tend to show very high effects of feedback on learning. However, some studies show that feedback can have negative effects and make things worse. It is therefore important, the EEF say, to understand the potential benefits and the possible limitations of feedback as a teaching and learning approach. In general, research-based approaches that explicitly aim to provide feedback to learners, such as Bloom's 'mastery learning', tend to have a positive impact.

One thing to note is that, just because the EEF toolkit says that feedback is good does not imply that teachers should do lots more of it. It does mean that, when done well, it can really benefit pupils and so feedback should be done better, which is to say that feedback should be meaningful and helpful to pupils.

In practice, effective feedback tends to:

- be specific, accurate and clear (e.g. "It was good because you..." rather than just "correct");
- compare what a learner is doing right now with what they have done wrong before (e.g. "I can see you were focused on improving X as it is much better than last time's Y...");
- encourage and support further effort;
- be given sparingly so that it is meaningful;
- provide specific guidance on how to improve and not just tell students when they are wrong; and

- be supported with effective professional development for teachers.

Broader research suggests that feedback should be about complex or challenging tasks or goals as this is likely to emphasise the importance of effort and perseverance as well as be more valued by the pupils.

It's also worth remembering that feedback can come from peers as well as adults.

In order to ensure marking and feedback don't become behemoths, we must sense-check our assessments for their purpose, process and validity, and ensure marking is always meaningful, manageable and motivating.

Evidence also tells us that **metacognition and self-regulation** are equally impactful. Indeed, they take equal top-billing on the EEF toolkit and, like feedback, are said to add an extra eight months of learning per year.

Also akin to feedback, metacognition can mean different things to different people.

The EEF say that metacognitive approaches aim to help pupils think about their own learning more explicitly, often by teaching them specific strategies for planning, monitoring and evaluating their learning.

Metacognition gifts pupils a repertoire of strategies to choose from and the skills to select the most suitable strategy for any given learning task.

Metacognition, then, describes the processes involved when learners plan, monitor, evaluate and make changes to their own learning behaviours. Metacognition is often considered to have two dimensions:

1. Metacognitive knowledge, and

2. Self-regulation.

Metacognitive knowledge refers to what learners <u>know</u> about learning. This includes:

- The learner's knowledge of their own cognitive abilities (e.g. 'I have trouble remembering key dates in this period of history')
- The learner's knowledge of particular tasks (e.g. 'The politics in this period of history are complex')
- The learner's knowledge of the different strategies that are available to them and when they are appropriate to the task (e.g. 'If I create a timeline first it will help me to understand this period of history').

Self-regulation, meanwhile, refers to what learners <u>do</u> about learning. It describes how learners monitor and control their cognitive processes. For example, a learner might realise that a particular strategy is not yielding the results they expected so they decide to try a different strategy.

Put another way, self-regulated learners are aware of their strengths and weaknesses, and can motivate themselves to engage in, and improve, their learning.

We approach any learning task or opportunity with some metacognitive knowledge about:

- our own abilities and attitudes (knowledge of ourselves as a learner);
- what strategies are effective and available (knowledge of strategies); and
- this particular type of activity (knowledge of the task).

When undertaking a learning task, we start with this knowledge, then apply and adapt it. This is metacognitive regulation. It is about "planning how to undertake a task, working on it while monitoring the strategy to check progress, then evaluating the overall success".

The learning environment

Once we've used research evidence to help us determine which teaching strategies will lead to long-term learning, we need to attend to the learning environment because we know with some degree of certainty that the physical, social and emotional conditions in which pupils learn really do matter.

Pupils need to feel comfortable if they are to accept the challenge of hard work, and their basic needs must be met if they are to attend to teacher instruction. And the environment must help ensure pupils focus on the curriculum content we need them to learn and avoid unhelpful distractions or detractions.

How we use our classroom space and the rules, routines and expectations we establish are therefore crucial considerations.

In terms of the **physical learning environment**, we should consider factors such as room temperature, light, noise, layout, and the use of displays.

In terms of the **social learning environment**, we should consider how we create a whole school culture which promotes good behaviour and positive attitudes to learning, tackles poor behaviour including low-level disruption, and protects all staff and pupils from harassment and harm.

In terms of the **emotional environment**, we should consider how to create a classroom culture in which pupils feel safe and secure enough to willingly take risks and make mistakes from which they can learn. Here, the first few days spent in a new learning environment are perhaps the most pivotal in determining a pupil's academic progress. Here are five ways to create a 'growth mindset' culture: 1. Use frequent formative feedback, 2. High levels of challenge for every pupil, 3. Explicitly welcome mistakes, 4. Engaging in deliberate practice, and 5. Reward effort not attainment.

The three steps of teaching for long-term learning

There are myriad factors that determine a pupil's success, not least their own hard work, diligence and, yes, innate intelligence. As we have just seen, environmental factors play their part, too, as does the amount of support and influence that a pupil receives from their community of friends and family.

However, there is a 3-step learning process that teachers can follow in order to maximise the chances of pupils acquiring and retaining knowledge over the longer term so that it can be applied in multiple contexts.

The act of acquiring new knowledge and skills is the start of the learning process, it is what happens (or begins to happen) in the classroom when a teacher - the expert - imparts their knowledge or demonstrates their skills (perhaps through the artful use of explanations and modelling, of which more later) to their pupils - the novices.

Next, pupils store this new information in their long-term memories (via their working memories) where it can be recalled and used later.

The process of storing information in the long-term memory is called 'encoding'. The process of getting it back out again is called 'retrieval'.

A pupil could demonstrate their immediate understanding of what they've been taught by repeating what the teacher has said or by demonstrating the skill they've just seen applied. But this immediate display is not necessarily 'learning'. Rather, it is a 'performance'. It is a simple regurgitation of what they've just seen or heard and takes place in the working memory, without any need for information to be encoded in the long-term memory.

We can all repeat, rote-like, something someone else has just said or mimic a skill they've just demonstrated. But unless we can retain that knowledge or skill over time, we haven't really learnt it. And if we can't apply that knowledge or skill in a range of different situations, then - similarly - we haven't really learnt it, or at least not in any meaningful sense.

However, if we simply repeat the information over and again verbatim, we will only really improve pupils' surface knowledge of that information. To improve and deepen pupils' understanding, we need to teach curriculum content in different contexts. We need to model examples of its use in a range of contexts. And when we repeat learning we should do so in different ways.

The process of learning, then, is the interaction between one's sensory memory and one's long-term memory.

Our sensory memory is made up of:

- What we see - this is called our **iconic** memory;
- What we hear - this is called our **echoic** memory; and
- What we touch - our **haptic** memory.

Our long-term memory is where new information is stored and from which it can be recalled when needed, but we cannot directly access the information stored in our long-term memory.

As such, the interaction that takes place between our sensory memory and our long-term memory occurs in our working memory, or short-term memory, which is the only place where we can think and do.

In summary, there are - to my mind - three steps to improve the process of teaching for long-term learning:

1. Stimulate pupils' senses to gain the attention of working memory
2. Make pupils think hard but efficiently to encode information into long-term memory

3. Embed deliberate practice to improve pupils' storage in and retrieval from in long-term memory

A 4-step teaching sequence

Coupled with this, I recommend we use a 4-step teaching sequence whenever pupils are introduced to new information.

Research by Kirschner, Sweller and Clark (2006) compared guided models of teaching, such as direct instruction, with discovery learning methods, such as problem-based learning, inquiry learning, experiential learning, and constructivist learning, and found that the latter methods didn't work as well as the former. It didn't matter, they argued, if pupils preferred less guided methods, they still learned less from them (see also Clark, 1989).

In his book, Visible Learning, Professor John Hattie found that the average effect size for teaching strategies which involved the teacher as a "facilitator" was 0.17, whereas the average effect size for strategies where the teacher acted as an "activator" was 0.60.

Direct instruction had an effect size of 0.59 compared to problem-based learning with an effect size of just 0.15.

Therefore, direct instruction – it seems – is more effective than discovery learning approaches. But what, exactly, does good direct instruction look like in practice?

Personally, I think direct instruction works best when it follows this four-step sequence:

1. Telling
2. Showing
3. Doing
4. Practising.

Telling – or teacher explanation – works best when the teacher presents new material to pupils in small "chunks" and provides scaffolds and targeted support.

Showing – or teacher modelling – works best when the teacher models a new procedure by, among other strategies, thinking aloud, guiding pupils' initial practice and providing pupils with cues.

Doing – or co-construction – works best when the teacher provides pupils with "fix-up" strategies – corrections and "live" feedback.

Practising – or independent work – works best when the teacher provides planned opportunities in class for extensive independent practice.

Ensuring equal access to teaching for long-term learning

When we talk about differentiation, we often have in mind ways of scaffolding learning for our 'less able' pupils. But pupils – like learning – are complex and no pupil is uniformly 'less able' than another. Rather, some pupils have acquired more knowledge and skills in one area than another pupil or have practised a task more often. Of course, some pupils have additional and different needs – such as those young people with learning difficulties or disabilities – and they require a different approach. But to say they are 'less able' is, I think, an unhelpful misnomer.

What's more, the term "less able" infers an immovable position – if you are 'less able' you are destined to remain so ad infinitum, living your life languishing in the left-hand shadow of the bell-curve.

I'm not suggesting that every pupil performs the same – or has the same capacity to do so. We are not all born equal. But defining someone as less able as a result of a test – whether that be Key Stage 2 SATs, Year 7 CATs or GCSE outcomes - means we are in danger of arbitrarily writing off some pupils by means of a snapshot taken through a pinhole lens.

When approaching differentiation, therefore, we would be wise to remember that all pupils – like all human beings – are different, unique, individual. Differentiation, therefore, should not be about treating 'less able' pupils – or indeed those with SEND or eligible for Pupil Premium funding – as a homogenous group. Rather, we should treat each pupil on an individual basis.

Nor should we assume that what works with one pupil will work with all and that what was proven to work with 'less able' pupils in another school, in another district, in another country, (according to research evidence and meta-analyses) will work in our classroom.

To promote challenge in the classroom for all pupils, we need to reduce the threat level, we need to ensure no one feels humiliated if they fall short of a challenge. Rather, they need to know that they will learn from the experience and perform better next time.

Once we've created a positive learning environment in which pupils willingly accept challenge, we need to model high expectations of all.

Having high expectations of pupils is not only a nice thing to do, it actually leads to improved performance.

It's common practice to talk about three waves of intervention for disadvantaged pupils and those with SEND.

According to the now-defunct National Strategies, Wave 1 is "quality inclusive teaching which takes into account the learning needs of all the pupils in the classroom". As such, if we do not first provide pupils with quality classroom teaching, then no amount of additional intervention and support will help them to catch up.

But even with the provision of 'quality first teaching', some pupils will require more - and more tailored - support in the guise of Wave 2 in-class differentiations and Wave 3 additional interventions which take place outside the classroom and off the taught timetable.

Such intervention strategies may take the form of one-to-one support from a teaching assistant (TA) or additional learning support (ALS), small group targeted teaching by a SEND or High Needs specialist, or support from external agencies such as speech and language therapists.

The ultimate aim of such additional support, in most cases, is for it to become redundant over time. In other words, we want pupils with SEND to become increasingly independent and for the scaffolds to fall away. Indeed, this is the stated aim of Education Health and Care Plans (EHCPs) and High Needs funding: over time, discrete funding should be reduced as its impact is felt and pupils require less and less support.

With this aim in mind, it is important to ensure that all strategic interventions aimed at pupils with SEND are monitored whilst they are happening and are:

- Brief (20– 50mins),
- Regular (3–5 times per week),
- Sustained (running for 8–20 weeks),
- Carefully timetabled,
- Staffed by well-trained TAs (5–30 hours' training per intervention),
- Well-planned with structured resources and clear objectives,
- Assessed to identify appropriate pupils, guide areas for focus and track pupil progress, and
- Linked to classroom teaching.

Motivating pupils to learn

As well as supporting pupils to access our curriculum we need to motivate them so that they want to learn. Motivation requires:

1. A destination to aim for – knowing what the outcome looks like and not giving up until you reach it.
2. A model to follow – an exemplar on which to base your technique provided by someone who is regarded as an expert and who sets high expectations.
3. Regular checkpoints to show what progress has been made and what's still to do, coupled with regular celebrations of ongoing achievements and timely messages about upcoming milestones.
4. Personalisation – the ability to make choices about how to carry out tasks in order to increase enjoyment and engagement

In the classroom, there are two types of motivation that matter most: intrinsic and extrinsic.

1. Intrinsic motivation - this is the self-desire to seek out new things and new challenges, in order to gain new knowledge. Often, intrinsic motivation is driven by an inherent interest or enjoyment in the task itself. Pupils are likely to be intrinsically motivated if they attribute their educational results to factors under their own control, also known as *autonomy*, they believe in their own ability to succeed in specific situations or to accomplish a task - also known as a sense of *self-efficacy,* and they are genuinely interested in accomplishing something to a high level of proficiency, knowledge and skill, not just in achieving good grades - also known as *mastery.*

2. Extrinsic motivation – this is the performance of an activity in order to attain a desired outcome. Extrinsic motivation comes from influences outside an individual's control; a rationale, a necessity, a need. Common forms of extrinsic motivation are rewards (for example, money or prizes), or - conversely - the threat of punishment. We can provide pupils with a rationale for learning by sharing the 'big picture' with them. In other words, we can continually explain how their learning fits in to the module, the course, the qualification, their careers and to success in work and life.

We can also motivate pupils to learn if we engender a culture of excellence in our classrooms...

The first step towards motivating pupils to produce high-quality work is to set tasks which inspire and challenge them, and which are predicated on the idea that every pupil will succeed, not just finish the task but produce work which represents personal excellence.

Second, we can make ensure classwork is personally meaningful – for example by triggering pupils' curiosity and by posing a big question that captures the heart of a topic in clear, compelling language, and we can give pupils some choice about how to conduct the work and present their findings. We can also ensure that classwork fulfils an educational purpose – for example by providing opportunities to build metacognition and character skills such as collaboration, communication, and critical thinking, and by emphasising the need to create high-quality products and performances through the formal use of feedback and drafting.

Supporting disadvantaged pupils

In order to help disadvantaged pupils to learn, we can follow a three-point plan:

1. Identify the barriers
2. Plan the solutions
3. Agree the success criteria

Identify the barriers

Before we can put in place intervention strategies aimed at supporting disadvantaged pupils, we must first understand why a gap exists between the attainment of disadvantaged pupils and non-disadvantaged pupils. In short, we need to ask ourselves: What are the barriers to learning faced by my disadvantaged pupils? Are these barriers always in place or only for certain subjects, skills, etc?

Plan the solutions

Once we have identified the barriers our disadvantaged pupils face towards learning, we need to plan the solutions. And one of the most effective solutions, though by no means the only one, is to focus on developing pupils' cultural capital...

Cultural capital takes myriad forms and is highly complex. There is not one single solution, but we have to start somewhere, and I would suggest we start with vocabulary because we know that a lack of early language and literacy skills is a major cause of disadvantage. The explicit instructions of tier 2 and 3 vocabulary is therefore advisable but this must be done in domain-specific ways and only when relevant to disciplinary learning.

In addition, I would suggest that strategies aimed to helping disadvantaged pupils work best when they focus on the following:

1. Improving pupils' transitions between the key stages and phases of education
2. Developing pupils' cross curricular literacy skills
3. Developing pupils' cross curricular numeracy skills

Agree the success criteria

The third and final action on our three-point plan is to *agree the success criteria*. Once we've identified the barriers to learning faced by our disadvantaged pupils and have planned the best solutions to help them overcome those barriers, we need to be clear about what success will look like. We need to ask ourselves: What is my aim here? For example, is it to: raise attainment; expedite progress; improve attendance; improve behaviour; reduce exclusions; improve parental engagement; or expand upon the number of opportunities afforded to disadvantaged pupils?

Whatever our immediate goal is, ultimately we should be seeking to diminish the difference between the attainment of disadvantaged pupils in our school and non-disadvantaged pupils nationally, as well as narrowing our within-school gap. As such, if our initial aim is pastoral in nature, for example to improve behaviour and attendance, or reduce exclusions, then we must take it a step further and peg it to an academic outcome.

Creating the culture for implementation

Senior leaders in schools and colleges have five key roles in terms of creating the right culture to implement an effective curriculum: firstly, they need to **agree the vision** for their whole school or college curriculum which involves defining what is meant by the term 'curriculum' and making decisions about the national, basic, local and hidden curriculums; secondly, they are key to determining how **broad and balanced** the whole school or college curriculum will be and why; thirdly, they need to **articulate the purpose of education** in their school or college – and therefore guide middle leaders in determining the broad 'end-points' (schools) or 'body of knowledge' (FE) to be taught; fourthly, they need to **create the culture** in which a curriculum can flourish; finally, they need to be the gatekeepers and defenders of **staff skills and time**.

The fourth and fifth roles are critical to our current purposes because, if we are not careful, curriculum intent and implementation are in danger of becoming a fad to which a considerable amount of time is dedicated. I am not suggesting improving curriculum design and ensuring teaching leads to long-term learning are not important endeavours and deserving of more of our time – I think they are – but I am saying that, if we decide we need colleagues to dedicate more time to these important processes, then we must also decide what they can stop doing in order that their overall workload does not increase; rather, that they focus their time on doing the things that will have the biggest impact on pupils.

As well as protecting our colleagues' workloads, we need to ensure they are helped to develop the knowledge and skills required to engage in effective curriculum thinking, design and delivery. This includes designing programmes of CPD that perform a dual function: firstly, that they help teachers and middle leaders to develop their pedagogical content knowledge so that they know more about effective teaching strategies and approaches; and secondly, that they help teachers and middle leaders to develop their subject-specific knowledge so that they know more about their chosen disciplines.

Creating the systems for implementation

A school also needs to attend to the following systems if their curriculum is to be effectively implemented: performance management and quality assurance.

Designing an effective ***performance management*** system might start by agreeing a set of expectations or standards against which teachers can be measured for the purposes of performance management. One solution is the professional portfolio approach, not to be confused with a tick-box approach which mandates teachers to self-assess against a fixed set of criteria, but rather about teachers taking genuine responsibility for their own development and taking their professional practice seriously. Another possible solution is the 'balanced scorecard' approach – this works when criteria are quantifiable rather than qualitative – which is a means of aggregating a range of data.

Designing a *quality assurance* system might start by consulting upon, agreeing and communicating a vision for the quality of education in your school or college. This vision is unique because it reflects your local context. The next stage might be to write a short mission statement which articulates how that vision will be realised. The third stage might be to set the priorities for the next one to three years. These priorities should help focus the school or college on the actions it needs to take in order to achieve its vision and mission. Next might come the 'quality standards', the everyday behaviours and values you need your school or college to embody.

The purpose of quality assurance is to critically reflect on past performance in order to improve future performance. Self-evaluation requires subject leaders to state their position at the end of each academic year, the actions they took in the previous year to get there, the positive impact of those actions on pupils, each with supporting evidence, and the areas for improvement that remain and that they therefore need to focus on in the year ahead. The areas for improvement contained within the self-evaluation document should then be carried forward to the curriculum improvement plan and form the objectives for the year ahead. The curriculum improvement plan should be a live document used to record the actions required in-year in order to improve the quality of education each subject discipline provides. Each action taken to improve the quality of provision should be added to the plan alongside emerging evidence of its impact on pupils.

To quality assure each subject's provision and to support their improvements, subject leaders might receive around three curriculum reviews during the academic year, roughly one per term. Each curriculum review should be a professional process used to support and challenge leaders. The process should begin and end with a curriculum improvement plan.

The plan should be used to determine the nature of the review and to identify key areas of focus for the review. The outcome of the review process should, in turn, be an updated plan.

Our systems also need to promote ***classroom consistency*** – to help pupils avoid cognitive overload – and ***collective autonomy*** - whereby teachers plan together.

We also need to address the issues of teacher recruitment and retention if we are to have qualified subject specialists teaching pupils. In addition to dealing with the issue of workload, we could start to do this by:

- Addressing the nature of teachers' workloads
- Providing more opportunities for flexible working
- Improving pay and rewards
- Improving the quality of school facilities
- Improving the support leaders give to staff
- Providing more encouragement to teachers and make expectations clearer
- Improving the quality of initial teacher training
- Improving the availability of continuing professional development
- Improving the quality and relevance of CPD
- Tailoring the support offered to new teachers
- Providing opportunities for career progression including into leadership positions
- Improving the professional recognition and social standing of teachers

ABOUT THE AUTHOR

Matt Bromley is an education writer and advisor with over twenty years' experience in teaching and leadership including as a secondary school headteacher and principal, FE college vice principal, and MAT director. He also works as a public speaker, trainer, and school improvement lead, and is a primary school governor.

Matt writes for various newspapers and magazines and is the author of numerous best-selling books for teachers. Matt's education blog, voted one of the UK's most influential, receives over 50,000 unique visitors a year.

He regularly speaks at national and international conferences and events, and provides education advice to charities, government agencies, training providers, colleges and multi-academy trusts. He works as a consultant and trainer with several companies and also provides a wide selection of direct-to-market consultancy and training services through his own company, Bromley Education, which he founded in 2012.

You can follow him on Twitter: @mj_bromley.

You can find out more about him and read his blog at www.bromleyeducation.co.uk.

.

ALSO BY THE AUTHOR

The IQ Myth
The Art of Public Speaking
How to Become a School Leader
Teach
Teach 2
Making Key Stage 3 Count
The New Teacher Survival Kit
How to Lead
How to Learn
How to Teach
School & College Curriculum Design Book One: Intent

PUBLISHED BY

Spark Education Books UK

© Matt Bromley 2020

The right of Matt Bromley to be identified as the author of
this work has been asserted by him in accordance with the
Copyrights, Designs and Patents Act 1988

ISBN: 9798645689537

Printed in Great Britain
by Amazon

57095100R00356